RESEARCH ON PREPARING PRESERVICE TEACHERS TO WORK EFFECTIVELY WITH EMERGENT BILINGUALS

ADVANCES IN RESEARCH ON TEACHING

Series Editor: Volumes 1–11: Jere Brophy
Volumes 12–20: Stefinee Pinnegar

Recent Volumes:

Volume 7:   Expectations in the Classroom

Volume 8:   Subject-Specific Instructional Methods and Activities

Volume 9:   Social Constructivist Teaching: Affordances and Constraints

Volume 10:   Using Video in Teacher Education

Volume 11:   Learning From Research on Teaching: Perspective, Methodology and Representation

Volume 12:   Tensions in Teacher Preparation: Accountability, Assessment, and Accreditation

Volume 13:   Narrative Inquiries into Curriculum Making in Teacher Education

Volume 14:   Places of Curriculum Making: Narrative Inquiries into Children's Lives in Motion

Volume 15:   Adolescent Boys' Literate Identity

Volume 16:   Narrative Inquirers in the Midst of Meaning-Making: Interpretive Acts of Teacher Educators

Volume 17:   Warrior Women: Remaking Post-Secondary Places through Relational Narrative Inquiry

Volume 18:   Emotion and School: Understanding How the Hidden Curriculum Influences Relationships, Leadership, Teaching, and Learning

Volume 19:   From Teacher Thinking to Teachers and Teaching: The Evolution of a Research Community

Volume 20:   Innovations in Science Teacher Education in the Asia Pacific

ADVANCES IN RESEARCH ON TEACHING   VOLUME 21

RESEARCH ON PREPARING PRESERVICE TEACHERS TO WORK EFFECTIVELY WITH EMERGENT BILINGUALS

EDITED BY

YVONNE FREEMAN
*The University of Texas at Brownsville,
Brownsville, TX, USA*

DAVID FREEMAN
*The University of Texas at Brownsville,
Brownsville, TX, USA*

United Kingdom – North America – Japan
India – Malaysia – China

Emerald Group Publishing Limited
Howard House, Wagon Lane, Bingley BD16 1WA, UK

First edition 2014

British Library Cataloguing in Publication Data
A catalogue record for this book is available from the British Library

ISBN: 978-1-78441-265-4
ISSN: 1479-3687 (Series)

ISOQAR certified
Management System,
awarded to Emerald
for adherence to
Environmental
standard
ISO 14001:2004.

Certificate Number 1985
ISO 14001

INVESTOR IN PEOPLE

CONTENTS

LIST OF CONTRIBUTORS   *vii*

ABOUT THE EDITORS   *ix*

INTRODUCTION   *xi*

PART I: CHANGING VIEWS OF EMERGENT BILINGUALS TO PROMOTE BEST PRACTICES

CHAPTER 1   PEDAGOGIES OF DISCOMFORT: SHIFTING PRESERVICE TEACHERS' DEFICIT ORIENTATIONS TOWARD LANGUAGE AND LITERACY RESOURCES OF EMERGENT BILINGUAL STUDENTS
Suniti Sharma and Althier Lazar   *3*

CHAPTER 2   DEVELOPING DEEPER UNDERSTANDINGS OF DIVERSITY: SERVICE LEARNING AND FIELD EXPERIENCES COMBINE FOR GENERATIVE LEARNING OF BILINGUAL/ESL PRESERVICE TEACHERS
Minda Morren López and Lori Czop Assaf   *31*

CHAPTER 3   *"PORQUE SÉ LOS DOS IDIOMAS."* BILITERACY BELIEFS AND BILINGUAL PRESERVICE TEACHER IDENTITY
Sandra I. Musanti   *59*

CHAPTER 4   MONOLINGUAL TEACHER CANDIDATES PROMOTING TRANSLINGUALISM: A SELF-STUDY OF TEACHER EDUCATION PRACTICES PROJECT
David Schwarzer and Mary Fuchs   *89*

CHAPTER 5   DISCOVERING BEST PRACTICES
FOR BILINGUAL TEACHER PREPARATION:
A PEDAGOGY FOR THE BORDER
Alcione N. Ostorga and Peter Farruggio   *113*

CHAPTER 6   MODELING COLLABORATIVE
TEACHING IN TEACHER EDUCATION: PREPARING
PRE-SERVICE TEACHERS TO TEACH *ALL* STUDENTS
Tatyana Kleyn and Jan Valle   *137*

PART II: INVESTIGATIONS TO SUPPORT BEST PRACTICES

CHAPTER 7   PREPARATION TO PRACTICE: WHAT
MATTERS IN SUPPORTING LINGUISTICALLY
RESPONSIVE MAINSTREAM TEACHERS
María Estela Brisk, Anne Homza and Janet Smith   *167*

CHAPTER 8   PREPARING LATINA/O BILINGUAL
TEACHERS TO TEACH CONTENT IN SPANISH TO
EMERGENT BILINGUAL STUDENTS ON THE
US–MEXICO BORDER
Alma D. Rodríguez and Sandra I. Musanti   *201*

CHAPTER 9   A SELF-STUDY OF TEACHER
EDUCATOR PRACTICE: STRATEGIES AND
ACTIVITIES TO USE WITH AUTHENTIC TEXTS
Mary Soto   *233*

CHAPTER 10   ANNOTATED LESSON PLANS: THE
IMPACT ON TEACHER CANDIDATE PREPARATION
FOR EMERGENT BILINGUAL STUDENTS
Craig A. Hughes   *257*

CHAPTER 11   "PERFORMING GOOFINESS"
IN TEACHER EDUCATION FOR EMERGENT
BILINGUAL STUDENTS
Mary Carol Combs   *287*

ABOUT THE CONTRIBUTORS   *313*

LIST OF CONTRIBUTORS

Lori Czop Assaf	Texas State University, San Marcos, TX, USA
María Estela Brisk	Boston College, Chestnut Hill, MA, USA
Mary Carol Combs	University of Arizona, Tucson, AZ, USA
Peter Farruggio	University of Texas Pan American, Edinburg, TX, USA
Mary Fuchs	American School of the Hague, Wassenaar, The Netherlands
Anne Homza	Boston College, Chestnut Hill, MA, USA
Craig A. Hughes	Central Washington Univ., Ellensburg, WA, USA
Tatyana Kleyn	City College of New York, New York, NY, USA
Althier Lazar	St. Joseph's University, Philadelphia, PA, USA
Minda Morren López	Texas State University, San Marcos, TX, USA
Sandra I. Musanti	University of Texas at Brownsville, Brownsville, TX, USA
Alcione N. Ostorga	University of Texas Pan American, Edinburg, TX, USA
Alma D. Rodríguez	University of Texas at Brownsville, Brownsville, TX, USA
David Schwarzer	Montclair State University, Montclair, NJ, USA

Suniti Sharma	St. Joseph's University, Philadelphia, PA, USA
Janet Smith	Edscape Consulting, Arlington, MA, USA
Mary Soto	California State University Chico, Chico, CA, USA
Jan Valle	City College of New York, New York, NY, USA

ABOUT THE EDITORS

Yvonne Freeman and **David Freeman** are professors emeriti at The University of Texas at Brownsville. Their research focuses on effective education for emergent bilinguals. They present regularly at international, national, and state conferences. The Freemans have published books, articles, and book chapters jointly and separately on the topics of second language teaching, biliteracy, bilingual education, linguistics, and second language acquisition. Their newest books are *Essential Linguistics: What You Need to Know to Teach Reading, ESL, Spelling, and Grammar*, 2nd edition (2014); *Between Worlds: Access to Second Language Acquisition*, 3rd edition (2011), *Academic Language for English Language Learners and Struggling Readers* (2009), the revised translation of, *La enseñanza de la lectura y la escritura en español y en inglés en clases bilingües y de doble inmersión* (2009), and *English Language Learners: The Essential Guide* (2007).

INTRODUCTION

This book is the first of a two volume set on teacher educators' research on how to best prepare teachers for the increasing linguistic diversity in schools. It is specifically dedicated to the preparation of preservice teachers. Preservice teachers are different from inservice teachers as they have not yet had classes of their own to teach, and they must plan for classes that, for them, are still only imagined. The reality is that many new teachers are not prepared for the diversity they find in today's students, particularly the linguistic diversity.

Although these future teachers take coursework that is designed to give them background on teaching, research, theory, and practice, many programs lack courses designed specifically to prepare teachers to teach students who come to school speaking a language or languages other than English. Even when such courses are included, there is a lack of research on how best to prepare preservice teachers to teach students who speak English as a second or third language. The chapters in this volume report on current research by teacher educators reporting on how they are working to prepare preservice teachers for classes with some or many students whose home language is not English.

The title of this book is *Research on Preparing Preservice Teachers to Work Effectively with Emergent Bilinguals.* Emergent bilinguals (EBLs) are those students who come to school speaking languages other than English. They have been referred to using many different terms including English Language Learners (ELLs), English Learners (ELs), culturally and linguistically diverse (CLD) students, and, a term used in government documents, Limited English Proficient students (LEPs).

An alternative term to refer to these students is *emergent bilinguals*, coined by García (García, 2009, 2010; García, Kleifgen, & Flachi, 2008). García has argued that this is a more appropriate way to refer to these students because it validates the language or languages students come to school speaking and acknowledges the fact that, as they learn English, they are becoming bilingual. They are not simply learning English, as the term EL implies; they are EBLs. In fact, many of these students learning English are becoming emergent multilinguals as they already speak more than one language before beginning to learn English. In this book, authors use the term emergent bilinguals as they describe their research with preservice teachers who will be working with EBLs in schools.

An estimated 25.3 million EBLs, ages 5 and older reside in this country. That is about 9% of the total K-12 school population and represents an 80% growth from 1990 to 2010. While the highest concentration of EBLs remains in the traditional immigrant destination states of California, Texas, New York, Florida, Illinois, and New Jersey, there are growing numbers of EBLs in all 50 states. Some states that previously had very few immigrants or second language learners, including Nevada, North Carolina, and Georgia, have experienced an almost 400% growth in the last twenty years. Arkansas, Tennessee Nebraska, South Carolina, Utah, Washington, and Alabama all experienced 200% or more growth in this same time period (Pandya, Bartalova, & McHugh, 2011).

Currently, the teacher workforce is 84% White and female (Feistritzer, 2011). As a result, there is a dramatic discrepancy between the cultural and language backgrounds of most teachers and the backgrounds of their students. There are presently approximately 5.3 million EBLs in U.S. schools (Whatley & Batalova, 2013) and estimates indicate that by 2020 half of all public school students will have non-English speaking backgrounds (National Center of Educational Statistics, 2013). With the growth in the numbers of EBLs that has occurred and is predicted to occur in schools, interest in these learners has encouraged research and publications. However, most of this research has centered on the students themselves and the politics surrounding their education. There is a need for more research from teacher educators who work with preservice teachers preparing them to meet the needs of EBLs. Teacher educators must know how to help future teachers provide effective instruction to the increasing number of linguistically diverse students in the schools.

The days of relegating the teaching of EBLs to specialist teachers are gone. Now all teachers, not only English as a Second Language (ESL) teachers or bilingual teachers, need pedagogical language knowledge (Bunch, 2013) to teach in classrooms with linguistically diverse students. As Bunch explains:

> I argue that efforts to prepare teachers for working with English learners (ELs) to engage with increasing language and literacy expectations across the curriculum requires development of *pedagogical language knowledge* (Galguera, 2011) not to "teach English" in the way that most mainstream teachers may initially conceive of (and resist) the notion, but rather to purposefully enact opportunities for the development of language and literacy in and through teaching the core curricular content, understandings,

and activities that teachers are responsible for (and, hopefully, excited about) teaching in the first place. (p. 298)

That is, teacher educators need to be able to not only teach preservice teachers how to teach literacy or language arts, math, social studies, or science, but also the language their students need to talk about, read about, and write about these subjects. In addition, teacher educators need to help preservice teachers appreciate and celebrate bilingualism and multiligualism. In our ever changing, global society, EBLs should be encouraged to celebrate and develop the languages they bring to school as they learn in English.

In this volume, we bring together the research of teacher educators from around the country. The chapters represent teacher education programs in the states of Pennsylvania, Massachusetts, New York, and New Jersey in the East, Texas and Arizona in the Southwest, and Washington and California in the West. The preservice teachers in these studies are preparing to work in large urban areas like New York, Boston, and Philadelphia, in suburban communities, and in rural border regions. In some cases the schools these future teachers will enter are multiethnic and multilingual. In Texas, Arizona, and California, especially along the border, student bodies are sometimes almost 100% Latino.

Most of the chapters report on research with future mainstream teachers, but some specifically deal with the preparation of future special education teachers or bilingual teachers. Many of the preservice teachers studied, like the present teaching population, were white females. However, the future bilingual teachers included in the chapters were almost all Latinas who were once EBLs themselves.

There are a variety of ways that teacher educators writing in this volume have approached their research. In all cases, they have pursued special passions and/or concerns they have related to the schooling of EBLs. The chapters are organized loosely into two sections: *Changing Views of Emergent Bilinguals to Promote Best Practices* and *Investigations to Support Best Practices*. All of these chapters help to inform teacher educators whose preservice teachers will be working in our linguistically diverse schools.

There are six chapters in the first section, *Changing Views of Emergent Bilinguals to Promote Best Practices*. Each chapter examines the ways that preservice teachers view EBLs and/or how they understand and embrace best practices for them. In the opening chapter, *Pedagogies of Discomfort: Shifting Preservice Teachers' Deficit Orientation toward Language and Literacy Resources of Emergent Bilingual Students*, Sharma and Lazar researched the effects of a course they taught on literacy, language, and culture that was grounded in pedagogies of discomfort (Zembylas, 2010). The researchers conducted the study with preservice elementary and secondary candidates in Philadelphia using both quantitative data from pre and post surveys, and qualitative data from responses, self-analyses, and participant interviews. Their goal was to see if the deficit orientations held by their preservice teachers changed after experiencing the course.

In the chapter *Developing Deeper Understandings of Diversity: Service Learning and Field Experiences Combine for Generative Learning of Bilingual/ESL Preservice Teachers*, López and Assaf asked, "In what ways does participating in a semester-long field-based university course combined with a service learning program shape preservice elementary teachers' views about effective literacy practices for emergent bilinguals?" This study, conducted in Central Texas, drew on Ball's (2009) generative change model and the four processes of change — metacognitive awareness, ideological becoming, internalization, and efficacy. In order to view the generative change that their research revealed, five types of ethnographic data were collected including observations, lesson plans, and reflections from the service learning project, transcripts, and interviews.

The chapter *"Porque sé los dos idiomas." Biliteracy Beliefs and Bilingual Preservice Teacher Identity* also reports on research from a literacy course, but this course is a course in biliteracy with Latino/a bilingual education preservice teachers living along the border. The goals of the course included helping the future elementary teachers understand literacy and biliteracy development and further develop their own linguistic academic competence through engagement in authentic opportunities to read, write, think, and talk in Spanish. In this chapter, Musanti explores both the past literacy experiences of her students and the beliefs they held about literacy using literacy autobiographies and a detailed questionnaire. The questionnaire data were analyzed to more accurately describe students' linguistic profiles and language use. Musanti also triangulated findings from students' autobiographies to explore the reasons students wished to become bilingual teachers and to examine the characteristics of their social and academic use of Spanish and English.

Schwarzer and Fuchs take readers a step beyond bilingualism in their report on a language and literacy course in which Schwarzer promoted translingualism with his preservice candidates in the greater New York City metropolitan area. Their goal was to help their students adopt a translingual ideology in which languages and literacies are explored and used as resources during content area instruction. In this chapter entitled

Monolingual Teacher Candidates Promoting Translingualism: A Self-Study of Teacher Education Practices Project, Schwarzer used a self-study methodology to research two questions. First he wanted to research how the class experiences he provided helped teacher candidates conceptualize a translingual approach to language and literacy development. He then worked with one monolingual secondary teacher candidate, Fuchs, to analyze how she developed her role as a translingual English teacher through the completion of the class experiences.

Discovering Best Practices for Bilingual Teacher Preparation: A Pedagogy for the Border is an in-depth report on the experiences and findings from a five-year research project that employed an innovative approach to higher education pedagogy used to teach bilingual preservice students how to provide research based, constructivist-oriented additive pedagogy to EBLs. This bilingual teacher educator research team examined the effects of their attempt to provide additive developmental learning opportunities to EBL students in the accountability-driven school system of schools along the border of Texas. Through an analysis of journal entry data and transcripts from focus group discussions, Ostorga and Farruggio analyzed the preservice teachers' developing awareness of themselves as bilingual, bi-literate professionals who have the potential of changing the present subtractivist teaching practices in the area.

The final chapter in the first section of the book on changing views of EBLs to promote best practices is Kleyn and Valle's *Modeling Collaborative Teaching in Teacher Education: Preparing Pre-service Teachers to Teach All Students.* The authors, professors of bilingual education and inclusive education/disability studies, respectively, combined their student teaching seminars in bilingual education and childhood education and team taught their course in an effort to better prepare preservice candidates to work with *all* students and to prepare them for the collaborative team teaching trend within New York City public schools. Kleyn and Valle had several goals for their self-study of teacher education practice (S-STEP) research. They wanted to provide a model of co-teaching as well as provide preservice teachers with the experience of being students in a classroom with two teachers. In addition, they wanted to provide preservice candidates with ongoing access to the expertise of two professors *during* their student teaching experience and to engage preservice teachers in critical conversations about identifying and resisting deficit constructions of both EBL students and students with disabilities. Using the co-instructors' weekly reflective journals and student evaluations as data, the researchers explored the benefits of team teaching in a teacher education course.

We open the second section of this volume, *Investigations to Support Best Practices* with a chapter by Brisk, Homza, and Smith entitled *Preparation to Practice: What Matters in Supporting Linguistically Responsive Mainstream Teachers*. In this chapter, the researchers employed a mixed method retrospective study to investigate the impact of their Teaching English Language Learners (TELL) teacher preparation program, a program that took place in the state of Massachusetts, one of three states that has passed legislation eliminating most forms of bilingual education. Attention to the needs of bilingual learners and the need to support the academic language development of EBLs were emphasized throughout the elementary and secondary subjects' preservice work. The researchers analyzed the perceptions their mainstream teacher graduates had about practices that support EBLs emphasized in their preparation program and the impact the program had on their current teaching.

The Texas border is the context for the next chapter, *Preparing Latina/o Bilingual Teachers to Teach Content in Spanish to Emergent Bilingual Students on the US–Mexico Border*. The researchers, Rodríguez and Musanti, investigated participants' understandings of teaching language through content to EBLs and the role of academic language in a content methods course taught in Spanish. The goals of the study were to gain insights into elementary preservice bilingual teachers' understandings of teaching language through content and academic language and to further bilingual teachers' academic language development in Spanish. The preservice candidates' lesson plans were used as data and were independently analyzed by the investigators. Studying different elements in the lesson plans, Rodríguez and Musanti looked for evidence of how the lessons helped EBLs develop language through content. They looked for strategies to support academic language development while teaching content. The researchers also analyzed the lesson plans to determine the preservice teachers' own use of academic Spanish.

Preservice secondary students studying at a university in northern California provides the context for *A Self-study of Teacher Educator Practice: Strategies and Activities to Use with Authentic Texts*. The goal of the S-STEP was to investigate the effect of the support Soto, the author and researcher, provided for secondary teacher candidates and first year teachers in planning reading, and writing activities around authentic texts. Teacher candidates were supported through a methodology class, class observations, informal meetings, emails, and text messaging. Data collected for the study included results of a survey, formal and informal interviews with the participants, observation notes, and anecdotal notes. The investigator analyzed the data to determine what strategies were effectively implemented which, in turn, will inform her own future teaching practices.

Preservice teachers are almost always required to submit lesson plans that reflect their understanding of how to put theory into practice. In *Annotated Lesson Plans: The Impact on Teacher Candidate Preparation for Emergent Bilingual Students*, Hughes conducted research to assess the impact of the use of annotated lesson plans with elementary education candidates at a university in central Washington. The students modified lesson plans they had previously written to include strategies to accommodate EBLs. They also annotated the plans by referencing the learning and language acquisition theory and research that guided their modifications. Two questions guided the research. (1) How do annotated lesson plans assist teacher candidates in connecting language and learning theories to the modifications made in their lesson plans? (2) What was the impact of creating the annotated lesson plan on the teacher candidates, as expressed through their self-reflection of the process? The data collected were the annotated lesson plans and reflection statements from the students on the impact of the lesson plan development and modification, and the results were coded to reveal themes.

The final chapter in this volume *Research on Preparing Preservice Teachers to Work Effectively with Emergent Bilinguals* is a research study on a unique approach to instruction in preservice classes called "goofiness pedagogy." Goofiness pedagogy is designed to model creative teaching to help EBL learners academically, linguistically, and socially. In her chapter *"Performing Goofiness" in Teacher Education for Emergent Bilingual Students*, Combs' discusses a multi-year study of goofiness pedagogy — theatrical drama, play and performance — that helps preservice teachers develop an alternative vision of exceptional teaching for and with EBLs. Combs' data consisted of student and author reflections on the practice of performed goofiness, video-taped performances of students engaged in drama and improvisation, and student written artifacts, Combs reports on how preservice teachers in Arizona, a state with highly restrictive language policies, respond to this innovative pedagogy.

The process of working with the teacher educators who have contributed to this book has been both informative and exciting. It is encouraging to know that teacher educators across the country are conducting research on ways to prepare preservice teachers to develop a positive view of EBLs and on ways to work effectively with these students. In the process of conducting their research, the authors of these chapters are also informing their own teaching. The goals of this book are to disseminate this important research and, at the same time, to encourage other teacher educators to conduct further research on the best ways to prepare preservice teachers to teach EBLs. We look for more publications like this one that will continue to support teacher educators as we all try to find effective ways to prepare teachers to meet the needs of the growing population of emergent bilinguals in our schools.

REFERENCES

Ball, A. (2009). Toward a theory of generative change in culturally and linguistically complex classrooms. *American Educational Research Journal, 46*(1), 45–72.

Bunch, G. (2013). Pedagogical language knowledge: Preparing mainstream teachers for English learners in the new standards era. *Review of Educational Research, 37*(February), 298–341.

Feistritzer, C. E. (2011). *Profile of teachers in the U.S. 2011.* Washington, DC: National Center for Education Information.

García, O. (2009). *Bilingual education in the 21st century: A global perspective.* Malden, MA: Wiley-Blackwell.

Garcia, O. (2010). Misconstructions of bilingualism in U.S. education. *NYSABE News, 1*(1), 2–7.

García, O., Kleifgen, J. A., & Flachi, L. (2008). *From English language learners to emergent bilinguals.* New York, NY: Teachers College.

National Center for Education Statistics. (2013). *English language learners.* Retrieved from https://nces.ed.gov/programs/coe/indicator_cgf.asp

Pandya, C., Bartalova, J., & McHugh, M. (2011). *Limited English proficient individuals in the United States: Numbers, share, growth, and linguistic diversity LEP data brief.* Washington, DC: The Migration Policy Institue.

Whatley, M., & Batalova, J. (2013). *Limited english proficient population in the United States.* Washington, DC: The Migration Policy Institute.

Zembylas, M. (2010). Teachers' emotional experiences of growing diversity and multiculturalism in schools and the prospects of an ethic of discomfort. *Teaching and Teachers: Theory and Practice, 16*(6), 703–716.

PART I
CHANGING VIEWS OF EMERGENT BILINGUALS TO PROMOTE BEST PRACTICES

CHAPTER 1

PEDAGOGIES OF DISCOMFORT: SHIFTING PRESERVICE TEACHERS' DEFICIT ORIENTATIONS TOWARD LANGUAGE AND LITERACY RESOURCES OF EMERGENT BILINGUAL STUDENTS

Suniti Sharma and Althier Lazar

Abstract

A major challenge in teacher education in the United States is how to address the academic and linguistic needs of the growing numbers of emergent bilingual students. A second challenge is how to prepare predominantly White monolingual preservice teachers with little exposure to speakers of languages other than English to educate culturally and linguistically diverse students. With these two challenges in mind, this study examines how a course on literacy, language, and culture grounded in pedagogies of discomfort shifts preservice teachers' deficit orientations

Research on Preparing Preservice Teachers to Work Effectively with Emergent Bilinguals
Advances in Research on Teaching, Volume 21, 3−29
ISSN: 1479-3687/doi:10.1108/S1479-368720140000021001

toward emergent bilingual students' language and literacy resources. Using Ofelia García's (2009) definition for emergent bilingualism, this mixed-method study was conducted from 2011 to 2013 with 73 preservice teacher participants enrolled at an urban mid-Atlantic university. Quantitative data consisted of pre and post surveys while qualitative data comprised written responses to open-ended statements, self-analyses, and participant interviews. Findings evidence preservice teachers' endorsement of monolingualism before coursework; however, pedagogies of discomfort during coursework provoke critical reflection leading to significant shifts in preservice teachers' dispositions toward teaching language diversity in the classroom with implications for teaching emergent bilingual students.

Keywords: Preservice teacher dispositions; emergent bilingual students; linguistic diversity; urban schools; pedagogies of discomfort; critical

Introduction

In the 21st century, the number of emergent bilingual learners continues to increase in classrooms across the United States making it an imperative for teacher education programs to prepare teachers for cultural and linguistic diversity. In addressing this area of educational change, two interrelated challenges have gained critical momentum. The first challenge is how to address the academic and linguistic needs of the increasing numbers of emergent bilingual students and build upon their language skills and literacy resources (García, 2009). The second challenge is how to prepare predominantly White monolingual preservice teachers with little exposure to bilingualism and bicultural literacies to teach in diverse classrooms. In addressing these two challenges, the last decade of school reforms, literacy programs, and language policies implemented as classroom practice have been unable to change the educational outcomes of culturally and linguistically diverse students (Gándara & Contreras, 2010). Teacher education literature documents the continued prevalence of teachers' orientations toward bilingual and bicultural students grounded in the deficit theory which perpetuates negative academic consequences for culturally and linguistically diverse students (Pollack, 2012). Hence, there is a critical need for preparing self-reflective teachers with the skills and dispositions necessary for working with diverse cultural and linguistic groups.

Proponents of the deficit theory in teacher education contend that racial minorities hold an inferior cultural, economic, social, political, and educational status because of a deficiency within the group themselves (Walker, 2011). Accordingly, minority groups are perceived with attitudes and beliefs that are drawn from a deficit value system being associated with a culture of poverty, a lack of work discipline and weak family structure, leading to a vicious cycle of poverty and educational inequality. Against this deficit landscape of teacher preparation, monolingual endorsement in public policy and exclusion of bilingualism in educational contexts not only restricts students from using their home language skills and literacy resources but conceals the social, economic, and political categories around which inequities in education are created and sustained (Zentella, 2005).

Rather than maintaining the deficit theory, research in bilingual teacher education suggests creating and maintaining classrooms that affirm linguistic diversity, which requires an awareness of bilingualism and bicultural literacy practices (Palmer & Martinez, 2013). Awareness of linguistic diversity includes recognizing the world views of bilingual and bicultural students, families, and communities, how bilingual speakers make meaning of the world around them, and an affirmation of their funds of knowledge as language and literacy resources (Moll, 2010). This awareness also includes teachers' examining their own values, beliefs, and assumptions, and the opportunities to practice in environments where the teacher's cultural and linguistic background differs from students' background.

Purpose

Keeping the two interrelated challenges in mind, this chapter examines how in a required course on literacy, language and culture, pedagogies of discomfort (Zembylas, 2010) emerge, provoking a shift in preservice teachers' deficit orientations toward emergent bilingual students' language skills and literacy resources. According to Zembylas, introducing preservice teachers to the ethics of discomfort and emphasizing the pedagogical role of conflict in the classroom has the potential for transforming teacher dispositions toward cultural and linguistic diversity. As a pedagogical tool, discomfort opens preservice teachers' classroom discussions toward the questioning of inequity and discrimination in educational contexts, unsettling taken-for-granted forms of classroom knowledge and practices that provoke critical reflection on their own beliefs and assumptions about cultural and linguistic diversity. Therefore, as teacher educators, designing courses across teacher education with the goal of transforming teacher dispositions toward cultural and linguistic diversity, reducing racism, and positively affecting student learning and outcomes through redesigned coursework, we support the philosophies underlying pedagogies of discomfort.

Redesigning coursework grounded in pedagogies of discomfort provides new opportunities for preservice teachers to experience bilingual and bicultural school communities, examine their own personal and professional values, beliefs, and assumptions, reflect on what these values, beliefs, and assumptions mean for teaching and student learning, and acquire the dispositions for building upon the language and literacy resources of emergent bilingual students. In other words, developing an engagement with pedagogies of discomfort introduces future teachers to a critical and historical awareness of cultural and linguistic devaluing and offers opportunities to future teachers for developing a teaching philosophy grounded in understanding bilingualism substantiating the teacher's role in affirming students' bilingual language and literacy practices as experiential classroom resources.

In what follows, we report on findings from a 3-year study of preservice teachers enrolled in a required course on literacy, language, and culture that included a field experience component and took place from 2011 to 2013. We begin with a brief review of literature followed by the theoretical framework for this study. Next, we give an overview of the course on literacy, language, and culture for preservice teachers, elaborate on our mixed methodology and report on findings from our study. We close with a discussion on the implications of our findings and conclude with some recommendations.

Literature Review

Literacy and language research within teacher education suggests teachers' background knowledge including their educational beliefs and assumptions about diversity guide their classroom decisions and practices with implications for teaching culturally and linguistically diverse students (Cummins, 2008). Research also suggests the prevalence of teachers' deficit thinking toward cultural and linguistic diversity and the need to address the underlying assumptions and beliefs influencing teachers' professional practice. Current research documents the need for challenging the assumptions that persist about bilingualism reflected in current approaches and models for preparing teachers for culturally and linguistically diverse students (Ceballos, 2012).

The literature on teaching bilingual students for whom English is not the home language instructs teachers to follow models advocating specific strategies for addressing the deficit in the language development of English language learners, English as a second language learners, and limited English proficiency learners rather than challenge the assumption of monolingualism and English-only practices (Cummins, 2007; García & Sylvan, 2011). The generalized and prescriptive nature of the models and frameworks do not work for all language learners; therefore, emergent bilingual students are more likely to be marginalized from school opportunities as their knowledge and skills remain misunderstood and underutilized by their teachers (Martínez, 2010). Along these lines are frameworks based on the monoglossic belief that linguistic practices are those validated by monolingual speakers of English (García, 2009), subtractive bilingualism whereby children lose their home language (Valenzuela, 2010), cultural deficiency theory that places minority culture as the source of poor school performance and low English language proficiency and the English-only movement in educational policy and reform that represses linguistic varieties and vitality (Ruiz, 2010; Stroud, 2009; Wee, 2011). García (2009) problematizes the cultural assumptions embedded in terms such as language dominance, mother tongue, second language learners, to promote the use of the term emergent bilingual which brings into play the broad and complex range of language practices in which bilingual students engage. Research evidence reveals such pedagogical perspectives do not challenge teachers' deficit orientations reflected in their assumptions about emergent bilingualism, nor do they problematize teachers' classroom practices based on normative discourses privileging monolingualism (Cummins, 2007; Gándara & Contreras, 2010).

On the other hand, research documents the need for shifting teachers' attitudes from the monolingual norm toward understanding bilingualism and biliteracy as a social and cultural practice (Pennycook, 2010). García and Kleifgen (2010) support bilingualism as a dynamic practice to be understood in the context of language as everyday practice in schools and society. Zentella (2005) suggests that rather than frame bilingual students within deficit theories, teachers should build upon the bilingual strengths of students to support teaching and learning. Further, effecting a shift from deficit thinking toward building upon the background knowledge and language skills diverse students bring with them must begin at the preservice level and continue to be a part of the professional development for in-service teachers. This growing body of scholarship suggests that the repertoire of biliteracy practices and language skills of emergent bilingual students is being recognized as a pedagogical resource not only by classroom teachers but teacher educators actively engaged in teacher preparation curriculum planning and implementation. These resources are described in terms of polylingual and polycultural literacies (Gutiérrez, Bien, Selland, & Pierce, 2011), code-meshing (Canagarajah, 2011), code-switching (Palmer, 2009a), hybrid learning spaces (Gutiérrez, Baquedano-López, & Tejeda, 2009), translanguaging (García, 2009), and sociocritical literacy (Gutiérrez, 2008).

According to Palmer (2009b), teachers' critical awareness of multilingual practices and being proactive in moving away from English-only domination supports emergent bilingual students' language learning processes. According to research challenging deficit orientations, teachers need a deeper engagement with bilingualism, the language practices of bilingual communities, and the sociocultural dynamics of bilingual classroom contexts (Palmer & Martinez, 2013). While the literature suggests the need for teachers to develop critical awareness of emergent bilingual learners' literacy and language resources, there remains a gap in the knowledge of how to assist future teachers beginning at the preservice level, to develop this awareness and link this awareness to their classroom practice as in-service teachers.

Theoretical Framework

We refer to the term emergent bilingual (García, 2005, 2009) to focus on the emergent character of bilingualism as an ongoing process of language proficiency and the strengths and capacities of students engaged in learning a new language as part of the schooling process. García (2009) calls for preparing teachers for emergent bilingual students beginning with offering opportunities and experiences to preservice for examining their perceptions, beliefs, and attitudes toward bilingual students, their literacy practices and learning skills. According to García, if teacher educators and policy makers are committed to promoting equity and equal opportunities for language other than English speakers, then three interconnected areas in critical literacy need attention: (1) designing coursework aimed at shifting teachers' deficit perceptions of bilingualism to support emergent bilingual literacy resources; (2) problematizing the use of labels such as English language learners, English as a second language and low English proficiency loaded with negative implications for emergent bilingual students; and (3) preparing future teachers for multilingual rather than monolingual and monoglossic pedagogies and classroom practices cognizant of the social and cognitive resource of emergent bilingualism (Cummins, 2007). Drawing from García's call, the course on literacy, language, and culture was based on critical literacy and bilingual pedagogies for questioning taken-for-granted theories and classroom knowledge.

Aligning with Garcia's call for designing coursework aimed at shifting preservice teachers' deficit perceptions of bilingual students, we employed discomfort as a pedagogical device for challenging issues such as racism, oppression, and social injustice in educational theory and practice. In other words, we used pedagogies of discomfort as classroom and research praxis to incite preservice teachers to question their own beliefs and assumptions about cultural diversity and reflect on their role in perpetuating deficit orientations toward students who are culturally and linguistically diverse (Sharma, 2014). Boler and Zembylas (2003) note that engaging educators in pedagogies of difference and reflecting on the discomfiting truths of one's own beliefs and assumptions is a step toward addressing discrimination in the classroom. Thus, as a teaching tool, pedagogies of discomfort are grounded in analyses of power, privilege, inequity, and discrimination in educational contexts. Accordingly, preservice teachers are prompted to examine their own personal and professional role within social and institutional practices in relation to multiple and interlocking systems of oppression such as race, class, gender, religion, sexual orientation, and academic ability. Within this framework, coursework includes reading and reflecting on language and literacy in terms of histories of domination and oppression, developing the skills of analysis for challenging social and institutional structures that privilege dominant cultural and linguistic groups, and reflecting critically on their own social locations in terms of power and privilege that have consequences for linguistically diverse students. Thus, the classroom becomes a powerful pedagogical site for preservice teachers to challenge power relations within existing ways of thinking, critical self-reflection on one's own beliefs, assumptions, and dispositions for effecting transformative educational change.

Aimed at shifting deficit orientations that marked many preservice teachers' dispositions toward emergent bilingual students, we examine the following questions:

1. How does the course on literacy, language, and culture where preservice teachers are engaged in pedagogies of discomfort shift and increase

awareness of the resources of culturally and linguistically diverse students?
2. What are preservice teachers' perceptions, beliefs, and attitudes toward bilingual students' literacy practices before and after the course?

Coursework Grounded in Pedagogies of Discomfort

As the planning and implementation of coursework was critical to effecting a shift in preservice teachers' deficit orientations, in the next section we give a detailed account of the experiential opportunities, content supports, and curricula outcomes embedded in the coursework. Course readings introduced preservice teachers to key theories, frameworks, issues, and practices for promoting language and literacy development of culturally and linguistically diverse students, with a special focus on emergent bilingual students. Coursework consisted of (1) reading and responding to scholarship on research, policy, and practice on language and literacy in K-12 school systems; (2) viewing and responding to contemporary films on the politics of literacy and language; (3) working directly with emergent bilingual students in culturally and linguistically diverse schools through field placements; (4) Participating in class discussions and critical analyses of course readings, films viewed, field experiences, preservice teachers' own locations in relation to social class, race, language and educational equity; and (5) critical reflection on their own growth and development as future teachers.

Coursework as pedagogies of discomfort was designed to move students outside their comfort zones and engage them directly with multiple and interlocking systems of oppression such as social class, race, and language and its relation to literacy practices and equity in education. Rather than an abstract concept, pedagogies of discomfort is both a tool and a critical literacy practice aimed at engaging preservice teachers in analyzing identity and culture, locating themselves within networks of power and privilege, challenging the systemic nature of institutional, social, and economic categories defining cultural differences that privilege or oppress, and promoting anti-racist pedagogies in the classroom.

Socialized within the mainstream or dominant culture of society many preservice teachers seldom have an opportunity to identify, reflect upon, or confront their biases' when it comes to teaching diverse student populations. Therefore, the aim of the course was to provoke preservice teachers to critically analyze their beliefs and assumptions and rethink their orientations toward linguistically diverse students. Coursework, class interactions, and field experiences were positioned to incite future teachers to move outside their comfort zones, leading to: (1) understanding bilingualism, (2) examining own beliefs that underlie their curricular choices, (3) viewing bilingual language and literacy practices as a pedagogical resource, and (4) making the shift from the language of deficit such as English language learners, English as a second language, limited English proficiency to emergent bilingualism as a complex language practice.

Course Reading

Preservice teachers were required to read and respond to three texts and several articles. The first text focused on giving preservice teachers an overview of the theories and principles of social equity literacy teaching in relation to racial identity and social justice (Lazar, Edwards, & McMillon, 2012). The second text engaged preservice teachers with standardized forms of English and American language variations in relation to power, privilege, and educational outcomes (Charity Hudley & Mallinson, 2011), while the third text focused on emergent bilingualism and its relation to critical literacy practices for transforming educational outcomes (García & Kleifgen, 2010). Preservice teachers were also required to analyze several articles on key concepts in language and literacy such as language as culturally situated (Heath, 1983; Maschinot, 2008), language identity (Delpit, 2002), and Funds of Knowledge and language as a resource (Moll, Amanti, Neff, & González, 1992). Preservice teachers were asked to respond in writing to these readings by identifying the key concepts/points contained in the articles, relating these to their own teaching/learning experiences, and generating critical questions for classroom discussion, analysis, and self-reflection.

Films

The course included two films as academic texts aimed at competencies that enable preservice teachers to analyze, evaluate and ask critical questions of dominant and accepted forms of knowledge as well as raise preservice teachers' awareness of the politics of language and its impact on linguistic minorities and their educational experiences. The documentary film "American Tongues" (1988), gives an overview of language variation and the roots of language as political and social power in the United States addressing how non-standardized varieties of language are used by minorities and perceived by the dominant culture. The film "Precious Knowledge" (2011), chronicles four high school seniors as they resist the banning of their Tucson high school ethnic studies program by the Arizona legislature. The film reveals how an ethnic studies curriculum, grounded on principles of critical pedagogy, improved graduation rates but was banned from schools by the Arizona government for being segregationist and anti-American.

Field Experience

Preservice teachers were placed in six different schools (five elementary, one secondary) serving large populations of emergent bilingual students in primarily underserved urban communities. Although most preservice teachers had attended suburban schools, urban placement was part of the course design to move preservice teachers out of their comfort zones, engage in bilingual school settings, and prompt critical reflection on their own perspectives, beliefs and assumptions about emergent bilingualism. In terms of the schools' language policy, the primary educational objective of all four schools was students' mastery of English. Preservice teachers visited the school for a full day or two half days once a week observing and assisting the cooperating teacher and working with emergent bilingual students. Preservice teachers were required to keep a field experience reflective log of their daily activities in the school and build a case study of one student documenting the student's culture, community capital, home and school language/literacy practices, Funds of Knowledge, student's educational experiences, parental involvement, classroom teacher's interaction with the student, and their own responses to working with the student.

Class Discussions

Class discussions served as a participatory and democratic format for pedagogies of discomfort useful in critiquing forms of knowledge established in school practice and policy and working inclusively toward the emergence of new alternative forms of knowledge. Preservice teachers were encouraged to discuss how language and literacy relate to broader social, cultural, and economic relations, share their own perspectives on the relationship between language domination and equity in education, and reflect on their

monolingual privileging of English over multilingual literacies and practices. Discussions offered preservice teachers opportunities for broadening
their own perspectives and bringing in examples from their everyday lives
to relate to the issue under discussion. Preservice teachers responded
to open-ended questions related to the concepts presented in their field
experiences.

Research Design

Participants and Setting

Drawing from García's (2009) call for bilingual teacher preparation and
using pedagogies of discomfort as the foundation for coursework, this
mixed-method study was conducted in 2013 with 73 undergraduate preservice teacher participants from an urban-based mid-Atlantic university in
the United States. All participants were enrolled in a required course,
Literacy, Language, and Culture focused on the intersection of race, class,
literacy, and language in relation to equity in education in general and
developing a more complex understanding of the language skills and literacy resources of emergent bilingual students, in particular. Participants
comprising 68 females and 5 males were enrolled in three course sections
during the spring of 2013 (43 freshman, 17 sophomores, 8 juniors, and 5
seniors). With the exception of one African American female and one
Brazilian male participant, all participants self-identified as white and
monolingual speakers of English. In keeping with IRB regulations, pseudonyms have been used for all participants and participation was voluntary
with the option to withdraw at any point in the course of the study.

Collection of Data

Two types of data were collected. First, quantitative data were gathered
from pre and post surveys using "Learning to Teach for Social Justice —
Beliefs" (LTSJ-B) (Enterline, Cochran-Smith, Ludlow, & Mitescu, 2008),
an instrument designed to measure key beliefs associated with social justice
such as participants' attitudes toward differences in socioeconomic class
and language. For the purpose of this chapter, we examine participants'
response to Items 6 and 9 on the survey designed to assess teachers' expectations of students whose home language is not English and who come

from high poverty communities. In the United States, 75% of emergent bilinguals live in high poverty communities (García & Kleifgen, 2010). This is the case for the majority of emergent bilinguals living in the Philadelphia area where our teacher education students are placed for their fieldwork. Most of our placement schools serve students in high poverty communities. Asking our preservice teachers to comment about their assumptions and expectations of children in poverty is relevant to our inquiry about their expectations of emergent bilinguals, although we acknowledge that poverty and emergent bilingualism do not always coincide.

Accordingly, the two selected items refer to participants' perceptions of students who do not speak English as their first language and the relationship between their socioeconomic status and the academic resources they bring into the classroom. Item 6 states: It's reasonable for teachers to have lower classroom expectations for students who don't speak English as their first language and Item 9 states: Economically disadvantaged students have more to gain in schools because they bring less into the classroom. Participants were asked to rank these statements using a Likert scale (Strongly Disagree = 1; Disagree = 2; Uncertain = 3; Agree = 4; Strongly Agree = 5). Scores reflecting disagreement (1 and 2) align with positive social justice orientation. Teachers with this view would reject the notion that it is reasonable to have lowered expectations of students who fit these descriptions. To prepare the data for analysis, scores for these negatively worded items were reversed such that higher scores correlated with a positive social justice orientation.

Second, qualitative data included written responses to the open-ended statement: Please describe the language and literacy abilities of students in high poverty urban communities. Placed in urban schools where most students were emergent bilingual students and came from high poverty communities, we asked participants to write a response to this statement in January and again in May. We also asked participants to write a self-analysis of their experience with coursework and the changes in their assumptions and perceptions during and after the course. In addition, a graduate student conducted a one-hour individual interview with 10 of the participants.

Analysis of Data

Analysis sought to triangulate findings from multiple data sources for validity and reliability. The analysis process entailed open-coding of themes to examine preservice teachers' responses across surveys, written statements, interviews, and self-analysis. We used axial coding to make connections between different data sources and check the integrity of emergent themes across the data ensuring internal validity and confirming similarities and differences between data (Corbin & Strauss, 2008).

Analysis consisted of three steps. First, pre and post survey data were examined quantitatively using the Wilcoxon rank sum test of significance for differences between the two samples from pre and post survey responses indicating a shift in rank in participants' educational beliefs and attitudes toward emergent bilingual students. We examined the rank shift looking at the qualitative responses to written statements using open-coding for themes and patterns to explore the shift. We focused on statements related to students' language and literacy abilities. The majority of codes generated from January's statements reflected deficit orientations of students' abilities and the factors that impacted them. These contrasted with codes taken from the May that tended to show capacity orientations toward students' abilities, with additional statements about teachers' responsibility to nurture students' growth. Representative samples of data from responses to written statements were used to evidence the shift of particular beliefs about bilingual students. In the third step we examined occurrences and co-occurrences of themes between the different types of qualitative data, that is, statement responses, interviews, written self-analysis followed by an evaluation of findings between quantitative and qualitative data. Examining relationships across data, we generated inferences from preservice teachers' beliefs and assumptions before, during and after the course; documented evidence on how course experiences shifted preservice teachers' beliefs and attitudes toward bilingualism and the literacy resources of emergent bilingual students; and identified key areas to address through redesigning coursework in teacher preparation.

Findings from the Study

In this section, first, we present findings from the quantitative analysis of pre and post surveys, followed by qualitative and quantitative analysis of response to statements, and qualitative data such as interviews and self-analysis. For the purpose of this study, we report findings from items six and nine on the pre and post survey data from all participants, response from one of the written statements of all participants, an interview from one participant as an exemplar representation, and self-analysis of two participants whose responses were representative of participants in this study.

Survey Items

In this section, we present a quantitative analysis using the Wilcoxon rank sum test applied to two items on the pre and post surveys. Item 6 states: "It's reasonable for teachers to have lower classroom expectations for students who don't speak English as their first language." Tables 1 and 2 show the frequency, percent, and cumulative percent of students' responses to this (reverse scored) statement in January and May, respectively.

There were highly significant differences ($p < 0.001$) between pre-course (January) and post-course (May) students' responses to Item 6. In January, 29% of students scored 1–3, representing a deficit orientation with lower expectations of emergent bilingual students. Note the large proportion of students (19.2%) who indicated "Uncertain" when responding to this item. In May, only 6.8% of students scored 1–3 reflecting a significant decrease in participants' deficit-oriented ratings of emergent bilingual students.

Table 1.   January Item 6.

Scale of 1–5		Frequency	Percent	Cumulative Percent
Valid	1.00	2	2.7	2.7
	2.00	5	6.8	9.6
	3.00	14	19.2	28.8
	4.00	31	42.5	71.2
	5.00	21	28.8	100.0
Total		73	100	

Table 2.   May Item 6.

Scale of 1–5		Frequency	Percent	Cumulative Percent
Valid	1.00	2	2.7	2.7
	3.00	3	4.1	6.8
	4.00	21	28.8	35.6
	5.00	47	64.4	100.0
Total		73	100.0	

Tables 3 and 4 show students' responses to Item 9, "Economically disadvantaged students have more to gain in schools because they bring less to the classroom" from January and May.

Applying the Wilcoxon rank sum test to Item 9, we found significant differences in students' responses to Item 9 between January and May ($p < 0.001$). In January, 8 preservice teachers agreed with Item 9, indicating a deficit orientation and 16 either did not know whether students in high poverty communities brought less to the classroom. This constitutes about 1/3 of the participants who either held a deficit or neutral orientation regarding what high poverty students bring to the classroom. In May, however, only two respondents held a deficit orientation and another 11 held neutral orientations; together they constituted 18% of the entire group – almost half the number of preservice teachers who responded either negatively or neutrally in January. Further, over 80% disagreed with this statement in May, reflecting an increase in the number of students who rejected a deficit premise about students in low poverty communities, many of whom are emergent bilinguals. Finally, the data also show a significant jump in the percentage of respondents who significantly disagreed with Item 9 in May, from 28.8% to 49.3%.

Table 3. January Item 9.

Scale of 1−5		Frequency	Percent	Cumulative Percent
Valid	2	8	11.0	11.0
	3	16	21.9	32.9
	4	28	38.4	71.2
	5	21	28.8	100.0
Total		73	100.0	

Table 4. May Item 9.

Scale of 1−5		Frequency	Percent	Cumulative Percent
Valid	1.00	1	1.4	1.4
	2.00	1	1.4	2.7
	3.00	11	15.1	17.8
	4.00	24	32.9	50.7
	5.00	36	49.3	100.0
Total		73	100.0	

Based on our analysis across both items from the pre and post survey, findings indicate a significant difference in most preservice teachers' beliefs and attitudes toward bilingual students between the time points January when the course started and May when the course ended. Findings evidence preservice teachers' endorsement of monolingualism before coursework; however, pedagogies of discomfort during coursework prompted critical reflection leading to significant shifts in preservice teachers' dispositions toward teaching language diversity. After coursework, preservice teachers demonstrated more positive dispositions toward students who do not speak English as a second language with implications for teaching bilingual students.

Response Statements

Findings based on students' response statements were consistent with the survey results in that candidates' orientations toward emergent bilingual students shifted from a deficit orientation to a capacity orientation. These data also show that candidates broadened their ways of describing students' language and literacy abilities. In response to the statement prompt, "Describe the language and literacy abilities of students in high poverty communities," we identified 89 separate comments that fit within five broad types. Table 5 shows the comment type, number, and percentage in relation to the total number of comments. The categories are arranged from most to least frequently generated by candidates.

As Table 5 indicates, a large portion of the comments (40%) related to students' having reduced or "lower" language and or literacy abilities relative to students in more economically privileged communities. Also included in 19% of the comments were references to the obstacles or hardships that students in high poverty communities would encounter, and these were often cited as the primary reasons why students were presumed to have underdeveloped language and literacy abilities. A relatively smaller proportion of comments indicated that students have varied abilities and that teachers should not have preconceptions of these students (18%) and another 17% of the comments reflected candidates' belief that students were capable. Only 6% of the comments related to the teacher and his/her responsibility to advance the literacy and language abilities of students.

Table 6 provides a summary of the findings for May. Again, the numbers of comments and their percentage relative to the total number are arranged from most to least frequent. These comments contrast with

Table 5. January Descriptions of Language and Literacy Abilities of Students in High Poverty Communities.

Categories	Recurring Comments in the Data	Number of Times Comments Occurred in Data	Percentage Relative to Number of Comments (#/89)
1.	Students probably have reduced language and or literacy abilities (than those in more affluent communities).	36	40
2.	Students face a number of hardships that constrain language and literacy development.	17	19
3.	Students have varied abilities; teachers must refrain from having pre-set expectations.	16	18
4.	Students are capable.	15	17
5.	Teachers are responsible to advance students' language and literacy development.	5	6

those produced in January, both in their orientation toward students and in their variation. We located a total of 141 comments that fit into 10 categories, twice the number of categories that emerged from the January response statements. Several of these categories reflect a capacity view of students.

The most striking difference in the response statements from January to May was the commentary on students' capacities, which are evident in categories 2, 3, 4, and 6. While similar in their orientation, each category is distinct. For instance, indicating that students have talents and knowledge (category 2) is different from indicating that they can succeed (category 4); the former category recognizes students' present positive abilities and intellectual worthwhile the latter reflects preservice teachers' belief that students have the potential for future academic achievement. Category 3 is distinct from these because the teacher is the primary subject, but it implies that students have the capacity to reach high levels of achievement if the teacher sets these expectations. Category 6 is most distinct because it recognizes the natural variation and legitimacy of the literacies and languages children bring to school.

What is particularly noteworthy is that none of these categories was generated by preservice teachers in January. While there were 15 comments (17%) indicating that children were capable in the first set of response

Table 6.   May Descriptions of the Language and Literacy Abilities of
Students in High Poverty Communities.

Categories	Recurring Comments in the Data	Number of Times Comments Mentioned in Data	Percentage Relative to Number of Comments (#/141)
1.	Teachers are responsible to advance students' language and literacy development.	31	22
2.	Students bring talents and knowledge to school (funds of knowledge).	30	21
3.	Teachers should have high expectations of students.	26	18
4.	Students can succeed.	13	9
5.	Students face a number of hardships that constrain language and literacy development.	10	7
6.	Students' language and literacy abilities may be different, but just as legitimate as those valued in school.	9	6
7.	Students probably have reduced language and or literacy abilities (than those in more affluent communities).	9	6
8.	Students should retain their home language.	5	3
9.	Students need to learn academic language.	4	3
10.	Students have varied abilities; teachers must refrain from having pre-set expectations.	4	3

statements, none described children as talented or knowledgeable, as was the case in the second set. This is more than a three-fold increase in the number of capacity-oriented comments made by preservice teachers in January. What is also striking is the difference in candidates' commentary about the responsibility of teachers in advancing the literacy and language abilities of students in high poverty communities. The January response statements contained five comments reflecting this theme (6% of the total); in May the response statements contained 31 such comments (22% of the total).

The response statements produced in May also included action-oriented statements taking ownership of the teacher's role in understanding bilingualism and becoming aware of students' language abilities. Five preservice teachers suggested that students should retain their home language, primarily because they considered it valuable for learning a new language and because loss of the home language compromises students' cultural and linguistic identity. Four commented that students need to learn academic language in order to succeed in school. The January response statements did not include any references to distinctions between "home" and "academic" language, or what students ought to do to develop their language capacities. The shift toward a capacity orientation toward linguistically nondominant students evidences an increase in preservice teachers' understandings about emergent bilingual language differentiation.

Interview and Self-Analysis

In this section, we present an excerpt from an interview conducted with a participant, Rebecca, followed by her self-analysis as well as excerpts from a self-analysis by Amy, to triangulate and provide further evidence of the shift from deficit orientation to perceiving the complexity of language and literacy practices outside dominant and standard English. While the quantitative data provides an overview of all 73 participants, qualitative excerpts offer thick descriptions of changes in individual perceptions that also served as examples.

Rebecca: Rebecca is a white monolingual first year preservice teacher placed in an urban elementary school that served primarily African American and Latino students from high poverty communities. This excerpt is taken from an interview at the beginning of taking the language and literacy course in which she was asked to describe the language abilities of students in the school. First, Rebecca speaks about the use of non-standard English by African American students and the importance of standard English as the language of academic success. Invested in the traditional notion of standard English, Rebecca's comments on African American English reflect a lack of awareness of its history and structure and the nuanced usage of English as a diverse language practice among many African Americans.

> They [African American] all speak English. They sing lyrics a lot and shorten words like take off the "g" on "−ing." They do double negatives a lot.

Rather than viewing African American English as a language with a particular history and structure, or recognizing the use of lyrics as a pedagogical resource, she rejects the language, reflecting a deficit orientation. In the same interview, referring to emergent bilingual students, specifically, students' whose home language is Spanish, Rebecca comments:

> I think they [emergent bilingual students] should still speak the home language at home but to function in society they need to speak English in school. I guess trying to have other students help them with understanding it and trying to get them to practice English. You need to respect them and not make them feel bad about their mistakes too. Give them more time to work on things. I think for it to work out better they should just speak English in the classroom because most students will be speaking English and that might be confusing.

In both excerpts Rebecca values monolingualism in the classroom endorsing English as the language of school and society. In the second excerpt, she asserts emergent bilinguals should make the transition from speaking Spanish to speaking English in school as the latter is the language of success saying, "to function in society they need to speak English in school."

In the following excerpt taken from a self-analysis after the course in which Rebecca indicates a shift from deficit orientation and monolingual endorsement of English stating that learning English should not mean compromising students' cultural identity or home language.

> I think it is important that they obviously learn English but I don't think that you should cut out their culture from that. I think that this would be more addressed at home than at school because I think (they) should come into school and learn and practice English more than their second language. There should just be a communication with the parents that they should continue to practice their language and English at home.

While Rebecca's comments reflect a shift, she emphasizes that language development is the primary responsibility of the home, rather than school. At the same time, when interviewed after the course, Rebecca is more hesitant to comment on the abilities of emergent bilinguals showing a movement away from a deficit orientation and recognizing the limits of her own knowledge and skills with regard to emergent bilingualism. According to Rebecca,

> The use of language depends on context ... I think in writing is a time to address language that needs to be formal and that there is a certain language that needs to be used in the school and the work force and that is when you can really teach them like standardized English but I think that if it's just conversational or its just reading that the students should be able to use the language that they use at home.

In this statement, Rebecca was explicit about the contextual use of language and she provided examples of what this might look like in the classroom. We can infer the effect of pedagogies of discomfort in Rebecca's use of the phrase "standardized English" reflecting her growing sense that there is no one standard way of using language; rather, the standardization of language is contextual and determined by those in power. She identified writing instruction as a space where standardized English can be taught and where conversations about the use of more formal language forms can be addressed. Another shift in Rebecca's thinking is indicated when she refers to the role of the teacher in the language development of students, not the sole responsibility of the home.

Amy: The next excerpt is taken from a self-analysis at the end of the course by Amy, a White, monolingual, first year preservice teacher who completed her field experience in a school that served high poverty communities of African American students and Spanish speaking emergent bilingual students. Reflecting on her perceptions, beliefs, and assumptions before she entered the course as well as the experiential learning throughout the semester, Amy states:

> This course taught me how difficult it can be to openly discuss these issues [race, social class and language differences in relation to educational inequity] If your teaching is culturally responsive you may have to address these issues. Originally, I did not think teaching students to challenge the state was justifiable in schools. In order to provide changes and social justice-this must happen.

After watching the two videos, "American Tongues" and "Precious Knowledge," Amy reflects upon the language and literacy development of all students in general, and notes the shift in her perceptions of the teacher's role in educating emergent bilingual students, in particular. Discussing the impact of the films on her changing attitude toward emergent bilingual students and the resources or "value" bilingual students bring into the classroom, Amy notes in her self-analysis:

> Originally I believed teachers should introduce students [emergent bilingual students from high poverty communities] to resources that are lacking in their communities. Now, I attribute value to all that these students bring to schools from their own experiences and I can see beyond stereotypes. The most impactful aspect of this course was the chapter readings and videos. The video we watched was particularly impactful on me. It gave me the feeling of discomfort which allowed me to change into an advocate for my students.

Amy's response to coursework, that is, course readings, field experiences, and videos clearly demonstrate shifts in her thinking about the language abilities of emergent bilingual students in high poverty communities, showing participants' growth toward a capacity-oriented view of students' language and literacy as an academic strength and classroom resource. From the qualitative data that included interviews, class discussions, and self-analysis, we found both participants, Rebecca and Amy, at the beginning of coursework displayed deficit orientations toward students who spoke languages other than English in schools that served high poverty communities. Their statements also showed that engaging in coursework has contributed toward shifting their perceptions of monolingual endorsement of English to engaging in conversations about the "value" that emergent bilingual students bring into the classroom. Both participants emphasized the academic resource of the emergent bilingual students they worked with in their field experience and their own earlier perception of bilingual students as English language learners coming into the classroom with a language and learning deficit. During the course, both participants grappled with their own language biases, recognized the error of having low expectations for students whose English language skills are emergent, how schools reinforce this deficit status, and asserted that teachers must make time to learn about cultures and languages different from their own so that they understand how emergent bilingual speakers make sense of the world.

The above excerpts also reflect preservice teachers' growing awareness of the role of the teacher in supporting students' language development and building upon the language and literacy resources of emergent bilingual students. The interviews show some individual variation among preservice teachers, from the rigid endorsement of English initially displayed by Rebecca when she asserted that students' should use English only in school to Amy's introspection on her own deficit perceptions, beliefs and assumptions of emergent bilingual students. As evidenced in the interviews and self-analysis, interactions with socially, culturally, and economically diverse communities brought further relevance to coursework through experiential learning and exposure to bilingual classroom contexts.

Conclusions and Recommendations

The challenge of preparing predominantly White monolingual preservice teachers for culturally and linguistically non-dominant communities can be accomplished by increasing their understanding of bilingualism and bicultural literacies through coursework grounded in pedagogies of discomfort that include critical course readings on language issues, videos on language debates and literacy practices, and strategic field placements in urban schools serving high concentrations of African American and emergent bilingual students from high poverty communities. This study demonstrates pedagogies of discomfort as part of coursework is key to shifting preservice teachers' deficit orientations supporting linguistic diversity. Viewing coursework not as a neutral body of curricular knowledge to be transmitted to students, pedagogies of discomfort provokes critical reflection on language and literacy research, theory and practice as a cultural, political, and educational construct to be examined, questioned, and changed. Pedagogies of discomfort aim to transform both teacher preparation and future teachers by combining critical self-reflection with intellectual analysis of educational research, policy, and practice in a historical context as a step toward preparing teachers with the skills and dispositions for educating all students including those who are culturally and linguistically diverse.

Implementation of pedagogies of discomfort as a pedagogical tool provide preservice teachers with theoretical understandings and practical strategies for questioning and challenging established forms of curricula knowledge and the beliefs and assumptions embedded in them that perpetuate inequities in education. With innovative curriculum such as pedagogies of discomfort promoting awareness of linguistic diversity through strategic field opportunities in diverse settings provokes questioning of deficit theories in teaching and school practices. Ongoing critical reflection framed within pedagogies of discomfort supports preservice teachers' understanding of themselves and the language and literacy resources of culturally and linguistically diverse students.

Our findings indicated that at the beginning of the course most participants assumed the importance of English-only instruction in contrast to bilingual and multilingual education. Participants' beliefs about the education of emergent bilingual students reflected federal and state policy favoring English-only instruction. Important themes that arose out of the analysis of participants' written response were: (1) preservice teachers' beliefs and attitudes represent educational policy and practice endorsing English-only instruction; (2) preservice teachers do not question the status quo nor do they question social and economic inequalities; and (3) preservice teachers' beliefs and attitudes toward emergent bilingual students has the potential for transformation through teacher education coursework with opportunities for critical reflection on their knowledge and assumptions about bilingual education and their future classroom practice. This study provides evidence of how teacher preparation curricula can be redesigned to support preservice teachers in developing a deeper understanding of bilingual language and literacies by offering experiential opportunities, content supports, and curricula outcomes embedded in coursework.

By drawing from the analysis, shifting preservice teachers' deficit orientations toward emergent bilingual students' language and literacy resources, framed around redesigned teacher education coursework prepares future teachers with the skills and dispositions for addressing the linguistic and academic needs of emergent bilingual students. A program of study in teacher preparation should build upon the growing research in bilingual and multilingual education that demonstrates the necessity to provide preservice teachers with experiential opportunities in schools serving emergent bilingual students.

Content supports such as current research in bilingual education, videos confronting policy and practice within the sociocultural contexts of bilingualism and biliteracies, serve as powerful pedagogical resources for engaging preservice teachers in analysis of historical inequities perpetuated in educational policy and practice disrupting the cycle of deficit underlying teachers' curricula choices and decisions. Curricula outcomes from redesigned and targeted coursework lead to teachers' ongoing critical reflection on their own assumptions and beliefs about cultural and linguistic diversity.

We observed strong shifts in preservice teachers' orientations toward emergent bilinguals; however, we recognize the limitations of teacher development based on a single education course. We identified challenges and areas of need within teacher preparation for teaching emergent bilingual students which include examining how changing attitudes and perceptions of future teachers toward diversity informs their pedagogical skills investigating how preservice teacher preparation and capacity building transfers into classroom skills for addressing the needs of linguistic diversity, and exploring the educational experiences of emergent bilinguals based on longitudinal studies for making generalizations that impact language policy and classroom practice.

In addition, even though many preservice teachers shifted toward a greater appreciation of emergent bilinguals' language abilities, their written statements and interviews did not include critical commentary about English-only policies in schools. We did not intentionally solicit preservice teachers' insights about the state of education for emergent bilinguals, but recommend doing so in future studies. To strengthen preservice teachers' critical understandings of schooling practices, we subsequently included a course exercise that allowed preservice teachers to work in groups to rate their school placements according to the level of acceptance of students' home language, with high ratings given to schools that invited students' home language with the end goal of bilingualism. Preservice teachers compared and contrasted their placements and rich discussions followed about how these different school settings align with current theories regarding second language acquisition and the empirical research that shows the benefits of bilingualism.

Our findings also indicate a need to strengthen particular course components, since only a small percentage of preservice teachers indicated a need for students to retain their home language. Following this study, we intend revising the course to extend the discussion of Cummins' theories of linguistic interdependence and common underlying proficiency, as described in García and Kleifgen (2010).

In closing, we offer a few recommendations for future research that address some of the gaps in our study and will inform teacher education programs in maximizing the learning opportunities of future teachers for serving the academic and linguistic needs of all bilingual students:

- Longitudinal research on the practical application of pedagogies of discomfort in emergent bilingual teacher preparation and implications for classroom change
- Multidisciplinary research on how disciplinary knowledge in the content areas such as social studies, science and mathematics is conceptualized and designed for bilingual speakers promoting equity in educational settings
- Comparative studies on the academic and linguistic differences and needs between bilingual and monolingual learners
- Research that focuses on preservice teachers' views of education for emergent bilinguals, including inequalities associated with current policies and practices.

References

Boler, M., & Zembylas, M. (2003). Discomforting truths: The emotional terrain of understanding difference. In P. Trifonas (Ed.), *Pedagogies of difference: Rethinking education for social change*. New York, NY: RoutledgeFalmer.

Canagarajah, S. (2011). Codemeshing in academic writing: Identifying teachable strategies of translanguaging. *Modern Language Journal, 95*, 401–417.

Ceballos, C. B. (2012). Literacies at the border: Transnationalism and the biliteracy practices of teachers across the US–Mexico border. *International Journal of Bilingual Education, 15*(6), 687–703.

Charity Hudley, A. H., & Mallinson, C. (2011). *Understanding English language variation in U.S. schools*. New York, NY: Teachers College Press.

Corbin, J. A., & Strauss, A. (2008). *Basics of qualitative research* (3rd ed.). Thousand Oaks, CA: Sage.

Cummins, J. (2007). Rethinking monolingual instructional strategies in multilingual classrooms. *Canadian Journal of Applied Linguistics*, *10*(2), 221−240.

Cummins, J. (2008). Teaching for transfer: Challenging the two solitudes assumption in bilingual education. *Encyclopedia of Language and Education*, *5*, 1528−1538.

Delpit, L. (2002). No kinda sense. In L. Delpit & J. K. Dowdy (Eds.), *The skin that we speak: Thoughts on language and culture in the classroom* (pp. 31−48). New York, NY: The New Press.

Enterline, S., Cochran-Smith, M., Ludlow, L. H., & Mitescu, E. (2008). Learning to teach for social justice: Measuring change in the beliefs of teacher candidates. *The New Educator*, *4*, 267−290.

Gándara, P., & Contreras, F. (2010). *The Latino education crisis: The consequences of failed social policies*. Cambridge, MA: Harvard University Press.

García, E. (2005). *Teaching and learning in two languages: Bilingualism and schooling in the United States*. New York, NY: Teachers College Press.

García, O. (2009). *Bilingual education in the 21st century: A global perspective*. Malden, MA: Wiley/Blackwell.

García, O., & Kleifgen, J. A. (2010). *Educating emergent bilinguals: Policies, programs, and practices for English language learners*. New York, NY: Teachers College Press.

García, O., & Sylvan, C. E. (2011). Pedagogies and practices in classrooms: Singularities in pluralities. *Modern Language Journal*, *95*, 385−400.

Gutiérrez, K. D. (2008). Developing sociocritical literacy in the third space. *Reading Research Quarterly*, *43*, 148−164.

Gutiérrez, K. D., Baquedano-López, P., & Tejeda, C. (2009). Rethinking diversity: Hybridity and hybrid language practices in the third space. *Mind, Culture, and Activity*, *6*(4), 286−303.

Gutiérrez, K. D., Bien, A. C., Selland, M. K., & Pierce, D. M. (2011). Polylingual and polycultural learning ecologies: Mediating emergent academic literacies for dual language learners. *Journal of Early Childhood Literacy*, *11*, 232−261.

Heath, S. B. (1983). *Ways with words: Language, life, and work in communities and classrooms*. Cambridge, UK: Cambridge University Press.

Lazar, A., Edwards, P., & McMillon, G. (2012). *Bridging literacy and equity: The essential guide to social equity teaching*. New York, NY: Teachers College Press.

Maschinot, B. (2008). *The changing face of the United States: The influence of culture on child development*. Washington, DC: ZERO TO THREE.

Martínez, R. A. (2010). Spanglish as literacy tool: Toward an understanding of the potential role of Spanish-English code-switching in the development of academic literacy. *Research in the Teaching of English*, *45*(2), 124−149.

Moll, L., Amanti, C., Neff, D., & González, N. (1992). Funds of knowledge for teaching: A qualitative approach to developing strategic connections between homes and classrooms. *Theory into Practice*, *31*(2), 132−141.

Moll, L. C. (2010, August/September). Sixth annual brown lecture in education research mobilizing culture, language, and educational practices: Fulfilling the promises of Mendez and Brown. *Educational Researcher*, *39*(6), 451−460.

Palmer, D. (2009a). Code switching and symbolic power in a second grade two-way classroom: A teacher's motivation system gone awry. *Bilingual Research Journal*, *32*, 42−59.

Palmer, D. (2009b). Middle-class English speakers in a two-way immersion bilingual class-room: "Everybody should be listening to Jonathan right now ...". *TESOL Quarterly*, *43*, 177–202.

Palmer, D., & Martinez, R. A. (2013). Teacher agency in bilingual spaces: A fresh look at preparing teachers to educate Latina/o bilingual students. *Review of Research in Education*, *37*, 269–297.

Pennycook, A. (2010). *Language as a local practice*. New York, NY: Routledge.

Pollack, T. (2012). The miseducation of a beginning teacher: One educator's critical reflections on the functions and power of deficit narratives. *Multicultural Perspectives*, *14*(2), 93–98.

Ruiz, R. (2010). Reorienting language-as-resource. In J. Petrovic (Ed.), *International perspectives on bilingual education: Policy, practice and controversy* (pp. 155–172). New York, NY: Information Age Publishing.

Sharma, S. (2014). Intercultural teaching and learning through study abroad experiences: Pedagogies of discomfort and oppositional consciousness for equity in education. In C. Schelin & B. Garii (Eds.), *Critical and narrative intercultural teaching and learning reader*. Charlotte, NC: Information Age Publishing.

Stroud, C. (2009). Towards a postliberal theory of citizenship. In J. Petrovic (Ed.), *International perspectives on bilingual education: Policy, practice and controversy* (pp. 191–218). New York, NY: Information Age Publishing.

Valenzuela, A. (2010). *Subtractive schooling: U.S.–Mexican youth and the politics of caring*. New York, NY: State University of New York Press.

Walker, K. L. (2011). Deficit thinking and the effective teacher. *Education and Urban Society*, *43*(5), 576–597.

Wee, L. (2011). *Language without rights*. Oxford: Oxford University Press.

Zembylas, M. (2010). Teachers' emotional experiences of growing diversity and multicultural-ism in schools and the prospects of an ethic of discomfort. *Teaching and Teachers: Theory and Practice*, *16*(6), 703–716.

Zentella, A. C. (2005). Introduction: Perspectives on language and literacy in Latino families and communities. In A. C. Zentella (Ed.), *Building on strength: Language and literacy in Latino families and communities* (pp. 1–12). New York, NY: Teachers College Press.

CHAPTER 2

DEVELOPING DEEPER UNDERSTANDINGS OF DIVERSITY: SERVICE LEARNING AND FIELD EXPERIENCES COMBINE FOR GENERATIVE LEARNING OF BILINGUAL/ESL PRESERVICE TEACHERS

Minda Morren López and Lori Czop Assaf

Abstract

In this qualitative study, we explore 31 preservice teachers' generative trajectories including how they built on instructional practices learned in the service-learning project, the university methods course, and the field-based experience. We addressed the question: In what ways does participating in a semester-long field-based university course combined with a service-learning program shape preservice teachers' views about effective literacy practices for emergent bilinguals? We identified four themes in our analysis: importance of choice in literacy pedagogy; learning from

Research on Preparing Preservice Teachers to Work Effectively with Emergent Bilinguals
Advances in Research on Teaching, Volume 21, 31–57
Copyright © 2014 by Emerald Group Publishing Limited
ISSN: 1479-3687/doi:10.1108/S1479-368720140000021000

and with our students; freedom to apply course methods and ideas; *and* growing confidence *and align them with Ball's (2009) generative change model and the four processes of change — metacognitive awareness, ideological becoming, internalization, and efficacy.*

We found the preservice teachers' ability to develop an awareness of diversity grew from their work with students both in their field-block experience and writing club. These opportunities provided them with a layering of learning — from course readings, collaborating with teachers, to problem solving and creating lessons that specifically met their students' needs. By moving in and out of different contexts, preservice teachers developed generative knowledge about ways to support writing for emergent bilinguals. Likewise, they became keenly aware of their own experiences and beliefs. Implications include the importance of providing a variety of opportunities for preservice teachers to work directly with students. This should be accompanied by written and verbal discussions to examine and critique their experiences and ideologies in relation to students' language and literacy needs.

Keywords: Teacher education; bilingual education; English as a Second Language; service learning; field experiences; clinical experiences

The roots of service learning lie deep in the mission of education. Educators commonly serve the needs of others; so it comes as no surprise that service learning, a teaching and learning strategy that integrates meaningful community service with instruction and reflection to enrich the learning experience, teach civic responsibility, and strengthen communities is commonly employed by teachers. (Zeller, Griffith, Zhang, & Klenke, 2010, p. 35)

Research on the importance of and impact service-learning projects have on preservice teachers' understanding of diversity has gained increased attention in recent years (Wade, 2007). Several studies (i.e., Cobb, 2005; Wade, 2000) have determined that service learning supports preservice teachers' knowledge, confidence, and ability to implement effective instructional practices as future teachers. However, less attention has been devoted to research documenting the value of participating in a semester-long, field-based university course combined with a service-learning program as a way to enhance preservice teachers' generative learning about emergent bilinguals' literacy learning. With a growing disparity between the largely White, monolingual teacher population and the increasingly linguistically diverse student body in the United States, national assessment data, reports, and literature reviews indicate this is an area sorely in need of exploration. The focus of this chapter is to examine preservice teachers' generative learning after participating in a university-based field experience and a service-learning literacy project with elementary language learners.

Purpose and Significance

According to the National Service Learning Clearinghouse (2009), service learning is defined as a teaching and learning strategy that integrates meaningful community service with instruction and reflection to enrich the learning experience. In teacher education, service learning includes thoughtful service experiences that meet community needs and are created in collaboration with schools and the community to enhance what is taught in classrooms while also fostering the development of care for others. Service learning integrates community service into the academic curriculum (Koliba, Campbell, & Shapiro, 2006) and can provide a context for preservice teachers to learn outside the traditional school building or curricular constraints (Wade, 2000).

Engaging in service learning can benefit prospective teachers in various ways. Service learning, such as school-based tutoring, can shape how preservice teachers confront their own biases and deficit views (Cobb, 2005), develop caring and responsive relationships with students, and increase multicultural awareness and a sense of social justice (McHatton, Thomas, & Lehman, 2006). In hopes of supporting our preservice teachers' understanding of diversity and helping them gain a deeper understanding of effective literacy instruction for emergent bilinguals, we sought to understand how participating in a field experience as well as a literacy after school program shaped preservice teachers' views about diversity and effective language and literacy instruction. Using generative change theories (Ball, 2009), we wanted to understand the ways in which, a continuous, semester-long service-learning project in addition to a field experience shaped teachers' metacognive awareness, ideological becoming, and efficacy about working with emerging bilinguals. We address the following question: In what ways does participating in a semester-long, supervised literacy service-learning program and a university-based field experience shape preservice teachers' views about diversity and effective literacy practices for emergent bilinguals?

Our research is in response to the call for teacher educators (Anders, Hoffman, & Duffy, 2000) to study our programs, our courses, our teaching, and our expectations and requirements" (p. 734) in order to prepare future teachers for the complexities of teaching. We used a "Teacher as Researcher" framework (Cochran-Smith & Lytle, 1999; Goswami & Stillman, 1987; Lieberman, 1988) because it is an important tool for all teachers (including teachers who are professors) to improve their craft and enhance student learning. Minda was the course professor and began this study as an interested Teacher Researcher. Lori was neither an instructor nor a student and began the study as an interested teacher educator wanting to learn more about supporting emergent bilinguals in field-based teacher education.

Literature Review

Much of the literature on service learning with preservice teachers is fairly recent. Of these studies, most suggest that service-learning opportunities are vital to helping preservice teachers become aware of their own beliefs and assumptions, particularly in relation to the students they will encounter in schools who are different from them (Cochran-Smith, 1995; Hale, 2008; Smylie, Bay, & Tozer, 1999). For example, in a qualitative study with 44 preservice teachers and a control group, Zeller et al. (2010) found that preservice teachers' awareness of diverse populations of students in public school settings was increased through their service-learning experience. The preservice teachers in the service-learning project developed a nuanced awareness of the commonalities as well as differences between themselves and their students and demonstrated a new understanding of their students' lives outside of school. They became more sensitive to students' needs both cognitively and affectively and viewed their relationship differently from stranger to friend.

Similarly, participants in a study conducted by Tellez, Hlebowitsh, Cohen, and Norwood (1995) reported "dramatic personal revelations regarding race and ethnicity and class" (p. 70) after participating in a service-learning project. Their study suggests preservice teachers shed deficit views of emergent bilinguals and adopted affirmative ideologies toward their students. Tellez et al. found that these preservice teachers had increased confidence in teaching diverse, urban youth. In fact, many of the participants indicated a commitment to working in urban areas with historically marginalized populations. Overall, the findings are clear: participating in service learning can enhance preservice teachers' pedagogical skills (Alt & Medrich, 1994; DeJong & Groomes, 1996; Sleeter, 1995; Tellez et al., 1995) while allowing university students to give back to the schools and institutions that help them develop as teachers (Wade & Saxe, 1996). In light of this positive research, we found few studies that explore preservice teachers' generative learning while participating in a teacher education field experience and a service-learning project. In this study, we highlight the experiences and generative learning of undergraduate preservice teachers who participated in an after school service-learning project in addition to their university field experience.

Theoretical Framework

Generativity and Generative Learning

Generativity has been studied in developmental psychology (Erikson, 1963), behavioral psychology (Epstein, 1993), and critical psychology (Strong, 2010). These multiple perspectives are built around Erikson's theory of psychosocial development and highlight three significant dimensions: responsibility, productivity, and creativity. Responsibility refers to the needs of other people, productivity to the professional domain, and creativity to new possibilities. In teacher education, generativity has been used to describe teacher knowledge (Ball, 2009; Franke, Carpenter, Levi, & Fennema, 2001). Generative knowledge refers to the ability of teachers to apply their knowledge and personal understandings to new topics and situations. Generative teachers are able to meet the educational needs of their students by integrating new knowledge with existing knowledge to consider the context and needs of their students (Ball, 2009).

Arnetha Ball's work with U.S. and South African teachers plays an important role in understanding the process of preservice teacher learning and generative learning. In her longitudinal study, Ball discovered that teachers built on the same instructional practices they experienced in their professional development course to inspire their students to become generative thinkers. Based on this research, Ball coined the term *generative change* to describe teachers' process of ongoing learning. She explained that knowledge becomes generative when a teacher continues new learning by "making connections with his or her students' knowledge and needs, and begins planning the teaching based on what he or she is learning" (p. 48). For Ball, generative learning is based on teachers' development and the use of generative knowledge, which consists of professional knowledge, personal knowledge, and knowledge gained from students.

Drawing on her research, Ball designed a model of generative change as a framework for future professional development and a heuristic to study how teachers become reflective, thoughtful, critical, and generative thinkers. In her model, Ball identified the importance of narrative writing (Bruner, 1994) and highlighted four theories and processes that shape a teacher's generative learning: metacognitive awareness (Bransford, Brown, & Cocking, 2000), ideological becoming (Bakhtin, 1981), internalization (Vygotsky, 1978), and efficacy (Bandura, 1997). Metacognitive awareness refers to one's ability to think about his or her thinking and to monitor current levels of mastery and understanding. Effective teachers are metacognitively aware of their strengths and weaknesses and have a "repertoire of tools and resources to assist them in attaining their goals" (Ball, 2009, p. 49). This repertoire includes a reconceptualization of their students as resources in the teaching process. As teachers reflect on their personal and professional lives, they become more aware of and responsive to their students' needs. At the same time, teachers grapple with previous beliefs and ways of being that challenge their ideologies. Ball (2009) notes that as teachers are exposed to multiple discourses and new perspectives through a variety of texts, they grapple with conflicting ideas and have the potential to develop new ways of being. Ball leans on Bakhtin's notion of ideological becoming (Bakhtin, 1981) to explain changes in teachers' identities or their progression toward ideological clarity.

Ideological Clarity

Ideological clarity can ultimately contribute to what becomes internally persuasive to teachers — shaping thoughts, beliefs, actions, and ways of theorizing about the world (Assaf, 2006). Recently, many teacher educators have addressed the notion of ideological clarity in preparing teachers, particularly when working with culturally and linguistically diverse students (Assaf & Dooley, 2010; Bartolomé, 1998; Expósito & Favela, 2003; King, 1991). Ideologies are more than beliefs — they are sets of beliefs that often go unexamined by individuals (vanDijk, 1998) and can manifest themselves in inner histories and experiences shaped by one's passions, needs, and perspectives in their own lives and society as a whole (Darder, Baltodano, & Torres, 2002). When teacher ideologies go unexamined, prospective teachers, regardless of ethnic or linguistic background, tend to unconsciously and uncritically hold beliefs and attitudes about the existing social order that reflect mainstream ideologies and can be harmful to many students, especially emergent bilinguals (Haberman, 1991; Macedo, 1994).

Moreover, when people believe the system is fair, they tend to engage in assimilationist practices rather than culturally responsive ones. They also tend to oppose policies and practices that have been shown to be effective for historically subjugated populations, such as bilingual education (Bartolomé, 2004) and the practice of utilizing all of students' linguistic repertoires. Increasing ideological clarity helps preservice teachers begin to recognize the positive and negative aspects of all cultures, shedding assumptions of superiority of their own cultures over those of the students they serve (Expósito & Favela, 2003). And "to open up students to a wide range of experiences so that they can expand, hold up to a critical light, and adjust their own ideological lens in ways that make the classroom more inclusive, exploratory, and transformative" (Bartolomé, 2004, p. 117).

Methodology

In the sections below, we describe the setting and participants and highlight the data and data analysis used in this study.

Setting and Participants

This study was conducted with 31 undergraduate preservice teachers who were enrolled in the Early-Childhood to grade 6 English as a Second Language (ESL) ($n = 23$) or Bilingual Education ($n = 8$) certification program at a large, public Hispanic Serving Institution (HSI) in the southwest over two consecutive semesters. Of the 31 preservice teachers, one is a Latino male; 30 are women. There were 16 white women, 12 Latinas, and 2 African-American women. All but two participants were in their early mid-twenties. The preservice teachers were enrolled in either the fall

($n = 15$) or spring ($n = 16$) semester field block at Antigua Elementary (all names are pseudonyms).

The field block is an integral part of this large teacher preparation program. In a study of faculty, teacher educators in this teacher preparation program expressed the belief that the field block is vital for preservice teachers to learn about multicultural pedagogy, connect theory to practice, and become more aware of and responsive to diversity (Assaf, Garza, & Battle, 2010). As a required component of their preparation, preservice teachers are immersed in a public elementary school setting for a semester in "the block" by attending three university courses onsite and interning in public school classrooms for approximately eight hours a week. The field block takes place prior to student teaching. Typically, preservice teachers take two literacy courses and one classroom management course during this semester. Usually, these courses are taught on the public school site by university faculty and include topics such as reading methods and theory, literacy assessments, curriculum design, and classroom management. There are several assignments consistent across all elementary field blocks in this teacher preparation program, including a preservice teacher led read aloud and direct teach. The direct teach lesson consists of the preservice teacher leading some kind of lesson agreed upon with their cooperating teacher and taught to a small group or the entire class. For this assignment, preservice teachers are to teach a concept to students and follow it up with guided practice and other activities. It is called a "direct teach" to distinguish it from the read aloud but to give preservice teachers some flexibility. Both of these assignments are designed to give preservice teachers more experience applying what they have learned about literacy pedagogy and curriculum planning while allowing for flexibility across grade levels and topics.

In addition to the common assignments, the preservice teachers in the Antigua Elementary block were assigned texts and projects designed to foster thinking about their own language and literacy development and use. We used texts such as Johnston's (2004) *Choice Words* to encourage students to think about the ways teachers talk about literacy and students. We also assigned Ayers and Alexander-Tanner's (2010) *Learning to Teach: The Journey, in Comics.* We chose to use a book in graphic form to foster thinking and awareness of multiliteracies and broaden students' views of what counts as text. The projects we assigned were also designed to foster reflection and awareness of language and literacy in diverse ways. In one assignment, preservice teachers created a "multiliteracies timeline" using online freeware (www.dipity.com or www.capzles.com) and wrote an accompanying reflection paper outlining critical moments or most influential experiences related to languages and literacies in their own lives (see López & Brochin, 2014 for more detail on this assignment). There was also a focus on understanding the language and literacy needs of diverse students, particularly emergent bilinguals.

To guide their reflections over the semester, preservice teachers kept a writer's notebook and completed an audit trail (Vasquez, 2004). The audit trails were similar to the multiliteracies timelines but specific to learning during the semester. For the audit trail assignment, preservice teachers made note of any important learning, understandings, insights or "a-ha" moments they experienced at any point during the semester. These included quotes from a reading, a class discussion, an observation in a classroom, or an experience interacting with an elementary student or their family. At the end of the semester, we gathered as a class and shared our audit trails in chronological order on the walls of our classroom, with visual representations, quotes and explanations. These guided introspections and class discussions were designed to reveal patterns of learning in individuals and as a group, and to aid students in their ideological becoming (Bakhtin, 1981) or in developing ideological clarity (Bartolomé, 2004), particularly in relation to working with diverse students.

Another unique aspect of the Antigua Elementary field block was the addition of a fourth literacy class added to the onsite coursework called "Integrating Reading and Writing." Preservice teachers typically take this required course separately from the field block as it is taught on the university campus. For the block at Antigua Elementary, this particular course was added to provide additional experience working with emergent bilinguals at the school site in teaching writing. In addition, administration and teachers at Antigua Elementary were interested in partnering with the university for enrichment opportunities for students in reading and writing, so adding the course was a way to meet the needs of the public school and the university at the same time.

While many teacher educators value multicultural exposure and field experiences for their preservice teachers, several teacher educators from this university described how they deliberately chose schools with bilingual, Two-Way Immersion, and ESL programs as sites for educating preservice teachers with the goal of effectively preparing teachers to work with emergent bilinguals (Assaf et al., 2010).

As former bilingual elementary teachers, Minda and a fellow colleague who led the block at Antigua Elementary purposefully selected a school with a high quality bilingual program and experienced bilingual teachers. First, the leadership at the school is very knowledgeable regarding bilingual education. The former principal (who was the principal when this field block was established) is a Latina with a doctorate in bilingual education. The current principal is a Latina with a master's degree in bilingual education. Both principals are former bilingual teachers and strong advocates for emergent bilinguals. The two current assistant principals are Latina, bilingual, and have extensive experience with emergent bilinguals. In addition to the supportive administration, there is strong leadership among the teachers. There are two bilingual teachers per grade level at the school and the majority of these teachers have a master's degree in bilingual education. The teachers are recognized locally and nationally as experts in the field and have presented widely at conferences and published articles related to teaching and bilingual education.

In addition to the strong advocacy for bilingual education and bilingualism, Antigua Elementary was also chosen as a field-based site to prepare teachers because of its diverse student and family population. There is both economic and ethnic diversity in this school of over 1,000 elementary students, with a population that is 75% Latino, 10% white, 8% African-American, 2% Asian, and 5% mixed race or other. Eighty percent are labeled "economically disadvantaged" and 36% are emergent bilinguals. This kind of setting provides rich opportunities for the preservice teachers to learn and also to give back to the community.

The "Writing Club" Service-Learning Project

The service-learning project resulted from conversations between administrators, teachers, and professors about the need to provide preservice teachers with more learning experiences with diverse students and their families in an unstructured and voluntary setting. Faculty from Antigua Elementary enthusiastically supported the program and viewed it as an opportunity for their students to receive additional literacy instruction and mentoring. The service-learning project was conceptualized as an enrichment opportunity for students, not as a tutoring program. For us, the distinction is important. The writing club was not designed to take struggling students and "fix" their writing so they would be better prepared for a standardized test or to mimic what was taught in the classroom. Instead, the writing club was meant to be a place where elementary students could get excited about writing, share their thoughts and feelings with others through writing, and interact with university students in a more intimate setting.

The practicing teachers at Antigua Elementary recommended students for the program but did not participate in it, as many were conducting their own tutoring or enrichment programs after school at the same time. The preservice teachers were encouraged to ask teachers questions about their students and to solicit teaching ideas (i.e., suggestions for literature to use or topics of writing to cover) and feedback from the practicing teachers but no formal arrangements were made for such communication or collaboration.

The "writing club" took place from 2:45 to 4:00 p.m. at Antigua Elementary one day a week for eight weeks (in the fall semester it only lasted seven weeks due to a scheduling conflict). In the spring semester, students from grades 3 to 5 participated; in the fall semester only fourth graders were invited to join the club. Elementary students were invited by their teachers to participate and criteria for selection decided by the teacher. The teachers chose students for various reasons including lack of participation in other clubs or tutoring, interest in writing, the need for additional academic or affective support and mentoring, and parent interest in the club. Students gained permission from their parents to participate and no transportation was provided, so it was limited to those who could provide transportation on their own. Each semester, approximately fifty students participated; about a third of the students were from the bilingual program. Groups of 3–5 students were assigned to preservice teacher pairs and effort was made so that each pair worked with at least one emergent bilingual who was serviced in either a bilingual or ESL classroom.

For the writing club, preservice teachers worked together in pairs designing and leading literacy experiences focused around writing. Each pair was assigned 3–5 elementary students to work with. The sessions began with a snack provided to students. Then preservice teachers worked with their small groups in various locations around the school. Some groups met outside, others worked in pods, hallways, or classrooms. Typically, one preservice teacher read a text or posed a question while the other preservice teacher observed, took notes, and supported any instruction or discussion. Preservice teachers were encouraged to use multicultural literature to foster writing and responses in whatever language the students chose to use (English or Spanish). The lesson plan for the first session was modeled for preservice teachers in their university class and it began with a reading of the bilingual book "I am René the boy/Soy René el niño" by Colato-Lainez (2005). Students were then asked to discuss their names and talk about the history of their name, a story related to their name, and their opinions regarding their name.

After using a text or quote, preservice teachers designed a writing activity, prompt, or assignment they all engaged in together. Preservice teachers presented mini-lessons on various writing strategies such as finding a topic, adding more detail through snapshots and thoughtshots (Lane, 2008), editing, revising, and conferencing. Students were guided through the reading and writing activities with constant interaction and discussion. During each session, preservice teachers led students out to meet their parents at pick up and many interacted with the families at this time. The final meeting of the writing club was a sharing celebration where students were encouraged to share their final writing piece with the whole group by reading it aloud and students received an anthology that included one published writing piece from every participant.

Preservice teachers created mini-lessons and planned activities for the majority of the club meetings. These were collected in a notebook along with observations and reflections, both weekly and overall. Participants were asked to reflect on their service-learning experience and to connect it to the literature or other experiences they had at Antigua Elementary.

Data Collection and Analysis

A qualitative framework (Lincoln & Guba, 1985) with emphasis on phenomenology, ethnographic methods, and teacher research served as the methodological landscapes for this study. A phenomenological approach was used to explore the way people experience their world and to understand their perspectives (Moustakas, 1994). In order to understand how the service-learning project, the university course, and field-block experiences shaped the preservice teachers' generative learning, we applied ethnographic methods over an extended period of time (Geertz, 1973). The ethnographic data collection procedures, such as multiple participant observations in the service-learning project and in their internship classrooms, interviews, reflective journals, and document analysis over five months, were adapted to corroborate participants' shifting experiences and practices. In terms of teacher research, we built on Cochran-Smith and Lytle's (1999) definition of teacher research as action-oriented and involving "reflecting on one's teaching and practice, inquiring about it, exploring it, and taking action to improve or alter it" (p. 78). As Hubbard and Power (1999) stated, "teaching is researching" (p. 20). We used this approach with our preservice teachers because it aligns with our ideologies about teacher education. We believe teacher education should include exploring and understanding our own practices along with taking action with the purpose of improving teaching and schools.

Five types of ethnographic data were collected: observations, lesson plans and reflections from the writing club, transcripts, and interviews. Data analysis was ongoing and took place over several stages during the semester, using the constant-comparative method (Lincoln & Guba, 1985). Along with a graduate assistant, we read and reread all data and inductively coded units of words that had meaning independently. We thoroughly read the lesson plans and reflections written by each preservice teacher and transcripts of the writing club and interviews, labeling words and phrases for open coding (e.g., "getting to know students," "choice," and "responsive pedagogy") in a technique designed to understand the text after multiple readings (Bogdan & Biklen, 1992). Documents were compared and codes were defined and categorized into emerging themes (Lincoln & Guba, 1985) as each category was reexamined, redefined, and combined with other similar categories. For example, initial codes were based on multiple or repeated occurrences of words or phrases with similar meanings (e.g., "getting to know students" and "interest inventories," and "asking students about themselves" came together as "learning from and with our students") and were grouped together to create themes.

From our analysis we identified four themes: *importance of choice in literacy pedagogy; learning from and with our students; freedom to apply course methods and ideas*; and *growing confidence*. In the following section, we present the findings organized around these four themes. We then align Ball's (2009) generative change model and the four processes of change — metacognitive awareness, ideological becoming, internalization, and efficacy with the findings from this study of preservice teachers. We examine these findings and the generative change model in relation to learning to teach literacy to emergent bilinguals. We conclude with implications for teacher education and outline some limitations of this study.

Findings

Importance of Choice in Literacy Pedagogy

We began the semester with a multiliteracies timeline project in order to facilitate awareness of the role of literacies and languages in the lives of our participants. As part of this assignment, participants chose positive and negative aspects of their language and literacy development both in and out of school. In their reflections, preservice teachers most often wrote about the importance of choice in their literacy development. Several students pointed to the lack of choice when they were learning to read and write and how this impeded their development.

In her timeline, Kelly depicted a love of reading and writing in her elementary school years due to teachers giving her freedom and choice. But she pinpointed the time this changed for her. She wrote,

> My sophomore year is when I began to really dislike writing. We wrote every day and we never had free choice. In class we were given prompt after prompt after prompt and writing was no longer fun or exciting but instead it was something that I dreaded.

After discussing and reflecting on the experience, Kelly understood that what made these kinds of rote and prescriptive literacy experiences dreadful for her was the lack of choice and the feeling that what she had to say was not important. Kelly wrote about the kind of teacher she wants to be, one who will foster choice and interest rather than forcing students to only respond to a prompt. She explained,

> I know not all students will enjoy writing but I hope I can give them reasons of why writing is important as well as fun and meaningful. Many students like myself found that what they wrote was not important and they need to be reminded what they have to say is valuable. Each student has a voice and their voice shines through their writing. Allowing students to write freely will not only provide better work from the students, but it will also be more enjoyable to read as a teacher. I know that prompts are required for certain assignments, but my main goal is to let students write about what is important to them because what they care about is important.

In her reflection, Kelly shows an awareness of the literacy pedagogies that impacted her both positively and negatively. She also demonstrates an understanding of the complexities of teaching literacy, that "prompts are required for certain assignments" but students can still write about what is important to them and have choices.

Similarly, Fran, a bilingual preservice teacher, wrote about her experiences in and out of bilingual programs in school. She recounted how she did not always feel motivated to read and write, particularly when the literacy activities did not seem to relate to her life. There was one teacher who gave her a choice in what she wrote about, however, and this had a dramatic effect on her desire to write. In reflecting about how that experience will impact her future pedagogy with emergent bilinguals, Fran wrote,

> I also want to be the teacher who will give a student the opportunity to write about anything they desire because choice is the key. I do not want to set limits on their

potential to create a published poem ... As a future teacher, I also want my students to feel free to create writing that relates to their lives whether they prefer to write in English or Spanish ...

Although Fran was not always encouraged to read and write on topics that were relevant to her or that included both of the languages she was proficient in, Fran recognized the importance of allowing students to choose from their linguistic repertoires. In turn, she is determined to give her emergent bilinguals opportunities to foster and create literacies in multiple languages.

Learning from and with Our Students

In the writing club, we asked preservice teachers to get to know their students (3–5 elementary students per pair) and to design lessons according to their students' needs and interests. The preservice teachers began with interest inventories and other activities to get to know their students. From there, they designed lessons that integrated reading and writing while incorporating the needs and interests of their students. This kind of teaching was designed to help our preservice teachers understand how to plan literacy instruction based on the unique backgrounds of the students. In their reflections, the preservice teachers indicated the importance of purposely getting to know their students' interests, learning preferences, and cultural and linguistic backgrounds. For many, this was the first time they had been guided in responsive teaching and there were strong emotions such as fear and excitement surrounding the experience. They felt they were learning to become better literacy teachers, and they began to view students as important assets to their learning. Tracy explained it this way,

> I really enjoyed getting to know my kids. Getting to talk to them about their day and interests was something I looked forward to every time. It helped me plan my writing lessons but it also helped me realize how important it is to listen to a child about their own lives and interests.

Not only was Tracy excited about working with her small group of students, but she used the knowledge she gained about them to plan her lessons responsively. Likewise, some of the preservice teachers described working with diverse students as a "puzzle" that they were learning to solve. Farah described the writing club as a learning experience that "forced me to think on my toes and really search the children for answers; what was or was not working was up to me!" These participants described learning from and with their students as positive and integral to literacy pedagogy.

And yet for some participants, there was fear associated with teaching writing and diverse students, particularly in the beginning. Betty wrote,

> We learned about the interests of all students and incorporated them into our lessons. I have so many ideas now. I cannot wait to teach writing to diverse students in my future classroom. This is something I would have been scared of two months ago but now it is something I am excited about!

Betty recognized her own growth as a novice literacy teacher. She had gone from fear to excitement in working with the interests and backgrounds of her students. Betty was able to describe her development as a novice teacher and although she may have not known how to be responsive or she may have even been "scared" of incorporating student interest into her lesson, she felt excited about the prospect of being a responsive literacy teacher now that she has more tools and a better understanding of how to do so.

This fear of teaching diverse students was also evident in some participants' views of linguistic diversity. Some preservice teachers reflected that before teaching emergent bilinguals in the writing club, they didn't see how students' native language could be used as an asset in an English speaking class. For example, Amanda wrote about the experience of working directly with emergent bilinguals for the first time in the writing club. She said working with emergent bilinguals allowed her to see how Spanish could be used as a resource in literacy teaching. She explained,

> The after school program will help me teach diverse students because it gave me a chance to work closely with a group of kids who are diverse. One was a fluent Spanish speaker and she helped us read books that had a few Spanish words in them. It helped all of us enjoy the book more and understand more of what it was saying.

Amanda's direct experience of working with emergent bilinguals in a small group setting showed her the value of incorporating linguistic diversity into literacy teaching. She found the students' linguistic resources to be beneficial to all students in the group, not only the Spanish speaker. Affirming linguistic diversity was also described by Leslie, a bilingual preservice teacher, While she understood the value of linguistic diversity in her own life, Leslie described her experience in getting to know her students as affirming students' background and culture in addition to helping students to see their own unique abilities as strengths. She stated,

One thing I will take away from this experience is the importance of establishing relationships with your students. Creating relationships with your students invites freedom of diversity in your classroom ... I love the fact that these students felt such pride for their language and culture. They were never afraid to speak English or Spanish with us, and they were able to write freely in both languages. When our student shared his writing piece [in Spanish] with the whole after school program he just made me want to stand tall. His passion was seen through his writing. His voice was felt through the audience. It was so beautiful it made me proud to know that he was one of my students.

The relationships they built with students helped them appreciate diversity and they realized the importance of relationships for fostering literacies. And while the context of teaching may change for these preservice teachers, an important learning for them was how to understand and develop literacy lessons based on the backgrounds, interests, and needs of their students.

Freedom to Apply Course Methods and Ideas

Fostering relationships and learning with diverse students was an area preservice teachers articulated as a strength of their writing club experience. Another asset of the service-learning project was the flexibility and freedom it offered them. The preservice teachers articulated that they felt "lucky" to have additional practice in the writing club, particularly in ways that were less structured than in the traditional classroom. Angela reflected,

We were always able to try different strategies out with our small groups. We were able to tell which students really took to our ideas and which ones didn't, and for those students we could modify the lessons and ideas to our liking. This setting made for a great learning experience.

The small group setting, working with a partner, and lack of prescriptive curriculum in the writing club facilitated the freedom preservice teachers experienced. They felt that they were able to apply knowledge from their coursework in ways that were different from their experiences in the classrooms during the school day. The teaching the participants were experiencing in classrooms during the school day was more structured and standards based, while the writing club was open to experimentation.

Some participants suggested the added flexibility of the writing club helped them learn more about literacy teaching than their traditional field-based experiences. One participant, Angela, remarked, "I enjoyed the ability to pick my own books so my group could relate to them." Another participant, Meredith, described it this way, "working with a small group of kids allowed me to test methods of reading and writing without being overwhelmed with trying something new with a whole class." Alex wrote, "The after school program provided a different setting and experiences with students that was more significant to my career than the intern classroom experience." Alex explained in a follow up interview that the service-learning program was more significant to her because it forced her to design lessons to accommodate the students she had, and she created the lessons on her own. This kind of autonomy was unlike what she experienced in the classroom.

Growing Confidence

As the preservice teachers planned and implemented their lessons and worked together with their partners to problem solve, they expressed *growing confidence* about their teaching. They wrote or commented about participating in the service-learning program as "invaluable," "priceless," and "unforgettable." While many initially questioned their knowledge and ability to teach reading and writing, some preservice teachers expressed *growing confidence* after working with small groups of students. They described the autonomy and responsibility as part of their growing confidence. At the end of the experience, Toni reflected on the program and wrote,

> Working in the service learning program really allowed me to be more relaxed and confident about teaching. The small group of diverse students and the autonomy my partner and I had was so important. We were able to accommodate our students more [than in the classroom] and figure out what they needed and fix our lessons so it would work for them. I learned a lot about time management and implementing a lesson plan smoothly. I think I am much better prepared to teach all students because of this experience.

Teaching small groups of diverse students in the after school program shaped how the preservice teachers saw themselves as teachers and also how they saw their students. The more the preservice teachers began to get to know the students and see the difference they were making in their learning, the more confident and comfortable they became with teaching, reading, and writing. Tracy said, "Although in order to be a good reading and writing teacher for all students I will need a lot more practice, this program gave me a good head start and a good glimpse into how to be involved with students and their writing."

Aligning the Phases of Generative Change

According to Ball (2009), there are four stages in the process of generative change. In phase 1, teachers develop increased metacognitive awareness through the narration of personal experiences. In phase 2, as teachers engage in thoughtful discussions about important issues related to diversity and literacy, they begin to look within themselves and their students' needs to determine their role within the teaching/learning community. By phase 3, teachers engage in action research and/or other thoughtful problem solving inquiries, and they begin to internalize and develop generative thinking skills. Finally, in the fourth and final phase, teachers combine theory, best practices, and their students' needs to facilitate their own theory posing and generative thinking. Using Ball's work as a framework, we wanted to determine the preservice teachers' generative trajectories and explore how they built on the instructional practices learned in the service-learning project, the university methods course, and the field-base experience.

In designing our field-based courses and experiences, we deliberately began with activities and readings designed to help preservice teachers understand self and moved towards society and social justice issues. It is important to note we were not familiar with Ball's generative change model at the beginning of this research, but we were familiar with each individual concept that makes up her model. We discussed how the preservice teachers' experiences may or may not be congruent with the students they will teach. Throughout the semester, our preservice teachers read texts, discussed, and wrote reflections regarding literacies and diverse students, particularly emergent bilinguals. We examined the larger sociohistorical context of teaching emergent bilinguals and we discussed issues of social justice. Participants were also asked to reflect on their experiences and to connect these experiences to the literature.

As we learned more about Ball's (2009) model, we were interested in how it fit with our preservice teachers' experiences. We outline the connections between her model and our study in Table 1. The first phase of metacognitive awareness was facilitated through reflection on the role of literacies and languages in both the preservice teachers' own lives and the lives of others (their future students, for example). For us, this aspect of the generative change theory was about awareness on the part of the preservice teachers of both their own lives as well as how literacies are conceptualized, how languages are learned and effective practices. The first step for many of our preservice teachers was to reflect on how literacies

Table 1.   How Ball's (2009) Generative Change Model Relates to Data
in this Study.

Concepts in Ball's Four Phases of Generative Change	Related Actions	How the Concept Was Mediated in Our Courses and Field Work/Service Learning	Findings
Metacognitive awareness	Identify strengths and weaknesses; reflection and awakening	Multiliteracies timeline project, reflections, readings and class discussions on literacies	Importance of choice in literacy pedagogy, learning from and with students
Ideological becoming	Engagement with multiple discourses; introspection and agency	Readings and class discussions, reflections	Importance of choice in literacy pedagogy, learning from and with students
Internalization	Social learning, application of new knowledge, and advocacy	Working with a partner and diverse students in the writing club; class discussions, sharing of ideas	Freedom to apply new learning, Growing confidence
Efficacy	Problem solving and continual learning; voice and efficacy	Responsive teaching, audit trails and other reflections on learning over semester	Importance of choice in literacy pedagogy, growing confidence

and languages were fostered in their own lives. We saw them identify their
own strengths and weaknesses. Many of them reflected on effective pedagogies they experienced as students and connected these to their views of
effective teaching.

Closely examining and questioning their own experiences and connecting
them to the larger context to determine their role(s) in the teaching/learning
community is emphasized in the second phase of Ball's (2009) generative
change as ideological becoming. We asked our preservice teachers to
engage in this kind of work through assigned readings, class discussions,
and additional reflections. Ayers and Alexander-Tanner's (2010) graphic
novel facilitated discussions around the teaching profession and various
ideologies surrounding diverse students. We also used excerpts from
Cummins' work on bilingual education and discussed current events related
to emergent bilinguals.

The two first phases of the generative change focus on preservice
teachers' understandings of self, pedagogy, and the larger context.

In the third phase of generative change, Ball recommends action research and group discussions to enhance the internalization of concepts. Although not action research, we used inquiry as a tool for the preservice teachers to deepen their understanding of their students' lives and the connection to their language and literacy learning. Our preservice teachers planned writing lessons on a weekly basis based on students' needs. This kind of responsive teaching was a way for the preservice teachers to apply new knowledge to their teaching context. As in Ball's work, the preservice teachers indicated an increased sense of efficacy after applying what they were learning in their coursework to the service-learning program. The freedom to apply new learning and growing confidence exemplifies the generativity that Ball describes in the fourth phase of the model.

Limitations of the Study

While there was some change of perspectives recorded and generative learning did take place, it would be beneficial to follow students into their teaching careers and experiences in a longitudinal study, much the way Ball (2009) did. This study took place over one semester and therefore may have been too short of a timeframe to see dramatic change in preservice teachers. Additionally, the data collection for this study was conducted by a professor of her students. The data included assignments and personal reflections. Data collected as part of a course can sometimes be skewed to fit the professor's viewpoints. If data was collected by an outside researcher who did not have a role in the course (i.e., is not the professor of record) may be less biased. However, it was beneficial to have a second researcher involved in data analysis who was not the professor of record.

Practical Implications and Recommendations

By closely examining how service learning supports generative learning, we call for the inclusion of more service learning to complement traditional field-based education in Colleges of Education and other practicum-based programs. The preservice teachers' ability to develop an awareness of diversity grew from their consistent work with students both in their field-block experience and the writing club. These two opportunities provided the preservice teachers with a layering of learning – from course readings, collaborating with their mentor teachers, to being able to problem solve and create lesson plans that specifically met the needs of their students. By moving in and out of different contexts (field-based block and service-learning project), the preservice teachers were developing generative knowledge about ways to support writing for emergent bilinguals. Likewise, the preservice teachers became keenly aware of their own experiences and beliefs as language learners. They focused on the importance of providing students choice in their language and literacy learning and came to view the complexities of writing instruction in new ways. Like the students studied by Zeller et al. (2010), our preservice teachers expressed clearer understandings of their students' lives outside of school. As they learned about the lives of their students, they developed affirming views of their students' abilities and began to nurture caring relationships (McHatton et al., 2006). By responding to their students' learning needs and personal experiences, the preservice teachers noticed that their new ways of teaching positively impacted their students' learning – in turn shaping their efficacy and agency particularly as teachers of culturally and linguistically diverse students.

In order to effectively prepare preservice teachers to instruct emergent bilinguals, it is critical to provide a variety of formal and informal opportunities for them to work directly with students. This work should be accompanied by opportunities to engage in written and verbal discussions in order to examine and critique their own experiences and ideologies in relation to students' language and literacy needs. Verbal and written discussions and reflections can mediate the preservice teachers' internalization of new learning (Ball, 2009). Ongoing written reflections that compare and contrast multiple experiences can help preservice teachers modify their teaching and learning strategies and question their effectiveness.

We recommend creating multiple assignments that explicitly guide preservice teachers to explore their past beliefs and experiences as language learners and connect those experiences to the lives of their students. Like the multiliteracies timeline, preservice teachers can create a variety of digital projects such as a glogster, digital story, or a website that highlight their experiences and compares their experiences to their students' lives. Not only do these reflective assignments help preservice teachers understand and challenge their beliefs about language and learning, they can also support their goals and pedagogical practices when they become teachers.

Learning about their students' lives and creating lesson plans that responded to their students' language needs, interests, and lives outside of class was an important finding from this study and one that was nurtured through course and service learning expectations. Designing responsive instruction can be difficult when preservice teachers are only working in their field-based course (Assaf & López, 2012). They can be overwhelmed with large classes, taking on new lessons and teaching assignments, and trying to keep up with the institutional goals and expectations of a school. Additionally, when preservice teachers only participate in field-base experiences they are required to engage in mandated curriculum planning and test-driven instruction that tends to be deficit focused (Dooley, 2005).

Unlike teaching to a mandated curriculum, responsive teaching involves building on students' responses, fostering flexibility, and developing teacher–student relationships (Dozier & Rutten, 2005/2006). The preservice teachers in this study did not simply adapt students to a particular method but instead took advantage of teachable moments by providing lessons in response to student needs and interests throughout the writing club session. A service-learning project such as the one highlighted in this research can provide an informal space for preservice teachers to understand students, their cultural and linguistic experiences, build caring relationships, and align learning and instructional tools to support student learning. We recommend providing explicit guidelines to help preservice teachers conduct interest inventories with the students they work with, to question their assumptions about diversity, and to engage in a responsive discourse driven by students' needs, interests, and abilities not test scores.

Equally important, working in small groups during a service-learning project and in a field-block experience (in the university seminar and in the classroom) can provide excellent opportunities for preservice teachers to engage in critical introspection and problem solving. Hollingsworth (1994) points to the importance of collaborative conversations where "collaboration and sustained conversations become the exchange and reformation of ideas, intimate talk, and reconstructive questions" (p. 6). We recommend creating spaces for preservice teachers to engage in problem solving activities and discussions that help them apply new knowledge and extend their understanding of literacy and language learning beyond their university classroom. We agree that "the real opportunities for learning to teach come from a combination of making decisions about instruction and having the time to interact with others to reflect and build knowledge and beliefs related to the area of literacy" (Mallette, Kile, Smith, McKinney, & Readence, 2000, p. 594).

Lastly, Ball (2009) describes the processes of generative change as taking place within an individual's zone of proximal development. The preservice teachers entered the field block at different stages of development and awareness and were challenged to apply their understanding of writing pedagogy and language learning with their students in the writing club. As teacher educators design and implement service-learning projects in their courses, they need to consider their preservice teachers' individual zones of proximal development and find ways to provide safe spaces where individuals can take risks and extend their professional and personal knowledge.

References

Alt, M. N., & Medrich, E. A. (1994). *Student outcomes from participation in community service.* US Department of Education Office of Research. Berkeley, CA: MPR Associates.

Anders, P. L., Hoffman, J. V., & Duffy, G. G. (2000). Teaching teachers to teach reading: Paradigm shifts, persistent problems, and challenges. In M. L. Kamil, P. B. Mosenthal, P. D. Pearson, & R. Barr (Eds.), *Handbook of reading research* (Vol. 3, pp. 719–742). Mahwah, NJ: Erlbaum.

Assaf, L. C. (2006). One reading specialist's response to high-stakes testing pressures. *The Reading Teacher, 60*(2), 158–168.

Assaf, L. C., & Dooley, C. (2010). Investigating ideological clarity in literacy teacher education. *The Teacher Educator, 45*(3), 153–178. doi:10.1080/08878730.2010.489144

Assaf, L. C., Garza, R., & Battle, J. (2010). Multicultural teacher education: Examining the perceptions, practices, and coherence in one teacher preparation program. *Teacher Education Quarterly, 37*(2), 115–135.

Assaf, L. C., & López, M. M. (2012). Reading rocks an after school literacy program: Responsive reading instruction. *Journal of Early Childhood Teacher Education, 5*(1), 55–62.

Ayers, W., & Alexander-Tanner, R. (2010). *To teach: The journey in comics.* New York, NY: Teachers College Press.

Bakhtin, M. M. (1981). *The dialogic imagination.* Austin, TX: University of Texas Press.

Ball, A. (2009). Toward a theory of generative change in culturally and linguistically complex classrooms. *American Educational Research Journal, 46*(1), 45–72. doi:10.3102/0002831208323277

Bandura, A. (1997). *Self-efficacy: The exercise of control.* New York, NY: Freeman.

Bartolomé, L. I. (1998). *The misteaching of academic discourses: The politics of language in the classroom.* Boulder, CO: Westview Press.

Bartolomé, L. I. (2004). Critical pedagogy and teacher education: Radicalizing perspective teachers. *Teacher Education Quarterly, 31*(1), 97–122.

Bogdan, R., & Biklen, S. (1992). *Qualitative research for education: An introduction to theory and methods* (2nd ed.). Boston, MA: Allyn and Bacon.

Bransford, J. D., Brown, A. L., & Cocking, R. R. (Eds.). (2000). *How people learn: Brain, mind, experience, and school.* New York, NY: National Academy Press.

Bruner, J. S. (1994). Life as narrative. In A. H. Dyson & C. Genishi (Eds.), *The need for story: Cultural diversity in classroom and community* (pp. 28–37). Urbana, IL: National Council of Teachers of English.

Cobb, J. (2005). Planting the seeds … tending the garden … cultivating the student: Early childhood pre-service teachers as literacy researchers exploring beliefs about struggling readers and diversity. *Journal of Early Childhood Teacher Education, 26,* 377–393.

Cochran-Smith, M. (1995). Color blindness and basket making are not the answers: Confronting the dilemmas of race, culture, and language diversity in teacher education. *American Educational Research Journal, 32,* 493–522.

Cochran-Smith, M., & Lytle, S. (1999). Learning to teach for social justice. In G. A. Griffith (Ed.), *The education of teachers: Ninety-eighth yearbook of the national society for the study of education* (pp. 114–144). Chicago, IL: University of Chicago.

Colato-Lainez, R. (2005). *I am René the Boy/Soy René el niño.* Houston, TX: Arte Publico Press.

Darder, A., Baltodano, M., & Torres, R. D. (Eds.). (2002). *The critical pedagogy reader.* New York, NY: Routledge/Falmer.

DeJong, L., & Groomes, F. (1996). A constructivist teacher education program that incorporates community service to prepare students to work with children living in poverty. *Action in Teacher Education, 18*(2), 86–95.

Dooley, C. M. (2005). One teacher's resistance to the pressures of test mentality. *Language Arts, 82,* 177–185.

Dozier, C. L., & Rutten, I. (2005/06). Responsive teaching toward responsive teachers: Mediating transfer through intentionality, enactment, and articulation. *Journal of Literacy Research, 37*(4), 459–492.

Epstein, S. (1993). Emotion and self-theory. In M. Lewis & J. Haviland (Eds.), *The handbook of emotions.* New York, NY: Guilford Publications.

Erikson, E. H. (1963). *Childhood and society* (2nd ed.). New York, NY: Norton.

Exposito, S., & Favela, A. (2003). Reflective voices: Valuing immigrant students and teaching with ideological clarity. *The Urban Review, 35*(1), 73–91.

Franke, M., Carpenter, T., Levi, L., & Fennema, E. (2001). Capturing teachers' generative change: A follow-up study of professional development in mathematics. *American Educational Research Journal, 38*(3), 653–689.

Geertz, C. (1973). *The interpretation of cultures: Selected essays.* New York, NY: Basic Books.

Goswami, D. & Stillman, P. R. (Eds.). (1987). *Reclaiming the classroom: Teacher research as an agency for change.* Montclair, NJ: Boynton/Cook.

Haberman, M. (1991). Can culture awareness be taught in teacher education programs? *Teacher Education, 4,* 25–31.

Hale, A. (2008). Service learning with Latino communities: Effects on preservice teachers. *Journal of Hispanic Higher Education, 7*(1), 54–69.

Hollingsworth, S. (1994). *Teacher research and urban literacy education.* New York, NY: Teachers College Press.

Hubbard, R. S., & Power, B. M. (1999). *Living the questions: A guide for teacher-researchers.* Portland, ME: Stenhouse.

Johnston, P. (2004). *Choice words: How language affects children's learning.* New York, NY: Stenhouse.

King, J. E. (1991). Dysconscious racism: Ideology, identity, and the miseducation of teachers. *Journal of Negro Education, 60*(2), 133–146.

Koliba, C. J., Campbell, E. K., & Shapiro, C. (2006). The practice of service learning in local school-community contexts. *Educational Policy, 20*(5), 683–717.

Lane, B. (2008). *But how do you teach writing? A simple guide for all teachers.* New York, NY: Scholastic.

Lieberman, A. (Ed.). (1988). *Building a professional culture in schools.* New York, NY: Teachers College Press.

Lincoln, Y. S., & Guba, E. G. (1985). *Naturalistic inquiry.* Beverly Hills, CA: Sage.

López, M. M., & Brochin, C. (2014). Transnational preservice teachers' literate lives and writing pedagogy in a digital era. In R. Ferdig & K. Pytash (Eds.), *Exploring multimodal composition and digital writing* (pp. 298–315). Hershey, PA: IGI Global. doi:10.4018/978-1-4666-4345-1.ch018

Macedo, D. (1994). *Literacies of power: What Americans are not allowed to know.* Boulder, CO: Westview.

Mallette, M. H., Kile, R. S., Smith, M. M., McKinney, M., & Readence, J. E. (2000). Constructing meaning about literacy difficulties: Preservice teachers beginning to think about pedagogy. *Teaching and Teacher Education, 16*, 593–612.

McHatton, P. A., Thomas, D., & Lehman, K. (2006). Lessons learning in service learning: Personnel preparation through community action. *Mentoring & Tutoring: Partnership in Learning, 14*(1), 67–79.

Moustakas, C. (1994). *Phenomenological research methods.* Thousand Oaks, CA: Sage.

National Service-Learning Clearinghouse. (2009). *Building effective partnerships for service-learning.* Scotts Valley, CA: National Service-Learning Clearinghouse.

Sleeter, C. E. (1995). Reflections on my use of multicultural and critical pedagogy when students are white. In C. E. Sleeter & P. McLaren (Eds.), *Multicultural education, critical pedagogy, and the politics of difference.* New York, NY: SUNY Press.

Smylie, M. A., Bay, M., & Tozer, S. E. (1999). Preparing teachers as agents of change. In G. A. Griffith (Ed.), *The education of teachers: Ninety-eighth yearbook of the national society for the study of education* (pp. 18–62). Chicago, IL: University of Chicago.

Strong, T. (2010). Collaboration, generativity, rigor, and imagination: Four words to focus and animate our practice oriented inquiries. *Human Systems: Journal of Therapy, Consultation & Training, 21*, 380–396.

Tellez, K., Hlebowitsh, P. S., Cohen, M., & Norwood, P. (1995). Social service field experiences and teacher education. In J. M. Larking & C. E. Sleeter (Eds.), *Developing multicultural teacher education curricula* (pp. 65–78). Albany, NY: State University of New York Press.

vanDijk, T. (1998). *Ideology: An interdisciplinary approach.* London: Sage.

Vasquez, V. (2004). *Negotiating critical literacies with young children.* New York, NY: Routledge-LEA.

Vygotsky, L. (1978). *Mind in society: The development of higher psychological processes.* Cambridge, MA: Harvard University Press.

Wade, R. (2000). Service learning for multicultural teaching competency: Insights from the literature for teacher educators. *Equity & Excellence in Education, 33*(3), 21–29.

Wade, R. (2007). Service-learning for social justice in the elementary classroom: Can we get there from here? *Equity & Excellence in Education, 40*, 156–165.

Wade, R., & Saxe, D. W. (1996). Community service-learning in the social studies: Historical roots, empirical evidence, critical issues. *Theory and Research in Social Education, 24,* 331–359.

Zeller, N., Griffith, R., Zhang, G., & Klenke, J. (2010). From stranger to friend: The effect of service learning on preservice teachers' attitudes towards diverse populations. *Journal of Language and Literacy Education, 6*(2), 34–50.

CHAPTER 3

"*PORQUE SÉ LOS DOS IDIOMAS.*" BILITERACY BELIEFS AND BILINGUAL PRESERVICE TEACHER IDENTITY

Sandra I. Musanti

Abstract

This study, carried out in the bilingual and bicultural border area of South Texas, is an exploration of bilingual preservice teachers' identity formation and their experiences and beliefs about literacy and biliteracy during an undergraduate class focused on learning about emergent literacy in the bilingual classroom. This study is based on a sociocultural approach to learning and identity development, and research that explores how bilingual teachers' identity is shaped through their participation in cultural and linguistic practices. The purpose of this practitioner research is to provide insights into preservice teachers' identities as they start to explore literacy and biliteracy practices. Two research questions guide the study: What experiences about literacy and biliteracy development do prospective teachers identify as meaningful? How do these experiences contribute to define bilingual preservice teachers' identities? Findings indicate that bilingual preservice teachers' identities are

Research on Preparing Preservice Teachers to Work Effectively with Emergent Bilinguals
Advances in Research on Teaching, Volume 21, 59–87
ISSN: 1479-3687/doi:10.1108/S1479-368720140000021002

shaped by cultural and linguistic experiences that define the bilingual and bicultural dynamics of the region. Two predominant types of experiences impact bilingual preservice teachers' beliefs about teaching, learning, and literacy/biliteracy development. Particularly significant in defining their perceptions are the lessons learned from meaningful others − especially mothers and teachers − and certain relevant memories regarding effective practices they experienced when learning to read and write. Implications for teacher education preparation of bilingual teachers are identified.

Keywords: Bilingual education; bilingual preservice teacher education; teacher identity; transnational identities; biliteracy development; literacy and biliteracy beliefs

Introduction

Reading does not consist merely of decoding the written word or language; rather, it is preceded by and intertwined with knowledge of the world. Language and reality are dynamically interconnected. (Freire & Macedo, 1987, p. 29)

Three years ago, I joined the faculty in a university located in the southernmost part of Texas on the border with Mexico. As a Latina, different aspects of the culture were familiar, especially the language. Spanish is my first language, so I felt a closeness to home as I discovered how much of the daily interactions in this part of Texas occur in Spanish. However, it was clear to me that I was still an outsider in many other ways. I needed to learn about the cultural and linguistic identity of the region. One of my first teaching assignments was the class, Emergent Literacy in the Bilingual Classroom. I immediately fell in love with this class, partially because it is taught in Spanish, and mainly, because I explore with preservice teachers how young emergent bilingual children learn to read the word while trying to make sense of the world around them (Freire & Macedo, 1987).

Students taking this class are pursuing a bilingual education teaching certification in the state of Texas. They are very eager to learn and are especially eager to learn about literacy and biliteracy development in Spanish. During my first semester teaching this class, I noticed how pleased they were when discussing the value of being bilingual; and how surprised they seemed when I explained the sophisticated linguistic competencies required to navigate between and within two languages so fluidly and seamlessly.

Acknowledging that being bilingual and bicultural are traits that identify my students, and living in the region has caused me to rethink some of my teaching practices, especially in regards to using language as a pedagogical resource in teacher preparation (Valdés, Bunch, Snow, Lee, with Matos, 2005). Using language as a pedagogical resource entails valuing students' bilingualism and integrating their language repertoire and biliteracy skills in the instructional approach (Moschkovich, 2002). Since teaching cannot be detached from the context in which it is taking place, it needs to be grounded in a deep understanding of students' needs and resources for learning (González, Moll, & Amanti, 2005).

Analysis of demographic data reveals the critical need for high quality bilingual teacher preparation programs to serve the growing population of low-income Latina/o bilingual learners (Flores, Sheets, & Clark, 2011). The South Texas border context has an even greater need to address these concerns than other parts of the country because it has one of the highest Latina/o populations in the country (95%). Many of the college students who are pursuing a teaching certification in bilingual education define themselves as bilingual and first generation college students, and many are from low-income family backgrounds.

This study contributes to an understanding of bilingual preservice teachers' identity formation in South Texas and their experiences and beliefs about literacy and biliteracy. Participants were students in an undergraduate class, Emergent Literacy in the Bilingual Classroom. The goals of the course included helping the preservice teacher understand literacy and biliteracy development, and further develop their linguistic academic competence by providing authentic opportunities to read, write, think, and talk in Spanish.

This study draws from theorists who highlight the impact of teacher education in the development of teacher identity and a view of learning as a sociocultural construction (Britzman, 1991; Clarke, 2008; Danielewicz, 2001; Morgan, 2004; Varghese, Morgan, Johnston, & Johnson, 2005) as opposed to the trend that conceptualizes teacher learning as the acquisition of a set of skills and the mastering of procedural knowledge (Duffy, Webb, & Davis, 2009). The study looks at teaching education practices from a perspective of identity development to help educators gain an understanding of the cultural and linguistic factors impacting bilingual teacher education. I started this study with two research questions that guided my inquiry and data analysis: What experiences about literacy and biliteracy development do prospective teachers identify as meaningful?

How do these experiences contribute to define bilingual preservice teachers' identity?

Theoretical Framework

This study draws from a sociocultural approach to understanding teacher learning and identity development, and from research that explores how bilingual teacher identity is shaped through participation in cultural and linguistic practices (Clark, Jackson, & Prieto, 2011; Clarke, 2008; Gee, 2001). From a sociocultural perspective, learning is a situated process that does not occur in a vacuum but as individuals become part of a community of practice (Wenger, 1998). Communities of practice involve a shared endeavor that engages individuals in negotiating meaning while, jointly, identifying goals and tasks. Prospective teachers become part of communities of practice as they face the challenge of learning to teach and learning about teaching (shared endeavor) while developing an in depth understanding of complex discourse practices such as educational policy, classroom discourse, school practices supporting different types of language use in the classroom, among others (Gee, 2008; Hornberger, 2004). Participation in different discourse practices shapes preservice teachers' actions and beliefs regarding language (Gee, 2008). It is important that teacher educators design instruction considering that preservice teachers learn through participation in different discourse practices, promoting activities that foster preservice teachers' reflection on their beliefs about language and learning as well as on the development of their teacher identity (Giampapa, 2010; Morgan, 2004; Smagorinsky, Cook, Moore, Jackson, & Fry, 2004).

Bilingual Teacher Preparation

Drawing from García and Kleifgen (2010), I contend that bilingual teacher preparation programs tend to follow a monoglossic ideology that translates into teaching instructional practices that promote the strict separation of languages during instruction, the development of English literacy over biliteracy or multiliteracies, and the avoidance of translanguaging as part of teaching and learning. Bilingual teacher education programs should be based on the understanding of bilingualism as dynamic and ever changing.

This entails focusing on building a teacher preparation pedagogy grounded in the candidates' own language use, enabling teachers to use their different languages extensively, and modeling how to develop academic abilities in both languages (García, Flores, & Woodley, 2012).

Guerrero, Farruggio, and Guerrero (2013) contend that helping prospective teachers in South Texas to succeed may require the development of a "border signature pedagogy" to better prepare bilingual preservice teachers in the region, most of whom have had K-12 schooling experiences almost exclusively in English. Identifying teacher education practices to address the needs of bilingual preservice teachers in this region of high Latino/a population is critical and long overdue. It requires revisiting teacher educators' instructional approach taking into account how preservice teachers' cultural and linguistic background influences their teaching identity (Clark & Flores, 2001; Clark et al., 2011; Flores, Ek, & Sánchez, 2011; Morgan, 2004).

Researchers have acknowledged the relevance of preservice teachers' accessing their language and literacy histories and reflecting and writing about them. Smith, Sánchez, Ek, and Machado-Casas (2011) examine the construction of ideas about teaching reading and writing through candidates' personal literacy trajectories. They conclude that students are able to "increase their understanding of personal linguistic ideologies and language varieties …. They become aware of the complexity of language learning and language teaching and confront the consequences of negative language ideologies and linguistic hegemony" (p. 184). Similarly, Edwards (2009) explains that writing autobiographies and reflecting about them could afford preservice teachers opportunities to critically think about their experiences as literate individuals while deepening their understanding about language and literacy.

Bilingual Preservice Teacher Identity

Teacher identity is an ongoing process of being and becoming a teacher (Britzman, 1991; Miller-Marsh, 2002). In this process of constructing a teacher identity, teachers develop their particular ways of understanding and experiencing the world. Teachers' perceptions about what learning is and how knowledge is constructed impact teachers' sense of self (Britzman, 1991). Understanding preservice teachers' construction of their identity as future bilingual teachers involves ascertaining: "what is valued as truth or discarded as fiction, how one defines her relationship to the world and to others, ... what is taken for granted in familiar and unfamiliar situations, and how one understands teaching and learning" (Britzman, 1991, p. 24). In other words, teacher education will benefit from preparing teachers to discern their own beliefs about how students learn and what are effective teaching practices. Teacher educators should promote critical reflection of what preservice teachers tend to take for granted or they assume are natural ways of doing in education. For instance, some preservice teachers tend to have a difficult time questioning the effectiveness of how they have been taught to read and write.

From a sociocultural perspective, the development of teacher identity is an intersection of different experiences and social interactions within self, the family, the community, and the schooling process. The development of identity begins before their teacher preparation program (Flores, Clark, & Guerra, 2008; Musanti & Pence, 2010; Varghese et al., 2005) and is influenced by the cultural, social, and historical context in which preservice teachers live (Smagorinsky et al., 2004).

Varghese et al. (2005) discuss how language teacher identity relates to participation in different social, cultural, and political contexts and discourses, and how this participation influences belief systems, attitudes, and shared values (Danielewicz, 2001; Gee, 2001). Therefore, cultural and linguistic experiences and relationships mediate preservice teachers' development and identity construction. Furthermore, the social construction of identity is at the core of preservice teachers' beliefs about bilingual education, literacy instruction, and the role of culture in learning (Clark et al., 2011).

Several studies have addressed teacher identity formation in relation to learning and development. From the perspective of a community of practice, Clarke (2008) presents an exploration of identity development in the first cohort of students to complete a new teacher education program. He concludes that learning to teach is a process of identity formation (p. 35). Preservice teachers become immersed in a community of practice, and they internalize ways of thinking, doing, interacting, and communicating that grant membership to that group. More recently, Ajayi (2011) conducted a qualitative exploration of 57 English as second language (ESL) teachers' identity development in California. He concluded that Latino and African-American ESL teachers' identities are intrinsically interwoven with their cultural and ethnic backgrounds. He explains that ESL teachers' sociocultural identities are negotiated in relation to their students' backgrounds, and they mediate their interpretations of practice in multiple and complex ways.

Studies of bilingual teacher identity development have also concluded that identity intersects with different sociocultural experiences and discursive practices. In a study of novice bilingual teachers, Varghese (2006) showed "how professional identities of teachers are created through an interaction of the structural influences surrounding them as well as how they respond to such influences" (p. 222). She concludes that conflicting discourses regarding bilingual education impact teachers' construction of a sense of self as bilingual teachers. Flores et al. (2008) examined the acculturation of Latino preservice bilingual teachers and also found that Latino teachers' identities are rooted in their ethnic origins and cultural identity. The researchers conclude that life experiences of ethnic minority educators "act as a 'bridging identity' toward their teacher identity formation" (p. 291) and affect the way preservice teachers see themselves and interact with students, parents, and colleagues.

Literacy and Biliteracy Beliefs

Literacy has been redefined as the competence to use language and images in multiple ways to access, represent, and critically think about ideas (Giampapa, 2010). Literacy is no longer thought of as the acquisition of a collection of technical skills to read and write. Being literate is the capacity to think and interpret the world beyond the printed text, and reading the world is a practice that empowers individuals (Freire & Macedo, 1987).

In the same way, biliteracy is more than the development of skills to read and write in two languages. Biliteracy development occurs in multiple contexts and through social interaction (García, Bartlett, & Kleifgen, 2007). Several authors have defined biliteracy as a process that entails the interweaving of two languages in a dynamic and continuous way, integrating skills development, knowledge construction, and experiences (Dworin, 2003; Hornberger, 2004; Reyes, 2006). Focusing on emergent bilinguals, Reyes (2006) explains that "*Biliteracy* is a term used to describe children's literate competencies in two languages, to whatever degree, developed either simultaneously or successively" (p. 35). Dworin (2003) contends that biliteracy is different from the literacy competence developed by monolinguals and is an important intellectual and sociocultural asset. Bilingualism, biliteracy, and biculturalism can be considered forms of cultural capital and a valuable resource in a diverse and rapidly changing society (Trueba, 2002 as cited in Manyak, 2006). When bilingual individuals develop literacy skills in either of their two languages, this development positively contributes to the growth of their literacy skills in the other language (Manyak, 2006; Moll, Saez, & Dworin, 2001).

More research is needed in the field of biliteracy development and the implications that it has for teacher preparation. Escamilla (2006) argues that most research has explored literacy and biliteracy development from a monolingual perspective with a major focus on reading and writing for second language learners. In addition, she claims that there is a scarcity of research exploring biliteracy development, and that studies of teachers' beliefs about what constitutes effective biliteracy teaching practices are almost non-existent. Many teachers and teacher candidates hold unexamined assumptions about biliteracy that are imprinted with a monoglossic ideology and a deficit view of the bilingual learner (Escamilla, 2006; García & Kleifgen, 2010). Even when caring for students, teachers tend to believe that the teaching practices proven effective with monolingual speakers should be equally effective with bilingual learners. As a result, they tend to hold a deficit view of bilingual students interpreting their academic struggle as a lack of skills. As Escamilla (2006) asserts

> In short, teacher beliefs that language, culture, and social class is a problem combined with a dearth of literature on the development of biliteracy, are enacted in teaching practices that often address the "problem of language" rather than the development of bilingualism and biliteracy. (p. 2332)

Pérez and Huerta (2011) discuss a dynamic biliteracy framework to approach bilingual teacher preparation. They propose a comprehensive model that promotes a holistic understanding of biliteracy processes, including an understanding of how biliteracy is socially and culturally mediated and the role biliteracy plays in disciplinary learning and in the academic achievement of emergent bilinguals. Moreover, Moll et al. (2001) suggest that educators consider becoming biliterate as a fluid process that is connected to children's experiences and impacted by schooling, and social and cultural contexts.

Transnational Literacies and Identity

Researchers noticed the unique ways in which literacy practices took place in transnational communities (i.e., immigrant families, borderland communities) and how they were interwoven and displayed, and important studies followed that explored "the lived experiences, human practices, and 'cultural logics' of people whose everyday lives are dramatically shaped by large-scale global and transnational processes ..." (Warriner, 2007, p. 202). Literacy and biliteracy practices in a transnational context express the dynamic nature of being part of two cultural and linguistic communities. Following this line of work, Sánchez (2007) analyzed the narratives of transnational Latino families and identified the different ways in which they used language and literacy practices to represent themselves. In her conclusion, she emphasized the importance of understanding the "transnational lives" (p. 278) of student teachers, and how their experiences impact and transform language and literacy practices. Bartlett (2007) examined the educational trajectories of newcomer immigrant students in a bilingual high school. He discussed how cultural artifacts (i.e., grades, labels such as "good student") and the bilingual literacy practices valued by schools are essential to identity construction and transnational students' achievement.

Researchers concur about the importance of understanding how individual life experiences, and the literacy and cultural practices people routinely engage in as members of a transnational community become part of the process of identity formation. This study contributes to this body of knowledge by exploring the literacy and biliteracy experiences and the transnational identities of preservice bilingual teachers in a borderland context.

Methods

In this qualitative study, I follow a practitioner researcher approach (Cochran-Smith & Lytle, 2009). As a teacher educator, I believe it is critical to engage in research that requires a reflective and critical attitude toward practice in terms of its goals, assumptions, activities, or outcomes. Practitioner research contributes to an understanding of preservice teachers' beliefs and learning needs, and, ultimately, to identify changes that can positively impact their learning. Therefore in this study, I focus on exploring the meanings of the autobiographical narratives preservice teachers wrote as part of a class I teach in a bilingual program. The intent is to identify student teachers' perceptions of literacy and biliteracy experiences and how these experiences contribute to their teacher identity.

In addition, this study includes a narrative inquiry approach to analyze preservice teachers' autobiographical narratives. The narrative approach "gives prominence to human agency and imagination, it is well suited to studies of subjectivity and identity" (Riessman, 1993, p. 5). The text as constructed by the narrator becomes a particular way of making meaning and interpreting an experience, event, situation or outcome. Therefore, for the purpose of this study, narratives are the written texts bilingual preservice teacher construct to express their literacy stories and their beliefs (Clandinin & Connelly, 2000). By examining students' reflective writing in their literacy autobiography, I identify different experiences they render important in their literacy development, and the impact on their identity formation.

Setting and Participants

The university where this study was conducted is located on the U.S.–Mexico border and serves a majority Latino population of Mexican descent. This university prepares most of the teachers in the region with teaching specializations in bilingual education and English as a second language. The selected course is one of the core courses for the baccalaureate degree program in the Early Childhood-6 (EC-6) Bilingual Generalist, entitled Emergent Literacy in the Bilingual Classroom. The program of study includes a series of three courses focused on bilingual classroom methodology that are taught in Spanish. The selected course is the first of the three, and it focuses on exploring current theories and methods of early literacy development in the bilingual classroom. Students take this course midway into their program of studies.

I designed instruction to engage prospective teachers in a variety of literacy related activities, including writing a literacy autobiography, engaging in multiple opportunities for cooperative and collective work analyzing literacy lessons from video cases, modeling and demonstrating teaching strategies, tutoring and interviewing students, and observing and reflecting on K-3 elementary classroom teaching, among others. The main goal for this course is for students to learn about the principles and foundations of bilingual education and how these apply to literacy and biliteracy development. The main textbook for this course is the Spanish version of Freeman and Freeman (2009), "La enseñanza de la lectura y la escritura en español en inglés en clases bilingües y de doble inmersión." [Teaching Reading and Writing in Spanish and English in Bilingual and Dual Language Classrooms.]

Participants ($N = 42$) in the study were students taking this course during the Summer 2013 and Fall 2013. The first round of data collection included 22 students during Summer 2013 and the second round of data was collected in the Fall 2013 and involved 20 students. All students were bilingual. Most students (71%) spoke Spanish as the first language, 12% spoke English as the first language, and 17% were simultaneous bilinguals. Schooling experiences were varied. Most students completed their schooling in South Texas where instruction is predominantly in English, and bilingual education programs are reduced to early-exit transition programs (67%). Some students completed all or part of the elementary education in Mexico, most commonly Pre-K (Pre-Kindergarten or preschool) K (Kindergarten) through third grade (33%). The names of students used in the narrative are pseudonyms and the inclusion of information that could allow identifying them has been omitted.

Data Collection

Data was collected during two consecutive semesters (Summer 2013 and Fall 2013) and included all course assignments and a questionnaire. For the purpose of this article, I analyze data from the students' literacy autobiographies and questionnaires.

Literacy autobiography. Tapping into preservice teachers' previous knowledge and learning experiences is at the core of this assignment. To write the literacy autobiography students revisit their initial experiences of learning to read and write at home or at school, identify meaningful learning experiences or painful ones, and reconstruct pieces of their schooling history. This assignment is grounded in the belief that teachers and teacher candidates tend to draw knowledge from their experiences as learners (Lortie, 1975) and from their internalization of practices modeled by their distant mentors (John-Steiner, 1997). At the beginning of the semester, the students are required to write a 2–3 pages long autobiography describing and reflecting on their literacy beliefs and experiences.

I describe the assignment requirements during the first class, defining it as an opportunity to reconstruct their initial literacy experiences both at home and at school. I also make explicit my belief regarding how these experiences tend to shape the way teachers understand teaching and learning. In addition, I initiate the reflective and writing process in class with an activity to promote a collective discussion of the students' lived experiences. Students take some time in class and write one initial paragraph for the literacy autobiography. Then, in small groups they read their initial paragraph, receive and provide feedback on academic writing style, and share other experiences that they believe are meaningful to their literacy story.

Typically, they claim that they do not remember their early experiences, so I ask them to do informal interviews with family members and to collect artifacts that provide evidence of their early experiences, such as books they used to like to read or samples of school writing. This way, they have the opportunity to reconstruct their early literacy experiences as well as to discover the early schooling experiences of siblings, parents, or grandparents. In addition, I ask them to reflect on how their literacy history might impact their beliefs about how children learn to read and write in one or more languages.

Questionnaire. I designed a questionnaire to collect information on students' bilingual profile, characteristics of their language uses both socially and academically, their perceptions of reading and writing skills in each language, reading habits, family demographic information, reasons to become a bilingual teacher and most beneficial learning activities implemented during the course. The questionnaire involved a series of 23 questions, 21 closed questions and 2 open-ended questions. One question asked about their reasons to become a bilingual teacher and the other one asked to identify the most helpful learning activities during the semester. This questionnaire was voluntary, not graded, and it was completed in the language of preference of the students at the end of the semester. For the purpose of this study, I analyze their responses to items on the bilingual profile, use of language, perceptions of reading and writing skills, and reasons to become a bilingual teacher.

Data Analysis

Analysis involved multiple readings of students' autobiographies in order to look for themes emerging from the narratives (Riessman, 1993). Initially, I read all the students' autobiographies after the semester was over, highlighting important information in relation to students' initial literacy experiences. An inductive inside-out approach to the data followed to explore the content of the autobiographies and to identify themes that appeared across the different narratives (Merriam, 1998; Riessman, 1993). Autobiographies were coded to identify: (a) literacy experiences at home, (b) literacy learning experiences at school, (c) meaningful distant mentors

(John-Steiner, 2000), (d) the meaning of being bilingual, and (e) beliefs about effective literacy teaching practices. Responses to the open-ended questions on the questionnaire were read multiple times and coded to identify references to self-perception about becoming a bilingual teacher. In this study, questionnaire data were used to more accurately describe students' linguistic profile and language use, and to triangulate findings from students' autobiographies especially in relation to the reasons to become a bilingual teacher.

I identified four major themes regarding bilingual preservice teachers' experiences and their beliefs about literary and biliteracy that shape their bilingual teacher identity. The first theme describes how preservice bilingual teachers in the U.S.–Mexico border bridge culture and language through the construction of narratives that express an image of themselves as transnational, bilingual, and bicultural. The second theme explores how bilingual preservice teachers value learning from meaningful others, such as family members or past teachers, and the impact on literacy and biliteracy beliefs. The third theme describes the meaning of being bilingual as portrayed in the autobiographies and questionnaires and identifies specific beliefs about literacy that intersect with preservice teachers' identities. The fourth theme highlights preservice teachers' understandings of becoming bilingual teachers. In the following section, I describe the findings for each theme. Each theme is illustrated with students' quotes that are transcribed verbatim.

Findings

Bridging Culture and Language

Analysis of the literacy autobiographies showed that all bilingual preservice teachers' narratives provided an initial safe space for reconstructing personal and meaningful learning experiences as well as reconnecting with their linguistic and cultural histories (Edwards, 2009). Two narratives can be identified as representative of bilingual preservice teacher's experiences in South Texas. Yolanda summarized one of these predominant narratives:

> *Yo nací y fui criada en [ciudad], Texas por mis dos padres. Al ser hija de padres mexicanos cuya lengua materna fue el español, naturalmente también fue la mía y las de mis cuatro hermanos. La mayoría del tiempo en mi casa se hablaba en español pero mis hermanos mayores también hablaban inglés porque lo aprendieron en a la escuela.* [I was born and raised in [city], Texas by my parents. Being the daughter of Mexican parents whose first

language was Spanish, of course, it was also mine and my four brothers' first language. Most of the time, Spanish was spoken in my house but my older brothers also spoke English because they learned at school]. (Yolanda)

Most bilingual preservice teachers' narratives (67%) told stories similar to Yolanda, having been raised and educated in the United States by Mexican immigrant parents. A second type of narrative portrays the complexity of the transnational dynamics of the region and the implications for individual lives (Warriner, 2007). This second type of narratives (33%) includes the stories of students who lived or went to school for some period of time in Mexico, and then moved across the border. Ramón who was born in the border town in Texas refers to this particular dynamic:

Yo nací en [ciudad] Texas hace 23 años, pero siempre viví en la ciudad vecina que se encuentra en el sur, [...] México. Es aún más extraño que solo he ido a escuelas americanas, mas sin embargo, mi lengua maternal es y fue siempre el español. [I was born in the city of ..., Texas 23 years ago, but always lived in the neighboring town located in the south,... Mexico. It is even stranger that I've only attended American schools, but yet, my mother tongue is and always was Spanish.] (Ramón)

As indicated by their narratives and the responses to the questionnaire, even when their cultural and ethnic roots are located in Mexico, most of their schooling experiences are located in the United States, in a state and region where Spanish is rarely used as language of instruction, and when it is used is only as a tool to transition students to English. This creates a tension between the academic discourse on the need for bilingual education that preservice teachers learn and the discourse of the schools districts promoting English only education. In order to put into dialogue these competing discourses, bilingual preservice teachers need opportunities to bridge their ethnic and cultural experiences with their bilingual preservice teacher identities as they complete their journey toward graduation (Clark et al., 2011).

Ana's narrative integrated these tensions when she recalled her experience in the bilingual Pre-K and Kinder classrooms. *"En mis primeros años de primaria recuerdo que no me permitieron hablar mi lengua materna en mis clases."* [During my first years in elementary school I remember I wasn't allowed to speak my first language in class.]

Despite the fact that Spanish was her first language and with disregard to her placement in a bilingual classroom, she was tested without explanations and placed in an English only classroom in the middle of first grade, uprooting her from her classmates and her familiar teacher. These narratives speak about bilingual preservice teachers' commitment to embrace their transnational self, bridging their culture and languages while trying to manage "the complexities of belonging both 'here' and 'there' simultaneously" (Suarez-Orozco, 2001 as cited in Warriner, 2007, p. 202).

Learning from Meaningful Others

As researchers have argued, bilingual preservice teachers need to gain awareness and learn from past meaningful experiences that can contribute to transforming their teaching (Clark & Flores, 2001; Flores, Ek, et al., 2011). The analysis of the autobiographies identified two predominant types of experiences that impacted bilingual preservice teacher's beliefs about teaching, learning, and literacy/biliteracy development. Particularly significant in defining bilingual preservice teacher perceptions are the lessons learned from meaningful others – especially mothers and teachers, and certain relevant memories of effective practices learning to read and write.

John-Steiner (2000) describes the critical role that meaningful others can have in shaping our ways of knowing and acting. Bilingual preservice teachers describe the critical role parents, and specially mothers, played in shaping their initial learning experiences with reading. Mothers are named almost exclusively when describing being read Spanish stories at night, buying books to read, or going to the library. As in Flores, Ek, et al.'s (2011) exploration of preservice teachers' "*trayectorias*" [trajectories], the autobiographies clearly depict how mothers are typically the ones assuming the role of teaching children to read in Spanish. This is especially relevant for bilingual preservice teachers who completed their schooling in the United States. For instance, Beatriz is a 36-year-old mother born to Mexican parents. She explains the central role her mother played in her access to literacy in Spanish.

> *Recuerdo que creo que tenía unos 7 o 8 años y mi madre me hacía leer libros en español y luego los tenía que copiar en un papel exactamente lo que estaba en el libro. Quizás fue así que aprendí a como leer y escribir en español. Aunque mi español no es perfecto, ni en lectura ni en escritura, se como comunicarme y lo entiendo muy bien.* [I remember I was about 7 or 8 years old and my mother made me read books in Spanish and then I had to copy on paper exactly what was in the book. Maybe doing that I learned to read and write in Spanish. Although my Spanish is not perfect, neither reading nor writing, I know how to talk and I understand it very well.] (Beatriz)

Beatriz's story is representative of many students who choose to become bilingual teachers in an attempt to reclaim the right to being bilingual and biliterate (Skutnabb-Kangas, 2008).

Beatriz and Raul's stories are similar in that their mothers played a key role in assuring they developed oral and reading skills in Spanish. Raul was born in a U.S. border town but spent his first years in the neighboring Mexican town where he completed at least two years of schooling in a bilingual private school. Raul's mother contributed to the development of her son's language skills in Spanish after moving back to the United States.

Mi mama siempre ha hecho el esfuerzo de reforzar mi conocimiento del idioma. El español que me enseñaron en la escuela fue muy limitado. Aprendí a leer y escribir un español muy básico en mi casa. [My mom has always made the effort to reinforce my knowledge of the language. The Spanish I was taught in school was very limited. I learned to read and write a very basic Spanish at home.]

Raul, like other bilingual preservice teachers, understood that he didn't have opportunities to further develop his language competence in Spanish. My effort throughout the course was to open a dialogue to reflect on this linguistic outcome, not as an individual deficit, but as the lack of opportunities they had to enhance their Spanish proficiency.

Bilingual preservice teachers learned important values from significant family members. Most bilingual preservice teachers believed families play a critical role in children's education and literacy development. Yolanda, who completed all her schooling in the United States, explains how she learned from her mother that parents' involvement as well as *"práctica, mucha práctica"* [practice, lots of practice] are needed for children to learn to read and write.

Alma expressed similar beliefs. She completed elementary and high school in Mexico, her mother was a teacher, and she is one of the students who indicated that Spanish was her first and dominant language even though she feels comfortable reading in both languages for classes. Her grandfather also played a key role:

Yo crecí viendo a mi abuelo leer libros y siempre me llamó la atención como él se apasionaba tanto en el mundo de la lectura y despertó en mí la curiosidad por leer. [I grew up watching my grandfather read books, and it always struck me how he was so passionate about reading, and this motivated my curiosity to read.]

Nelly learned about the value of books from her grandmother in Mexico. She lived with her *"abuelita"* [little grandmother] for a year while her mother took care of an ill sibling in the United States. Before she returned to live with her parents, *"abuelita"* gave her a fable book collection with audiocassettes. As she still did not know how to read, she listened to her first fable "*El Flautista de Hamelin*" [The Pied Piper]. These are some examples of the critical role different family members play in helping children to become literate, and to value literacy.

Even in the midst of adverse circumstances and when parents could not provide the type of experiences that some identify as positive to promote learning and literacy development, some students found a source of inspiration. Julie shared how she might become the first one in her family to graduate from college. This was made possible because her single mother at that time made the decision to leave Mexico looking for different opportunities for herself and her daughters.

> *Yo crecí sin recursos por que desafortunadamente no se pudo quebrar el ciclo conmigo. Tuve obstáculos y dificultades durante mi aprendizaje de lectoescritura pero la decisión de mi madre mejoró mis posibilidades. Mi madre fue una gran inspiración para mí y creo que mi determinación de querer aprender fue lo que me ayudó (sic.).* [I grew up without resources because unfortunately it failed to break the cycle with me. I had obstacles and difficulties during my literacy learning but my mother's decision improved my chances. My mother was a great inspiration to me and I think my determination to want to learn is what helped me.] (Julie)

Julie's narrative is representative of many preservice bilingual teachers. Poverty and a search for better opportunities for their children is what motivated many of bilingual preservice teachers' parents to immigrate to the United States. This message is clearly evident in students' stories about uprooting and pride for parents' sacrifices and efforts to provide for a better life for them.

Meaningful experiences with past teachers either in Mexico or in the United States tend to shape the way teacher candidates perceive what it means to be a bilingual teacher. Bilingual preservice teachers' experiences as learners underscore the importance of affect in learning (Flores, Ek, et al., 2011) and the understanding of students' learning needs. Norma remembered her Pre-K teacher, who despite "*siendo una señora anglo que no hablaba el español a la perfección*" [being Anglo and not speaking very good Spanish] reached out to her students so they all could learn about "*un mundo nuevo y maravilloso*" [the new and wonderful world] of reading. This teacher showed Norma how to care about students' learning and literacy development.

Mónica clearly described how her second grade teacher, Mrs. S used to read aloud while students were sitting at the carpet. Mónica highlighted how important it was for her to have the opportunity to read to her peers and how this motivated her to practice reading aloud. Similarly, Angie completed kindergarten in Mexico, and she recalled loving school, especially because of the teacher who taught her to read and write in Spanish. Marcia words' underscored the meaning and the impact that a teacher can have on the way students' see themselves: "*La importancia de un maestro para hacer la diferencia en nuestras vidas*" [the relevance of a teacher to make a difference in our lives]. These narratives show how bilingual preservice teachers' learning and identity development are mediated by social interaction and experiences with meaningful others and add support to other similar research in the field (Flores et al., 2008; Flores, Ek, et al., 2011; Miller-Marsh, 2002).

Being Bilingual and Beliefs about Literacy

Preservice teachers' answers to the questionnaire provide important insights into their perception of their linguistic profile and literacy skills and the impact of their schooling opportunities. Most student teachers believe they have stronger writing skills in English (59%) than in Spanish (41%). This follows from the fact that most students completed most of their schooling in South Texas (67%) in school districts where access to quality bilingual programs is almost non-existent. Most students (69%) received instruction in Spanish for a short period of time, mostly in early-exit programs (K-1 or PreK-2) in South Texas or in private schools in Mexico (number of years varied). Only 12% of the students reported they achieved an equivalent level of writing skills development in both languages. These data can be better understood in relation to bilingual preservice teachers' narratives of their literacy and biliteracy early experiences.

The autobiographies illustrate how literacy beliefs and practices are fully shaped by the sociocultural contexts in which students live and interact (Gee, 2008; Hornberger, 2004). Bilingual preservice teachers' narratives indicate that the belief system that supports their understanding of literacy and biliteracy development is strongly rooted in their lived experiences. The narratives that included a direct reference to how children learn to read and write showed that these bilingual preservice teachers understood literacy as the acquisition of decoding skills (Freeman & Freeman, 2009).

Claudia explained "*Desde que estamos chiquitos tenemos que familiarizarnos con las letras, no solo el sonido si no también con la forma de las letras*" [Since we are little we need to become familiar with the letters, not only the sound but also the shape of the letters]. This perception comes from early learning experiences both at home and at school. At home, parents used strategies they experienced as learners and thought were effective, such as learning the alphabet, identifying syllables, playing different games of word recognition, doing "*planas*" [worksheets], writing several lines copying the same word, and practicing writing their name, among others.

From early schooling experiences both in the United States and Mexico, student teachers draw on the emphasis placed on word recognition and decoding skills. Alejandra's experiences in Mexico learning to read reflect the traditional techniques corresponding to the alphabetic and syllabic methods (Freeman & Freeman, 2009):

> ... *al memorizar las letras del alfabeto y su fonética, empecé a unir consonantes y vocales para formar silabas como ba,be,bi,bo,bu,..... Esto me ayudo a dar el siguiente paso que fue hacer uniones de estas combinaciones como oraciones 'mi mamá me mima mucho' o simples como 'casa, caso, cosa' (sic)*. [Memorizing the letters of the alphabet and the sounds, I started to put together consonants with vowels to form syllables like ba, be, bi, bo, bu,... This helped me to take the next step linking these combinations in sentences (example) and simple words like (examples)....]

Memories of meaningful moments learning to read in English are similar. Bilingual preservice teachers described elementary teachers teaching different aspects of phonemic awareness and phonics development. Felicia remembered how she was taught to "read" decoding the sound of the short or long vowels in different words. Her narrative of that experience also showed an emphasis on decoding abilities and word recognition.

> *Por ejemplo la palabra "cut," sabia como leerla haciendo el sonido de las letras c ŭt. Un ejemplo de una palabra con una "long vowel," es la palabra cake. Sabia como leerla sonando cada letra y por el símbolo cā k e.* [For instance the word *cut*, I knew how to read it sounding out the letters c ŭu t. An example of a word with a long vowel, is the word *cake*. I knew how to read it sounding out each letter and because of the symbol cāke.]

Views of Biliteracy and Bilingualism

Bilingual preservice teachers reflected on their perceptions of the implications of developing biliteracy. They narrated stories that highlighted the lack of opportunities to develop their literacy skills in Spanish, describing their language loss as they were immersed in the U.S. schooling system, and comparing their experiences of learning to read and write in Spanish and English.

There were three distinct emphases in the bilingual preservice teachers' narratives: becoming biliterate as mastering reading in Spanish and English, learning in Spanish as a way to transition to English, and a vision of bilingualism and biliteracy as an asset.

Students' narratives emphasized the importance of learning to read and write in two languages. For Natalia, becoming bilingual involves literacy skills in both languages. After describing her schooling experiences learning to read and write, she reflects on the challenges involved in mastering reading in the native language, and then in the second language. Her view clearly shows the struggles many of these bilingual preservice teachers have experienced as bilingual learners.

> *Muchos niños que son bilingües aprenden de esta forma, empezando con su lengua natal y consecutivamente, siguiendo con la segunda lengua que es el inglés para muchos de nosotros. Es importante reconocer que ser bilingües implica mucha más sabiduría pero también mucho esfuerzo.* [Many bilingual children are learning in this way, starting with their native language and consecutively, following the second language that is English for many of us. It is important to recognize that being bilingual means a lot more intelligence but also more effort.]

A second emphasis found in narratives shows how preservice teachers also view Spanish instruction as a way to transition to English. This view is a reflection of the monoglossic ideology of early-exit programs predominant in the region that use native language instruction as a tool to mainstream students into English classrooms (García & Kleifgen, 2010). Alicia, who works as a teacher aide in a Pre-K classroom, defined emergent literacy highlighting the centrality of transitioning students to English:

> *En la etapa inicial de alfabetización los niños (…) pueden (…) aprender (…), siempre [usando] como base su lengua materna y hacer una transición paso a paso al segundo o más idiomas ….* [In the initial stage of literacy development, children can learn always using their mother tongue and doing the transition step by step to the second or more languages.] (Alicia)

Bilingual preservice teachers' perception of what bilingual education means is shaped and narrowed by their experiences with bilingual programs in the region (mostly early-exit programs) either as a student themselves, as parent of a child attending a program, or as a teacher aide.

A third emphasis appears in narratives that include a vision of bilingualism as a personal and professional asset, and an understanding of biliteracy linked to academic achievement. Yamila believes her academic achievement is partially the result of the fact that she attended bilingual classrooms until fourth grade. She explained that what students learn in the first language is transferred to the second language. She ended her reflection stating that *"El niño que es bilingüe tiene más oportunidades de triunfar en lo personal, en lo académico y en lo profesional"* [The bilingual child has more opportunities to succeed at the personal, academic, and professional level].

Each emphasis represents a way to understand language in relation to learning and literacy development. While bilingual preservice teachers clearly value bilingualism and biliteracy, their views of bilingualism and biliteracy reflect the context of bilingual preservice teachers' schooling experiences, and the prevalent and conflicting views of bilingual education in the region.

Becoming a Bilingual Teacher

Autobiographies and questionnaires indicate that preservice teachers believe they did not have meaningful learning opportunities to develop reading and writing skills in Spanish. Preservice teachers wrote about their feelings of frustration and explained how these experiences shaped their perceptions of the role of bilingual education and bilingual teachers. Ana explained her anguish and fear after being moved in first grade from a bilingual classroom to an English only classroom. This experience influenced the way she perceives bilingual education and her decision of becoming a bilingual teacher:

> *Ahora miro atrás a esta experiencia, después de perseguir una carrera en educación bilingüe, y no puedo sino sentir una sensación de culpa al sistema escolar por la razón de no aumentar mi idioma español. Aunque tengo la capacidad para hablar, leer y escribir en español, creo que yo podría haber sido mejor si mi educación temprana fuera tomado una ruta diferente. Especialmente porque yo ya comprendí todo los beneficios de ser bilingüe.* [Now I look back at this experience, after pursuing bilingual education as a career, I believe the educational system is responsible for not doing what is necessary to develop my Spanish, I think I could do better if my early education would've taken a different path. Specially, because now I understand the benefits of being bilingual.] (Ana)

Ana's narrative integrates some of the reasons expressed by bilingual preservice teachers as to why they decide to become a bilingual teacher. She highlights the significance of opportunities to develop literacy in both languages and the perception that the educational opportunities afforded to emergent bilinguals are not sufficient or adequate.

These reasons were also explicit in preservice teachers responses to the questionnaire. Most students (42%) indicated that they want to help students learn two languages acknowledging the advantages of being bilingual. Forty-two percent explained that their goal is to support English language learners and to help students who, like them, have difficulties at school because of their struggle with language. Very few (5 students out of 42) indicated that their main goal was to teach in Spanish or to support native language development, only two students made explicit references to the importance of biliteracy development or teaching to read and write in two languages, and only one bilingual preservice teacher indicated the reason to choose the bilingual certification program was to improve her Spanish.

Bilingual preservice teachers believe in the importance of being bilingual and bilingual education, and they value their potential contribution to developing the linguistic assets students bring with them.

> *Quiero ser maestra bilingüe porque yo tome clases en bilingüe comparado a mis hermanas que no. Yo creo que yo soy o tengo un (asset)...[por]que tuve la oportunidad de aprender los dos idiomas.* [I want to be a bilingual teacher because I had bilingual classes compared to my sisters who did not. I believe I am or have an asset ... because I had the opportunity to learn both languages.] (Cristina)

Holding high expectations for students, understanding students' needs and providing adequate scaffolding for their learning process are core beliefs for bilingual preservice teachers who struggled adapting to the ESL classrooms. Isabel recalls:

> *Un maestro que era bilingüe me ayudo a mejorar y a darme cuenta cuanto potencial tengo. Quisiera de igual manera ayudar a alumnos a descubrir su potencial en la escuela.* [A bilingual teacher helped me to improve and to realize my potential. Likewise, I would like to help students to discover their school potential.] (Isabel)

Becoming a bilingual teacher entails the motivation to promote and help maintain the development of the native language. This student chose to express herself in English while she acknowledges the importance of supporting the development of students' first language: "*I wish to be a bilingual teacher because I believe it is important to help those children increase their mother tongue*" (Ana). Evidently, most student teachers' responses reveal important aspects of their bilingual teacher identity, especially culturally responsive teaching beliefs and the understanding that children can learn when provided the adequate support.

Discussion

The analysis of the literacy autobiographies illustrates how bilingual preservice teachers' identities are shaped by their individual beliefs, their experiences, and by their participation in social and cultural language practices, such as the teacher preparation process (Danielewicz, 2001; Gee, 2001). As a teacher educator, I learned new things from and about my students as I engaged in a systematic analysis of their narratives. Most importantly, I gained an in depth understanding of the individual stories and how they form part of a collective transnational narrative of self that grounds the identity development process of bilingual teachers in the region.

Preservice teachers were influenced by meaningful others, especially mothers and teachers. Their narratives account for different significant experiences learning to read and write, and developing competencies in Spanish and English that grounded their beliefs about bilingual education, and about literacy and biliteracy (Clark & Flores, 2001; Flores et al., 2008; Flores, Ek, et al., 2011). These beliefs reveal conflicting discourses that bilingual preservice teachers have to negotiate as they construct their teacher identity. On one hand, they learn about the discourse supporting the positive effects of bilingual education. On the other hand, they need to make sense of the social and political discourses that privilege mainstreaming students in English only classrooms. Stories of exclusion, marginalization, and academic failure were accompanied by descriptions of feelings of guilt for what they perceive is a lack of Spanish development, and a sense of loss of language and opportunities (Guerrero et al., 2013). Preparing bilingual teachers requires opportunities for them to understand and reflect on the conditions of schooling and to analyze implications for practice.

The findings highlight that bilingual preservice teachers hold high expectations for emergent bilingual students, they are committed to support instruction in the native language, and they are advocates of bilingual education. However, some beliefs about literacy and effective practices need to be challenged. Even when caring about emergent bilinguals, bilingual preservice teachers initially perceive reading and writing as essentially a decoding process, and tend to identify language as a problem that needs to be amended through practice of isolated skills (Escamilla, 2006). Following Giampapa (2010), preparing bilingual teachers to deal with the literacy demands of a globalized and multicultural world, teacher educators should advance ways to integrate biliteracy and bilingual identities not only as content but also as resources for learning.

Narratives showed that bilingual preservice teachers' chose to become bilingual teachers as a result of the impact of their own experiences as emergent bilingual learners and the scarce opportunities afforded to them to develop biliteracy. Seeing bilingualism as a personal asset encouraged them to become advocates for emergent bilingual students. Teacher preparation needs to take into account the reasons preservice teachers have to become bilingual teachers.

Implications for Bilingual Teacher Preparation

Several implications for practice can be derived from the previous discussion:

First, given that most bilingual preservice teachers were afforded few opportunities to fully develop their biliteracy skills, it is important that teacher preparation fosters the development of academic literacy in Spanish and English. Teacher preparation programs should include opportunities beyond course work to engage students in multiple literacy practices in Spanish (i.e., service learning in community centers, designing informal learning activities, dialogue journal with students or peers, arts and performing activities, among others). They provide opportunities for bilingual preservice teachers to learn about the critical role that literacy and biliteracy experiences play in both, academic learning and identity formation. Moreover, the findings show the importance of integrating opportunities to reflect on their literacy experiences in English and Spanish, and to develop awareness of the similarities and differences between languages (Cummins, 2007). "Lived experiences, coupled with theoretical understandings from their preparation, potentially provides candidates with deeper conceptualizations of the role of language as a cultural tool for learning and as a critical societal resource." (Flores, Ek, et al., 2011, p. 54).

Second, teacher preparation should acknowledge the conflicting discourses about literacy and biliteracy development that preservice teachers need to understand and negotiate as they become bilingual teachers. It is critical to move away from conceptualizations of literacy and biliteracy that only emphasize a skill-based approach to instruction. For instance, teacher educators can model and demonstrate instruction centered on integrating language and culture as resources for learning. One approach is the implementation of translanguaging practices in bilingual teacher education programs (Escamilla, 2006; García & Kleifgen, 2010).

Third, it is important to provide safe spaces for bilingual preservice teachers to share, explore, and reflect on their lived experiences. Following Morgan (2004), I contend that bilingual teacher preparation needs to include the perspective of teacher identity as pedagogy. For instance, the literacy autobiography assignment was intended as a tool to promote bilingual preservice teachers' reflections on their experiences with language and literacy development. In addition, it calls for bilingual preservice teachers to critically consider how this can shape their understanding of effective practices and their future teaching (Edwards, 2009; Flores, Sheets, & Clark, 2011). Using life histories, autobiographies or reflective accounts of experiences, teacher educators can model the importance of knowing the learner while assisting in their identity formation.

In conclusion, teacher preparation can benefit from a closer look at how we are preparing future teachers and from recent theorizations of teacher education as a process of identity formation (Morgan, 2004; Varghese et al., 2005). Transforming bilingual teacher preparation requires conceptualizing learning as shaped by belief systems and cultural and linguistic identities through practices that provide preservice teachers with tools for exploration of beliefs and identity.

Study Limitations and Future Research Directions

Several limitations hinder findings generalizability. This study analyzed data from a limited number of participants. In addition, the sample included bilingual preservice teachers from a region with a predominantly bilingual population. As with any qualitative study, there are limitations related to self-reported data that cannot be verified and reflect individual idiosyncratic interpretations of the world. It is important to point out that my role as researcher and as course instructor could have biased my interpretations. Nevertheless, this is a risk worth taking if we consider that being an insider affords a privileged position to observe and collect valuable data (Merriam, 1998). My role and the rapport I established with the participants allowed me to gather information that could not be collected otherwise.

There is a great need for more practitioner studies that examine the complexities of teacher educator practices through the exploration of students' beliefs and identity if we aspire to transform bilingual teacher preparation (Duffy et al., 2009). Among other topics, teacher educators could engage in exploring: the effectiveness of bilingual teacher preparation programs in promoting understanding of biliteracy development, the impact of different instructional approaches in bilingual preservice teachers' understanding of effective biliteracy practices, and different aspects of teacher preparation curriculum that can impact bilingual preservice teachers' identity development.

References

Ajayi, L. (2011). How ESL teachers' sociocultural identities mediate their teacher role identities in a diverse urban school setting. *Urban Review: Issues and Ideas in Public Education, 43*(5), 654–680.

Bartlett, L. (2007). Bilingual literacies, social identification, and educational trajectories. *Linguistics and Education, 18*, 215–231.

Britzman, D. P. (1991). *Practice makes practice. A critical study of learning to teach.* Albany, NY: State University of New York Press.

Clandinin, D. J., & Connelly, F. M. (2000). *Narrative inquiry. Experience and story in qualitative research.* San Francisco, CA: Jossey-Bass Publishers.

Clark, E. R., & Flores, B. B. (2001). Who am I? The social construction of ethnic identity and self-perceptions in Latino preservice teachers. *The Urban Review, 33*(2), 69–86.

Clark, E. R., Jackson, L. G., & Prieto, L. (2011). Identity: A central facet of culturally efficacious bilingual education teachers. In B. B. Flores, R. S. Hernández, & C. E. Riojas (Eds.), *Teacher preparation for bilingual student population* (pp. 27–39). New York, NY: Routledge.

Clarke, M. (2008). *Language teacher identities. Co-constructing discourse and community.* Tonawanda, NY: Multilingual Matters.

Cochran-Smith, M., & Lytle, S. (2009). *Inquiry as a stance. Practitioner research in the next generation.* New York, NY: Teachers College.

Cummins, J. (2007). Rethinking monolingual instructional strategies in the multilingual classroom. *Canadian Journal of Applied Linguistics, 10*(2), 210–240.

Danielewicz, J. (2001). *Teaching selves. Identity, pedagogy, and teacher education.* Albany, NY: State University of New York Press.

Duffy, G., Webb, S., & Davis, S. (2009). Literacy education at a crossroad. Can we counter the trend to marginalize quality teacher education? In J. Hofmann & Y. Goodman (Eds.), *Changing literacies for changing times.* New York, NY: Routledge.

Dworin, J. E. (2003). Insights into biliteracy development: Toward a bidirectional theory of bilingual pedagogy. *Journal of Hispanic Higher Education, 2*(2), 171–186. doi:10.1177/1538192702250621

Edwards, D. (2009). Tracing literacy journeys: The use of the literacy autobiography in preservice teacher education. *Australian Journal of Teacher Education, 34*(4), 51–61. Retrieved from http://dx.doi.org/10.14221/ajte.2009v34n4.6

Escamilla, K. (2006). Semilingualism applied to the literacy behaviors of Spanish-speaking emerging bilinguals: Bi-illiteracy or emerging biliteracy? *Teachers College Record, 108*(11), 2329–2352.

Flores, B. B., Clark, E. R., & Guerra, N. S. (2008). Acculturation among Latino bilingual education teacher candidates: Implications for teacher preparation institutions. *Journal of Latinos and Education, 7*(4), 288–304.

Flores, B. B., Ek, L. D., & Sánchez, P. (2011). Bilingual education candidate ideology: Descubriendo sus motivos y creencias. In B. B. Flores, E. R. Clark, & R. Hernández-Sheets (Eds.), *Teacher preparation for bilingual student populations: Educar para transformar* (pp. 40–58). New York, NY: Routledge.

Flores, B. B., Sheets, R. H. R., & Clark, E. R. (Eds.). (2011). *Teacher preparation for bilingual student populations: Educar para transformer.* New York, NY: Routledge.

Freeman, Y. S., & Freeman, D. E. (2009). *La enseñanza de la lectura y la escritura en español y en inglés en clases bilingües y de doble inmersión* (2nd ed.). Portsmouth, NH: Heinemann.

Freire, P., & Macedo, D. (1987). *Literacy: Reading the word and the world.* New York, NY: Bergin & Garvey.

García, O., Bartlett, L., & Kleifgen, J. A. (2007). From biliteracy to pluriliteracies. In P. Auer & L. Wei (Eds.), *Multilingualism* (Vol. 5, pp. 207–228). Handbook of Applied Linguistics. Berlin: Mointon/de Gruyter.

García, O., Flores, N., & Woodley, H. (2012). Transgressing monolingualism and bilingual dualities: Translanguaging pedagogies. In A. Yiakoumetti (Ed.), *Harnessing linguistic variation to improve education* (pp. 45–75). Bern: Peter Lang.

García, O., & Kleifgen, J. A. (2010). *Emergent bilinguals. Policies, programs, and practices for English language learners.* New York, NY: Teachers College Press.

Gee, J. P. (2001). Identity as an analytic lens for research in education. In W. G. Secada (Ed.), *Review of research in education* (Vol. 25, pp. 99–126). Washington, DC: American Educational Research Association.

Gee, P. (2008). *Social linguistics and literacy. Ideology in discourses* (3rd ed.). New York, NY: Routledge.

Giampapa, F. (2010). Multiliteracies, pedagogy and identities: Teacher and student voices from a Toronto elementary school. *Canadian Journal of Education, 33*(2), 407–431. Retrieved from http://files.eric.ed.gov/fulltext/EJ895577.pdf

González, N., Moll, L., & Amanti, C. (2005). *Funds of knowledge: Theorizing practices in households, communities, and classrooms.* Mahwah, NJ: Lawrence Erlbaum.

Guerrero, M. D., Farruggio, P., & Guerrero, M. C. (2013). Conceptualizing a border signature pedagogy for Mexicana preservice bilingual educators. *Radical Pedagogy, 10*(2), 1–15. Retrieved from http://www.radicalpedagogy.org/

Hornberger, N. H. (2004). The continua of biliteracy and the bilingual educator: Educational linguistics in practice. *International Journal of Bilingual Education and Bilingualism, 7*(2–3), 155–171. Retrieved from http://repository.upenn.edu/cgi/viewcontent.cgi?article=1008&context=gse_pubs

John-Steiner, V. (1997). *Notebooks of the mind. Explorations of thinking* (Rev. ed.). New York, NY: Oxford University Press.

John-Steiner, V. (2000). *Creative collaboration.* Oxford: Oxford University Press.

Lortie, D. C. (1975). *Schoolteacher. A sociological study.* Chicago, IL: The University of Chicago Press.

Manyak, P. C. (2006). Fostering biliteracy in a monolingual milieu: Reflections on two counter-hegemonic English immersion classes. *Journal of Early Childhood Literacy, 6*(3), 241–266. doi:10.1177/1468798406069798

Merriam, S. B. (1998). *Qualitative research and case study applications in education*. San Francisco, CA: Jossey Bass Publishers.

Miller-Marsh, M. (2002). The shaping of Ms. Nicholi: The discursive fashioning of teacher identities. *Qualitative Studies in Education, 15*(3), 333–347.

Moll, L. C., Saez, R., & Dworin, J. (2001). Exploring biliteracy: Two student case examples of writing as a social practice. *Elementary School Journal, 101*(4), 435–450.

Morgan, B. (2004). Teacher identity as pedagogy: Towards a field internal conceptualization in bilingual and second language education. *International Journal of Bilingual Education and Bilingualism, 7*(2&3), 172–188.

Moschkovich, J. N. (2002). A situated and sociocultural perspective on bilingual mathematics learners. *Mathematical Thinking and Learning, 4*, 189–212.

Musanti, S. I., & Pence, L. (2010). Collaboration and teacher development: Unpacking resistance, constructing knowledge, and negotiating identity. *Teacher Education Quarterly, 37*(1), 73–90.

Pérez, B., & Huerta, M. E. (2011). Dynamic biliteracy. Teacher knowledge and practice. In B. B. Flores, E. R. Clark, & R. Hernández-Sheets (Eds.), *Teacher preparation for bilingual student populations: Educar para transformar* (pp. 115–130). New York, NY: Routledge.

Reyes, I. (2006). Exploring connections between emergent biliteracy and bilingualism. *Journal of Early Childhood Literacy, 6*(3), 267–292. doi:10.1177/1468798406069801

Riessman, C. K. (1993). *Narrative analysis*. Newbury Park, CA: Sage University Paper.

Sánchez, P. (2007). Cultural authenticity and transnational Latina youth: Constructing a meta-narrative across borders. *Linguistics and Education, 18*, 258–282.

Skutnabb-Kangas, T. (2008). Human rights and language policy in education. In S. May & N. Hornberger (Eds.), *Encyclopedia of language and education* (2nd ed., Vol. 1, pp. 107–119). Language Policy and Political Issues in Education. New York, NY: Springer.

Smagorinsky, P., Cook, L., Moore, C., Jackson, A., & Fry, P. (2004). Tensions in learning to teach: Accommodation and the development of a teacher identity. *Journal of Teacher Education, 55*(1), 8–24.

Smith, H., Sánchez, P., Ek, L. D., & Machado-Casas, M. (2011). From linguistic imperialism to linguistic conscientización: Learning from heritage language speakers. In D. Schwarzer, M. Petrón, & C. Luke (Eds.), *Research informing practice – Practice informing research: Innovative teaching methodologies for world language teachers* (pp. 177–198). Charlotte, NC: Information Age Publishing, Inc.

Suarez-Orozco, M. (2001). Globalization, immigration, and education: The research agenda. *Harvard Educational Review, 71*(3), 345–365.

Trueba, H. (2002). Multiple ethnic, racial, and cultural identities in action: From marginality to a new cultural capital in modern society. *Journal of Latinos and Education, 1*(1), 7–28.

Valdés, G., Bunch, G., Snow, C., Lee, C., with Matos, L. (2005). Enhancing the development of students' language. In L. Darling-Hammond & J. D. Bransford (Eds.), *Preparing teachers for a changing world: What teachers should learn and be able to do* (pp. 126–168). New York, NY: National Academy of Education.

Varghese, M. (2006). Bilingual teachers-in-the-making in Urbantown. *Journal of Multilingual and Multicultural Development, 27*(3), 211–224.

Varghese, M., Morgan, B., Johnston, B., & Johnson, K. (2005). Theorizing language teacher identity: Three perspectives and beyond. *Journal of Language, Identity, and Education, 4*(1), 21–44.

Warriner, D. S. (2007). Transnational literacies: Immigration, language learning, and identity. *Linguistics and Education, 18*, 3–4.

Wenger, E. (1998). *Communities of practice: Learning, meaning, and identity.* New York, NY: Cambridge University Press.

CHAPTER 4

MONOLINGUAL TEACHER CANDIDATES PROMOTING TRANSLINGUALISM: A SELF-STUDY OF TEACHER EDUCATION PRACTICES PROJECT

David Schwarzer and Mary Fuchs

Abstract

This chapter is based on a self-study of teacher education practices (S-STEP) project that explored the pedagogical practices of a teacher educator and the impact of such practices on a teacher candidate engaged in the process of becoming a translingual teacher. This S-STEP study includes David, a professor in a teacher education program in the greater New York City metropolitan area, and Mary, a teacher candidate enrolled in the program. The purpose of the study was to discover how different class activities influenced the philosophical and pedagogical views of one teacher candidate in the program. The following are the two research questions of the study:

1. *How did the class experiences that a teacher education professor, David, designed help teacher candidates conceptualize translingual approach to language and literacy development?*

Research on Preparing Preservice Teachers to Work Effectively with Emergent Bilinguals
Advances in Research on Teaching, Volume 21, 89–112
Copyright © 2014 by Emerald Group Publishing Limited
ISSN: 1479-3687/doi:10.1108/S1479-368720140000021003

2. *How did a monolingual teacher candidate, Mary, develop her role as a translingual English teacher through the completion of these experiences?*

The findings of this S-STEP project demonstrate that the Sociocultural Reflection, the Community Study, and the Linguistic Landscape fostered a translingual approach to language and literacy in the classroom. Moreover, the findings suggest that upon the completion of the projects, one teacher education candidate was able to better define translingualism as a phenomenon of study, ideology, and pedagogy.

Since this investigation is based on a S-STEP project of a single teacher educator and a single teacher candidate, more research with larger populations is needed. Practical implications for teacher educators and teacher candidates in other settings are explored.

Keywords: Multilingualism; translingualism; linguistic landscape; culturally responsive teaching; mainstream teacher candidates; second language

Introduction

The joy is about enabling other peoples' stories to be heard at the same time. You have the story of the orchestra as a professional body. You have the story of the audience as a community. You have the stories of the individuals in the orchestra and in the audience ... Now it's about you, the player, telling the story. Now it's a reverse thing: you're telling the story and you're telling the story and even briefly, you become the storyteller, to which the community, the whole community listens to [sic]. And Bernstein enables that. (Itay Talgam, 2009, TED Talks)

In this analogy, the classroom is a concert hall and the teacher is the conductor. Some conductors view their role as giving the orchestra specific directions and tasks to carry out. Itay Talgam observes that others, like Leonard Bernstein, showed musicians the process and the behavior required to produce evocative and emotive sounds. Using his facial expressions, Bernstein demonstrated to the orchestral members how their music was making him feel. But he didn't expect the oboe to sound like the flute or even the bassoon. Nor did he try to persuade the drums to the sound like trumpets or violins. He allowed the musicians to tell their stories in their own way, using their own voices and their own language.

More and more students in our schools are multilingual and transnational, bringing their own voices to our concert halls — the classroom. However, our teacher candidate population remains mostly White, female, monolingual, and middle class (National Center for Education Statistics, 2011a). It is therefore, the role of the teacher educator to prepare teachers for these changing environments. In an analogous way to the orchestra conductor, a monolingual teacher in a multilingual classroom can orchestrate experiences for the learners in which different languages and literacies are explored and fostered under the teacher's leadership. The orchestra conductor may be an expert playing one of the instruments in the band. However, it is up to the conductor to create a safe and harmonious environment in which each instrument is heard and the fluid combinations of instruments are appreciated. Monolingual teachers can also create a safe and harmonious environment in which each one of students' native languages and literacies is heard and where fluid combinations among the languages are appreciated.

The purpose of this chapter is to investigate the activities used by one teacher educator at a large university in the New York City metropolitan area to promote a translingual approach to teaching and learning and their impact on one teacher candidate in the program. Translingualism (in contrast with monolingualism, bilingualism, and multilingualism) is a more fluid interpretation of language and literacy in transnational and multilingual environments. According to Schwarzer, Petron, and Luke (2009), translingualism is the "development of several languages and literacies in a dynamic and fluid way across the life span, while moving back and forth between real and imagined borders and transacting with different cultural identities within a unified self" (p. 210).

Purpose

As a professor in a teacher education preparation program, David has been concerned about his teacher candidates' ideology regarding second language issues in general and their role as educators in multilingual and transnational learning communities in particular. David believes that part of his role is to design meaningful classroom experiences to help his students develop a more sophisticated view of their craft. This reflection impacted the design of this Self-Study Teacher Education Practices (S-STEP) project carried out with one of the teacher candidates in the program.

Following are the research questions that guided this S-STEP project:

1. How did the class experiences that a teacher education professor, David, designed help teacher candidates conceptualize a translingual approach to language and literacy development?
2. How did a monolingual teacher candidate, Mary, develop her role as a translingual English teacher through the completion of these experiences?

Significance

Mainstream classrooms in the United States increasingly include large numbers of immigrant students who speak languages in addition to English at home. In 2009 alone, 11.2 million U.S. children spoke a language other than English at home; 8 million of these children spoke Spanish (U.S. National Center for Education Statistics, 2011b). However, our teacher candidate population remains mostly White, female, and middle class (National Center for Education Statistics, 2011). The linguistic resources of communities often go unnoticed by schools and teachers and should be part of teacher education coursework. It is the role of the teacher educator to prepare White middle class teacher candidates to teach mostly multilingual, transnational, and poor children in school districts.

The experiences that most teacher education programs currently provide for teacher candidates look at language and literacy development as a static phenomenon. The S-STEP project described here is based on the premise that teacher educators need to provide more experiences for teacher candidates to adopt a more fluid conceptualization of language and literacy development by engaging in a translingual approach to teaching and learning.

Participants

David is a multilingual and transnational university professor at a large university in the New York Metropolitan area. David was born in Argentina, completed his B.A. and M.A. in Israel and came to the United States to complete his Ph.D. He and his family moved back to Israel for two years and then returned to the United States. His family is multilingual (since Hebrew, English and Spanish are used on a regular basis) and transnational (since the family moves back and forth between Israel and the United States). He teaches a course on sociocultural perspectives on teaching and learning in a graduate level teacher candidate education program at a large university in the New York metropolitan area. The class is the second class in the professional sequence, and as part of the NCATE accreditation process, it requires all professors teaching a section of the class to conduct a Community Study of a school district in the area.

Mary is a monolingual secondary English teacher candidate who was living in Harrison, New Jersey at the time of the study – a multilingual and transnational community 10 miles from New York City. Mary was a teacher candidate in the program and subsequently became David's graduate assistant.

Course Design

The course David teaches centers on the characteristics of schooling, teaching, and learning for students from diverse social, linguistic, and cultural backgrounds. Students in David's class were seeking certification in secondary education in 17 different content areas ranging from English to science and physical education to music. The students in David's class were required to complete three major assignments for the class: a Sociocultural Reflection, a Community Study, and a Linguistic Landscape.

Sociocultural Reflection

As part of the Sociocultural Reflection Project students reflected on their own schooling experiences and compared them to the experiences of students in other schools. Students were then asked to critically reflect on their assumptions and beliefs about their personal experiences. Moreover, they were required to reflect and write on the impact of the increasing linguistic, social, and cultural diversity in K-12 schools in general and in their content areas in particular. Students reflected on issues such as their own privilege (or lack of it); and their own race, ethnicity, or sexual orientation and how it affected their schooling experiences.

Community Study

The Community Study assignment involved an in-depth investigation of a diverse community and its schools. Specifically, this investigation focused on a racially/ethnically diverse and economically impoverished district from among those formerly designated as Abbott districts. These districts are the product of approximately 30 years of frequent and controversial dialogue, litigation, and 13 decisions of the New Jersey Supreme Court. There are about 30 school districts that have received the Abbott designation in the state's history – a title that brings with it a considerable amount of financial support. In New Jersey, teacher candidates traditionally view former Abbott districts as urban districts with large emergent bilingual populations and high poverty rates.

The purpose of the Community Study assignment is to help students: (a) develop a framework for understanding the relationship between schools, communities, and society; (b) promote the skills needed to familiarize students with diverse communities and their residents; and (c) envision ways in which teacher candidates can help their future students see connections between their in- and out-of-school experiences. David decided to require students to complete two visits in their target community. The first visit was open-ended. There was not a clear agenda other than getting acquainted with the community and spending some time there. The second visit was much more focused since students were looking for the phenomenon of translingualism in the target community.

This Community Study assignment required students to participate in a variety of activities: to spend time in the community they choose to study, to speak with people that lived or worked there, and to review and interpret online data available about the community through different sources including the U.S. Census Bureau, School Report Cards published by the New Jersey Department of Education, and local educational agencies or organizations. The final section of this assignment required students to develop one culturally responsive learning activity using the resources they researched for the project.

Linguistic Landscape

The purpose of this assignment is to document how written languages reside in the community. Students research how languages and literacy in different languages are present in the print environment of the community, by taking 20–25 digital pictures of multilingual artifacts. As students in the class take these pictures, they start to reflect on the unconventional ways in which languages intersect in the public space. Students then organize and analyze their pictures, in order to find a common thread among them. The purpose of this project is to see how schools are (or are not) reflecting the realities of languages used by its members in the community. Moreover, this assignment is designed to promote students' reflections on translingualism as an important construct for their teaching in multilingual and transnational learning communities in the United States.

Literature Review

In this section, we elaborate on the concept of translingualism and contrast it with bilingualism and multilingualism. Translingualism is a more fluid conceptualization of language and literacy development. The first scholar to publish about a trans-language learner is Jonietz (1994) who writes about the students in the international school settings she was working in:

> If the traditional terms are not really applicable, is there a more appropriate term? Is it possible that these learners are 'trans-language learners' (TLL)? 'Trans-language learner' is a term which describes an individual who moves from a maternal/native language to competence in an additional environmental/instructional language and culture. (p. 43)

Jonietz explains that "trans-language" does not mean a traditional bilingual/ multilingual student; rather, a trans-language learner moves between two or more languages based on the reality of their present situation. For example, a trans-language learner might be a student at an American international school in Portugal who was born in a Spanish-speaking country to a Hebrew-speaking father and an Italian-speaking mother. Therefore, the movement among languages and literacies in this student's life is much more fluid than a traditional bilingual or multilingual student.

Shell and Sollors (1998) further explain this view of translingualism as a hybrid tongue, as a crossing between language boundaries, and the movements between existing languages in the introduction to *The Multilingual Anthology of American Literature: A Reader of Original Texts with English Translations*:

> The collection presents new views of multilingualism as a historical phenomenon and as an ongoing way of life. It does so by taking seriously the task of examining the history of discrete language groups and their literary productions, as well as by crossing language boundaries (in a comparative work centering on shared themes or genres) and paying attention to the many superimpositions of existing languages onto one another (in code-switching, bilingual puns, and in 'hybrid tongues'); by investigating newly invented languages; and by reflecting on the effects of multilingualism on English writing in the United States. (pp. 9–10)

Kellman in his anthology (2003) further explains the concept of translingualism as a fluid movement from one's mother tongue to a second language. He particularly focuses on authors who became famous for their literary work in their second language. Kellman refers to translingual authors as "those who write in more than one language or in a language other than their primary one" (p. ix). Kellman also states that "by expressing themselves in multiple verbal systems, they [translingual writers] flaunt their freedom from the constrains of the culture into which they happen to be born" (p. ix).

Pennycook (2006) uses the concept of translingualism from an activist perspective and as a possible goal for language education in general. He explains how the movements between languages and cultural understandings may craft an important space in all classrooms.

> As educators we need to understand that the spaces and cultures our students inhabit are to be found not so much in predefinitions of cultural and linguistic background, as in the transcultural flows with which our students engage. By seeing language education as a practice of translingual activism, we open up an important space for both to oppose the incursion of homogenous discourses and to look for multiple sources of cultural renewal. (p. 114)

Pantano (2005) helps us understand that in our present mobile, multicultural, multilingual society "translingualism is a phenomenon that is destined to become the norm in this age of globalization and increased migration, and its cultural importance is enormous" (p. 97).

The differences between bilingualism, multilingualism, and translingualism still need to be addressed. Although translingualism has been used in the literature reviewed here it has not been clearly defined in a way that it is clearly differentiated from the others (see Cutter, 2005 for more information on this topic).

Most recently, Canagarajah (2013a, 2013b) has expanded on and contributed to the conceptualization of translingualism. He states:

> I must emphasize that the neologism of 'translingualism' is indeed needed. Existing terms such as *multilingual* or *plurilingual* keep languages somewhat separated ... the term translingual enables a consideration of communicative competence as not restricted to predefined meanings of individual languages, but the ability to merge different language resources in situated interactions for new meaning construction. (pp. 1–2)

As explained above, the definition of translingual education used in this chapter is one developed by one of the authors and his colleagues as:

> The development of several languages and literacies in a dynamic and fluid way across the life span while moving back and forth between real and imagined borders and

transacting with different cultural identities within a unified self. (Schwarzer et al. 2009, p. 210)

Methodology

This chapter describes the S-STEP project in which David and Mary reflect on their practice. David's reflection centers on the activities he provided to students in his classes in order to promote a translingual approach to teaching and learning. Mary's reflection centers on her Sociocultural Reflection and Community Study that was completed as part of her prerequisite education course, and her Linguistic Landscape projects that she conducted as part of her ongoing exploration of the translingual approach.

According to Pinnegar, Hamilton, and Fitzgerald (2010) there are three phases to the S-STEP project: the Authority Experience, the so-what question, and when the study turns back on itself. In the Authority Experience phase, the research is grounded in the teacher's own experiences and understandings of the phenomenon being studied. In the second phase, the so-what question, it is important to clearly articulate not only what was learned from the inquiry project based on the teacher's own practice, but how these insights are significant and valuable for the teacher education field. The third and final phase is the most useful to practitioners in the field reading the account because it provides empirical evidence in support of the author's understanding of the phenomenon studied.

According to LaBoskey (2004), there are five characteristics of any S-STEP project:

1. They are self-initiated and focused − the researcher is studying himself/ herself therefore the dichotomy between the researcher and the informants are central to the inquiry.
2. Improvement Aimed − the inquiry project is conducted to improve the personal practice of the researcher while contributing to impact the field.
3. Interactive − the inquiry project requires collaboration and dialogue with others in different formats and capacities (practitioners, researchers, research texts, etc.).
4. Multiple, Primarily Qualitative, Methods − the researcher utilizes whatever methods will provide the best evidence for understanding the practices that are being studied.

5. Exemplar-Based Validation — the validity of the study is largely based on the researcher's own expertise in the field studied and when other researchers and practitioners incorporate the insights gained into their own practice.

Finally, according to Pinnegar and Hamilton (2009), an S-STEP is designed around four sets of questions: what concerns the researcher as a practitioner; who to involve in the project; what methods to use; and the theories/pedagogies/philosophies that will guide the research. The S-STEP project described in this chapter followed this framework.

The researcher was concerned that the pre-service teachers in the teacher education program had life experiences that are very different from the experiences of the students they will teach. Therefore, David asked himself, "What are some educational practices that will impact students' ideologies about learning and teaching in multilingual and transnational learning environments?" He wanted to see if the projects he designed for his class could help teacher candidates reflect, change their attitudes, and implement translingual practices into their own teaching.

David chose to work with Mary as a co-researcher because of her understanding of translingualism and her close work with him as a graduate assistant. Data was collected through a variety of sources and included anecdotal records of Mary and David's weekly meetings for three semesters; all email exchanges between Mary and David regarding their experiences in the class, as a curriculum developer, and as a student in the program; and participant observation notes from Mary and David's presentations at several regional and national forums. A selective analysis of the emergent themes from the data guided Mary's ongoing reflection on her transformation as a translingual educator.

Data Collection and Analysis

Data for this S-STEP project was collected throughout the three semesters of collaboration between Mary and David. According to Luke (2004), the current climate in U.S. schools demands a transcultural and cosmopolitan teacher who is able to "to shunt between the local and the global, to explicate and engage with the broad flows of knowledge and information, technologies and populations, artifacts, and practices that characterize the present historical moment" (p. 1438). For this reason, all written communications and artifacts produced as part of the collaboration, such as email, notes from meetings, PowerPoint presentations, and drafts and comments on students' work, were used as part of this S-STEP project. According to Owocki and Goodman (2001), through observing and recording what informants do on a regular basis, researchers also develop new understandings of their ways of thinking and learning. This theory was particularly relevant to the S-STEP project and evidenced in our almost daily reflection on our practice.

Findings

Research Question #1

This section will report on each of the research questions. The first research question is, "How did the class experiences that a teacher education professor, David designed help teacher candidates conceptualize a translingual approach to language and literacy development?" The three experiences were a Sociocultural Reflection, a Community Study, and a Linguistic Landscape. Based on David's analysis of Mary's three projects, and his conversations and email exchanges with her, it appears that David was able to help students conceptualize translingualism in three distinct ways: translingualism as a phenomenon of study, translingualism as an ideology, and translingualism as a pedagogy.

Translingualism as a Phenomenon of Study. David found that the Sociocultural Reflection was very instrumental in revealing that students such as Mary viewed language and literacies in different communities as a rigid and clear-cut phenomenon. Mary thought that the signs in a community would either be in English or in Spanish, and that the languages would be separated or presented in a sequence. However, after visiting the target community as part of the Community Study, Mary started noticing and commenting on how languages in a multilingual and transnational environment behave in very fluid ways. The Linguistic Landscape provided opportunities for her to further analyze the fluidity of language choices in the community she studied. Fig. 1 shows one picture she took.

The picture in Fig. 1 displays a combination of words and phrases from Spanish and English. The store offers a variety of services: it is a travel agency and bank, which the owners have signified with English words like

Fig. 1. Harrison Storefront. *Source*: © 2014 Google.

"travel" and "money transfer." The store also advertises access to the Internet with Spanish words and phrases like "internet café" and "cyber café." Other phrases like "fax, copias & P.O. Box," are a mixture of English and Spanish. Most importantly, the storeowner purposely created this as a permanent sign by affixing adhesive letters to glass and ordering a printed plexi-glass sign. We are assuming that the design of a permanent marquee, or a sign that was designed to stay for a while in a community, might have been carefully reviewed. It may not be unusual to imagine that a number of people were engaged in the approval process to make sure that the sign was correct.

It is interesting to analyze the "foto passaporte" section of the sign – the word "foto" is the Spanish form of "photo" while the linguistic form of "passaporte" is what we call a translingual version. It moves back and forth between the English version (passport) and the Spanish one (pasaporte) and creates an original version (passaporte). During one of our presentations Mary mentioned: "Now I understand that languages are not neatly separated in Harrison, they intersect with each other in many interesting ways. I am wondering how can I use these resources from the Linguistic Landscape into my English classroom."

In conclusion, the Community Study and the Linguistic Landscape projects that David instituted in his class promoted the understanding of translingualism as a phenomenon of study. Mary, for example, witnessed how different languages and literacies intermingle in real life situations. The assignments also helped Mary think about possible uses of these resources in content area instruction.

Translingualism as an Ideology. Worden (2013) in the conclusion section of Canagarajah's volume about translingualism states:

> The introduction to this volume starts with the question: what does "trans" do to language? In one sense, the answer is, nothing ... A new term, a new approach, do nothing about this ... But if we change the question slightly by asking ... what it does to us as literacy scholars and teachers? What happens then? (p. 235)

Reflecting on how translingualism impacts teachers and teaching and based on the conversations David and Mary had during the three semesters, it appears that the Sociocultural Reflection helped students reflect on their ideologies about English as the main language of instruction. The chapter helped students ask, "What are our unmarked and sometimes unresearched ideologies about the best ways to help our students develop their emergent language and literacy in different languages?"

During the first experiences David provided in his class, students seemed to view English as the only key for students' success. Even foreign language, ESL, and bilingual teacher candidates often held a monolingual view of language and literacy development. They believed that their students would be confused if language and literacy experiences in their class were fluid and merging. They believed that complete separation between languages is needed. Mary's early comments reveal some of these same perceptions about language separation: "I think that all the signs are either in English or in Spanish – but they are never mixed ... That will be too confusing for the reader, wouldn't it?" (notes from weekly meeting).

However, after visiting the community as part of the Community Study, students started noticing and commenting on how languages and literacy in different languages seemed to be a common phenomenon when they visited churches, libraries, restaurants, and other public places. Then, the careful analysis required by the Linguistic Landscape forced students to think about how these rich linguistic resources were available in the community.

Some of the findings show that Mary started to develop a translingual ideology as she conducted the Linguistic Landscape of Harrison (where she was living at the time). Drawing from the music metaphor discussed earlier, Mary might compare the translingualism approach to leading an orchestra. Although she only knows how to play one instrument, (speak one language, English, fluently), she can craft spaces in her class where different instruments can play together (all other languages spoken and written in her class). However, Talgam's metaphor could be pushed further for the purposes of this discussion. Whereas an orchestra director has pre-assigned roles that can be played only in one particular version, the jazz band leader allows musicians a space for improvisation — a space where their instrument can flourish while it works in harmonious ways with others. Therefore, a teacher with a translingual ideology, like a jazz band leader, allows students to experiment with their languages and literacies while creating an overarching structure that is conducive to learning.

In conclusion, the three experiences David instituted in his class promoted the understanding of translingualism as an ideology. Mary started reflecting on her own un-marked ideologies about the separation of languages. Originally, she thought it would be important to keep languages separate to prevent confusion. After completing the projects, she started to adopt a translingual ideology in which languages and literacies are explored and used as resources during content area instruction.

Translingualism as a Pedagogy. Reflecting on the conversations David and Mary have had during this S-STEP project, it appears that the different experiences teacher candidates completed helped them to develop a translingual lens to reflect on their pedagogical beliefs in general and their beliefs about language and literacy in particular. As they wrote their Sociocultural Reflection, teacher candidates commented on special language and literacy experiences that their teachers had provided for them. Some vividly remembered a translation project for their Spanish class, and some remembered a meaningful project interviewing World War II veterans for their Social Studies class.

The Community Study helped students reflect on how landmarks and other resources that are unique to the community can serve as material for student learning and engagement. Teacher candidates begin to realize that, for example, the civil war cemetery that is part of their community might serve as a very useful tool for their Social Studies curriculum. They also started to realize that some of those unique resources might include languages and literacies.

While conducting the Linguistic Landscape of Harrison, it is evident that Mary began to make pedagogical connections between the language and literacies in the community and her content area, English. As part of a joint presentation for a conference, Mary constructed a unit plan in which she used community members as well as other linguistic resources readily available in Harrison as a way to include students' native tongues in a fluid way into her curriculum.

In conclusion, the three assignments helped Mary and other students develop an understanding of translingualism as a pedagogy. In the Sociocultural Reflection, Mary reflected on her own pedagogical views in light of her own experiences as a student in high school classrooms in which language and literacy seldom were at its center. After conducting a Community Study, Mary started to see how community-specific landmarks and other resources could be used to engage students as they studied different content areas. The Linguistic Landscape helped Mary develop a clear sense of how languages and literacies that reside in the community in a fluid and unique way can inform any teacher's curriculum.

Mary's experience is typical. Comments from former teacher candidates, such as, "Every time I go to any federal office I pay attention to all the signs in languages other than English;" emails with pictures of translingual signs; and even articles about multilingualism in NYC sent to David to use in his class are commonplace.

Research Question #2

The second research question addressed in this study was, "How did a monolingual teacher candidate, Mary, develop her role as a translingual English teacher through the completion of these experiences?"

A careful analysis of Mary's class assignments shows that the Linguistic Landscape was the one that promoted the most reflection on her view of language and literacy as a fluid phenomenon with implications for teaching and learning. According to Gutierrez, Baquedano-Lopez, and Tejeda (1999), conversations between teachers and students in the classroom are part of a negotiated third space of discourse where social norms in language can be upheld or redefined. Through discussion of her written assignments, her visits to the community, and her reflections, Mary was able to enter into a third space with David where she could reflect on her linguistic experiences in schools and change her perspective as a translingual educator.

Sociocultural Reflection: Mary's Experiences. The Sociocultural Reflection assignment was instrumental in starting a deeper reflection about some aspects of Mary's sociocultural upbringing. Mary had become critical of her schooling experiences at a young age but had not deeply questioned how her experiences were different from those of other teacher candidates. She was different from her peers in that she had pursued study abroad opportunities, was intrigued by diversity from a very young age, and as a teacher candidate, became puzzled by its implications for both general and special education settings. Her understanding of social justice and democracy as a political issue that should be pursued in both policy arenas and pedagogical ones always drove her search towards greater insight.

During class discussions about the chapter, Mary realized her schooling experiences, and therefore many of her sociocultural experiences, were different than her peers, despite the fact that many of them grew up in Northern New Jersey, just a few towns away. Through conversations with David, Mary started to reinterpret her Sociocultural Reflection as evidence of a translingual ideology. As a child, she had gone to schools that provided some interaction with other languages in addition to discussions of diversity. Her reflections on the phenomena of translingualism in light of those schooling experiences, and the attitude and approach she had adopted as a result of learning alongside students from different language backgrounds, helped her understand how she was now changing her ideology as a practitioner. She realized she wanted to provide students with more opportunities for third spaces within her classroom so that one language would not be preferred over another. Mary began to see for herself how language and literacies could be used in addition to race and socioeconomic status to segregate students in the classroom. In this regard, the Sociocultural Reflection helped to cement Mary's adoption of a translingual ideology.

A Community Study of Harrison. In the Sociocultural Reflection, Mary reflected on her childhood schooling experiences in the town she grew up in. In the Community Study, Mary analyzed the data from schools she had not attended and in a community she had just moved to, Harrison, NJ. She knew Harrison was diverse, but as a result of her data analysis, she could now better understand the complexities of schooling there: many children were first and second generation immigrants and spoke different languages at home and school. Therefore, the evidence or phenomenon of translingualism, due to the sheer number of students with different language backgrounds, could not be ignored.

Mary became more intrigued by the Community Study data and its effect on teaching as ideology and lesson planning as methodology. She began to ask questions about how students in Harrison saw their world and whether their experiences, walking to school, talking to friends and family, and the languages they used to express themselves, were supported and/or appreciated in school.

Mary had previously compared her own schooling experiences with her teacher candidate peers in the Sociocultural Reflection. In the Community Study, she reflected on how student experiences in Harrison may have also differed from those of her teacher candidate peers. In conversations with other teacher candidates, Mary questioned whether her peers had the same insights into language use in communities and how students might feel, learning in a monolingual English classroom. The questions Mary asked in conversations with David focused on how the schooling experiences of White monolingual teachers different from translingual students in monolingual settings. She wondered how monolingual teachers could support the layers of language and literacies in the translingual classroom. These questions led her to complete the Linguistic Landscape project as part of her exploration of translingualism. As part of the reflection on the Community Study, Mary routinely discussed with David her concerns about implementing translingual pedagogies in the classroom as a monolingual teacher. In the following semesters, while David was administering a similar assignment to students in his class, Mary and David discussed several practical ways in which some of the theoretical insights they were discussing could become part of an English class in a local high school.

Mary's Linguistic Landscape. A careful analysis of the weekly conversations between Mary and David showed that Mary's initial perceptions about language artifacts were quite conventional at the outset of the S-STEP project. Mary did notice environmental print in languages other than English in her community. However, she rarely analyzed its content and other features that were more fluid in nature.

Mary's access to students in Harrison was limited as a monolingual teacher candidate. But she did have access to public spaces and linguistic objects. Through weekly conversations, David encouraged Mary to take a closer look at languages in her neighborhood. Mary was starting to understand the nature of languages and literacy in her neighborhood as a more translingual phenomenon. Mary reported that she "started to pay more and more attention to the signs she regularly saw in her community, written in Chinese, Spanish, Portuguese, Polish, and English." Mary was surprised by David's comments such as: "Which language appeared first or on top ...?" "What language(s) were preferred over the others ...?" "Was each language given the same amount of space on a sign or were some languages used more than others ...?" As a result of David's questioning, Mary decided to engage in a more in-depth analysis of the signs in her neighborhood by taking pictures of linguistic objects – signs displayed in store windows, parks, and above commercial establishments (Ben-Rafael, Shoami, Amara, & Hecht, 2006).

Mary was particularly struck by one sign advertised in a restaurant window on a paper printout, "Seafood Arroz Chaufa," which was an amalgamation of Chinese, Peruvian, and American traditions. Chaufa is a fried rice dish created in Peru by Chinese immigrants who were looking for ingredients to cook their traditional foods. Through conversations about the sign and its language, David helped Mary to elucidate the fluidity of the language choices (e.g., the sign could have said "Seafood Fried Rice" or "Arroz Chaufa con Mariscos"). The actual sign made translingualism evident: "Chaufa" for Peruvian residents and "Arroz Chaufa" for other Spanish-speaking individuals who may have heard of Peruvian-Chinese fusion food. Most interestingly, perhaps, is the inclusion of English word *seafood*. David and Mary asked, "Why did the owner, who presumably made this sign, include the word in English? Why not Chinese or Spanish?"

Mary could not know for certain why individuals chose to arrange languages in a particular order in their store signs. But she continued to be intrigued by the phenomena of translingualism in Harrison. As evidenced in conversations with David, Mary persistently asked how individuals decide which languages to use and how the signs were designed and made in order to convey the intended message to their audience. Mary and David discussed two types of signs in her Linguistic Landscape: public signs issued by government officials or entities and private signs, made by individuals, associations, or firms acting more or less autonomously in the limits authorized by official regulations (Ben-Rafael et al., 2006). Mary and David also considered the materials used to create signs. Some were temporary signs, such as computer printouts, and others were permanent signs made with adhesive lettering, printed on awnings, billboards, or metal.

These considerations led Mary to additional questions: "What significance does this have for residents of Harrison? What about for secondary school students walking around their neighborhood? For teachers preparing to engage students in their lessons? And for teacher trainers, hoping to encourage teacher candidates to gain insight about a community with rich and storied backgrounds?" Thus, the process of conducting the Linguistic Landscape gave Mary the idea of designing activities that had the potential to create a third space in her own future practice where both Mary and her students could move between languages without creating a hierarchy of language and power.

Through an analysis of Mary's Linguistic Landscape, it is clear that she developed a more sophisticated view of language and literacies as they are portrayed in the public domain. She documented examples of translingualism in the community and began to formulate a more concrete approach to teaching through a translingual ideology that was specific to the community she would be teaching in. In other words, she realized that the unique Linguistic Landscape of Harrison would not necessarily translate to nearby Newark or Jersey City. Each community brought with it a new set of data, cultural history, traditions, and languages. To her, this no longer meant teaching all students as if they were monolingual or bilingual, just as she previously understood she could not teach all students as if they shared her exact ethnic, racial, or socioeconomic experiences. Instead, Mary began to understand her role as an orchestra conductor in the classroom with students who were capable of playing multiple instruments with varied tones, pitches, and notes. Her role as a monolingual teacher would be to orchestrate experiences in which students' native languages and literacies could thrive in a fluid third space that she had crafted for them. Her final steps as a teacher candidate would require her to consider the practical applications for her newfound insights.

The Linguistic Landscape yields the most powerful and intentional reflection on the role of the mainstream teacher in her role as the orchestrator of a translingual learning community. Mary became intrigued with Linguistic Landscapes as a way to research the language resources available for teachers in the different communities. She completed a Linguistic Landscape of her town. She documented English, Spanish, Portuguese, and Chinese environmental print as they appeared in the community. Finally, she used these funds of knowledge as a catalyst for the development of a unit plan that could be used in her future secondary English class.

In conclusion, Mary's reflection on all class projects reveals that each one of the projects created a distinct a third space where she reflected on her role as a translingual teacher. The Sociocultural Reflection helped Mary refine her understanding of translingualism as an ideology; the Community Study impacted her understanding of translingualism as a pedagogy and finally the Linguistic Landscape cemented her understanding of translingualism as a phenomenon of study.

Conclusions and Practical Implications

Throughout the research, David continued to reflect on his responsibility as a teacher educator committed to preparing teacher candidates who could create translingual experiences within their own classrooms. He determined that teacher educators, like himself, could provide teacher candidates with meaningful experiences to foster their reflection on their role in translingual classrooms. Courses such as the one David teaches are designed to help teacher candidates reflect on their socioeconomic, ethnic, cultural, and religious experiences. Yet, there are many opportunities in the course curriculum for teacher candidates to design lesson plans or develop alternative projects or assignments where students could include their own languages or linguistic experiences.

Fig. 2 summarizes the new insights gained through this S-STEP project about translingualism as a pedagogy that David's teacher candidates explore in his class.

When discussing language and literacy development within the different compartmentalized views in a literacy development class, a biliteracy development class, an ESL literacy development class, a foreign language

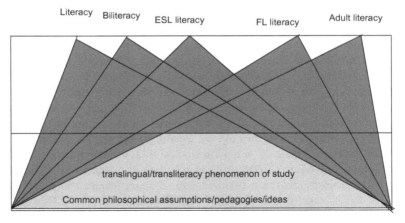

Fig. 2.   The Multiple Representations of Transliteracy Development.

literacy development class, or an adult literacy class, teacher candidates may only see the top of the iceberg. Each one of its peaks is quite different and isolated from the other which demonstrates why teacher candidates learn about language and literacy in different contexts.

However, a translingual pedagogy asserts that underneath the distinct peaks of the iceberg, there are common underlying pedagogical principles that are shared by conscientious teachers interested in fostering a fluid view of language and literacy in their multilingual and transnational learning communities. Defining the pedagogical underlying principles shared across distinct areas of expertise is crucial to the success of schooling in the twenty-first century.

The findings of the current study suggest that the Sociocultural Reflection, the Community Study, and the Linguistic Landscape are worthwhile experiences for teacher educators to assign in order to foster a translingual approach to language and literacy in the classroom. Moreover, the findings show that upon the completion of the projects, teacher candidates were able to better define translingualism as a phenomenon of study, an ideology, and a pedagogy.

A translingual approach to teaching and learning will allow students to tell their stories in their own way, using their own voices and in their own languages. It is the role of every teacher to craft such a meaningful space, as an orchestra or jazz band conductor, in the class where students can flourish and develop. This S-STEP project reflects a two-year partnership for David and Mary. We are hoping more teacher candidates and teacher educators will join us in this important and rewarding endeavor.

Limitations of the Study

This study has limitations. Since the investigation is based on a S-STEP project of a single professor and a single teacher candidate in a particular context and geographical region, the results might not be replicated in other situations. Since Mary is trained as an English teacher, more research conducted by other content area teachers interested in promoting a translingual approach to teaching and learning is needed. Additional studies by teacher educators in different contexts throughout the world, as well as in different content areas, promoting a translingual approach to teaching and learning, and using S-STEP or other methods of inquiry, should be carried out to see if the findings of this study can be generalized.

Acknowledgment

The authors wish to thank Christian Acosta for his willingness to offer suggestions and feedback on earlier versions of this chapter as well as for his help with the references.

References

Ben-Rafael, E., Shoami, E., Amara, M., & Hecht, N. (2006). The symbolic construction of the public space: The case of Israel. *International Journal of Multilingualism, 3*(1), 7–30.

Canagarajah, S. (2013a). *Literacy as translingual practice: Between communities and classrooms.* New York, NY: Routledge.

Canagarajah, S. (2013b). *Translingual practice: Global Englishes and cosmopolitan relations.* New York, NY: Routledge.

Cutter, M. J. (2005). Review of book switching languages: Translingual writers reflect on their craft. *College Literature, 32*(2), 199–201.

Gutierrez, K. D., Baquedano-Lopez, P., & Tejeda, C. (1999). Rethinking diversity: Hybridity and hybrid language practices in the third space. *Mind, Culture, and Activity, 6*(4), 286–303.

Haglund, C. (2008). Linguistic diversity, institutional order and sociocultural change: Discourses and practices among teachers in Sweden. In J. E. G. Budach & M. Kunkel (Eds.), *Écoles Plurilingues — Multilingual Schools: Konzepte, Institutionen und Akteure. Internationale Perspektiven* (pp. 147–168). Frankfurt: Peter Lang.

Haglund, C. (2010). Transnational identifications among adolescents in suburban Sweden. In P. Quist & B. A. Svendsen (Eds.), *Multilingual urban Scandinavia: New linguistic practices* (pp. 96–110). Tonawanda, NY: Multilingual Matters.

Jonietz, P. (1994). Trans-language learners: A new terminology for international schools. *International Schools Journal,* (27), 41–45.

Kellman, S. (2003). *The translingual imagination* (1st ed.). Lincoln, NE: University of Nebraska Press.

LaBoskey, V. K. (2004). Afterword: Moving the method of self-study forward: Challenges and opportunities. In *International handbook of self-study of teaching and teacher education practices* (pp. 1169–1184). Dordrecht, The Netherlands: Kluwer Academic Publishers.

Luke, A. (2004). Teaching after the market: From commodity to cosmopolitan. *Teachers College Record, 106*(7), 1422–1443.

National Center for Educational Statistics. (2011a). *Digest of education statistics, 2010.* Retrieved from http://nces.ed.gov/pubs2011/2011015_2a.pdf. Accessed on July 23, 2014.

National Center for Educational Statistics. (2011b). *Digest of education statistics, 2010.* Retrieved from http://nces.ed.gov/pubs2011/2011033_2.pdf. Accessed on July 23, 2014.

Owocki, G., & Goodman, Y. (2001). *Kidwatching: Documenting children's literacy development.* Portsmouth, NH: Heinemann.

Pantano, D. (2005). Review of switching languages: Translingual writers reflect on their craft (Kellman, G. (Ed.), University of Nebraska Press, 2003). *Style: A Quarterly Journal of Aesthetics, Poetics, and Stylistics, 39*, 95–97.

Pennycook, A. (2006). Language education as translingual activism. *Asia Pacific Journal of Education, 26*(1), 111–114.

Pinnegar, S., Hamilton, M., & Fitzgerald, S. (2010). *Self-study of practice as a genre of qualitative research: Theory, methodology, and practice.* New York, NY: Springer.

Schwarzer, D., Petron, M., & Luke, C. (2009). Conclusion. In D. Schwarzer, M. Petron, & C. Luke (Eds.), *Research informing practice—practice informing research: Innovative teaching methodologies for world language teachers.* Charlotte, NC: Information Age Publishing.

Shell, M., & Sollors, W. (1998). *The multilingual anthology of American literature: A reader of original texts with English translations.* New York, NY: New York University Press.

Sollors, W. (1998). Introduction: After the culture wars; or, from "English Only" to "English Plus". In W. Sollors (Ed.), *Multilingual America: Transnationalism, ethnicity and the languages of American literature* (pp. 1–16). New York, NY: New York University Press.

Talgam, I. (2009). *Lead like great conductors* [Web]. Retrieved from http://www.ted.com/talks/itay_talgam_lead_like_the_great_conductors

Worden, D. (2013). Afterword: Reflection from the ground floor. In *Literacy as translingual practice: Between communities and classrooms.* New York, NY: Routledge.

Appendix: Linguistic Landscapes

Purpose

Document the Linguistic Landscape of the community you are researching by taking 20–25 digital pictures of multilingual artifacts representing the languages in the community. Organize and analyze pictures trying to find a common thread among them. Remember, the purpose of this project is to see how schools and communities relate (or do not relate to each other ...).

Format

Introduction. Explain in detail what is a Linguistic Landscape and why should teachers and schools be aware of this issue.

Data collection and analysis. Contextualize where the pictures were taken and why you believe multiple languages were used for each artifact. Analyze data in accordance to the twist you are trying to incorporate in your final project.

Conclusion. *(These are options — you do not need to do them all)*

- Provide practical implications and detail curricular changes for teachers/ classrooms in the particular communities you visited in general and in your content area in particular.
- Suggest to teachers what they can do with such artifacts in their classrooms.
- Explain why incorporating such artifacts in the classrooms are important for linguistically diverse children.
- Choose a particular grade and describe in detail three (3) practical changes for this classroom based on your findings.

Possible Places to Gather Data

Restaurants (look at menus, signs, paintings, wall decorations, etc.).
Government offices, Association offices, & Organizations

Important Note: Please keep in mind that you may need to secure permission to take pictures in some places. Ask before you take a picture!

CHAPTER 5

DISCOVERING BEST PRACTICES FOR BILINGUAL TEACHER PREPARATION: A PEDAGOGY FOR THE BORDER

Alcione N. Ostorga and Peter Farruggio

Abstract

As members of a team of bilingual preservice faculty in the South Texas borderlands, we have observed a consistent, pattern of inappropriate pedagogy offered to the emergent bilingual learners (EBLs) in the region's inadequate PK-12 system, where subtractivist teaching practices and school policies undermined their academic development and their personal and professional identities as bilinguals and linguistic minorities. Our task is to teach our preservice students about best practices as we help them develop an awareness of themselves as bilingual, bi-literate professionals who can navigate within the accountability-driven school system and provide additive developmental learning opportunities to their emergent bilingual students.

In this chapter, we describe the experiences and findings from a five-year research project that employed an innovative approach to higher education pedagogy to teach 63 bilingual preservice students how to provide

Research on Preparing Preservice Teachers to Work Effectively with Emergent Bilinguals
Advances in Research on Teaching, Volume 21, 113–136
ISSN: 1479-3687/doi:10.1108/S1479-368720140000021004

research-based, constructivist-oriented additive pedagogy to emergent bilinguals. Analysis of data from journals and focus group discussions suggest the development of the critical stance necessary for the development of an additive approach needed for the optimal development of emergent bilinguals. Although the study is limited to the specific context of South Texas US–Mexico border communities, the findings have implications for the preparation of bilingual education settings across the nation.

Keywords: Constructivist pedagogy; preservice bilingual teachers; critical stance; academic Spanish; cultural and professional identities

Hi Guys, the purpose of this email is to inform everyone about an idea that several UTPA students and staff have been thinking about putting into action. As we all know the best type of education a person could have is bilingual education, not necessarily Spanish and English, BUT being the case that we are in the valley, that is exactly what is lacking here; a school that can properly teach students and help them be the best they can be. Several of us have been meeting with professors and other interested people on creating a Dual language school in the valley, because it is long overdue.

Introduction

A preservice bilingual teacher in our research project at the University of Texas Pan American (UTPA) sent this message to her fellow students and to us, two project professors, asking for a meeting to plan a dual language school. Our South Texas borderland region, the Rio Grande Valley (RGV), has many nominally dual language schools; but apparently this student was aware of the contradictions between the authentic dual language education taught in her college courses and what she saw in the local elementary classrooms. In the planning meeting, students said they feared it would be difficult to practice real dual language teaching in the existing schools and asked for our help to create a school where they could implement what they had learned in our courses. Their initiative suggests that our program gave them an ideological clarity about how to promote learning for emergent bilingual learners (EBLs).

To best serve EBLs' learning needs, we must discover how to prepare bilingual teachers to apply effective teaching practices in their classrooms.

At the same time, we must transform and focus their consciousness to appreciate the importance of professional values and a concern for children's personal and cultural identities. To teach effectively in two languages, bilingual teachers must achieve an awareness of the sociopolitical implications of language use in the United States, and must develop a determination to maintain and develop their emergent bilingual students' mother tongue.

Located along the US–Mexico border, ours is the largest bilingual teacher preparation program in Texas. Most of our preservice students are Mexican Americans, and many experienced bilingual education as children. As bilingual teacher educators, we strive to promote in our students strong teacher identities that integrate professional and personal values with a knowledge of best practices for teaching EBLs. Because these practices differ from much of the teaching of 15–30 years ago, we struggle to overcome our students' preconceived notions of what it means to be a teacher, particularly a bilingual teacher. Most of our students have been indoctrinated with the "apprenticeship of observation," as documented in Lortie's classic sociological study of schoolteachers (Lortie, 1975) and substantiated by others (Belmonte, 2009; De Courcy, 2007). During their years as elementary students, they experienced their bilingual and ESL teachers' culturally and linguistically subtractivist pedagogical practices, and accepted them as normal teaching. Unfortunately, these practices predominate today in our region's transitional bilingual education (TBE) classrooms, where EBLs are quickly transitioned into English Only (EO) instruction as early as kindergarten. TBE results in the loss of the mother tongue and the weak development of the second language (García & Kleifgen, 2010).

As outlined in previous chapters of this book, the predominantly mainstream teachers who will serve EBLs across the United States must acquire an awareness of the special capabilities and needs of linguistic minority children. Equally important is the need to increase the diversity of the teaching workforce, especially for EBLs. However, providing these children with teachers from their home communities and cultural backgrounds does not guarantee that these teachers will offer culturally and linguistically relevant pedagogy, especially in our borderlands schools.

Many of our local schools offer a behaviorist, teacher-centered, pedagogical approach with minimalist skills-based instruction. The goal is to quickly transition EBLs into monolingual EO classrooms. Teachers are pressured to follow scripted curricula with practices detrimental to students' academic and linguistic development. In TBE programs, students are subjected to skills-based teaching and predominantly English instruction.

These practices contrast with the holistic and linguistically additive instruction needed by EBLs for academic growth. Unfortunately, such didacticism and linguistic subtractivism (Valenzuela, 2004) is common for the instruction of EBLs throughout the United States because school administrators mistakenly believe that such practices produce higher test scores (Ravitch, 2010). Since these flawed pedagogical practices resemble what our preservice teachers experienced as children, they tend to replicate them instead of implementing the constructivist and linguistically additive approach learned in our teacher preparation program. In the local schools, our novice bilingual teachers rarely see lessons that promote EBLs' linguistic and conceptual development practiced coherently, and many become assimilated into the subtractivist professional cultures of their schools. To avoid such negative assimilation, teacher preparation must include transformative learning and critical reflective dialogue (Brookfield, 2009) in its curriculum.

Given their acculturation as schoolchildren in the behaviorist, subtractivist pedagogy of the borderlands schools, our preservice students' archetype of a bilingual teacher contrasts diametrically with our program's philosophy and mission, which stresses the value of a culturally and linguistically additive pedagogy. Murillo (2010) found that they generally devalue the use of Spanish to communicate in academic settings. They struggle to integrate their cultural and professional identities. The borders between their multiple identities inhibit their sense of self-efficacy and empowerment. They must overcome these identity conflicts to become effective bilingual teachers and change agents within a subtractivist school system that imposes hegemonic control over the borderlands Latino communities.

Purpose

In this chapter, we present the results of a federally funded research project called the Curriculum Assessment for Successful Students Outcomes (CASSO). Our faculty research team designed a context-specific signature pedagogy (Shulman, 2005) for bilingual teacher education based on the characteristics and learning needs of our working class Latino preservice teachers. We approached this design with two objectives:

1. to develop specific practices for bilingual teacher preparation that would promote within our context, effective bilingual teachers, capable of applying a principled approach in their teaching practices.

2. to counteract the negative effects of subtractive EO and TBE programs on the linguistic and affective development of the teacher candidates in our program.

Significance of the Study

Although our research was conducted in a specific borderlands context, we believe our contribution to bilingual teacher preparation may impact such programs across the United States. Our preservice teachers' voices bring an important message to those who lead our nations' public schools. Furthermore, teacher educators in bilingual education should become aware of the preservice pedagogy that addresses the specific needs of Latino preservice teachers. To populate classrooms for Latino EBLs with teachers familiar with their students' culture and language is insufficient. We must prepare and support bilingual teachers who

1. have political and ideological clarity about the hegemonic oppression of US Latino communities and the need to resist this oppression through social justice pedagogy (Bartolomé, 1994, 2000); and
2. are willing and able to engage in principled practices for EBLs and advocate for their rights as learners (Gandara & Contreras, 2009; García, & Kleifgen, 2010).

The Context of the Study

RGV spans the Texas–Mexico border along the northern margin of the Rio Grande in the southernmost tip of the United States. School districts along the Texas border are more impacted by lower social class status and linguistic marginalization than non-border districts (Sloat, Makkonen, & Koehler, 2007). The RGV contains a high concentration of economically disadvantaged students. More than 90% of its students are Latinos who speak Spanish at home, 28.8% are classified as Limited English Proficient (LEP), the state's term used to identify EBLs, and 79.3% are economically disadvantaged. Educational attainment is below state and national averages. Only 26% of adults 25 years or older have a high school diploma, suggesting that the parents of most school age children did not complete high school.

RGV school districts employ a greater proportion of Latino teachers than most other areas with Latino-majority school communities (Sloat et al., 2007). Some infer from this greater proportion of Latino teachers a beneficial impact on student learning because of student-teacher ethnic compatibility (Hanushek, Kain, O'Brien, & Rivkin, 2005). However, a relatively high proportion of borderlands teachers have less than seven years of professional experience, and their students' academic achievement is low compared to students in non-border districts.

Like other communities with large Latino populations, RGV communities experience ethnic segregation and linguistic isolation (Gandara & Contreras, 2009). But a notable distinction for the RGV's schools is that, unlike most Latino-majority schools in the US, their bilingual teachers largely teach in their own or neighboring communities. They are thoroughly familiar with the issues encountered by their pupils, since many of them faced the same challenges as schoolchildren. This familiarity, however, comes with a drawback. Many of our teacher candidates were poorly served by the area's weak K-12 educational system, especially those who as EBLs experienced the low-quality English immersion and early exit TBE programs. These programs' ineffective pedagogical practices hampered the development of our teacher candidates' academic language in both Spanish and English, and weakened their conceptual knowledge in all subject areas. When they return to teach in the local communities, their academic deficiencies often contribute to the perpetuation of the region's cycle of underachievement.

Though this picture seems bleak, there are many positives. Our bilingual preservice students have demonstrated resilience and a strong commitment to make a difference for the children in the local schools. Many of them attend college while raising their own children. Several even have babies while in college. Some also work to help support their families. Despite the many obstacles they face, they graduate and become certified bilingual teachers by passing three or four state certification exams. Their persistence is exemplified by the fact that many require several attempts to pass these exams.

In exploring how to best address our students' learning needs, the CASSO faculty team considered the local schools context, where our students would attempt to apply the concepts learned in our courses. Our preservice program is founded on a constructivist theoretical framework that values student-centered instruction, integrated thematic units, a balanced approach to reading instruction and additive bilingualism/biliteracy development. This framework contrasts with the pedagogical culture of the local schools, which emphasizes scripted curricula, teacher-centered, skills-based instruction and the early transition of EBLs into EO classrooms.

TBE programs, known as early exit programs, prematurely remove young emergent bilingual children from bilingual instruction and place them into EO classrooms, often as early as first grade, before their second language has developed sufficiently for them to understand the curriculum. While promoting academic failure and hindering intellectual growth, this policy also harms children's emotional development by devaluing their parents' language and inhibiting their cultural and linguistic identity formation. Such marginalization of EBLs' identities leads to their withdrawal from academic participation and their intellectual disempowerment (Cummins, 2001).

Literature Review

Although much has been published about the best practices for teaching emergent bilingual children (Freeman & Freeman, 2009; Ovando & Combs, 2012), or best practices for preparing teachers in general (AERA, Cochran-Smith, & Zeichner, 2005), there is an absence of empirical evidence about specific practices that promote the development of effective bilingual education teachers (August & Hakuta, 1997). Nevertheless, the CASSO faculty team collaborated to synthesize an innovative teaching approach derived from a knowledge base that served as the theoretical underpinning of our work with our preservice bilingual teachers. We focused on developing a signature pedagogy (Shulman, 2005) not only to achieve a coherence between the content and delivery of our courses, but also to promote in our students the formation of character and values that lead to effective pedagogy for EBLs. Content and pedagogical knowledge is necessary, but by itself insufficient; teacher educators must facilitate the transformation of their preservice teachers' consciousness so they become advocates for schoolchildren and seek to achieve social justice in their classrooms (Shulman, 2005). A signature pedagogy refers to a set of distinctive instructional practices that promote our students' successful professional preparation and carry over to their students' learning. It requires that preservice teachers be accountable for their learning by contributing their thought processes to a transparent discourse that becomes routine, habitual, and pervasive in their professional practice.

In CASSO, we incorporated a form of narrative research into our theoretical framework because it facilitated a collaborative relationship with our students as we listened to their concerns and feedback about our instruction, and it created a variety of dialogic interactions. Narrative research opens discourse spaces that go beyond data collection by promoting the formation of character, values, and identities (Galindo, 2007). In CASSO, it helped our students to become advocates for their future emergent bilingual students. Given the politicization of bilingual education in the United States, exemplified by the history of the Bilingual Education Act (Crawford, 2008), and the heightened contradictions between theory and practice in the RGV schools, our students' character development centered around increased sociopolitical awareness.

Design of the Modified Program

Since we were required to teach the state-approved curriculum, our modifications centered on how we taught that content, and represented the beginnings of a signature pedagogy (Shulman, 2005) adapted for our students' particular characteristics. We retained the content of the existing bilingual preservice program: socio-constructivist principles of learning, a socio-psycholinguistic approach to literacy development, and a dual language/additive pedagogical orientation. Our modifications derived from the pedagogical approaches to college teaching and adult learning developed by Fink (2003) and Michaelsen (2004).

CASSO faculty used Fink's Significant Learning approach (2003) to redesign our course structures. We analyzed the preservice program's situational factors and the socioeconomic, linguistic, and academic characteristics of our students to guide us in creating course activities and assignments tailored to our students' unique learning needs. Significant Learning meant leading the students in learning how to apply pedagogical knowledge to authentic teaching situations and resolving problems typically encountered in the teaching profession. In addition, our course activities helped our students to understand themselves as learners and to develop caring values.

We used Michaelsen's team-based learning (TBL) approach (2004) to complement Significant Learning. Some preservice instructors had been using collaborative learning activities sporadically, but TBL provided CASSO instructors with a consistent structure to create coherent, functional student teams, rather than loosely assembled groups. TBL provides for (1) fostering group cohesiveness by creating teams heterogeneous in characteristics and abilities, (2) maintaining groups intact during the course of the semester, and (3) providing the means for group accountability. TBL activities promote critical discussions of newly learned concepts by having the teams apply them to practical problem-solving situations with continuous feedback from the instructor. Problems posed to the teams require evaluation of a range of possible solutions, based on concepts in the coursework, at the higher levels of thinking described in Bloom's taxonomy (Bloom, 1979). A typical TBL activity posed to the teams followed these criteria:

• was based on a significant problem or situation,
• was the same problem for all teams,
• required a forced choice (only one solution could be chosen) based on analysis and application of concepts learned, and
• required simultaneous response from all teams, followed by discussion and immediate instructor feedback.

Though the kinds of TBL activities varied across our courses, at least some aspects of the TBL approach were used in our CASSO courses. Each of our two CASSO student cohorts was divided into heterogeneous teams that remained intact for the duration of each semester and were the same across all courses within each semester.

Curricular coherence, generally identified as an important component in quality teacher preparation (Darling-Hammond, 2006; Levine, 2006), was used in the CASSO project to promote learning that integrated the three areas of the preservice program: (1) literacy development, (2) general curriculum, and (3) bilingual education. The use of Fink's (2003) and Michaelsen's (2004) conceptual frameworks across the CASSO courses helped to achieve curricular coherence. In addition, faculty collaborated in course design by including discussions and learning activities that connected across courses. For example, a reading assignment was used for different purposes across two courses such as a bilingual methods and a curriculum methods course. Furthermore, whenever possible, the same faculty team members taught key sequential courses from one semester to the next, such as the two courses in reading methods, two of the courses in general curriculum methods, and two of the courses in bilingual education methods. Also, some of the faculty who taught program courses supervised the student teachers in their last semester.

Beyond Curriculum Modification

In addition to curricular modifications, CASSO was impacted by elements that occurred naturally as a result of the research activities and the ideology of faculty team members. As it often occurs in exploratory research, some of our emergent findings point us in unanticipated directions. It is important to highlight these factors since they suggest possible elements to be included in bilingual teacher preparation for Latino bilingual teachers.

An important aspect of bilingual teacher preparation for Latinos is the need to develop their identities and to promote the integration of personal and professional values.

Identity is generally explained as the set of values, attitudes, dispositions, and belief systems of an individual (Abt-Perkins, 1993). It is understood as a fluid concept of oneself and is constructed through social interaction and discourse (Varghese, Morgan, Johnston, & Johnson, 2005). In reality, an individual's identity is complex and people have multiple identities that are classified in different ways (Campbell, 2000). For example, cultural and professional identities are of significance in our study of bilingual teacher development. Since identity development is a social process that develops from our participation in certain communities and from our positioning within that community, for preservice teachers of language minority groups, cultural identities are hybrid responses to their development in two worlds: the cultural world of their families and communities, and the world of mainstream culture that they begin experiencing as schoolchildren. Thus for Latinos, identity exists in a multilayered space of plural discourses; its formation comes as a result of cultural shocks and conflicts, creating a synthesis that at times rejects or affirms previously formed identities (Canen, Arbache, & Franco, 2001). The formation of professional identities is also of significance for bilingual teacher educators since cultural and professional identities are in constant opposition to each other as discovered through narrative research of Latino preservice teachers (Aguilar, MacGillivray, & Walker, 2003; Galindo, 2007; Gomez, Rodriguez, & Agosto, 2008) Yet, the narrative research process is also a form of discourse that can mediate the formation of professional identities for Latino preservice teachers, whereby they become advocates for social justice (Galindo, 2007; Urrieta, 2007).

A space for narrative discourse as being beneficial for linguistic minority students is also supported by Rodriguez and Cho (2011) who argue that incorporating narratives of lived experiences can help to legitimize the students' experiential knowledge and promote agency. Though narrative research has often been associated with narratives of students' experiences prior to entering teacher preparation programs, it also subsumes narratives of learning and academic experiences.

Our research confirms findings from these previous studies suggesting that, particularly for our context, the creation of narrative spaces is important for the preparation of Latino bilingual teachers. Emergent themes in this study suggest that the relationships developed between students and the CASSO faculty illustrate how the space for narrative and critical discourse can be a potent mediator in the development and integration of cultural and professional identities. The narrative space was created both within the courses and as part of data collection. Within the courses, students were required to critically reflect on their experiences through online discussions and journals. In these assignments, they were often asked to find relationships between what they learned in the coursework about appropriate practices, what they had experienced as EBLs in bilingual education programs, and what they observed in our local schools as preservice teachers.

The narrative discourse space was also created through the data collection that took place each semester in student focus group discussions. In these focus groups, students shared their perspectives about the course activities they liked or disliked. They also shared the challenges and obstacles they experienced while going through the program, and analyzed the concepts learned in a more personal and relaxed setting. These discussions took place outside of coursework by research assistants who were not identified as their professors, so their dialogue was not associated with course grades and represented informal free expressions of their frank perspectives about the CASSO courses and instructors.

Finally, we note that the impact of the narrative space would have been lessened had it not been for the trust and *cariño* (affection) that developed between the students and the CASSO faculty as a result of the instructors' efforts to create a signature pedagogy based on caring and respect. Consistent with the concept of armed love (Freire, 1998), this pedagogy was "based on respect and focused on providing students with academically rigorous and liberatory education" (Bartolomé, 2008, p. 3). What evolved from our practice exemplified a way to develop "counter-hegemonic pedagogies" to help students move "towards agency and change" (Murrillo, 2010, p. 284).

The combination of curricular modifications, the space for narrative and critical discourse and the pedagogy of authentic *cariño* and respect, created the means to promote the transformative learning necessary in the preparation of Latino bilingual teachers. Transformative learning is the expansion of consciousness resulting from the transformation of basic worldviews, facilitated through conscious analysis of premises (Elias, 1997). Facilitating this transformation of worldviews, or meaning perspectives, should be the most fundamental goal of adult education (Mezirow, 1997).

Although college students are adults, many teacher educators attempt to teach them by applying learning principles developed to teach children. If we want to transform Latino preservice teachers' values about teaching to improve emergent bilingual children's learning, we must provide them with opportunities for perspective transformation. Such transformation usually results from a *disorienting dilemma*, such as that posed by critical examination of the contrast between appropriate practices for EBLs and what they themselves had experienced as schoolchildren. We believe that through narrative spaces and discourse, through TBL problem-solving assignments, and through open student-faculty dialogue, based on respect and *cariño*, Latino bilingual preservice teachers can develop the ideological clarity (Bartolomé, 2000) needed for effective teaching of EBLs.

Methodology

The research project used a mixed methods approach to study each of the two cohorts of students. The qualitative data set included the transcripts of student and faculty focus group discussions, course assignments, and student reflective journals, and video recordings of students working with emergent bilingual children. We focus here on the transcript analyses of student teachers' reflective journals and focus group discussions recorded near the end of the student teaching semesters to explore how the CASSO curriculum may have impacted our students.

Setting and Participants

The CASSO student participants consisted of 63 bilingual preservice teachers divided into two treatment cohorts, named Cohort 2 and Cohort 3. Cohort 1 was a control group that is not the subject of analysis. Cohort 2 consisted of 28 students who went through the program in 2009–2010. Cohort 3 consisted of 35 students who participated in 2010–2012. Although both cohorts completed the program in 4 semesters, cohort 2's third semester occurred during the summer, therefore their program spanned a shorter time frame. Cohort 3 attended the usual 15-week fall and spring semesters. Cohort 2's third semester included a unique summer reading program for EBLs, offered in a public library, that afforded them the opportunity to apply their learning with children unfettered by the constraints imposed by the mandated curriculum in the public schools.

Data Collection

Both cohorts were taught exclusively by project faculty, and CASSO faculty members supervised their student teaching. They wrote bi-weekly reflective journals during their student teaching semester, where they described and analyzed their experiences as they related to principles and concepts taught in the program. Representative cohort members participated in videotaped end-of-semester student focus groups in which they reflected on their own and their team members' experiences in the program and were encouraged to give feedback on the modified curriculum. CASSO instructors were not present during the student focus groups, and participants' identities were kept confidential from the faculty team during their tenure in the program to encourage a frank expression of opinions. Pseudonyms are used in written transcripts and surveys of all data sources.

Data Analysis

Qualitative data were obtained from several thousand pages of transcripts of student feedback from reflective journals, focus groups, and asynchronous online discussions. Students articulated numerous issues related to the challenges they faced in completing college coursework, the evolution of their personal and professional identities, and the sharpening of their sociopolitical awareness about the state of public education in the RGV and the nation.

The principal sources for our qualitative analysis were the bi-weekly student teacher journals and the student focus groups held at the end of the third and fourth (student teaching) semesters. In these sources, students tended to be more articulate in describing their own professional and personal growth and in evaluating the influence of the CASSO curriculum on that growth, especially on their increased awareness of effective pedagogy and of the sociopolitical situation of the public school system. Because these sources consisted of self-reported material, their analyses focused on the evolution of students' academic and professional identities and their sociopolitical consciousness. CASSO student teachers were supervised and observed by faculty team members so that the post-semester faculty focus groups confirmed details from students' reflective journals and focus groups.

Partner dyads of researchers applied qualitative content analysis (Sandelowski, 2000; Zhang & Wildemuth, 2009), within and across transcripts, and identified recurring topics raised by the students about their own learning and their perceptions of the local schools and the preservice program. Periodic discussions among the dyads compared the topics identified and honed down the lists of topics to the most salient issues raised by students. Next, Charmaz's (2006) version of constant comparative analysis and constructivist grounded theory was applied by each dyad, in collaboration with the other dyads, to find deeper themes embedded within relationships among these topics. This analysis was used continuously from earliest data collection, and initial findings were shared with course instructors each semester. This application of humanistic program evaluation (Cronbach, 1980) enabled the faculty team to periodically adjust their teaching in accordance with students' expressed needs.

Findings

After careful analysis of the focus group discussions and online journals as described above, we found a set of themes that emerged that illustrate some of the impact of our modified program. The emergent themes included response to the pedagogy of *cariño*, sense of community, critical analysis of curriculum in schools, professional autonomy, internalization and application of the CASSO curriculum, and the acquisition of academic Spanish.

Pedagogy of *Cariño*

Among the themes that emerged from this set of data was their positive response to the pedagogy of authentic *cariño* outlined by Bartolomé (2008) and employed by the project faculty This theme reflected the quality of caring for students that the CASSO students perceived in their instructors and other project faculty, and that was understood as a model of how to demonstrate teachers' concern for the welfare of their emergent bilingual students. Students often noted that their instructors would listen to their feedback by adjusting their teaching and course design from one semester to the next, which was an application of Cronbach's humanistic principle for conducting ongoing research (Cronbach, 1980).

Prior to student teaching, students' comments centered on the CASSO curriculum, mostly appreciating their instructors for their caring qualities. Many said that professors went the extra mile to adapt their teaching for students' learning needs, and help students to solve personal problems that interfered with learning. Several students noticed that such caring and attention was NOT usually provided outside of CASSO (e.g., in previous courses, in non-CASSO EC6 sections). For example, in a student focus group, in reaction to a non-CASSO student's criticism of her preservice experience, Julissa said.

> ... there's another student teacher ... She hates her experience through the blocks [semesters]; she's always ... talking bad about them. Oh, you know, they are bad, and the teachers don't care about us. ... She hates her program through here. I'm over here thinking, well, ... like, I had a good time ... because we were in CASSO, you know. Just in regular bilingual programs, they might not have the same relationship that our professors in CASSO have, so our experience through CASSO was like, awesome, I think it was awesome, like I wouldn't change anything ... I had a really good time with everything. Everything was perfect. Everything fit in at the end.

Sense of Community (Familia)

The structure of one continuous, enduring CASSO student and faculty cohort that stayed together throughout the program's four semesters, led many students to compare CASSO to a family, and to appreciate the closeness engendered by this approach. There was a general appreciation of how the use of teams and TBL enhanced this sense of community.

Students recognized the continuity, curricular cohesion, and articulation they found in CASSO, especially the familiarity and rapport they established with their instructors and fellow students who "carried over" from one semester to the next. They appreciated that the instructors worked as a team, offering integration among courses within and across the semesters, and commented favorably about working in teams. The family metaphor arose several times, as in this focus group exchange:

> Regina: Well, that's what I think really helped us 'cause I knew that even if Julissa wasn't in my same block, group, that semester, I could still ask her questions because I knew her from the previous semesters. So that's what I liked, we had the same group of students the entire time.
>
> Elisa: We made friends, like familia.
>
> Mariela: ... I think it's easier to work with a group the semester, and you already know their habits and everything, and I don't know, it just seems easier to be with the same group the whole semester than ... I like the way CASSO did it.

Critical Analysis of Curriculum in Schools

Almost all CASSO students expressed criticism of the curriculum of the local schools, what children were taught, how they were taught, and how they were treated. In various ways, this criticism was expressed by contrasting what they had learned in CASSO with what they observed in the schools.

As students had more opportunities to work directly with children, they expressed more detailed and critical analyses of the observed PK-6 curriculum and pedagogy, comparing and contrasting their field experiences and observations with direct references to CASSO's constructivist curriculum. They criticized the scripted, test-prep curricula, the teachers' unwillingness to resist these curricula, the absence of teachers' professional autonomy, and the authoritarian, top-down atmosphere in the region's schools, as exemplified in the following quotes from reflective journals:

> Aurora A: ... these are important points my mentor teacher and many teachers are forgetting about. This is why the students are not performing as good. This is something real that is not being taken care of properly in the classrooms. **Teachers** are now more worried about **teaching by the manual book guide** which are most of the time ineffective lesson plans and it's the kids who are being hurt.

> Alma A: ... it is difficult for me to watch the students become frustrated due to ... the way ... they are being taught ... which is causing them to feel that education and learning is routine, pointless, and terribly mundane.... especially in the lower grades such as pre-kindergarten and kindergarten. It is extremely important as a teacher to put forth an extra effort to make learning fun and interesting for the students.

Where some mentor teachers resisted authoritarian pressures, students linked their positive practices to the CASSO curriculum. The topic of professional autonomy arose frequently as students expressed dismay that their professionalism would be constrained as new teachers.

Professional Autonomy

Students expressed appreciation of the rare instances when the teachers they observed, or when they themselves, were free to implement aspects of CASSO's constructivist principles and practices in the classroom. Several voiced dismay at the prospect of not having such autonomy when they became teachers. They celebrated the few teachers who had autonomy, or who at least tried to exercise it, and criticized the many teachers who were controlled and seemed content to merely follow orders.

Another theme that emerged is the students' development of a sense of professional autonomy and critical resistance to the authoritarian, anti-developmental ethos of the public schools. In all the data sources, students frequently described and sharply criticized the prevailing school practices that contradicted what they were learning in CASSO. Transcript analysis revealed the growth and reinforcement of these qualities as the students chose to remain in CASSO and internalize its pedagogical and sociopolitical values. The increased explicitness and intensification of topics related to these values over time suggest that students' internalized the CASSO curriculum into their growing professional identity. The following quotes from journals are illustrative of the theme.

> Alma A: ... based on what I have observed, that students are not getting anywhere near the quality of education that they should be getting. This is not to say educators don't have good intentions ... they just do not know any better. In my educational courses we have often discussed how it seems that educators are brainwashed, robots that have been brainwashed to think that instruction should be focused around worksheets and phonics.

> Andrea D: ... my mentor asked me what she could do to teach all the material needed before the district benchmark got here. ... teachers feel so overwhelmed by the pressure, that they even plan on taking the students' PE (physical education class time) for two to three days out of the week. ... I mentioned to my mentor, "the curriculum and schools have been changing drastically and for worse." Now a days everything is timed and controlled ... It is a shame how teachers do not have the privilege to teach and do what they believe is better for the students' education.

In their third semester, cohort 2 students had the unique experience of unfettered autonomy in a non-school-based library summer reading program. That semester's student transcripts are filled with a universal sense of liberation for the freedom to apply the CASSO curriculum. The following are quotes from a focus group discussion:

> Lidia B: ... we get to work with children ... (on our own) without having a certified teacher monitoring all the time. ... we are free, ... to try out new stuff and make mistakes without being penalized or judged.

> Andrea D: ... I feel free put into practice what I have been learning without others telling me not to do it because it is wrong or it won't work.

> Diana D: ... The freedom we are getting to do our activities ... feels more natural and we are enjoying it better.

Internalization and Application of the CASSO Curriculum:

Whenever they found or created an opportunity to implement aspects of CASSO's constructivist pedagogy in their work with children, the CASSO students took advantage of that opportunity. In at least trying to apply what they had learned in CASSO, students demonstrated that they had internalized and appropriated the broader version of the modified curriculum, including not only how they taught lessons, but also how they organized social relationships and treated children.

A key part of the development of their professional identities was the students' ability and dedication to apply the CASSO curriculum when given the opportunity in their work with children. Examples of these applications included explicit displays of caring for students, integrated curriculum, projects, hands-on activities, social interaction, and thematic teaching. Such applications were difficult to perform, given the anti-constructivist ethos of the schools, but CASSO student teachers persisted in finding or creating opportunities to practice what they had learned. This persistence suggests students' internalization of our pedagogy deeply enough to seize the opportunity to use it.

During the final semester, in their journals, student teachers often discussed how they applied CASSO's pedagogical concepts to their work with children, sometimes with the permission of mentor teachers, at other times as substitutes, or by the strength of their creativity and self-assuredness.

Sonia V: ... I was lucky to get a mentor who follows the same research as CASSO. She understands that children can learn without the way they're teaching in the school system. So I can do what I've been taught to do, not what the administration is telling us to do.

Mayra C: For science, my mentor was expecting for me to read the pages from the science book and hold a discussion. But I tried to ... go beyond it. ... What I have learned in the blocks helped me so much in being able to plan and prepare the lesson .... I have being able to incorporate all the activities I learned in Dr. Dominguez' class. ... the science experiments we did in her class have helped me ... to think of projects ... to reinforce a science concept.

Jimena G: On Wednesday ... I focused on biographies. I created a power point with the different genres and also included a little game, which the students loved. They were so engaged they wanted to keep playing the game over and over again. Even on Thursday, they would ask if they could play it again. I was so happy to see them that engaged. And not only that, to see they were actually learning and working in their teams. For this activity I had the student pair up with a partner in which they were going to interview them and create a biography on them, and also draw a portrait about the person they interviewed. Their final work was a total success; the students were actively engaged the whole time and not only that they were very creative.

Andrea D: In one of the subjects that I have seen an improvement is in the students writing. From being straight to the point, not interesting, not entertaining some of them have modified their writing .... I did not follow my mentor's way of teaching writing ... Every day that they would turn in their "borrador" (draft). I would read it and would write notes and questions about something I did not understand. Also I would write that they needed to add more details. I would tell them that, 'as a writer, you need to write a story as interesting as it can be and full of details'. ... Most importantly, I let them know that "writing is more than the transcription of spoken words onto paper; it's a tool for discovery, self-expression, and communication."(Thompkins, 115) All I can say is that the improvement I have seen in the students' writing is great. Each day they would add more interesting details to their "borrador" and would even make it longer than usual. Some would even write up to two pages.

The Acquisition of Academic Spanish

Many students raised topics focused on their awareness of the need for bilingual teachers to master academic Spanish, on their own feelings of inadequacy in this area, and on their appreciation of CASSO instructors' efforts to help them develop stronger Spanish language skills. Many students eventually transferred their feelings of inadequacy to a sociopolitical awareness of the systemic roots of their weak language competencies. They articulated their appreciation of CASSO instructors' efforts to help them develop stronger Spanish language skills and an understanding that, to better serve the region's EBLs, they needed to improve their own language skills.

As they progressed through the program, students increasingly commented on the subtractivist nature of local bilingual programs, and connected this subtractivism to their own weak language and academic skills as products of the region's school systems. Many students eventually transferred their sense of personal inadequacy about language to a broader sociopolitical awareness of the systemic roots of their weak language competencies. The theme that tied these topics together was that CASSO students had developed an understanding that making a difference for the region's schoolchildren meant that as teachers, they needed to improve their own language skills and provide additive bilingual education opportunities for their students, as illustrated in the following excerpts from a focus group discussion:

Regina: ... they prepared, us, I think academically, they did a very good job of preparing us with everything that we need to know and we need to teach, but they also ... prepared us ethically, like, before, bilingualism you're gonna do English and you're gonna do Spanish, but now that we've been through CASSO and we've been with all of the professors it's like, well yeah, you're gonna do English and Spanish but you also need to be aware that you need to teach these kids that Spanish is good and

Spanish is ok, and it's good that they know two languages, no matter what anybody else says, and I think that that's something that some of us weren't aware of before ...

Julissa: ... they help you valorar your language because in the schools they take it away and it's so unfair because, like, now with the testing and all that, they want you to have academic Spanish, like, for the BTLPT and it's like, how do you want us to be perfect teachers if you take it away from us when we're little. Like, how do you expect us to know it when you yourselves are taking it away from us? ... with CASSO, they helped us love it again, like, they make you ... like a spark, you know, ... they teach you why you actually should be a bilingual teacher, what it really means to be a bilingual teacher, not just because you kind of speak it, no, you have to know strategies and the background, where they're coming from, and to love it. You have to love it in order to teach it correctly.

The analysis of focus group discussions and reflective journals suggest that students developed a sense of community and seemed to benefit from the pedagogy of authentic *cariño* provided in the project. They seemed to have developed a critical stance and a professional autonomy to make pedagogical decisions based on the additive approach to teaching EBLs they internalized from the curriculum provided. They also became aware of the need to develop academic Spanish in order to properly teach EBLs.

Additional topics focused on the anti-developmental, behaviorist treatment of children as test-takers, the lack of social interaction and caring in classrooms, and the dearth of positive professional interaction among teachers and administrators.

Limitations of the Study

As stated earlier, this study is limited to the context of border communities and preservice teachers who are Latinos. Yet, this focus on the professional development of Latino preservice teachers continues to be an area of concern for bilingual teacher educators (Clark, Jackson, & Prieto, 2010). Furthermore, this study is limited to findings as a result of data that is self-reported and lacks an examination of the impact of the modified curriculum by examining the practices of these participants after they became teachers in our local schools. This study is of importance for our understanding of the level of impact of the CASSO experience, and we are therefore currently engaging in this kind of research by following our participants after they graduated. The results of this ongoing research will be reported in the future.

Practical Implications and Recommendations

As suggested by the findings in the analysis of data presented here, the preparation of Latino teachers for work with EBLs requires a context-specific pedagogy where faculty work collaboratively to facilitate the integration of preservice teachers' cultural and professional identities, which in turn can promote the transformation of their consciousness, as explained by Shulman (2005) and supported by Murrillo (2010).

Preservice teachers need to deconstruct their preconceived concepts of what constitutes appropriate practices in order to embrace the newly acquired ideas. Therefore, it is important for them to have opportunities to experience opposite practices, and to then provide them with opportunities where they are free to apply what they learned in the coursework and pair these opportunities with time to engage in critical reflection of the contradictions present in the school settings where they will eventually become professionals. The space for narrative and dialogue along with opportunities to examine the contradictions between theory and practice, is an important medium through which they can forge their professional identities, build the character to become advocates for the EBLs they will eventually teach, and acquire the strength of conviction to work against the hegemonic conditions of the local public schools.

Furthermore, the voices of our preservice teachers illustrate how the methods used to create a space for narrative and discourse, can support their learning in meaningful ways. The use of Fink's Significant Learning framework and Michaelsen's TBL were in harmony with the creation of the spaces for dialogue that promoted the critical reflection evidenced by the students' statements. But these frameworks also provided a medium through which our faculty created curricular coherence, an essential factor in promoting transformative learning.

Let us again examine a portion of the email quoted at the beginning of this chapter:

> ... what is lacking here; a school that can properly teach students and help them be the best they can be. Several of us have been meeting with professors and other interested people on creating a Dual language school in the valley, because it is long overdue.

This excerpt from the email exemplifies our students' synthesis of their experiences and development at the preservice phase of their preparation, culminating in their desire to create a new school where they could freely apply what they had learned and considered important in their professional practice. This would be a new space where they could be allowed the agency to work with EBLs in an additive fashion, which they believed was lacking in the local schools. This critical stance has not been usually exhibited by preservice teachers (Ostorga, 2006), and we believe is an example of the kind of formation of character and values that Shulman (2005) refers to as essential in the development of teachers. For bilingual teachers, these values and critical stance can promote the principled, additive teaching practices necessary for the optimal development of emergent bilinguals. Nevertheless, a true test of the impact of the CASSO project can only be derived from an in-depth investigation of our graduates teaching practices in the local bilingual classrooms. We are currently conducting case studies of some of our graduates, but much work is left to be done.

References

Abt-Perkins, D., & Gomez, M. L. (1993). A good place to begin — Examining our personal perspectives. *Language Arts, 70,* 193–202.

AERA Panel on Research and Teacher Education, Cochran-Smith, M., & Zeichner, K. M. (2005). *Studying teacher education: The report of the AERA panel on research and teacher education.* Mahwah, NJ: Lawrence Erlbaum Associates.

Aguilar, J., MacGillivray, L., & Walker, N. (2003). Latina educators and school discourse: Dealing with tension on the path to success. *Journal of Latinos and Education, 2*(2), 89–100.

August, D., & Hakuta, K. (1997). *Improving schooling for language minority children: A research agenda.* Washington, DC: National Academy Press.

Bartolomé, L. I. (1994). Beyond the methods fetish: Toward a humanizing pedagogy. *Harvard Educational Review, 64,* 173–194.

Bartolomé, L. I. (2000). Democratizing bilingualism: The role of critical teacher education. In Z. F. Beykont (Ed.), *Lifting every voice: Pedagogy and politics of bilingualism* (pp. 167–186). Cambridge, MA: Harvard Education Publishing Group.

Bartolomé, L. (2008). Authentic cariño and respect in minority education: The political and ideological dimensions of love. *International Journal of Critical Pedagogy, 1*(1), 1–17.

Belmonte, D. (2009). *Teaching from the deep end: Succeeding with today's classroom challenges.* Thousand Oaks, CA: Corwin Press.

Bloom, B. S. (Ed.). (1979). *Taxonomy of educational objectives, Book I: Cognitive domain.* London: Longman.

Brookfield, S. D. (2009). *The skillful teacher: On technique, trust, and responsiveness in the classroom.* San Francisco, CA: Wiley.

Campbell, A. (2000). Cultural identity as a social construct. *Intercultural Education, 11*(1), 31–39.

Canen, A., Arbache, A. P., & Franco, M. (2001). Pesquisando multiculturalismo e educação: O que dizem as dissertações e teses. *[Investigating multiculturalism and education: What is stated in dissertations and thesis].* Educação e Realidade, 26(1), 161–181.

Charmaz, K. (2006). *Constructing grounded theory: A practical guide through qualitative analysis*. Thousand Oaks, CA: Sage.

Clark, E. R., Jackson, L. G., & Prieto, L. (2010). Teacher preparation for bilingual student populations: Educar para transformar. In B. B. Flores, R. Hernandez, R. Sheets, & E. R. Clark (Eds.), *Teacher preparation for bilingual student populations: Educar para transformar* (pp. 27–39). New York, NY: Routledge.

Crawford, J. (2008). *Advocating for English learners selected essays*. Buffalo, NY: Multilingual Matters.

Cronbach, J. L. (1980). *Toward reform of program evaluation*. San Francisco, CA: Jossey-Bass.

Cummins, J. (2001). *Negotiating identities: Education for empowerment in a diverse society*. Los Angeles, CA: California Association for Bilingual Education.

Darling-Hammond, L. (2006). Constructing 21st-century teacher education. *Journal of Teacher Education, 57*, 300–314.

De Courcy, M. (2007). Disrupting preconceptions: Challenges to Pre-service teachers' beliefs about ESL children. *Journal of Multilingual & Multicultural Development, 28*(3), 188–203.

Elias, D. (1997). It's time to change our minds: An introduction to transformative learning. *ReVision, 20*(1), 2–6.

Fink, L. D. (2003). *A self-directed guide to designing courses for significant learning*. Retrieved from http://deefinkandassociates.com/GuidetoCourseDesignAug05.pdf

Freeman, Y. S., & Freeman, D. E. (2009). *Academic language for English language learners and struggling readers: How to help students succeed across content areas*. Portsmouth, NH: Heinemann.

Freire, P. (1998). *Teachers as cultural workers: Letters to those who dare teach*. Boulder, CO: Westview Press.

Galindo, R. (2007). Voices of identity in a Chicana teacher's occupational narratives of the self. *The Urban Review, 39*(3), 251–280.

Gandara, P. C., & Contreras, F. (2009). *The Latino education crisis: The consequences of failed social policies*. Cambridge, MA: Harvard University Press.

García, O., & Kleifgen, J. A. (2010). *Educating emergent bilinguals: Policies, programs, and practices for English language learners*. New York, NY: Teachers College Press.

Gomez, M. L., Rodriguez, T. L., & Agosto, V. (2008). Life histories of Latino/a teacher candidates. *Teachers College Record, 110*(8), 1639–1676.

Hanushek, E. A., Kain, J. F., O'Brien, D. M., & Rivkin, S. G. (2005). *The market for teacher quality*. Working Paper No. 11154.National Bureau of Economic Research, Cambridge, MA.

Levine, A. (2006). *Educating school teachers*. Washington, DC: The Education Schools Project.

Lortie, D. (1975). *Schoolteacher: A sociological study*. Chicago, IL: The University of Chicago University press.

Mezirow, J. (1997). Transformative learning: Theory to practice. *New Directions for Adult and Continuing Education, 74*, 5–12.

Michaelsen, L. (2004). Getting started with team-based learning. In L. Michaelsen, A. Knight, & L. Fink (Eds.), *Team-based learning: A transformative use of small groups in college teaching* (pp. 27–52). Sterling, VA: Stylus Publishing.

Murillo, L. A. (2010). Local literacies as counter-hegemonic practices: Deconstructing anti-Spanish ideologies in the Rio Grande Valley. In V. J. Risko, R. T. Jiménez, & D. W. Rowe (Eds.), *59th yearbook of the national reading conference* (pp. 276–288). Oak Creek, WI: Literacy Research Association.

Ostorga, A. N. (Fall 2006). Developing teachers who are reflective practitioners: A complicated process. *Issues in Teacher Education, 15*(2), 5–20.

Ovando, C. J., & Combs, M. C. (2012). *Bilingual and ESL classrooms: Teaching in multicultural contexts.* New York, NY: McGraw-Hill.

Ravitch, D. (2010). *The death and life of the great American school system: How testing and
choice are undermining education.* New York, NY: Basic Books.

Rodriguez, T. L., & Cho, H. (2011). Eliciting critical literacy narratives of bi/multilingual
teacher candidates across U.S. teacher education contexts. *Teaching and Teacher
Education, 27*(3), 496–504. doi:10.1016/j.tate.2010.10.002

Sandelowski, M. (2000). Whatever happened to qualitative description? *Research in Nursing &
Health, 23*, 334–340.

Shulman, L. (2005, February). *The signature pedagogies of the professions of law, medicine,
engineering, and the clergy: Potential lessons for the education of teachers.* Paper
delivered at Math Science Partnerships Workshop. National Research Council's Center
for Education, Irvine, CA.

Sloat, E., Makkonen, R., & Koehler, P. (2007). *La Frontera: Student achievement in Texas
border and non-border districts.* (Issues & Answers Report, REL 2007-No. 027).
Washington, DC: U.S. Department of Education, Institute of Education Sciences,
National Center for Education Evaluation and Regional Assistance, Regional
Educational Laboratory Southwest. Retrieved from http://ies.ed.gov/ncee/edlabs

Urrieta, L. (2007). Identity production in figured worlds: How some Mexican Americans
become Chicana/o activist educators. *The Urban Review, 39*(2), 117–144.

Valenzuela, A. (2004). *Leaving children behind: How "Texas-Style" Accountability fails latino
youth.* Albany, NY: SUNY press.

Varghese, M., Morgan, B., Johnston, B., & Johnson, K. (2005). Theorizing language teacher
identity: Three perspectives and beyond. *Journal of Language, Identity and Education,
4*(1), 21–44.

Zhang, Y., & Wildemuth, B. M. (2009). Qualitative analysis of content. In B. Wildemuth
(Ed.), *Applications of social research methods to questions in information and library
science* (pp. 308–319). Westport, CT: Libraries Unlimited.

CHAPTER 6

MODELING COLLABORATIVE TEACHING IN TEACHER EDUCATION: PREPARING PRE-SERVICE TEACHERS TO TEACH *ALL* STUDENTS

Tatyana Kleyn and Jan Valle

Abstract

In an effort to better prepare pre-service candidates to work with all *students and to respond to the current collaborative team teaching trend within New York City public schools, the authors who are professors of bilingual education and inclusive education/disability studies, respectively, combined their student teaching seminars in bilingual education and childhood education, in order to: (1) provide a model of co-teaching as well as an experience and perspective of being a student in a classroom with two teachers; (2) provide pre-service candidates with ongoing access to the expertise of two professors* during *their student teaching experience; (3) engage pre-service teachers in critical conversations about identifying and resisting deficit constructions of both emergent bilingual students and students with disabilities; (4) engage in a self-study of*

Research on Preparing Preservice Teachers to Work Effectively with Emergent Bilinguals
Advances in Research on Teaching, Volume 21, 137–164
Copyright © 2014 by Emerald Group Publishing Limited
All rights of reproduction in any form reserved
ISSN: 1479-3687/doi:10.1108/S1479-368720140000021005

teaching practice within this collaborative context; (5) consider how well our respective programs currently prepare pre-service teachers. The Self-Study of Teacher Education Practices approach gleaned data from the co-instructors' weekly reflective journals and student evaluations to reveal multiple benefits of a collaborative classroom context for pre-service teachers as well as the professors. These benefits included a rethinking of academic structures, spaces for interconnectedness across fields, and increased professor and student learning. The findings challenge teacher educators to consider whether or not a traditional approach to teacher preparation truly offers pre-service teachers the tools to serve diverse students. The authors call on schools of education to transgress traditional academic boundaries to adequately prepare pre-service teachers for the 21st century classroom.

Keywords: Students with disabilities; emergent bilinguals; student teaching; co-teaching; inclusive education; higher education .

I have wanted to try some cross-disciplinary work and this is the perfect opportunity. It makes sense (at least in my head) that we could better address the complexities that our teacher candidates encounter in public schools by dissolving our own traditionally rigid disciplinary boundaries at the university level. Moreover, our students increasingly are being placed into co-teaching contexts. It seems significant that our teacher candidates will have the opportunity to experience co-teaching from the perspective of students as well as to observe a co-teaching model "in action." I am eager to see what emerges from our partnership! (JV)

Introduction

Adequately preparing teachers for the increasing complexity and diversity of 21st century public schools − and, in particular, the urban context − requires teacher education programs that reflect and address contemporary realities. The authors, a professor of bilingual education and a professor of inclusive education/disability studies (DS) respectively, prepare pre-service teachers to work within one of the largest and most diverse urban school districts in the country. In response to the large numbers of public school students identified as needing bilingual, English as a Second/Additional Language (ESL) and/or special education services, Collaborative Team

Teaching (CTT) classrooms (e.g., general education classrooms co-taught by a general education teacher and a special education teacher or a special education teacher and a bilingual education teacher) have become increasingly commonplace as a primary service delivery model within the school district. A range of terms are used to describe these settings. Although we use CTT, terms such as Integrated Co-Teaching (ICT), and Co-Teaching, among others, are also used to describe the same instructional model.

In an effort to respond to the current CTT trend, we combined our childhood education and bilingual education student teaching seminar classes to mirror the CTT instructional model. We established the following objectives for our collaboration: (1) provide a model of co-teaching as well as an experience and perspective of being a student in a classroom with two teachers; (2) provide pre-service candidates with ongoing access to the expertise of two professors *during* their student teaching experience; (3) engage pre-service teachers in critical conversations about identifying and resisting deficit constructions of both emergent bilingual students and students with disabilities; (4) engage in a self-study of teaching practice within the collaborative context; (5) consider how well our respective programs currently prepare pre-service teachers to work with *all* students.

Reflecting the school district's recent trend toward a more inclusive response to students with disabilities and emergent bilingual students, our collaborative student teaching seminar likewise merged traditionally separate academic disciplines of childhood education, inclusive education/DS, and bilingual education. We reasoned that co-teaching at the college level would provide an opportunity not only to demonstrate a current instructional model, but also to create a collaborative context within which to engage pre-service teachers in identifying and resisting assumptions and practices that contribute to deficit constructions of students with disabilities (Connor, Gabel, Gallagher, & Morton, 2008; Dudley-Marling, 2010; Linton, Melio, & O'Neill, 1995; Valle & Connor, 2011; Ware, 2006) as well as emergent bilingual students (Crawford, 2004; Freeman, 1998; García, 2009; Nieto, 2002; Valenzuela, 1999).

The following research questions guided the self-study.

1. How does a CTT seminar for pre-service student teachers impact learning for the professors and students?
2. What are the advantages and challenges to teaching across fields?
3. How can teacher education programs prepare educators to serve all students, including emergent bilinguals and students with disabilities?

Our new seminar configuration reflected Harris and Harvey's (2000) assertion that college students, particularly those never before exposed to collaborative contexts, given the opportunity to "see instructors responding to concepts or theories differently, taking risks, and taking distinct positions in relationship to the material studied, an implicit value is being lived out in front of them: that differences in perspective are beneficial to learning, acceptable, and encouraged. Diversity is experienced as being valuable" (p. 29). Beyond providing a co-teaching model within the seminar context, we reasoned that the presence of two instructors speaking from their respective disciplines would enhance the knowledge base of our pre-service teachers (Anderson & Speck, 1998) as well as encourage them to more deeply consider diversity issues within their student teaching placements.

Historical and Theoretical Perspectives on Co-Teaching

Reflective of the areas of expertise that we brought to CTT, our historical and theoretical framework likewise incorporates perspectives from inclusive education/DS and bilingual education.

Contextualizing Co-Teaching for Students with Disabilities

How to best meet the educational and social needs of students with disabilities within American public schools remains an ongoing debate among educational communities. Although federal special education law requires that students with disabilities be placed in the least restrictive environment (LRE), it has long been documented that public schools have over-relied upon segregated special education settings ranging from pull-out programs to self-contained classrooms to segregated special education schools, particularly in regard to students of color from lower socioeconomic backgrounds (Blanchett, 2006; Brantlinger, 2006; Harry & Klingner, 2006; Karagiannis, 2000). Over the last three decades, evidence of the negative effects of labeling – and the subsequent deficit constructions associated with labeling – has been widely documented (Connor et al., 2008; Dudley-Marling, 2010; Ware, 2006).

As early as the 1980s, the less than satisfactory outcomes for students with disabilities in special education programs raised concerns (e.g., Garvar & Papania, 1982; Will, 1986). By the 1990s, families and their advocates began to promote the slogan "Special Education is a Service, Not a Place" to express dissatisfaction with the predominance of segregated educational settings for students labeled with disabilities (Valle & Connor, 2011). Likewise, there began an educational movement away from the practice of *mainstreaming*, wherein a student with a disability could participate in general education *only* if he or she required no assistance to perform like his or her peers without disabilities toward the philosophy and practice of *inclusion*, wherein it is assumed that a student with a disability will benefit academically and socially from general education, even if his or her goals are different from the goals of non-disabled students (Villa & Thousand, 1995).

In an influential article co-authored by Bauwens, Hourcade, and Friend (1989), the notion of cooperative teaching, known today as co-teaching or CTT, was conceptualized as a service delivery model with a focus upon supporting students with disabilities in the general education setting. In the more than 20 years since, the number of inclusion classrooms with co-teachers has increased nationwide, primarily in response to two pieces of legislation — No Child Left Behind (2001) and the reauthorization of The Individuals with Disabilities Education Improvement Act (2004). In particular, the former requires that *all* students have access to the general education curriculum taught by highly qualified teachers, while the latter emphasizes that students with disabilities *must* be educated in the LRE. Thus, the recent federal emphasis upon placing students with disabilities within general education classrooms has given rise to more co-teaching at the K-12 levels.

Cook and Friend (1995) define co-teaching as "two or more professionals delivering substantive instruction to a diverse, or blended, group of students in a single physical space" (p. 2). In other words, two certified teachers, typically a general education teacher and a special education teacher, share instruction in a general education classroom of diverse students with and without disabilities (Friend & Cook, 2010). Moreover, we also might understand such a partnership between teachers with different areas of expertise as

> a reasonable response to the increasing difficulty of a single professional keeping with all the knowledge and skills necessary to meet the instructional needs of the diverse student population attending public schools and the complexity of the problems that they bring. (Friend, Cook, Hurley-Chamberlain, & Shamberger, 2010, p. 11)

While co-teaching is a practice that appears to be beneficial for students and teachers alike (Hang & Rabren, 2009; Solis, Vaughn, Swanson, &

McCulley, 2012), it is also the case that some teachers in these settings, as well as their administrators, are not adequately prepared in collaborative methods and approaches. Thus, it can be left up to chance whether or not a partnership becomes an effective one that benefits the learning of *all* students (Friend, 2007; Valle & Connor, 2011). It is our belief that pre-service teachers as well as in-service teachers and administrators, need sufficient exposure to strong models of collaborative teaching in order to effectively engage in such partnerships.

Contextualizing Co-teaching for Emergent Bilinguals

When considering the education of emergent bilinguals, co-teaching has not historically been an approach for this group of students. Within most bilingual education classrooms, one teacher who is proficient in both languages of instruction and knowledgeable in the content area(s) has generally been *the* classroom teacher. Emergent bilinguals in ESL models are often in general education classes for the majority of the school day and are either pulled out to work with an ESL teacher in a small group at their grade or English proficiency level, or the ESL teacher pushes in to their classroom and assists the teacher in supporting the students (Reyes & Kleyn, 2010). Although the latter approach does consist of two teachers working together, the amount of collaboration between the content and ESL teacher ranges significantly by factors such as lack of planning time, high numbers of teachers and grades, and a limited understanding of collaboration as a pedagogical approach (Honigsfield & Dove, 2010). Power dynamics between the ESL teacher and the content teacher often impede true collaboration because the ESL teacher may be subordinated to an assistant level, whereas content teachers are viewed as having "a real academic discipline" (Flores, 2012, p. 186). Arkoudis (2003) found a *pseudo-collaboration* present in such settings where the ESL teacher felt forced to yield to the content teacher, thereby obstructing possibilities for authentic collaboration.

Within bilingual education the growth of dual language bilingual (DLB) programs has given way to teacher collaboration. Within the side-by-side DLB model, one teacher takes on the English component in one classroom whereas the other teacher has the language other than English/target language component in a different classroom (Freeman, Freeman, & Mercuri, 2004). Two groups of students move between the two teachers, usually switching every other day. This type of collaboration is centered on planning, to ensure the content students learn builds from one day to next, rather than repeating. Although teachers are in separate classrooms, a considerable level of collaboration is required on a regular basis.

As special education has moved toward a more inclusive approach, emergent bilingual students with disabilities at the elementary level also may be served in ICT classes with a bilingual education teacher and a bilingual special education teacher, who work together on a daily basis to provide bilingual instruction to all students *and* individualized instruction for students with disabilities. Thus, students who require both language and special education services have their needs meet within a single setting.

Only within the last 10 years has research identified and focused on collaboration within the classrooms for emergent bilinguals — as opposed to students with disabilities (Honigsfeld & Dove, 2012). During this decade, the research has centered on areas such as inclusive practices and social justice (Theoharis, 2009), designing standards-based curriculum and instruction (Short, Cloud, Morris, & Motta, 2012), teacher leadership focused on instruction (Honigsfeld & Dove, 2010), and instructional approaches for emergent bilinguals and students with disabilities (Capper & Frattura, 2008).

The Problem of Normativity for Both Fields

In considering the current state of special education, it is worth noting that the field's parent disciplines of medicine, science, and psychology are deeply rooted in understanding human difference as dysfunctional, deficit-based, and abnormal (Danforth & Gabel, 2007). Given these disciplinary underpinnings, it is rather predictable, in hindsight, that special education became institutionalized in a way that segregated students with disabilities from students without disabilities, as previously discussed. As such, normativity became the principle around which schools organized themselves, giving rise to the now legendary parallel systems of general and special education. Although inclusive classrooms are more commonplace now than ever before, the presence or absence of disability, normal or abnormal, continues to determine how and where a student is taught and by whom (Brantlinger, 2004).

Within our collaborative student teaching seminar, it is noteworthy that we chose to contrast the "medical model" of disability that undergirds the deficit orientation of special education with a DS perspective of disability — an interdisciplinary field that conceptualizes disability as a marker of identity that intersects with race, ethnicity, language, class, gender, and sexual orientation (Gabel, 2005). Students were encouraged to consider disability as natural human variation rather than pathology. We placed particular emphasis upon understanding disability within cultural, historical, and social contexts.

Just as special education is centered on the normativity, emergent bilinguals are also judged against native English speakers. This rarely achievable standard centers not only on speakers having English as their maternal language, but this being their only language, thereby positioning English monolingualism as the norm and the ultimate goal. However, this native English speaker notion has been problematized on a variety of levels: (1) with the regional and cultural diversity across our nation, there is no one way of speaking English that is native; (2) it is usually speakers of Standard Academic English that are affiliated with this label, whereas speakers of other varieties of English — often from minoritized groups — are not seen within this label (Blommaert, 2010); and (3) when applying English as native to some speakers, it implies that it can never be appropriated by speakers of other languages (García, 2014). Therefore, our students were also encouraged to consider that as emergent bilinguals are developing a linguistic repertoire that includes features from two or more languages, their perceived non-nativeness creates an obstacle to being or even becoming part of the societal norm.

A Case for Modeling Co-Teaching in Higher Education

In an effort to better prepare our students to teach diverse students, we decided to combine and co-teach our student teaching seminars. We reasoned that our respective students would benefit from a semester-long exposure to a co-teaching model as well as two professors with expertise in bilingual education, TESOL, special education, childhood education, and DS. Moreover, it was our assumption that students would be better prepared to teach in public schools if the pedagogy in teacher education reflected the current practice of co-teaching.

Methods

This research was guided by the Self-Study of Teacher Education Practices (S-STEP) approach (LaBoskey, 2004; Pinnegar & Hamilton, 2009).

Because we were afforded a unique opportunity to co-teach across fields — a practice rarely implemented at the tertiary level, S-STEP allowed us to better understand our own experiences while contributing to a larger conversation across our fields. The qualitative methods permitted us to systematically study ourselves through reflection and dialogue that spanned the semester of our CTT student teaching seminar.

The Self-Study Process

Co-teaching at the college level requires a fundamental change in the long-standing tradition of strict disciplinary boundaries and single authority within the academy (Harris & Harvey, 2000). Such an instructional transition requires of co-instructors "a learning (or reacculturation) process to incorporate the new skills and assumptions into their existing mental structures" (Henderson, Beach, & Famiano, 2007, p. 117). In order to facilitate and document our re-acculturation process, we wrote and exchanged weekly entries about our individual and shared practice in reflective journals. The reflective entries were purposefully open-ended so that each instructor could write freely about her perspectives, experiences, and observations. The topics addressed ranged from student learning to collaborative approaches to general concerns. The presence of a critical other (Ghaye & Ghaye, 1998) served to deepen the reflective process. It is worth noting that our commitment to reflective practice through dialogue — a well-established benefit for professionals (Schon, 1983) — mirrored the reflective journaling required of our student teachers. In this way, we validated the collective responsibility for teaching and learning that grounds a collaborative classroom context. For the final reflection, we responded to the same questions asked of seminar participants on the course evaluation.

Following the completion of the semester we each reviewed the data to come up with preliminary themes that arose in the journals. We compared our themes to develop a coding scheme that was used to analyze the data and determine key findings (Cohen, Manion, & Morrison, 2011).

Participants and Setting

This study requires our positioning as key participants in the research. Jan Valle, a faculty member in the Childhood Education program with a specialization in inclusive education/DS, regularly teaches the childhood education student teaching seminar. She has worked within the field of special education for over thirty years and in various collaborative settings. Tatyana Kleyn, a faculty member in the Bilingual Education & TESOL program with a specialization in multicultural education and immigration, has taught the bilingual student teaching seminar for seven years. Until this experience, Tatyana had not formally taught in a CTT class, but often collaborated with educators in informal ways and wanted to experience such partnerships within her classes and teaching.

Our combined student teaching seminar had a total of 17 female students in their twenties and thirties who were a mix of graduate and undergraduate students earning their first certification in either childhood education or bilingual childhood education (grades 1–6). The students came from U.S.-born and immigrant backgrounds, mainly from Latin America. Many had graduated from the school system where they were student teaching.

The New York City school district (where our students were student teaching) boasts a diverse student body with 15.5% of emergent bilinguals (referred to English Language Learners) and 17% of students with disabilities. Students from these two backgrounds are served in bilingual education settings (22%), ESL classes (71%), and special education classes (6.8%) (NYC Independent Budget Office, 2013). Figures for students in CTT classrooms are not available, but from our own work in schools and Jan's annual collaboration with the school district on a summer Co-teaching Institute we have observed first-hand an increase in this teaching approach.

Findings and Discussion

Three broad themes emerged from our findings and frame the discussion that follows:

(a) Impact upon Structures of Academia,
(b) Discipline Dis/connections, and
(c) Reciprocal Learning.

Impact upon Structures of Academia

After our planning session I am very excited about the semester that lies ahead. I can already see that I am going to be learning a lot (such as the different models of team teaching). I am also looking forward to having conversations with a colleague that are not about programming, scheduling or meetings, but that really get at the teaching and learning process and what happens (and does not happen) in the classroom. After our first meeting I realized that many of the conversations at the "office" are around more administrative issues than educational ones, so this is going to be a refreshing change. (TK)

You are so right, Tatyana, about how our collegial conversations primarily revolve around administrative issues! I am really looking forward to being stimulated by your ideas and learning from you. The fact that it seems like a "luxury" to talk with a colleague about teaching reveals a lot about how skewed our time is toward creating and maintaining administrative structures. I am so glad that we have this opportunity. Perhaps it will inspire us to think about ways to make this kind of engagement happen more often among faculty. (JV)

From the time that we began talking about co-teaching, we were aware of the transgressive nature of such an arrangement within our School of Education. As is common in most colleges and universities, our colleagues almost always teach within their respective disciplinary programs. Over the years, however, there have been a few instances of team teaching — to be distinguished from co-teaching in that the instructors taught their own courses, then switched at mid-term to teach their respective content to each other's class. Currently there is no structure in place at our university to pay two professors to share a single course. Thus, we were able to co-teach only by merging our relatively small student teaching seminars in bilingual education and childhood education into a shared classroom space rather than teaching in two separate classrooms.

From the onset of our shared project, we recognized how the structure of co-teaching dramatically altered the content of our usual collegial conversations. As reflected in the journal excerpts above, it was immediately clear how much traditional academic structures dictate the nature of exchanges between colleagues. Changing how we typically work opened up rich avenues for pedagogical conversations that otherwise do not take place.

Implementing co-teaching in higher education. In planning for co-teaching, we identified a shared commitment to connecting theory to practice in meaningful ways. In light of the steady increase in the number of CTT classrooms within our respective fields, we shared a mutual concern for preparing our students to teach within this model. As CTT classrooms become more commonplace, our students are more likely to be placed in such settings for student teaching. Moreover, our graduates are more likely than ever to secure teaching positions in classrooms with two teachers.

Thus, we reasoned that modeling a co-teaching relationship might help prepare our students for the kind of work required in the field:

> It seems significant that our teacher candidates will have the opportunity to experience co-teaching from a student perspective as well as to observe a co-teaching model "in action" ... I am wondering what the students think about having two professors. It will be interesting to see how everything unfolds through the semester. Tatyana and I have our ideas about why **we** chose to co-teach. It will be interesting to see how students experience and respond to the co-teaching model. (JV)

Not only did co-teaching enhance our students' understanding of this pedagogical model, but also we gained deeper insight into the benefits and challenges of co-teaching and its application to higher education. Here Tatyana reflects on her oscillating position within a session Jan led on differentiation:

> As a co-teacher, I found myself moving between the role of a facilitator and the role of a student myself during this activity, and I really loved the flexibility I had in doing so. It also made me think about how we differentiate at the college level, or if we do at all. Maybe that's for another reflection paper!! (TK)

In the following journal excerpt, Jan reflects on what she experiences as a challenge of co-teaching at the higher education level:

> Given that I am working in the field with CTT teachers while co-teaching with Tatyana, I find it interesting that the biggest challenge for both the CTT teachers and ourselves is finding adequate time to co-plan. In light of our erratic schedules, we struggle to find a consistent time and day of the week to meet. At times, we have no other choice but to make "phone dates." I wonder if time to co-plan could be blocked as part of the seminar – both before and after class? (JV)

Through the practice of co-teaching, we found new opportunities for self-reflection at the level of higher education:

> Reflecting back upon the semester, not only would I have liked more planning time but I also would have liked to have integrated the instructional needs of individual students into our planning. Had we done this, I think that we would have gotten to know each other's students better and we might have used "flexible grouping" more effectively. (JV)

Our experience of modeling a current pedagogical practice within public schools certainly reinforced us how important it is for Schools of Education to maintain relevancy to the field.

> In light of the recent trend toward CTT classrooms in New York City public schools, I believe that our students benefited from seeing an effective co-teaching relationship "in action." The class seemed to enjoy the natural energy and humor between Tatyana and

myself which contributed to a positive classroom climate. Moreover, the students seemed to gain a lot from having access to the expertise of two professors from different academic fields. (JV)

Disrupting disciplinary boundaries.

I can't wait to find out what Tatyana and I can do together! She and I have had many conversations about the parallels between special education and bilingual education — on so many levels. As we went through our syllabi together, the intersections between our disciplines became apparent — and yet, there is much to contribute from our respective disciplines. (JV)

As reflected in the journal excerpt above, co-teaching afforded us the opportunity to disrupt traditional disciplinary boundaries and explore related outcomes within a sustained context. Doing so enabled us to forge new territory in regard to pedagogy and collaborative research in ways that traditional structures have not. Moreover, we began to consider how traditional structures might actually impede student learning:

Our collaboration does put into question the rigid divides in academia, and I agree that we must start rethinking the ways such separations hurt our students in terms of preparing them to teach ALL students. Perhaps this is something that can be addressed in a larger School of Ed. specialized meeting and/or when we have to rethink our program designs based on the new certification structure. (TK)

As the semester progressed, we began to identify specific ways that permeable disciplinary boundaries enhanced the education of our students:

I feel like yesterday's class really took advantage of the combination of students and the strengths they bring. By starting out mixing our students in the lesson sharing groups, we had students break out of their comfort zones and the results were positive. In my group the childhood education students were able to see how objectives for language and content are important when working with emergent bilinguals. (TK)

During announcements this week, Tatyana spoke about an upcoming conference regarding Mexican-American students. I love how co-teaching increases the information flow to both bilingual and childhood education students. It seems significant that childhood education students understand the relevance of such a conference to their work given the persisting (and increasing) categorizations of student populations within public schools, I think that Tatyana and I can demonstrate resistance to such ideas by helping our students conceptualize all students as everyone's responsibility. (JV)

The activity where students worked in groups to discuss different aspects of classroom culture really brought out the similarities (e.g., social networks, management, routines) and differences (e.g., schedules, class layout) between bilingual and general education classrooms. I was glad that **all** the students now know a little more about how dual language classrooms work. (TK)

It also appeared that our mutual orientation to sociocultural approaches to education from within our respective disciplines influenced our students to think more critically:

> The fact that we both approach education from a socio-cultural lens that is critical of systems that maintain the status-quo and oppression of certain groups, especially those who are in bilingual and special education, helped to anchor us regardless of the topic or student groups we discussed with our student teachers. I think our critical lens showed them that they need not blindly accept deficit views of children. There were many times over the semester where they showed surprise and even disgust at the system and its structures that go against what is best (or even just good) for children...I think we were effective in helping to prepare all our student teachers about the realities of teaching EBLs and students with special needs, tools to teach them and some apprehension about "support" structures that do just the opposite. The degree to which we did this, however, is not clear to me. (TK)

The dissolution of disciplinary boundaries, however, also exposed the degree to which our students have come to identify with their respective disciplines. It is of interest to us to consider if and how disciplinary boundaries within higher education might unwittingly reinforce the opposite of what we are teaching about inclusive practices:

> I also like that we are mixing the groups for the Lesson Share. It does seem, however, that the two groups retreat back among "their own kind" if we do not "impose integration" upon them. I am wondering why this might be the case. They giggle in acknowledgment when we point out their self-imposed physical segregation in the classroom, yet they persist in their seating arrangements. Have we somehow unwittingly reinforced this notion somehow? Or maybe it is just the nature of students to sit where they always sit? Should we have "imposed integration" from the first time that we met as a class? (JV)

> I think the question of segregation across programs versus "forced integration" is an interesting one. It mirrors the larger issues of segregation in our society in many ways, but specifically along racial/ethnic lines. I also notice that within the bilingual ed. students there is intra-group segregation by undergrad and grad students too. I think part of the reason for this is human nature, we are creatures of habit and comfort, so once we get used to something (where we sit) and someone (who we sit and interact with) we stick with that. While I do think there is a time and place for segregation, I also see it as very problematic if it's the norm. For instance, in our class there are definitely times when we needed students to separate into bilingual or childhood groups to provide them with instruction specific to their field. However, we have created many opportunities where students must collaborate across groups. I guess the question becomes to what degree must it be forced and if it only happens in that setting, why is that? (TK)

Identifying program gaps. An unexpected outcome of our collaboration is the identification of gaps within and across our programs. This most likely occurred because co-teaching afforded us the opportunity to engage in sustained conversations about pedagogy. Discussion of programmatic issues is evident in the following journal exchanges:

> I have become increasingly aware of persisting patterns and gaps in the childhood education program _ particularly in regard to students with disabilities and differentiated instruction ... I am wondering if Tatyana sees similar issues in the bilingual education program and, if so, how their program addresses such issues. (JV)

> I also notice gaps where students do not have the basic knowledge required to successfully work with bilingual children. My question about that is what have they simply forgotten or never really had to apply until this point. It seems many of the concepts they've learned don't really "click" until they get into the classroom. That said, I also realize there are areas that are either not taught or not taught well to our students. A significant concern I have is that all of their methods classes are not taught with emergent bilinguals in mind. Therefore, they never really consider how to scaffold for language and content. Another area where they need support is how to negotiate between two languages in various bilingual education models. Hopefully my co-authored book will help clarify this ☺ (TK)

> I could not agree more that students across ALL programs and departments should be exposed to the kind of discussion you facilitated during class. Are you as concerned as I am about childhood education majors (much less all of the other majors) being adequately prepared to teach students with disabilities and students whose first language is not English? I wonder if we should think about doing a faculty presentation to discuss the gaps in curriculum we have identified through our partnership? (JV)

Discipline Dis/connections

> I approached my partner to co-teach this seminar because I felt educators should be prepared to work with students with exceptionalities as well as emergent bilinguals, regardless of their certification areas. I also see a lot of socio-political connections between the fields and the way they and the students they serve are stigmatized on so many levels. However, I see conflating the fields as problematic in some ways too. I think this is because there are concrete differences, and I want those to come out as well. Emergent bilingual students and programs that serve them are often confused for remedial programs and the students as having language disabilities. For example, once I was shown a classroom where emergent bilinguals were combined with students who had hearing difficulties. I guess what I am trying to say is that these are two separate fields with students with distinct differences and I want to make sure that they comes across in our seminar as well. (TK)

> I so appreciate that you shared your uneasiness about "conflating the fields" in a way that might reinforce rather than challenge persisting underestimations about the capability of English Learners. Your legitimate concern reflects much about the negative status of special education within public schools. Someone in my field coined the term "disability creep" to describe how non-disabled people who are associated with "the

disabled (including special education teachers and parents) likewise come to be regarded by others as less competent. A pause for thought! I am wondering how we might engage our students in the conversations we are having with each other? (JV)

Before our semester began, we came with some understanding that there are clear connections between bilingual education and DS. And it was this basis that led us to come together to co-teach a seminar. However, Tatyana voiced hesitations about focusing only on similarities without teasing out the differences. In fact, her first and last journal entry as described earlier reiterated this point. Bilingual education is a stigmatized field in many respects, and special education is even more so. This could be Tatyana's way of separating the two as a way to protect emergent bilinguals from a field where deficits — as opposed to differences — are prevalent.

Assessment and labels. Labels that are imposed upon students drive both fields. Much has been written about the power of assigning labels when it comes to self-perception, outcomes, and stereotypes (Golash-Boza & Darity, 2008; Pollock, 2004). Within both fields the labels stem from assessments, which have also been deemed problematic on a variety of levels (Dudley-Marling, 2010; Menken, 2008; Valencia & Villarreal, 2005; Valle & Connor, 2011). Being aware of the challenges labels pose in the field of bilingual education such as the federal term of Limited English Proficient (LEP), Tatyana was aware of both her minimal knowledge of terminology in inclusive education/DS and the potential for harm when labels are used haphazardly:

My last challenge I am facing as I look ahead is my VERY limited knowledge of the field of disability studies. I already fear I have used offensive terminology or perpetuated stereotypes in this very reflection that the field is working so hard to overcome. (TK)

In the two fields, assessments are the centerpiece by which labels are prescribed. Over the semester we looked at these assessments, what they consisted of and their problematic nature when it came to validity, cultural and linguistic bias, and overall ethics. The common issues began to present themselves:

I was unaware that there was such a thing as a state language test [for students labeled English language learners]. Again, I am struck by the parallels between disability studies and emergent bilingualism...I am interested in the gatekeeping aspect of this test and the consequences it holds for students. (JV)

When I moved into the accommodations part of standardized assessment [for emergent bilinguals], I was curious as to the overlap with special ed. accommodations. I imagine there are many. Perhaps we could have created some kind of Venn diagram to show what modifications are allowed for both groups and which are only for one or another. (TK)

With the issues that assessments present and the potential negative consequences of labeling, these two areas dictate who becomes a part of each field and often times determine the educational and life trajectories of students who are forced into labels that act as obstacles to opportunities.

Pinpointing the similarities and differences. Although we had both come into the semester with a baseline understanding of how our fields compare and contrast, there were moments in the class that illuminated these areas. Students played a role in heightening our awareness:

> Jan's discussion about students who are identified as "special ed" started with a question about the difference between a student with an IEP and a struggling reader. I thought that was a great question and I appreciated the way one of the students in the bilingual program answered it. She said that a student with an IEP has learning difficulties that are diagnosed and a struggling reader could be someone learning the language so they simultaneously have difficulty when it comes to reading in that language. I thought this was very insightful and starts to tease apart the two fields, although I know it's much more complex than that. (TK)

Through the sharing of lesson plans across fields, the issue of language arose as a central defining feature within both bilingual education and inclusive education/DS:

> Your point about how "the childhood students were able to see how objectives for language and content are important when working with emergent bilinguals" is striking to me because these same objectives apply to students with learning disabilities — a disability with presumed neurological etiology that impacts language processing in one's native language. Given that learning disabilities are considered to be "language-based", I am wondering how similar the teaching methods in our respective disciplines are? And might it be that "our methods" are, in fact, basically grounded in tenets of "good teaching" that would benefit all students? (JV)

The questions Jan ends with show that our understanding of our similarities have begun to crystallize, but one semester of collaboration is nowhere near enough to truly see all the intersections that may exist between bilingual education and inclusive education/DS.

Contextualizing the coming together of the fields. During the semester that we co-taught, we also saw our respective fields come together within the school system where our student teachers were placed.

Ironically, as our collaboration was taking place the Department of Education restructured the Office of English Language Learners. It has been disassembled and is now a part of the newly formed Office of Special Education and English Language Learners. If I was optimistic about how the system worked I could tell myself that this new office is going to work with all teachers to support students in both these areas (which I feel we did and tried to do over this semester) that would be fine, but my more pessimistic side sees more problems than opportunities with such a structure. (TK)

I share your pessimism regarding the likely outcome of such a pairing. Administrators may have the best of intentions for these students, but it is the belief system of teachers that will determine the outcome. Quite frankly, it is simply EASIER to believe that certain groups of children do not belong and that other people can teach them better and in other places that benefit them more. It is of no surprise to me that similar issues plague both special education and bilingual education. Unless we change how we "do" school (and who benefits from the way school "is"), I do not think that significant change can take place. However, I do believe in the power of grassroots organizing and the capacity of individuals to engender change at multiple levels. I think that our collaboration this semester is one example of resisting the status quo in that we actively challenged our students to consider the consequences of "how things are" for two categorized groups of students. Yet I know that they need MUCH more support in developing effective resistance strategies as future teachers. Maybe our collaboration is a first step in that direction. (JV)

Regardless of the issues that undermine each field, the key underlying issue is one of social justice where students are seen for the strengths they bring rather than for what they lack. Furthermore, the fields are fighting to be seen as a part of a holistic education system, rather than a peripheral aspect of schooling that relegates students who do not fit within an ascribed normativity or English proficiency as outsiders and others. There are clearly differences that the fields engender, but their struggle for inclusion − in the full sense of the term − is what brings them together. And this thread was what evolved for students and the professors over the course of the seminar.

Reciprocal Learning

This semester I probably had my highest learning curve in terms of learning when I teach. Although I always learn from my students, there is something more intense about learning from a colleague who comes from a different field. While I know I have a long way to go in terms of my understandings around disability studies and special education (and now I know the difference between the two!) I at least feel I can have a knowledgeable conversation and a more in-depth awareness of the issues and inequities in the field. (TK)

As co-teachers, we both admittedly began the semester with minimal knowledge about each other's field. But by the conclusion of the semester, we had developed an increased awareness and understanding of our fields and their intersections. Although far from claiming expertise, we became more attuned to the issues of each other's field and more confident addressing them within our other teacher education courses.

Learning through meeting, co-teaching, writing, and reflecting.

Not only are all of our students gaining knowledge about dual language classrooms, so am I. Co-teaching is such a great way to increase our respective knowledge by learning from one another in the classroom. I think we are on to something! (JV)

It is rare that professors have the chance to continue to learn about disciplines not directly related to the boundaries of their classes, programs, and research. However, this co-teaching opportunity gave us a range of ways to continue our professional growth and learning. For example:

Each week, we had the privilege to give and receive feedback about our respective and collective teaching practices – a luxury in our otherwise hectic academic lives. We did this through informal conversation as well as weekly journals to one another. The process of writing a weekly entry and receiving Tatyana's written response to the entry as well as reading and responding in writing to Tatyana's weekly entry provided multiple opportunities to not only focus upon our practice but also to challenge each other's thinking. (JV)

The opportunity to make sense of new ideas through writing as a way of thinking and then receiving feedback from an expert in the field certainly expanded our understandings in ways that merely reading a book or journal article could not foster. Learning side-by-side with our students was another way we were able to take advantage of each other's expertise during class time:

Something I found unique to our co-teaching class was the ability to sit back in the role of the student during the time Jan discussed differentiated instruction. I found it very effective to take on a different position as it allowed me to reflect more about how we are instructing our students as well as to learn from my co-teacher. (TK)

I am eager to know more about what you were able to observe about our students. I loved that you freely commented and asked questions within this model – it felt very natural to me. (JV)

This type of learning was not only evident to us, but to our students as well. One noted, "You two work well together, feeding off each other's thoughts and asking for support in reference to your specialties."

Learning about each other. As faculty members in different programs, the opportunities we had to get to know about each other have been limited and largely left to our own devices. Most of our interactions are in meetings where the agenda is set beforehand. We connect around the needs of students, but rarely have a chance to engage in conversations about our interests, research, and teaching. This experience drastically changed our discourse patterns and allowed each of us to gain a fuller understanding about each other as people and professionals:

> As we described our professional backgrounds to the class, I learned much about Tatyana that I did not know. I am reminded again of Tatyana's earlier journal entry in which she reflected upon the functional nature of most faculty exchanges. There is so much talent and experience among the faculty that remains untapped — and even unknown. I am hoping that what results from our "experiment" of partnership might help all of us think about how to more mindfully engage with one another. (JV)

Although our department has held Brown Bag Lunches for colleagues to share their research, these one-shot approaches only skim the surface in introducing faculty to each other's expertise. In contrast, the sustained nature of co-teaching a course provided varied opportunities for us to learn about each other and our fields in ways that are rarely possible during the functions of regularly scheduled university life.

Pedagogical approaches. After teaching the same class for numerous years, it is possible to become tied to one's pedagogical approaches, especially if something appears to work. Co-teaching requires each person to confront other teaching styles, whether it means watching a new approach in action or trying out an unfamiliar strategy with her partner. The latter was our case when Tatyana suggested using the Collaborative Descriptive Inquiry (CDI) model to structure how students support one another in their lesson planning (for more on the process see Himley & Carini, 2000):

> Tatyana explained the process very clearly to the class. I love learning new strategies from my partner! I think the lesson plan sharing is going to become a vital part of the seminar … I plan to incorporate the journal and Lesson Plan Share into my fall seminar. Thank you, Tatyana! (JV)

Our combined student teaching context gave us the opportunity to go beyond reading or learning about a new instructional approach to *seeing* one another put practice into action with our own students. Observing first-hand the positive impact of an instructional approach upon student learning fostered an eagerness for us both to incorporate new approaches within our respective teaching repertoires.

Increased understandings across fields with a lot left to learn. Each field has its own way of functioning, which to an outsider may seem like business as usual. However, it is not until we learn more about established practices from someone in the field who has studied and experienced these traditions that we can start to better understand and question the status quo. This was precisely what happened when Tatyana was able to listen to Jan's presentation on the assessments used to refer students into the special education system:

> I was completely appalled, as was the rest of the class, at the types of questions students are presented with in the assessment schools use to determine services, placement and/or labels. It was way beyond just cultural bias; it was utterly ridiculous!! It almost seemed like a joke, I was wondering if you were going to stop and say "gotcha!" But this is real and an embedded part of our institutional practices in special education. It is also shocking and disgusting. I heard a few of our students say, "I am not referring anyone!" With this nonsense for an assessment, we might as well just flip a coin to see if students are really in need of services. What is being done to change this? And what can I do to help? (TK)

This type of learning is critical to understanding the larger inequities of our educational system. It is also the type of learning that can lead to collaboration and action as we are much more powerful when our voices come from across fields.

Within the arena of emergent bilingual students, the program to prepare teachers to serve them is called Bilingual Education & TESOL. Although faculty outside this program are familiar with these two models in name, few can truly explain the goals of each and how the approaches differ. This was also the case for Jan, who finished the semester with a much more nuanced understanding of each:

> I finally understand the difference between bilingual education and TESOL!... I increased my knowledge about bilingual education through weekly exposure to Tatyana's professional expertise. What a treat it was to hear Tatyana's presentations in class and to engage with her in planning meetings! Not only do I feel better prepared to engage with childhood education students around bilingual issues (although, admittedly, I have a long way to go but boy is it on my radar now!), I also feel more connected to the bilingual education program. (JV)

To sum up, what is clear from this experience is a strong recognition of the benefit of the experience for us both and the realization of just how much knowledge is within our reach.

> I have also learned that I have a lot to learn from my colleagues! Wouldn't it be amazing if everyone was required to team teach, just think about how much we'd learn from one another's area(s) of expertise, pedagogical approaches and their general

personalities and backgrounds. Granted, I am sure they wouldn't all be equally successful, but it would build a certain culture of interconnectedness on a variety of levels.
(TK)

Conclusion/Implications for Teacher Educators

It felt like a gift to be able to reflect in such a deep way, and do so with the feedback
of an invested colleague. It's a rather sad statement to make, because that should be
the norm, not a special treat! I also feel fortunate to work at a university where such
"experiments" are allowed and encouraged and to have done this with a colleague
who is so smart, witty, committed and a talented writer (guess who will be editing
out papers ;-) I learned a lot about CTT and special ed. (although I too agree I have
a long way to go!) and I believe all our students came out of this experience having
learning a lot about two specific populations of students, and teaching and learning
in general. (TK)

As stated elsewhere in this chapter, we conceptualized this study based
upon a mutual desire to (1) better prepare student teachers to teach *all*
students, (2) provide student teachers with the experience of learning within
a classroom context led by two instructors with unique and intersecting
areas of expertise, and (3) conduct a self-study of our co-teaching processes
at the university level. We now return to our research questions to synthesize our findings and offer implications for teacher educators and schools
of education.

Collaborative Teaching Impacting Professor and Student Learning

The CTT offered a rich learning venue for all involved in ways that differed
from traditional classes taught by one professor within a specific program.
As faculty members with two different areas of specialization, we were able
to learn more about each other's fields. This led to a greater understanding
of areas of intersections and disconnections, thereby not only expanding
our respective knowledge base and that of our seminar students, but also
the knowledge base of future students as we integrate our new knowledge
into other courses. It is worth noting that our seminar students expressed
gratitude for the opportunity to learn about children who inevitably will be
students in their future classrooms, but who are not the focus of their chosen majors and teaching certification.

Advantages and Challenges to Teaching across Fields

Our experience highlighted a range of advantages to teaching across our fields of bilingual education and inclusive education/DS. First, our areas of expertise are artificial in many ways and do not reflect the diversity of students and experiences teachers face. A broader approach to understanding students with different linguistic and ability backgrounds reflects the realities of 21st century schools. We must be willing to acknowledge that perhaps the biggest challenge to co-teaching at the university level is our own rigidity of thinking and being that keeps us in our traditional disciplinary boxes. It is of interest that our seminar students persisted in over-identifying with their respective majors within our shared classroom context − no doubt a reflection of the deeply entrenched university system of disciplinary isolation. This particular finding reinforces the need for courses that contextualize learning within the larger field of education and make explicit connections to related disciplinary areas.

**Developing Schools of Education that Prepare Educators to
Teach All Students**

Based upon our experience of co-teaching at the university level for one semester, we offer fellow teacher educators our (1) "lessons learned" gleaned from our particular co-teaching experience and (2) suggestions for creating spaces for co-teaching within the current university structure.

Lessons learned. With the advantage of hindsight, we see that we might have been more mindful about actively facilitating community among our students. In this regard, we seriously underestimated the impact of traditional disciplinary boundaries upon our students' capacity to see themselves in any other way. In order to increase cohesion among students, we suggest the following strategies for enhancing community in a co-taught bilingual and childhood education setting at the university level: (1) begin the semester with community building exercises that teachers typically use in CTT classrooms to bring seminar students together and to provide a model of co-teaching strategies; (2) rotate seating and/or groupings each week; (3) pair a childhood education student with a bilingual education student to serve as each other's expert resource partner throughout the semester; (4) insist that everyone learn each other's names and use them during discussions; (5) talk much more about the importance of classroom community in a CTT classroom; and (6) provide ample opportunities for "turn and talk" and small group discussion in "mixed groups."

Not only did we discover how entrenched our students were in their disciplinary areas, we also surprised ourselves by the realization of our own attachment to our respective disciplines. In hindsight, it appears that we acted in ways that reflected responsibility at some level for our "own students" – although we were not aware of it at the time. For example, we did not engage in any kind of in-depth conversation about our students' individual and collective needs – a hallmark feature of co-teaching. Had we done this, we would have gotten to know each other's students better and used "flexible grouping" more effectively. Moreover, it did not occur to us to read papers from each other's students. We graded our respective students' papers without considering the message it sent to our class community and the limitation it placed on our capacity to know all of our students. Early in the semester, Tatyana commented in her journal that maybe we should have created a new syllabus rather than pulling aspects from our respective syllabi. In retrospect, we believe that creating a shared syllabus might have "set the stage" for our own sense of collaboration. Lastly, we have considered how we might have enhanced a sense of community with our students had we read some of our journal entries aloud to them and solicited their insights and input as part of our meaning making.

Suggestions for creating spaces for co-teaching. The co-teaching seminar at the center of this discussion was made possible through our own initiative. There are no institutional supports or incentives within our School of Education to offer a course that integrates educational disciplines. Such a structure is certainly not unique to our university and for that reason we pose the following suggestions for moving toward a more inclusive approach to teaching at the university level: (1) cultivate relationships with colleagues outside of your own discipline; (2) begin collegial conversations about the intersections and disconnections within your respective disciplines; (3) jointly study the literature about co-teaching; (4) present research about the benefits of co-teaching to the administration along with research possibilities; and (5) look for contexts within which to launch co-teaching easily. For example, combining our seminars gave us a space to co-teach at an initial level and provided data to share with administration and faculty for the purpose of growing more inclusive practices within our own School of Education.

Our findings challenge teacher educators to consider whether or not a traditional approach to teacher preparation truly offers pre-service teachers the tools to serve students with all the social and human differences they may bring to the classroom. In the current climate in which schools of education are increasingly under the microscope for evidence of quality and effectiveness, this work pushes us to rethink traditional boundaries and approaches for teacher education programs. It is clear that divisions and specialties in academia are not as clear cut as we believe them to be, or even reflective of the reality of K-12 classrooms. Therefore, there is a need for faculty to teach across programs/areas of specialty and to collaborate with one another not only to increase individual knowledge, but also as a means to integrate knowledge across the teacher education curriculum. In light of the current trend toward collaborative classroom contexts within public schools, we contend that it is imperative for schools of education to dare to transgress traditional academic boundaries in order to adequately prepare pre-service teachers for the 21st century classroom.

Limitations

Although we contend that the results of this study contribute much-needed knowledge about co-teaching at the tertiary level, we also acknowledge its limitations. First, our data is derived solely from our observations and reflections. Although we had planned to include student voices and perspectives, the data we collected from a brief student survey distributed at the end of the course were less robust (although very positive) than we had hoped. Second, this S-STEP took place within one classroom during one semester, offering a window into a singular experience. Despite these limitations, we contend that our findings make a valuable contribution to the literature and could be applied to multiple contexts that prepare teachers to work with emergent bilinguals and students with disabilities including those who may also be emergent bilinguals.

References

Anderson, R. S., & Speck, B. W. (1998). Oh what a difference a team makes: Why team teaching makes a difference. *Teaching and Teacher Education, 14*(7), 671–686.

Arkoudis, S. (2003). Teaching English as a second language in science class: Incommensurate epistemologies? *Language and Education, 17*, 161–173.

Bauwens, J., Hourcade, J., & Friend, M. (1989). Cooperative teaching: A model for general and special education integration. *Remedial and Special Education, 10*(2), 17–22.

Blanchett, W. (2006). Disproportionate representation of African American students in special education: Acknowledging the role of white privilege and racism. *Educational Researcher, 35*(6), 24–28.

Blommaert, J. (2010). *The sociolinguistics of globalization.* Cambridge, UK: Cambridge University Press.

Brantlinger, E. (2004). Confounding the needs and confronting the norms: An extension of Reid and Valle's essay. *Journal of Learning Disabilities, 37*(6), 490–499.

Brantlinger, E. (2006). *Who benefits from special education? Remediating (fixing) other people's children.* Mahwah, NJ: Lawrence Erlbaum.

Capper, C., & Frattura, E. (2008). *Meeting the needs of all students: How leaders go beyond inclusion* (2nd ed.). Thousand Oaks, CA: Corwin Press.

Cohen, L., Manion, L., & Morrison, K. (2011). *Research methods in education* (7th ed.). New York, NY: Routledge.

Connor, D., Gabel, S., Gallagher, D., & Morton, M. (2008). Disability studies and inclusive education – Implications for theory, research, and practice. *International Journal of Inclusive Education, 12*(5–6), 441–457.

Cook, L., & Friend, M. (1995). Co-teaching: Guidelines for creating effective practices. *Focus on Exceptional Children, 28*(3), 1–16.

Crawford, J. (2004). *Educating English learners: Language diversity in the classroom* (5th ed.). Los Angeles, CA: Bilingual Educational Services.

Danforth, S., & Gabel, S. (2007). *Vital questions facing disability studies in education.* New York, NY: Peter Lang.

Dudley-Marling, C. (2010). *The myth of the normal curve.* New York, NY: Peter Lang.

Flores, N. (2012). Power differentials: Pseudo-collaboration between ESL and mainstream teachers. In A. Honigsfeld & M. Dove (Eds.), *Co-teaching and other collaborative practices in the EFL/ESL classroom: Rationale, research, reflections, and recommendations* (pp. 185–194). Charlotte, NC: Information Age Publishing.

Freeman, R. (1998). *Bilingual education and social change.* Philadelphia, PA: Multilingual Matters.

Freeman, Y., Freeman, D., & Mercuri, S. (2004). *Dual language essentials for teachers and administrators.* Portsmouth, NH: Heinemann.

Friend, M. (2007). *Co-teach!* Greensboro, NC: Marilyn Friend.

Friend, M., & Cook, L. (2010). *Interactions: Collaboration skills for school professionals* (6th ed.). Columbus, OH: Merrill.

Friend, M., Cook, L., Hurley-Chamberlain, D., & Shamberger, C. (2010). Co-teaching: An illustration of the complexity of collaboration in special education. *Journal of Educational and Psychological Consultation, 20*(1), 9–27.

Gabel, S. (Ed.). (2005). *Disability studies in education: Readings in theory and method.* New York, NY: Peter Lang.

García, O. (2009). *Bilingual education in the 21st century: A global perspective.* Malden, MA: Wiley-Blackwell.

García, O. (2014). TESOL translanguaged in NYS: Alternative perspectives. *NYS TESOL Journal, 1*(1), 2–10.

Garvar, A. G., & Papania, A. (1982). Team teaching: It works for the student. *Academic Therapy, 18*, 191–196.

Ghaye, A., & Ghaye, K. (1998). *Teaching and learning through reflective practice.* London: David Fulton.

Golash-Boza, T., & Darity, W. (2008). Latino racial choices: The effects of skin colour and discrimination on Latinos' and Latinas' racial self-identifications. *Ethnic and Racial Studies, 31*(5), 899–934.

Hang, Q., & Rabren, K. (2009). An examination of co-teaching: Perspectives and efficacy indicators. *Remedial and Special Education, 30*(5), 259–268.

Harris, C., & Harvey, A. (2000). Team teaching in adult higher education classrooms: Toward collaborative knowledge construction. *New Directions for Adult and Continuing Education, 87,* 25–32.

Harry, B., & Klingner, J. (2006). *Why are so many minority students in special education?* New York, NY: Teachers College Press.

Henderson, C., Beach, A., & Famiano, M. (2007). Diffusion of educational innovations via co-teaching. In L. McCollough, L. Hsu, & P. Heron (Eds.), *2006 Physics education research conference* (pp. 117–120). American Institute of Physics. Retrieved from http://homepages.wmich.edu/~chenders/Publications/PERC2006 Henderson.pdf

Himley, M., & Carini, P. (Eds.). (2000). *From another angle: Children's strengths and school standards: The prospect center's descriptive review of the child.* New York, NY: Teachers College Press.

Honigsfeld, A., & Dove, M. G. (2010). *Collaboration and coteaching: Strategies for English learners.* Thousand Oaks, CA: Corwin Press.

Honigsfeld, A., & Dove, M. G. (Eds.). (2012). *Co-teaching and other collaborative practices in the EFL/ESL classroom: Rationale, research, reflections, and recommendations.* Charlotte, NC: Information Age Publishing.

Karagiannis, A. (2000). Soft disability in schools: Assisting or confining at risk children and youth? *Journal of Educational Thought, 34*(2), 113–134.

LaBoskey, V. K. (2004). The methodology of self-study and its theoretical underpinnings. In J. J. Loughran, M. L. Hamilton, V. K. LaBoskey, & T. Russell (Eds.), *International handbook of self-study of teacher education practices* (pp. 817–869). Dordrecht: Kluwer Academic Publishers.

Linton, S., Melio, S., & O'Neill, J. (1995). Disability studies: Expanding the parameters of diversity. *Radical Teacher, 47,* 4–10.

Menken, K. (2008). *English learners left behind: Standardized testing as language policy.* Clevedon, Avon: Multilingual Matters.

New York City Independent Budget Office. (2013, May). *New York City Independent public school indicators: Demographics, resources, outcomes.* Retrieved from http://www.ibo.nyc.ny.us/iboreports/2013educationindicatorsreport.pdf

Nieto, S. (2002). *Language, culture, and teaching: Critical perspectives for a new century.* Mahwah, NJ: Erlbaum.

Pinnegar, S. E. & Hamilton, M. L. (2009). *Self-study of practice as a genre of qualitative research: Theory, methodology, and practice.* New York, NY: Springer.

Pollock, M. (2004). *Colormute: Race talks dilemmas in an American school.* Princeton, NJ: Princeton University Press.

Reyes, S., & Kleyn, T. (2010). *Teaching in two languages: A guide for K-12 bilingual educators.* Thousand Oaks, CA: Corwin Press.

Schon, D. A. (1983). *The reflective practitioner: How professionals think in action.* New York, NY: Basic Books.

Short, D. J., Cloud, N., Morris, P., & Motta, J. (2012). Cross-district collaboration: Curriculum and professional development. *TESOL Journal, 3,* 402–424.

Solis, M., Vaughn, S., Swanson, E., & McCulley, L. (2012). Collaborative models of instruction: The empirical foundations of inclusion and co-teaching. *Psychology in Schools, 49*(5), 498–510.

Theoharis, G. (2009). *The school leaders our children deserve: Seven keys to equity, social justice, and school reform.* New York, NY: Teachers College Press.

Valencia, R., & Villarreal, B. (2005). Texas' second wave of high-stakes testing: Anti-social promotion legislation, grade retention, and adverse impact on minorities. In A. Valenzuela (Ed.), *Leaving children behind: How 'Texas-Style' accountability fails Latino youth* (pp. 113–152). Albany, NY: State University of New York Press.

Valenzuela, A. (1999). *Subtractive schooling: US-Mexican youth and the politics of caring.* Albany, NY: State University of New York Press.

Valle, J., & Connor, D. (2011). *Rethinking disability: A disability studies approach to inclusive practices.* New York, NY: McGraw-Hill.

Villa, R. A., & Thousand, J. S. (Eds.). (1995). *Creating an inclusive school.* Alexandria, VA: Association of Supervision and Curriculum Development.

Ware, L. (2006). A "look" at the way we look at disability. In S. Danforth & S. Gabel (Eds.), *Vital questions facing disability studies in education* (pp. 271–288). New York, NY: Peter Lang.

Will, M. (1986). Educating children with learning problems: A shared responsibility. *Exceptional Children, 52,* 411–415.

PART II
INVESTIGATIONS TO SUPPORT
BEST PRACTICES

CHAPTER 7

PREPARATION TO PRACTICE: WHAT MATTERS IN SUPPORTING LINGUISTICALLY RESPONSIVE MAINSTREAM TEACHERS

María Estela Brisk, Anne Homza and Janet Smith

Abstract

This chapter investigates the impact of a teacher preparation program that includes specific attention to the needs of bilingual learners on participants' subsequent teaching practices. Specifically, this mixed methods retrospective study examines graduates' reports of their current teaching practices as well as their perceptions of the Teaching English Language Learners (TELL) program's impact on these practices. Multiple-choice survey data were analyzed quantitatively to identify trends among reported practices and perceptions. Open-ended survey and interview data were analyzed qualitatively to identify interrelated themes within teachers' detailed, first-hand accounts of their pre-service and in-service experiences. The results showed that there was variety with respect to whether particular linguistically responsive practices were routine, used occasionally, or rarely. There was also a difference with respect to whether such practices were perceived to be the result of having

Research on Preparing Preservice Teachers to Work Effectively with Emergent Bilinguals
Advances in Research on Teaching, Volume 21, 167–199
ISSN: 1479-3687/doi:10.1108/S1479-368720140000021006

participated in the program. Notably, the most frequently used practices attributed to the TELL program involved teaching language (TL) to facilitate content learning. Other aspects of the teacher preparation program supported effective practices for academic content learning, but only TELL coursework and experiences facilitated practices that emphasized academic language development. These results suggest that programs created to improve the preparation of teachers to work with bilingual learners in mainstream classroom contexts must make a special effort to develop teachers' skills in regard to language teaching, especially practices that focus on language beyond the word-level. There are limitations to the study because of the small number of participants and the fact that they were self-selected as program participants.

Keywords: Teacher preparation; sheltered English immersion; linguistically responsive teaching; teacher preparation for diverse learners

Introduction

Bilingual learners represent a growing population in Massachusetts classrooms, with a 13 % increase in the last 10 years. Approximately 58,000 students in Massachusetts, speaking 112 languages, were identified as being limited in English proficiency in 2010 (The Biennial Report to Congress on the Implementation of the Title III State Formula Grant Program School years 2008–10, 2013). At the same time, Massachusetts is one of three states that passed legislation eliminating most forms of bilingual education. (In this chapter the term bilingual learner refers to all students who function in more than one language regardless of proficiency, and emergent bilingual is applied to students who are in the process of learning English if the context requires that distinction.) This restrictive language policy, coupled with the barrage of standards and test requirements mandated by state and federal agencies, has placed an increasing strain on schools with bilingual learners. This is the context that many new teachers are entering.

In Massachusetts, as in other states, language policies that place bilingual students in mainstream classrooms increasingly create a context in which the specific linguistic and cultural needs of bilingual learners are overlooked, with teachers operating under the mistaken assumption that "[t]eaching ELLs is considered a matter of applying 'just good teaching'

(JGT) practices developed for a diverse group of native English speakers, such as activating prior knowledge, using cooperative learning, process writing, and graphic organizers or hands-on activities" (de Jong & Harper, 2005, p. 102). In such a context, specific linguistic and cultural features of the curriculum are invisible to those acquiring English as an additional language because most teachers have not been prepared to explicitly teach those features while teaching content.

To competently perform in the academic registers required of mainstream monolingual classrooms, bilingual learners must learn a second language at the same time and in addition to learning literacy and learning content knowledge (Bernhardt, 1991). If teachers ignore the specific teaching of language in the classroom, students develop a dialect that may allow them to cope with everyday communicative challenges (Fillmore & Snow, 2002). However, such a dialect does not provide sufficient emphasis on the linguistic requirements of academic content, limiting bilingual learners' ability to effectively engage in content area classes. Indeed, "when lexical and grammatical development does not keep pace with school expectations, students are unable to meet the reading and writing demands of disciplinary learning" (Schleppegrell, 2004, p. 80). The challenge of learning the academic English is not a problem only of bilingual students, but may be exacerbated in the case of the emergent bilingual in a monolingual classroom when the teacher has not been trained to utilize the student's native language to identify and build on the intellectual capacity the student may have already developed but cannot yet express (de Jong, Arias, & Sánchez, 2010).

The purpose of this chapter is to investigate, from the point of view of new teachers, the impact on participants of a teacher preparation program that includes specific attention to the needs of bilingual learners. The teacher preparation program under study is the Teaching English Language Learners (TELL) certificate program, comprised of two courses and a practicum experience that Boston College students majoring in the reading program and elementary and secondary education can choose to incorporate in their program of studies.

A group of graduates of this teacher preparation program who had completed the TELL certificate and are now practicing teachers reported on their current daily practices with bilingual learners. They also expressed their opinions with respect to which practices the program had prepared them to implement, what they found helpful, and what was lacking.

In 2005 Zeichner observed that "(r)esearch on the preparation of teachers to teach underserved populations should pay special attention to the preparation of teachers to teach English language learners because almost no research has been conducted on this aspect of diversity in teacher education" (Zeichner, 2005, p. 747). This study contributes much-needed research about the actual teaching practices of new teachers early in their professional role in relation to the preparation they had received in a specialized program. It focuses on outputs, that is, what teachers do in the classrooms with the knowledge and skills acquired, rather than only on inputs, that is, what programs should offer (Lucas & Villegas, 2013). Moreover, the program at the center of this study specializes in explicitly preparing participants to teach academic language to ELLs to meet the latter group's complex educational needs, rather than "subsuming the preparation of classroom teachers to teach English language learners within the more general considerations of the preparation of teachers for diverse populations" (2008, p. 606).

Political Context of the Study

The political context of this study is important because it imposes constraints on the potential of the program under study and, by extension, on the impact the program had on participants. In 1971 the Massachusetts legislation approved the first state-level law mandating bilingual education for districts that included a certain number of students of the same language background who were assessed as limited English proficient (LEP). English as a second language (ESL) courses were part of the bilingual education curriculum or were offered when the numbers of students were too small to support a bilingual program. Transitional Bilingual Education (TBE) provided education to a large percentage of emergent bilinguals throughout the state. Some students did not participate because of small concentrations of students of any one language or because of parental choice. Although the policy served those who participated well, it did not address the challenge of bilingual classes that included students of varying levels of English language proficiency. Moreover, over decades, the policy created a culture where standard curriculum teachers did not feel that they had to change their instruction because bilingual learners were taken care of by the teachers in the bilingual and ESL programs notwithstanding the fact that 15% of bilingual learners were enrolled in mainstream classes (Sánchez, 2006).

In 2002, a referendum vote passed in Massachusetts replacing bilingual education with Sheltered English Immersion (SEI) (General Laws of Massachusetts, Chapter 71A, 2003). This legislation, which still stands today, allows for a minimum use of the native language in standard curriculum classrooms, mostly for clarification. In current practice, the interpretation of how much native, or heritage language to use varies and in some districts is highly discouraged. In practice, the only alternative programs for bilingual students are two-way programs, which enroll a minimal number of the state's bilingual learners, only 822 out of close to designated 50,000 LEP (Massachusetts Department of Elementary and Secondary Education (MA DESE), 2005).

As the 2002 legislation resulted in an increase of the number of bilingual learners in standard curriculum classes, the state promoted initiatives to prepare teachers in standard curriculum classes to work with bilingual learners. However, neither professional development for in-service teachers nor preparation for pre-service teachers was mandated. Ultimately, after a decade, the federal government deemed the services to emergent bilinguals in Massachusetts to be inadequate. Under pressure from the Department of Justice, the Massachusetts Department of Elementary and Secondary Education (DESE) started a statewide effort to better prepare both in-service and pre-service teachers by establishing a mandatory "Sheltered English Immersion" (SEI) endorsement for all licensed core academic teachers. Given the daunting task of preparing the teachers already in schools, the DESE has approved one professional development course for in-service teachers to obtain the SEI endorsement. Many universities have followed suit adding one state-approved university course to their teacher preparation programs.

This political context has affected current participants and recent graduates of teacher preparation programs in two ways. First, current participants of teacher education programs are often given a practicum placement in standard curriculum classes that include bilingual learners — sometimes the majority of students. In these classrooms, the cooperating or mentor teachers from whom the candidates are meant to learn often have had little or no knowledge of effective practices for teaching bilingual learners. Other candidates may be given a practicum placement in one of the few designated SEI classrooms, where the cooperating teachers may have received only the minimal training for working with bilingual students.

Second, newly licensed teachers with emergent knowledge of how to work with bilingual students often find themselves in less than an ideal position as teachers. Due to the dearth of expertise in schools, these new teachers may not receive the school-based support to put into practice their knowledge of theory and methods for teaching bilingual learners. In addition, newly licensed teachers may be seen by school personnel as the de facto experts in teaching bilingual learners at a point in time when those teachers are still very new to the practice and to running their own classrooms. This expectation may be particularly difficult to meet if the new teachers' practicum experiences were with cooperating teachers who lacked an SEI endorsement.

Teacher education programs that focus on bilingual learners strive to impart to teacher candidates knowledge about the particular linguistic needs of bilinguals, particularly emergent bilinguals, and also to provide and demonstrate teacher practices that effectively teach both language and academic content. These two key elements – teacher knowledge and teacher preparation – are necessary but may not be sufficient, since learning to teach is "a process that is highly mediated by the social context of schools" (Cochran-Smith et al., 2012, p. 31). The social context of schools in some states, profoundly political in nature and shaped by language policies that govern what schools can and cannot do, can impede the success of teacher preparation focused on bilingual learners.

Teacher Preparation

Teacher preparation programs have struggled for a long time with the process of preparing teachers, especially when they want them to approach teaching in ways that are different from what they experienced themselves in their own education. One of the constant dilemmas is deciding what contributes most to effective teacher preparation: pedagogy courses or field experiences. Researchers question the value of courses on pedagogy because "speaking about new practices for the classroom is said to be much easier than really implementing them with students. Many teachers can talk about ways of acting in a very developmental way; however, they cannot act accordingly when in real situations" (Liberali, 2013, p. 237). Rather than rejecting theory or practice, Olsen (2008) argues that teacher knowledge develops in the intersection of formal theory, informal prior knowledge, and context of situation, thus adding as an important component to the teacher's own background. Clayton's (2013) model of effective teachers of bilingual learners also includes teachers' background as an important influence in successful teachers' practices, specifically the experience of learning a second language and being immersed in a culture other than their own.

Effective practices for teaching bilingual learners are more likely to be implemented when teacher candidates observe cooperating teachers, already well into their professional roles, implementing such practices in their field experiences (Schall-Leckrone, 2013). However, in contexts such as the one in Massachusetts, in which the education of bilingual learners was for many years seen as the responsibility solely of bilingual and ESL teachers, it is unlikely to find standard curriculum teachers who are strong models for the effective teaching of bilingual learners. Therefore, one challenge of teacher preparation programs is to break the cycle of ineffective practices and start creating opportunities for future teacher candidates to observe excellent models of teaching bilingual learners.

Teacher Knowledge

Being prepared to work with bilingual learners in a mainstream curriculum classroom is not simply having a tool kit brimming with good teaching ideas applicable to any learner. These indeed are useful with bilingual learners, but they are not enough. First and foremost "standard curriculum teachers need to embrace the role of *language* teacher" (de Jong & Harper, 2008, p. 137, emphasis added). To carry out this role effectively, they need to know about the structure of English at the discourse, sentence, and word levels, to understand the process of second language (L2) acquisition, and also to recognize the linguistic demands of their academic content area. Most teacher candidates tend to be monolingual native speakers of English (Kindler, 2002; Lucas & Grinberg, 2008) with little or no training in working with bilingual learners (Samson & Collins, 2012). Moreover, the vast majority has not experienced to learn rigorous academic content in a second language. Therefore, they may bring limited knowledge of explicit features of language and limited experiential knowledge to their teacher preparation program.

To provide guidance to teacher preparation programs, several researchers have been working to define and describe the knowledge and skills needed to be an effective teacher of bilingual learners. Lucas and Villegas (2011) have developed a model of "linguistically responsive" teaching that highlights language in a way that "culturally responsive" teaching typically does not (p. 56). Recently, these scholars have mapped elements of the linguistically responsive model onto Feiman-Nemser's (2001) developmental continuum that suggests "tasks for learning to teach" (Lucas & Villegas, 2013, p. 103). This effort both recognizes the developmental nature of learning to teach and also stimulates discussion about the tasks teacher education programs need to help teacher candidates develop effective linguistically responsive practices.

Effective practices with bilingual learners are influenced by teachers' disposition, knowledge, and background (Clayton, 2013). Key dispositions that underscored teachers' success were: "1) sensitivity, 2) encouragement, 3) positive attitude toward teaching ELLs, and 4) humor about themselves" (p. 47). Effective teachers know their students, the content they teach and the language needed by students to engage with the content, or "linguistic content knowledge" (p. 42). They need to know practices that do not rely completely on language to facilitate learning and understanding.

Within the present political context of trying to prepare teachers to effectively teach bilingual students, and given the limitations of the existing research on teacher preparation, this study spotlights those practices of teaching academic language to ELLs that novice teachers actually use in their classrooms. The novice teachers' experiences provide insight about the context in which they are implementing those practices as well as the impact of their preparation on their actual implementation of those practices.

Participants

The population of this study were teachers who participated in TELL from 2008–2012 and who received funding from Project Teaching Academic Language in the Content Areas (TALCA) ($n = 70$). The director of Project TALCA emailed all 70 teachers to participate in an online survey. In an effort to maximize response rate and to counter sampling bias, the director of Project TALCA offered potential study participants incentives as part of the recruitment efforts: the names of TELL teachers who agreed to take the survey would be included in a raffle to win an iPod Nano ($100 value each). The incentive for participating in a follow-up interview was also included a chance to win an iPod Nano.

Among the 70 TELL teachers contacted, a self-selected group of 27 teachers agreed to be in the study from an initial response rate of 39%. However, questions on the survey screened out six teachers who were not teaching emergent bilinguals in AY 2011–2012, thus 21 TELL teachers comprised the final response rate of 30%, an acceptable response rate for online surveys (Assessing teaching: Response rates, n.d., section 2). Another question in the survey invited survey respondents to participate in an optional telephone interview to be conducted within a month of the survey. Six of the TELL teachers who completed the survey agreed to participate in follow-up interviews by telephone some three weeks later.

TELL teachers who completed the survey, including the subset that participated in follow-up interviews, were all teaching emergent bilinguals at the time of the study, with well over half teaching students coming from homes where a language other than English was spoken, and almost half teaching at least 10 students designated as emergent bilinguals. All but one taught in an urban school, and all but three taught in Massachusetts; those not in Massachusetts taught in Georgia ($n = 1$) and in New York ($n = 2$). It is interesting to note that the language policy in Georgia is similar to that in Massachusetts as it emphasizes English language acquisition through options that do not include bilingual education (Curriculum and instruction, n.d.). The options for emergent bilinguals offered in New York public schools are different from those in Massachusetts, as they include TBE and two-way bilingual programs (Bilingual education, n.d., section 13). Almost half of the participants reported that they worked at the secondary level (grades 9–12) and among those, over half taught English Language Arts (ELA) or Math. All participants were under 35 years old at the time of the study, and over half were under 25 years old. All, except for three, were female.

Methods

This was a retrospective study of a cohort of TELL teachers in which they connected their pre-service preparation for teaching bilingual learners to actual practices in their professional role. Using a mixed methods approach for data collection and analysis using a survey and interviews, we considered together the trends and themes across data types both to enrich the findings and to test validity through triangulation of findings (Cresswell & Clark, 2007).

We collected data via a survey about classroom activities that support bilingual students. The survey had two parts: in one part respondents were asked about their use of the activities in their daily practice, and in the second part they were asked about the impact of the TELL program on their ability to use the activities. Both sections had Likert scale and open-ended questions (see Appendix A). All classroom activities we asked about in the survey had been presented in the TELL program and are referred to here as TELL practices, and many survey items referring to those activities were based on Hopkins's (2012) survey of Arizona teachers who completed mandatory SEI training in that state. We then conducted follow-up one-to-one 30-minute telephone interviews with a group of six self-selected teachers using a protocol of open response questions (see Appendix B).

We quantitatively analyzed the survey scale item responses to identify trends in respondents' use of the teaching practices listed in the survey and trends in responses about the impact of the TELL program vis-a-vis using those practices. The Likert-type scale yielded ordinal data that the electronic survey software tallied, and from those tallies we calculated frequencies.

Specifically, to learn which practices were used most often, we collapsed the scale ratings and corresponding frequencies to more clearly delineate frequencies at both ends of the scale. That is, we collapsed the five response categories into three categories: (1) *never/rarely*, (2) *sometimes*, and (3) *often/all the time*. To identify the impact that participating in the TELL program had on respondents' ability to use specific TELL practices, we collapsed the five response categories into three categories: (1) *no impact/small impact*, (2) *neither small or large impact*, and (3) *large impact/100% impact* (i.e., no other experience outside the TELL program had an impact on respondents' teaching).

Then we ranked by frequency from high to low the TELL practices that teachers said they used *often/all the time* and that teachers said they implemented as a result of the *large impact/100% impact* of their participation in the TELL program. We report on the practices that were on the top half of the ranking separately from those that were in the bottom half.

To identify which practices TELL teachers were able to implement but did not implement daily; we did a second analysis of the group of practices that fewer than 50% of TELL teachers used daily, looking at whether TELL teachers reported using those practices *sometimes*.

We also assigned the specific TELL practices to one of four categories: those practices that teach language (e.g., teaching new words), facilitate content learning (e.g., connecting lessons to bilingual learners' life experiences), facilitate language learning (e.g., engaging bilingual learners in oral language activities), and support bilingualism (e.g., encouraging students to communicate in their native language to facilitate classroom work), allowing us to consider their broader function as well.

We analyzed the text from open responses in the survey and from interviews using two components of the constant comparative method – identifying categories within the data and integrating multiple categories – to arrive at themes (Glaser & Strauss, 1967). Examples of themes that emerged included teachers' insights connecting theory to practice, and their

Table 1. Data Collection Methods and Information Gained in Each.

Method	Data Collection Format	Analysis
Survey	1. Likert-type scale items about teaching practices and preparation 2. Open-ended questions	1. Analyzed ordinal data (i.e., responses to scale items) to identify trends 2. Analyzed text using constant comparative methods, to identify themes and explanations of survey responses
Interviews	3. Open-ended questions about teaching practices and preparation	3. Analyzed text using constant comparative methods, to identify themes and key anecdotes

realization that some literacy strategies were effective with all students. From these sources we also learned of respondents' reasons for their choices on the survey and identified anecdotes about their experiences with the practices itemized in the survey (Table 1).

The results that follow, about practices and impact, indicate respondents' rankings of TELL practices they currently implement on a daily basis, TELL practices they are able to implement but do not do so daily, and the amount of impact that their learning from the TELL program had on their use of these practices. This means that the analysis teased out variation in two factors: (a) dosage, that is, how often they used the TELL practices and (b) degree, that is, the extent to which the TELL program prepared them to use the TELL practices.

Results

The purpose of this study was to investigate the classroom practices of a group of novice teachers who had attended the TELL program. The study also explored the teachers' perspectives on the connection between their preparation in the TELL program and their ability to implement practices.

Findings from surveys and interviews are used to report TELL teachers' most-frequently implemented practices and least-frequently implemented practices as well as the TELL program's impact on their ability to enact these practices. Within these practice-focused areas we present several themes: teaching academic language, facilitating content learning (FCL), use of students' native languages, and building on bilingualism.

Most-Frequently Implemented Practices: Teaching Academic Language and Facilitating Content Learning

Graduates were asked on the survey how frequently they integrated particular activities into the instruction of bilingual students in the classes they teach. Participants most frequently reported that they routinely implemented practices in two areas: (1) teaching academic language and (2) FCL by connecting to bilingual students' life experiences and prior knowledge and by building background knowledge. They were also asked to rate the impact that participating in the TELL program had in preparing them to implement those practices (see Table 2).

Teaching academic language. TELL graduates most frequently reported routine practices included teaching words namely, teaching academic vocabulary specific to the content as well as those more general academic vocabulary terms that are used across content areas. All of the respondents reported teaching words often or all the time, 95% taught content-specific academic vocabulary and 86% taught vocabulary that transfers across content. Eight-six percent of TELL teachers also routinely gave students opportunities for oral academic language development by promoting interaction among students within the classroom. Many (76%) also included a focus on academic language development in their content instruction by preparing language objectives for their lessons and units.

Teachers who participated in the study most frequently attributed to the TELL program their ability to engage in activities that focus on teaching language (TL) (indicated in Table 2 in bolded font). Indeed, among practices that they implemented, more teachers indicated that participation in TELL had a "large" or "100%" impact on their ability to teach language (indicated by the code TL) than any other practice. Specifically, 86% of the participants noted that they teach academic language that transfers across content areas "often" or "all the time" and 95% of participants said that the TELL program had a "large" or "100%" impact on preparing them to be able to engage in this particular practice.

Although not among the most highly ranked practices used "often" or "all the time," practically all TELL teachers did report teaching academic language other than vocabulary. For example, with the exception of one teacher, all indicated that they taught language at least "sometimes" by breaking up words into morphemes to discuss meaning (see Appendix A, survey item H). Similarly, all teachers reported teaching academic language such as sentence structures and discourse level structures at least

Table 2. Practices Most Frequently Implemented "Often" or "All the Time" and the TELL Program's Impact on Preparedness to Implement the Practice.

Classroom Practice	Code[a]	Percentage of Participants Who Implemented This Practice "Often" or "All the Time"	Percentage of Participants Who Reported that the TELL Program Had "a Large Impact" or "100% Impact" on Preparing Them to Implement Particular Practices
C. Teaching new words	**TL**	**100**	**76**
D. Teaching content-specific academic vocabulary	**TL**	**95**	**81**
N. Building background knowledge for content lessons	FCL	95	70
O. Linking new information to ELLs' prior knowledge (e.g., concepts learned in school, even if learned in L1)	FCL	90	70
E. Teaching academic language that transfers across content (also known as "mortar" or "Tier 2" vocabulary)	**TL**	**86**	**95**
M. Connecting lessons to ELLs' life experiences (e.g., concepts learned outside school, even if learned in L1)	FCL	86	60
G. Engaging ELLs in oral language activities (e.g., promoting interaction among students in the classroom)	**FLL**	**86**	**86**
Q. Preparing language objectives for lessons and/or units	**TL**	**76**	**95**

[a]Key: TL (teaching language); FCL (facilitating content learning); facilitating language learning (FLL). Practices that focus on teaching language (TL) are in bold.

"sometimes" (see Appendix A, survey item F). They rated the impact of the TELL program in preparing them to implement these within-word and beyond-word teaching strategies as 52% and 76%, respectively.

In the open response section of the survey and in the interviews, some graduates indicated their awareness of the important role they have as teachers in developing academic language among their bilingual students.

They are identified here using pseudonyms. They noted the need to serve as models: "as a teacher, you are modeling academic language for the most part" (Matt, 2013). One of the high school content-area teachers affirmed in an open response that the TELL program led her to understand "that we are language teachers." Some shared this knowledge beyond their own classrooms: one teacher reported pushing his colleagues to become more aware of the academic language they use and expect of their students and another noted in the survey that she shared "handouts and strategies" with her colleagues "who did not receive this kind of training and have a high number of ELL students in their respective classrooms."

Facilitating content learning. Teaching content was a priority for all teachers. However, TELL teachers frequently reported using activities that allowed them to get to know their bilingual students to facilitate content learning. As indicated in Table 2, teachers routinely took note of life experiences and of school learning that took place in their students' first language. Connecting lessons to pupils' life experiences, linking new information to their prior knowledge and building background knowledge for content lessons often were routine activities used by 86%, 90%, and 95% of the graduates, respectively. These are all practices that relate to and depend on knowing one's pupils well. As noted in Table 2, 60–70% of the TELL graduates rated the impact of the TELL program on preparing them to engage in these activities as a "large" or "100%."

Four of the teachers interviewed talked about the importance of getting to know their pupils to facilitate learning. Katherine, Matt, and Neil noted the importance of knowing and affirming pupils' prior knowledge as a starting point for instruction. Neil said that "figuring out where students are and how they learn" is key (August 7, 2013), while Matt noted the importance of not "making assumptions about what students know" in terms of language (August 5, 2013). Katherine shared how she chose readings that were culturally relevant to her students. She stated that knowing and building on students' prior experiences and background knowledge was "certainly something the TELL program was always talking about, pulling on prior knowledge, pulling on their past experience" (August 12, 2013). Amy's purpose for getting to know her students included a focus on affirming their home cultures and languages.

In addition to the activities noted in the surveys, TELL graduates named a number of other specific classroom activities, strategies, and approaches to facilitate language and content learning – all tied to the TELL program preparation – that they use in their practice (see Table 3). They discussed

Table 3. Specific Activities Mentioned in Interviews.

Specific Strategy or Instructional Approach	FCL or FLL[a]	T1	T2	T3	T4	T5	T6
Small groups	Both	x[b]	x	(x)[c]	x	x	x
Oral language practice	Both		x	(x)	(x)		
Socratic seminar	Both		x				
Culturally relevant reading	Both		x				
Project-based learning	Both			x			
Carrousel	Both				x		
Differentiation	Both				x		x
Informal assessments	Both						x
Anchor charts (models)	Both						x
Interactive games	FLL				x		
Sentence starters	FLL		x				
Visuals	FCL			x			(x)
Sheltered Instruction/SIOP[d]	FCL				x	(x)	x
Multiple modalities	FCL						x
Total number of strategies		1	5	4	6	2	7

[a]FCL – Facilitating content learning, FLL – Facilitating language learning.
[b]An x denotes explicit mention to a strategy.
[c]An (x) denotes implicit reference to a strategy.
[d]SIOP – Sheltered Instruction Observation Protocol.

some of these strategies very explicitly in the interviews and others were noted implicitly. For example, when Amy talked about the project-based approach she used, she was implicitly noting small group work and oral language practice. As the table indicates, teachers varied in the number of specific strategies they mentioned, with Katherine noting only one and Neil referring to seven. The most-frequently mentioned activities that teachers implemented were group work, oral language practice, and general sheltering techniques.

Teachers' intention of incorporating these specific activities and strategies into their practice was to enhance bilingual students' learning. However, many participants believed that a number of these activities benefited all their students, and in particular children with special needs. For example, teachers noted that helping student's access material in various ways, presenting content material in a variety of modalities to support comprehension and instruction of academic vocabulary, and including examination of the roots of words were beneficial to many students. One English teacher claimed that the literacy strategies he employed to support bilingual learners, were needed by all his students (Matt, 2013).

Least-Frequently Implemented Practices: Use of Students' Native Languages

Among the least-frequently implemented practices were those that involved the use of students' native languages (see Table 4). These practices included the teacher's use of the students' languages, students' use of their native language, and building on bilingualism to facilitate learning, for example, the use of code-switching and the examination of cognates. Less than 50% of teachers in the study reported using these practices "often" or "all the time." However, looking at this practice in less absolute terms, the

Table 4. Least Frequently Implemented Practices and the TELL Program's Impact on Preparedness to Implement the Practice.

Survey Item (Denoted by Letter) and Description	Code	Percentage Often or All the Time	Percentage Sometimes, Often, or All the Time	Percentage of Participants Who Reported that the TELL Program Had a "Large Impact" or "100% Impact" on Preparing Them to Implement Particular Practices
A. Instructing in a language other than English	FCL	5	19	7
B. Interacting with ELLs in a language other than English for non-instructional purposes	Neither	14	33	6
J. Asking ELLs to share their experiences about their everyday uses of language	**FLL**	**24**	**62**	**53**
K. Examining similarities or differences between students' native language and English (e.g., cognates)	**FLL**	**43**	**81**	**61**
P. Building on students' code-switching abilities during academic lessons	**Both**	**43**	**90**	**70**
L. Facilitating students' use of their native language(s) during lessons (e.g., to access background knowledge and to process new information)	FCL	48	81	58

percentage of teachers who reported using these strategies "sometimes," "often" or "all the time" is notably higher (see Table 4).

Use of students' native language(s). Only 5% of the teachers reported using the students' native languages for instruction (item A) and only 14% reported interacting routinely with students in their native language (item B). Few of the teachers were bilingual in the native language(s) of their students, and, while some experience of learning another language was part of the selection criteria for the TELL scholarships, neither proficiency or fluency in a language other than English was a requirement. Given the design of the TELL program and the restrictive language policy context of the Massachusetts schools, it was no surprise that teachers reported using students' languages infrequently and that only 6% or 7% reported that the TELL program had a "large" or "100%" impact on their use of students' native languages in these ways. It is interesting to note, however, that teachers reported that they facilitated student use of the native language to facilitate content learning (item L). For example, 48% of the teachers reported facilitating students' use of their native language(s) during lessons (to access background knowledge, to process new information). However, again looking at this practice in less absolute terms, the percentage of teachers who reported using these strategies "sometimes," "often" or "all the time," 81% of the respondents allowed their students to use their native languages in class to engage in classroom work. More than half of the respondents (58%) noted that the TELL program had a "large" or "100%" impact on preparing them to facilitate the use of students' native languages in these ways.

Two teachers mentioned the use of pupils' native language during the interviews. Amy discussed how she used what she called "same language groupings" revealing her appreciation of the benefits of allowing pupils to process concepts in their first language.

> My first semester I paired a bunch of Haitian French-speaking students together and they were phenomenal as a group. They would all teach each other and speak to each other in French when one of them did not understand me in English. [It was] just excellent, they worked really well together. [That was] something I would not have known if I had not taken the TELL courses.

Christa noted that while she "never taught in Spanish" to her Spanish speakers, she never stopped them from speaking Spanish to each other to try to explain meaning because she felt that was the way to help the students in that instant.

Building on bilingualism. Some teachers took advantage of students' bilingualism even if they themselves did not regularly use the students' languages. Less than half of the teachers reported routinely engaging in activities that facilitated academic language and content learning by examining similarities or differences between students' native language and English (e.g., cognates) or building on students' code-switching abilities during academic lessons (items K and P in Table 4). However, similar to the trend noted above, when those who engaged in these practices "sometimes" were considered, then a different picture emerged, with 81% and 90% of the teachers, respectively, reporting that they engaged in these activities at least some of the time. Sixty-one percent of the participants credited the TELL program with a "large" or "100%" impact on their ability to engage their students in comparing their native language and English and 70% credited the program with preparing them to build on students' code-switching abilities. Interestingly, teachers did not comment directly in their interviews on building on bilingualism through activities (items K and P, Table 4). However, one teacher mentioned code-switching when asked in the open-ended portion of the survey to "identify the single most crucial component currently missing from the TELL program that you recommend we add, in order to better prepare teachers for working with ELLs."

The results of this study show that participants in the TELL program engaged in daily practices to teach language and facilitate content to bilingual learners. Almost unanimously they attributed to the program their ability to implement practices involving language teaching, while fewer attributed their abilities to implement practices related to teaching content to the program. In relation to native language use, more teachers reported allowing students to use their language than using native language for instruction.

Discussion and Implications

This study aimed to identify the practices used by TELL program graduates in their role as novice teachers of bilingual students and to understand the impact of participating in the TELL program on those teachers' ability to implement such practices. The data looked at teachers' practices and whether they attributed such practices to what they learned in the TELL program. The results showed that there was variety with respect to whether practices were routine, used occasionally, or used rarely. There was also a difference with respect to whether practices were mostly the result of having participated in the program. Thus, these practices can be divided into four categories:

- Daily practices learned in the TELL program.
- Daily practices not specifically attributed to the TELL program.
- Less frequent practices attributed to the TELL program.
- Less frequent practices not emphasized by the TELL program.

The program succeeded in making participants aware of the importance of teaching academic language to facilitate content. Daily language practices especially focused on vocabulary. The program also made participants aware of the importance of exploring students' background knowledge as an important factor in FCL.

Facilitating content knowledge was also a major feature of their daily practices. However, participants attributed this knowledge to a lesser degree to the TELL program. Other courses in the program, especially method courses, equipped the participants with approaches to facilitate content learning.

Teaching language beyond vocabulary to include language analysis at the word, sentence, and discourse levels was also attributed to the TELL program. In addition, participants claimed that taking advantage of students' bilingualism was also learned by participating in the program. For example, some participants let students communicate in their native languages to support classroom engagement. Others report focusing on cognates and language contrast. These practices, however, were not part of the daily routine, but a number of participants reported using them at least sometimes. Finally, a small percentage of participants reported using the students' native language for instruction and even fewer attributed this knowledge to the TELL program.

These results suggest that programs created to improve the preparation of teachers to work with bilingual learners in mainstream classroom contexts must make a special effort to develop teachers' skills in connection to language teaching. Teachers need to recognize the characteristics of the language in their content area that could pose barriers to bilingual learners (Lucas & Villegas, 2013) and incorporate it into their instruction. However, language instruction has to go beyond the word level (de Jong & Harper, 2008). Therefore, programs need to make an extra effort to make teachers capable and aware of the need to go beyond vocabulary and teach the function and form of language in relation to word formation as well as sentence and discourse structures.

Teacher education programs need to consider the context when promoting practices. In Massachusetts because of the restrictive policies with respect to bilingual education, most teachers are being prepared to teach in English-only classrooms. However, a number of the TELL participants demonstrated that even when teachers cannot use a student's native language to teach, they can promote its use among students and can integrate bilingualism and the bilingual experience with content learning.

In addition, the attitude that good teaching practices are good enough for bilingual learners in mainstream settings has resulted in many schools with teachers who are neither fully prepared to teach all students in their classrooms, nor able to support novice teachers seeking examples of teachers who use practices that are effective for bilingual learners. Therefore, graduates of a teacher education program that prepares teachers with this much-needed knowledge may find themselves in the role of instant expert, while they struggle to succeed as novice teachers. Although challenging, this is a position offering new teachers the opportunity to advocate that all teachers support students' bilingualism and cultural experiences, regardless of whether the context promotes bilingual or English-only education. To take positive advantage of this potential leadership role, it may be necessary to extend teacher preparation programs' support to graduates in the initial years of teaching while finding ways to increase the level of expertise among peers in the teacher workforce (Schall-Leckrone, 2013).

In conclusion, teacher education programs focused on preparing mainstream teachers to work with bilingual learners and the graduates of these programs hold the key to substantially changing teacher preparation and, ultimately, changing teaching by emphasizing the important role that academic language knowledge plays in the education of bilingual learners. Teacher preparation programs can teach participants to be language teachers in addition to content teachers. Teaching language as well as content redefines the idea of good teaching because it is not only crucial for ELLs, but also necessary and effective for mainstream students.

Limitations and Considerations for Future Research

The participants recruited for this study included only TELL teachers who had been funded through Project TALCA, introducing a source of bias.

Project TALCA awarded scholarships to students in TELL based on students' characteristics, including commitment to and/or likelihood of working with bilingual leaners, border-crossing experiences (Anzaldúa, 1987), that is, knowledge of more than one language and culture, and commitment to social justice. Thus, these characteristics are more likely to be found in this study sample than in a randomly selected group of TELL program participants. Also, the sample size is too small to conclude with any certainty that the experiences of the study participants are representative of those of all TELL participants. Both of these issues could be addressed in future iterations of this study by broadening the participant population to include all graduates of each TELL cohort, regardless of scholarship status. Additionally, future research could delineate the experiences and practices of participants who are themselves bilingual compared to monolingual participants.

Self-selection of participants also introduced a potential source of bias: it may be that those who are more successful in their professional role are more likely to offer to be participants, although we attempted to offset that potential by offering an incentive to make participation attractive to all. This potential bias could be lessened further in the future by reformulating the research to include a post-study support component as an incentive, explicitly inviting teachers to identify the successes and the problems they are experiencing and then immediately following completion of their participation in the study they would receive coaching from program staff to address those problems.

The use of self-report data introduces at least four possible areas of bias: incomplete or selective memory; inaccuracy in recalling time and order of events; inaccuracy attributing positive and negative events to oneself and others; and exaggeration (Brutus, Aguinis, & Wassmer, 2013). The risk of such bias is offset by the opportunity to learn specifically about teachers' personal experiences in their professional role and perceptions of their pre-professional training. Such information and perceptions provide insights about future support the TELL program may be able to offer teachers once in the field. Nonetheless, such bias should be addressed and may be lessened in the future by implementing periodic data collection throughout the preparation of pre-service teachers and extending during their early year(s) in the professional role. This offer would also provide a more nuanced view of the longitudinal development of their skills for teaching bilingual students.

There was variation in the uniformity of participants' pre-practicum experiences during the TELL program that may have affected the results of this study. Although identifying more fairly similar classrooms for pre-practicum experiences would be ideal, the political context may prove that a near impossible undertaking. Thus, to address this variation, future research might identify a typology of the differences in pre-practicum experiences and compare the results of study participants according to the type of pre-practicum they experience. This would potentially provide further insight into both the political context in public schools as well as the impact of various pre-practicum experiences on participants' specific practices of teaching bilingual students once in their own classrooms.

Another important variable to consider in future research that was not addressed in this study is the location in which participants teach once they complete the TELL program. Classroom experiences may vary in the following ways: number of bilingual students versus number of native English speaking students; bilingual students from many different linguistic backgrounds versus bilingual students that share a heritage language; schools where participants are assigned the role of "expert" in teaching bilingual students versus schools with several other teachers well-versed in effective practices for teaching bilingual students. Research into the challenges and opportunities that graduates of the TELL program experience would offer important insights to the field of teacher education.

References

Anzaldúa, G. (1987). *Borderlands/La frontera: The new mestiza.* San Francisco, CA: Aunt Lute Books.

Assessing Teaching: Response Rates. (n.d.). *Instructional assessment resources.* Retrieved from https://www.utexas.edu/academic/ctl/assessment/iar/teaching/gather/method/survey-Response.php

Bernhardt, E. B. (1991). A psycholinguistic perspective on second language literacy. Reading in two languages. *AILA Review, 8,* 31–44.

Bilingual Education: Frequently Asked Questions. (n.d.). *NYSED.gov OBE-FLS.* Retrieved from http://www.p12.nysed.gov/biling/bilinged/faq.html#bilingual

Brutus, S., Aguinis, H., & Wassmer, U. (2013). Self-reported limitations and future directions on scholarly reports: Analysis and recommendations. *Journal of Management, 39*(1), 48–75. Retrieved from http://jom.sagepub.com/content/39/1/48

Clayton, C. (2013). Exemplary teachers of English language learners: A knowledge base. *The Journal of Research in Education, 2,* 35–64.

Cochran-Smith, M., Caannady, M., McEachern, K. P., Mitchell, K., Piazza, P., Power, C., & Ryan, A. (2012). Teachers' education and outcomes: Mapping the research terrain. *Teachers College Record, 114,* 31.

Cresswell, J. W., & Clark, V. L. (2007). *Designing and conducting mixed methods research.* Thousand Oaks, CA: Sage.

Curriculum and Instruction. (n.d.). Georgia Department of Education. Retrieved from https://www.gadoe.org/Curriculum-Instruction-and-Assessment/Curriculum-and-Instruction/Pages/English-to-Speakers-of-Other-Languages-(ESOL)-and-Title-III.aspx

de Jong, E. J., Arias, M. B., & Sánchez, M. T. (2010). Undermining teacher competencies: Another look at the impact of restrictive language policies. In P. Gándara & M. Hopkins (Eds.), *Forbidden language: English learners and restrictive language policies* (pp. 118–136). New York, NY: Teachers College Press.

de Jong, E. J., & Harper, C. (2008). ESL is good teaching "plus": Preparing standard curriculum teachers for all learners. In M. E. Brisk (Ed.), *Language, culture, and community in teacher education* (pp. 127–148). New York, NY: Routledge.

de Jong, E. J., & Harper, C. A. (2005). Preparing mainstream teachers for English-language learners: Is being a good teacher good enough? *Teacher Education Quarterly, 32*, 101–124.

Feiman-Nemser, S. (2001). From preparation to practice: Designing a continuum to strengthen and sustain teaching. *Teachers College Record, 103*, 1013–1055.

Fillmore, L. W., & Snow, C. (2002). What teachers need to know about language. In C. T. Adger, C. Snow, & D. Christian (Eds.), *What teachers need to know about language* (pp. 7–54). McHenry, IL: Center for Applied Linguistics.

Glaser, B. G., & Strauss, A. L. (1967). *The discovery of grounded theory: Strategies for qualitative research*. New York, NY: Aldine DeGruyter.

Hopkins, M. (2012). Arizona's teacher policies and their relationship with English learner instructional practice. *Language Policy, 11*, 81–99.

Kindler, A. L. (2002). *Survey of the states' limited English proficient students and available educational programs and services 2000–2001 summary report*. Washington, DC: National Clearinghouse for English Language Acquisition & Language Instruction Educational Programs.

Liberali, F. (2013). Student-teachers and teacher-educators experience new roles in pre-service bilingual teacher education in Brazil. In C. Abello-Contesse, P. M. Chandler, M. D. Lopez-Jiménez, & R. Chacón-Beltran (Eds.), *Bilingual and multilingual education in the 21st century* (pp. 231–255). Bristol, UK: Multilingual Matters.

Lucas, T., & Grinberg, J. (2008). Responding to the linguistic reality of mainstream classrooms: Preparing all teachers to work with English language learners. In M. Cochran-Smith, S. Feiman-Nemser, D. J. McIntyre, & K. E. Demers (Eds.), *Handbook of research on teacher education* (3rd ed., pp. 606–636). New York, NY: Routledge.

Lucas, T., & Villegas, A. M. (2011). A framework for preparing linguistically responsive teachers. In T. Lucas (Ed.), *Teacher preparation for linguistically diverse classrooms: A resource for teacher educators* (pp. 55–72). New York, NY: Routledge.

Lucas, T., & Villegas, A. M. (2013). Preparing linguistically responsive teachers: Laying the foundation in preservice teacher education. *Theory Into Practice, 52*(2), 98–109.

Massachusetts Department of Elementary and Secondary Education. (2005). LEP Students by District and Major Language. Retrieved from http://www.doe.mass.edu/ell/default.html?section=archive. Accessed on December 9, 2013.

Olsen, B. (2008). *Teaching what they learn, learning what they live: How teachers' personal histories shape their professional development*. Boulder, CO: Paradigm Publishers.

Sánchez, M. T. (2006). *Teachers' experiences implementing English-only educational legislation*. Doctoral dissertation, Boston College, Chestnut Hill, MA. Retrieved from Dissertations and Theses database (UMI No. 3238839). Chestnut Hill, MA: Boston College.

Samson, J. F., & Collins, B. A. (2012). *Preparing all teachers to meet the needs of English language learners: Applying research to policy and practice for teacher effectiveness.* Washington, DC: Center for American Progress.

Schall-Leckrone, L. (2013). *From coursework to classroom: Learning to teach history to bilingual students.* Retrieved from ProQuest Digital Dissertations (AAT 3587595).

Schleppegrell, M. (2004). *The language of schooling: A functional perspective.* Mahwah, NJ: Lawrence Erlbaum Associates.

The Biennial Report to Congress on the Implementation of the Title III State Formula Grant Program: School Years 2008–10. (2013). Retrieved from http://www.ncela.us/files/uploads/3/Biennial_Report_0810.pdf

Zeichner, K. M. (2005). A research agenda for teacher education. In M. Cochran-Smith & K. M. Zeichner (Eds.), *Studying teacher education: Report of the AERA panel on research and teacher education* (pp. 737–759). Mahwah, NJ: Lawrence Erlbaum.

Appendix A: Online Survey Questions –
Tell Teachers

Boston College Lynch School of Education
TELL Certificate Program and Project TALCA Study
TELL Program impact: The instructional activities and perceptions of TELL-trained teachers
Researchers: Anne Homza (Ed.D.) and Janet M. Smith (Ph.D).

Are you currently employed as a teacher this year?
[ ] Yes
[ ] No

Are you currently employed as a teacher in the United States?
[ ] Yes
[ ] No

How old are you?
[ ] Under 22
[ ] 22–25
[ ] 26–30
[ ] 31–35
[ ] Over 35

What is your gender?
[ ] Male
[ ] Female
[ ] Other

From which institution did you earn your undergraduate degree? (If more than one, provide the most recent.)
[ ] Boston College
[ ] Other (please indicate the name of the institution).

What undergraduate degree did you earn?

In what subject area was your major?

In what subject area was your minor?

Are there any English Language Learners (either identified or unidentified) in your class this year?
[ ] Yes
[ ] No

In what state do you currently teach?

At what level do you currently teach? (Check all that apply.)
[ ] Pre-kindergarten
[ ] Kindergarten − 5th grade
[ ] 6th grade − 8th grade
[ ] 9th grade − 12th grade
[ ] Other

What is the location of the school where you teach?
[ ] Urban
[ ] Suburban
[ ] Rural
[ ] Other

At what type of school do you teach? (check all that apply)
[ ] Public (non-charter)
[ ] Charter
[ ] Private
[ ] Religious affiliation
[ ] Non-religious affiliation

What subjects do you teach? (check all that apply)
[ ] English language arts
[ ] Math
[ ] Science
[ ] Social Studies
[ ] History
[ ] English as a Second Language
[ ] Foreign language
[ ] Other

How many students in total do you currently teach (or co-teach)?
[ ] Less than 10
[ ] 10−19

[ ] 20–29
[ ] more than 30
[ ] I do not know

How many of your students come from households where a language other than English is regularly spoken?
[ ] Less than 10
[ ] 10–20
[ ] 21–30
[ ] More than 30
[ ] I do not know

How many of your students are designated as English Language Learners (ELLs)?
[ ] Less than 10
[ ] 10–19
[ ] 20–29
[ ] More than 30
[ ] I do not know

How many of your students are NOT designated as ELLs but should have been (i.e., they are undesignated ELLs)?
[ ] 0
[ ] 1–9
[ ] 10–19
[ ] 20–29
[ ] More than 30
[ ] I do not know

How do you know which students are undesignated ELLs?

Teaching Activities
In a typical day, how often do you integrate the following activities into the instruction of English language learners in the class(es) you teach or co-teach? These are activities that you conduct in English or any other language, unless specified. We are interested in learning what you actually do in the classroom, not what you are required to do.

Likert-type scale ratings: Never/Rarely/Sometimes/Often/All the time

Items to rate:

A. Instructing in a language other than English
B. Interacting with ELLs in a language other than English for non-instructional purposes
C. Teaching new words
D. Teaching content-specific academic vocabulary
E. Teaching academic language that transfers across content (also known as "mortar" or "Tier 2" vocabulary)
F. Teaching academic language beyond words (e.g., sentence structure, discourse level structure)
G. Engaging ELLs in oral language activities (e.g., promoting interaction among students in the classroom)
H. Breaking up words into basic units (i.e., morphemes) to discuss meaning
 I. Discussing with ELLs specific ways to use language for different purposes or in certain situations
 J. Asking ELLs to share their experiences about their everyday uses of language
K. Examining similarities or differences between students' native language and English (e.g., cognates)
L. Facilitating students' use of their native language(s) during lessons (e.g., to access background knowledge, to process new information)
M. Connecting lessons to ELLs' life experiences (e.g., concepts learned outside of school, even if learned in L1)
N. Building background knowledge for content lessons
O. Linking new information to ELLs' prior knowledge (e.g., concepts learned in school, even if learned in L1)
P. Building on students' code-switching abilities during academic lessons
Q. Preparing language objectives for lessons and/or units

Impact of TELL on current practice
How would you rate the impact that participating in the TELL program had in preparing you to implement the following activities in the class(es) you teach or co-teach?
Likert-type scale ratings: No impact/Small impact/Neither large nor small impact/Large impact/Very large impact/100% impact: all my preparation came from the TELL program

Items to rate:

A. Instructing in a language other than English
B. Interacting with ELLs in a language other than English for non-instructional purposes
C. Teaching new words
D. Teaching content-specific academic vocabulary
E. Teaching academic language that transfers across content (also known as "mortar" or "Tier 2" vocabulary)
F. Teaching academic language beyond words (e.g., sentence structure, discourse level structure)
G. Engaging ELLs in oral language activities (e.g., promoting interaction among students in the classroom)
H. Breaking up words into basic units (i.e., morphemes) to discuss meaning
I. Discussing with ELLs specific ways to use language for different purposes or in certain situations
J. Asking ELLs to share their experiences about their everyday uses of language
K. Examining similarities or differences between students' native language and English (e.g., cognates)
L. Facilitating students' use of their native language(s) during lessons (e.g., to access background knowledge, to process new information)
M. Connecting lessons to ELLs' life experiences (e.g., concepts learned outside of school, even if learned in L1)
N. Building background knowledge for content lessons
O. Linking new information to ELLs' prior knowledge (e.g., concepts learned in school, even if learned in L1)
P. Building on students' code-switching abilities during academic lessons
Q. Preparing language objectives for lessons and/or units

In what other way(s), if any, did participating in the TELL program impact your role as a teacher of ELLs?

Current Support
[ ] Yes
[ ] No

Do you currently discuss the strategies you use for supporting the learning of ELLs with anyone else?
[ ] Yes
[ ] No

Please identify anyone with whom you discuss strategies for supporting the learning of ELLs. Check the appropriate group below.

[ ] Faculty or staff at BC
[ ] TELL colleagues
[ ] Colleagues at your school
[ ] Cooperating teachers from pre-practicum
[ ] Former supervisor(s)
[ ] Former student(s)
[ ] Family of former student(s)
[ ] Other

Name (used while in TELL program)
Current telephone number that you use most often — please indicate if it is your mobile phone or home phone
Current email address that you use most often.

Please describe the single most useful component of the TELL program for preparing you to support the learning of ELLs in your classroom.

Please identify the most crucial component currently missing from the TELL program that you recommend we add, in order to better prepare teachers for working with ELLs.

Please add here any ideas for improvement or areas of concern you have regarding the TELL program. Please answer openly and honestly.
Would you like to participate in a random drawing for an iPod as a thanks for completing this survey? If you choose YES, you will be asked to give your contact information. This information will be held in another database and not linked to the data from this survey.
[ ] Yes
[ ] No

Would you be willing to answer a few questions about what you learned from the TELL program in a brief (30−40 minutes) telephone interview with a researcher conducting this study?
[ ] Yes
[ ] No

If you choose YES, you will be asked to give your name and contact information. This information is held in another database and not linked to the data from this survey.

Would you like to participate in a random drawing for an iPod nano as a thanks for completing this survey?
[ ] Yes
[ ] No

Name (used while in TELL program)
Current telephone number that you use most often − please indicate if it is your mobile phone or home phone.
Current email address that you use most often.

Would you be willing to participate in a brief telephone interview with Janet Smith, Ph.D., one of the researchers from this study? If you choose YES, you will be asked to give your name and contact information. These data are held in another database and not connected to this survey. If you are among those selected for the interview, you will be eligible to win another iPod Nano. If you are among those selected for the interview, you will be eligible to win an iPad Nano. We will let you know if you were selected for the follow-up telephone call by mid-May, 2013.
[ ] Yes
[ ] No

Name (used while in TELL program)
Current telephone number that you use most often − please indicate if it is your mobile phone or home phone.
Current email address that you use most often.

(End of survey questions)

APPENDIX B: INTERVIEW PROTOCOL – FOLLOW-UP WITH SUBSET OF TELL TEACHERS

1. Please tell us about yourself: where you teach, what you teach, how long you have been teaching.
2. Please tell us about the students you teach, including the ELLs.
3. Overall, how would you describe your experiences of teaching ELLs so far?
4. Did you ever try to implement in your classroom any of the strategies you had learned about in the TELL certificate program?

   If yes:

   Which ones? How did it go?

   > Probes: What one activity was easiest to implement?
   > Why do you think it was easy?
   > Which one activity was the hardest to implement?
   > Why do you think it was hard?

   If no:

   Did you try to implement activities you had learned in the TELL certificate program and encounter barriers? Please explain.

   > Probes: Which was the most difficult barrier to grapple with?
   > Were there other reasons you did not implement activities from the TELL certificate program? Please explain.

5. In the TELL certificate program we combined several types of coursework: the TELL courses and other LSOE coursework, infused courses (secondary Math and Science only), practicum work with ELLs (elementary – Read Aloud; secondary – Academic Language Project), supervision from GAT/Clinical Faculty, guidance from cooperating teachers.

   In hindsight, what stands out the most for you about the TELL certificate program?

   What component(s) ended up being most useful in your professional role? Least useful?

   Would you characterize the TELL certificate program components as being well-aligned?

   > Probe: Did they ever contradict one another?

6. Do you think the TELL certificate program had any impact on your professional practice so far? Please explain.
   Probe: Was there some kind of broad impact?
   Was there some kind of limited impact?

7. What one piece of advice would you give to others just finishing the TELL certificate program but who have not yet started in their professional teaching role — in other words, what one thing do you wish you knew then that you know now about teaching ELLs?

8. Are there any additional comments you'd like to make

CHAPTER 8

PREPARING LATINA/O BILINGUAL TEACHERS TO TEACH CONTENT IN SPANISH TO EMERGENT BILINGUAL STUDENTS ON THE US–MEXICO BORDER

Alma D. Rodríguez and Sandra I. Musanti

Abstract

This chapter discusses the findings of a qualitative study conducted on the US–Mexico border to investigate preservice bilingual teachers' understandings of the effective practices needed to teach content in bilingual classrooms. Specifically, participants' understandings of teaching language through content to emergent bilinguals and the role of academic language in a content methods course taught in Spanish for preservice bilingual teachers were explored. The results of the study show that preservice bilingual teachers struggled to internalize how to develop language objectives that embed the four language domains as well as the three levels of academic language into their content lessons. Although participants emphasized vocabulary development, they integrated multiple scaffolding strategies to support emergent bilinguals. Moreover, although

Research on Preparing Preservice Teachers to Work Effectively with Emergent Bilinguals
Advances in Research on Teaching, Volume 21, 201–232
ISSN: 1479-3687/doi:10.1108/S1479-368720140000021007

preservice bilingual teachers struggled with standard Spanish, they used translanguaging to navigate the discourse of education in their content lessons. The use of academic Spanish was also evident in participants' planning of instruction. The authors contend that bilingual teacher preparation would benefit from the implementation of a dynamic bilingual curriculum that: (a) incorporates sustained opportunities across coursework for preservice bilingual teachers to strengthen their understanding of content teaching and academic language development for emergent bilinguals; (b) values preservice bilingual teachers' language varieties, develops metalinguistic awareness, and fosters the ability to navigate between language registers for teaching and learning; and (c) values translanguaging as a pedagogical strategy that provides access to content and language development.

Keywords: Academic language; bilingual teacher preparation; content teaching for emergent bilinguals; contextualization strategies; language objectives; translanguaging

La meta es que los estudiantes ingresen el desarrollo de lenguaje además del contenido por una variedad de actividades. Los estudiantes tendrán oportunidades de trabajar en grupos (heterogéneos), crear historias, construir organizadores gráficos, medir y comparar tamaños de dinosaurios, construir un gráfico de barras, excavar usando pinceles y brochitas, construir una línea de tiempo, investigar la demografía, explicar oralmente el orden de eventos, usar vocabulario específico para describir, escribir párrafos usando oraciones completas en tiempo presente y describir oralmente diez datos sobre su terrario. La maestra usara una variedad de tipos de andamiajes como modelando, contextualización, pensando en voz alta, uso de caja de apoyo, think pair share, etc. [The goal is for students to begin to develop language in addition to content through a variety of activities. The students will have opportunities to work in (heterogeneous) groups, create stories, build graphic organizers, measure and compare sizes of dinosaurs, build a bar graph, dig using small brushes, build a timeline, investigate demographics, explain orally the order of events, use specific vocabulary to describe, write paragraphs using complete sentences in the present tense, and describe orally ten facts about their terrarium. The teacher will use a variety of types of scaffolds such as modeling, contextualization, think alouds, reading boxes, think pair share, etc.]

The above is a quote from one of our Latina preservice bilingual teachers who developed lessons as a requirement for a course in her bilingual teacher preparation program. Although the student's written Spanish quoted above is not always conventional, her words clearly illustrate how she is grappling with the idea of how to teach language through content to emergent bilinguals. This chapter will describe a study we conducted on the US—Mexico border to identify effective bilingual teacher preparation practices for Latinas/os. Our review of the literature indicates that bilingual teacher preparation programs would benefit from studies that investigate preservice bilingual teachers' understandings about effective practices during their undergraduate work.

Purpose and Significance

With the growth of the Latino population, there has been an increased need for well-qualified bilingual and ESL teachers (Schneider, Martinez, & Owens, 2006). Many emergent bilingual students are attending low-quality and low-performing institutions. Most of these schools are staffed with underprepared or non-credentialed teachers (Sheets, Flores, & Clark, 2011). Moreover, Menken and Antunez (2001) state that only a small number of higher education institutions offer programs to prepare bilingual teachers. Clearly, then, it is critical to re-envision traditional teacher preparation, which is characterized by "fragmentation, weak content, poor pedagogy, disconnect from schools, and inconsistent oversight of teachers in-training" (Darling-Hammond, 2006, p. 6).

At the core of bilingual teachers' task is the ability to design and deliver instruction in the content areas in English and in the first language of their students (Davis, n.d.). Given that the home language of the majority of emergent bilingual students in Texas and the United States is Spanish (Batalova & McHugh, 2010; Davis, n.d.; Texas Education Agency, 2012—2013), it is vital for bilingual teacher preparation programs to include the development of academic Spanish as one of their program goals. This need is especially evident in regions with predominantly Spanish-speaking populations such as the US—Mexico border.

The current study was designed to identify effective practices in bilingual teacher preparation that can build teacher capacity among Latina/o preservice bilingual teachers to meet the instructional needs of emergent bilingual students. Specifically, this chapter focuses on exploring preservice bilingual teachers' ability to design content area instruction in Spanish for emergent bilingual students. This ability requires not only content and pedagogical knowledge, but also knowledge of effective instructional practices for emergent bilingual students and proficiency in Spanish as the language of instruction. Therefore, we identified the following research questions:

(1) How do preservice bilingual teachers apply their understanding of teaching language through content into their instructional planning?
(2) What is the role of academic language in a content methods course taught in Spanish for preservice bilingual teachers?

Review of Related Literature

This study is framed by related literature on three topics. First, we address the literature that discusses the trends in bilingual teacher preparation identifying needs and challenges. Second, we look into the work that explores the role of academic language in bilingual teacher preparation. Finally, we turn to the research done in the field of language development through content instruction.

Bilingual Teacher Preparation

The literature reveals a great need for research that explores how to better prepare preservice bilingual teachers. Research in the education has mostly focused on defining effective practices for mainstream teacher preparation programs with little attention to programs that are preparing teachers to educate the largest ethnic minority school population (Sheets et al., 2011). Capella-Santana (2003) explored changes in preservice teachers' multicultural attitudes and knowledge. The author concludes that "the discussion of issues related to the education of language minority students during the teacher preparation program can promote positive changes in teacher candidates' attitudes and knowledge regarding this issue" (p. 189). In particular, she contends that teachers of emergent bilinguals need to become more aware of the unique features of the language required in different content areas to plan instruction that is more strategic and nuanced for content learning.

De Jong and Harper (2005) discuss the dimensions of knowledge and skills related to language and culture that teachers need to effectively meet the needs of emergent bilinguals. They argue that teachers need to understand bilingualism and literacy development and how they can build on students' native language resources. Supporting language development requires that teachers identify the linguistic demands in the content areas and integrate this knowledge in the identification of appropriate language and content objectives. Further, Menken and Antunez (2001) examined the depth and quality of preparation for English as second language (ESL) and bilingual teachers and argue that such programs must strengthen the preparation in linguistics and the process of language development, as this is critical knowledge for what bilingual teachers are intended to teach.

Academic Language for Preservice Bilingual Teachers

Literature in the field of bilingual and ESL education identifies the importance of developing emergent bilingual students' academic language as a factor to improve student achievement and to narrow the gap between low- and high-performing students (Freeman & Freeman, 2007; Zwiers, 2008). Krashen and Brown (2007) define academic language as "the special language used in school and the professions" (p. 1). Cummins (2008) explains that academic language is acquired in school, and is needed for students to make academic progress. Freeman and Freeman (2009) argue that emergent bilinguals must learn the oral and written registers of schooling. Moreover, Zwiers (2008) concludes that academic language is linked to higher order and critical thinking skills, and its teaching is more complex than acknowledged by most educators.

A widespread misconception regarding academic language reduces it to content words, which translates into an emphasis on practices that focus on teaching vocabulary (Zwiers, 2008). Authors such as Scarcella (2003), Zwiers (2008), and Egbert and Ernst-Slavit (2010), among many others have identified the multiple and interrelated components of academic language, requiring the use of a varied spectrum of vocabulary, as well as syntactic structures, and discourse elements. Teachers must understand these three aspects of academic language to design and deliver instruction in a bilingual classroom.

However, as Egbert and Ernst-Slavit (2010) explain, developing academic language cannot be reduced to learning a variety of linguistic features. It involves cultural knowledge about "ways of being in the world, ways of acting, thinking, interacting, valuing, believing, speaking, and sometimes writing and reading, connected to particular identities and social roles" (Gee, 1992, p. 73). For instance, the way to express mathematical ideas, the representation of notations, procedures, and algorithms vary in different cultural and linguistic contexts. Even though in Latin America and the United States numbers are written using the same symbols, there are differences in "the names that are read for numbers, in the use of the decimal point, and in the separation of digits in large numbers" (Perkins & Flores, 2002, p. 347). It is important that teachers as well as students understand and value these differences. In bilingual classrooms, emergent bilinguals must acquire academic language in both English and Spanish. Therefore, bilingual teachers also need to develop academic competency in both English and Spanish to support their students' academic language development.

Spanish for Bilingual Teachers in the United States and Translanguaging

Even though the United States has "the fifth-largest Spanish speaking population in the world" surpassed only by Mexico, Spain, Colombia, and Argentina (Barnwell, 2008, p. 239), the development of academic Spanish among preservice bilingual teachers is complicated by their own conflicting histories of language development (Ek & Sánchez, 2008; Guerrero, 2003a). Ek and Sánchez (2008) explain how historically, schools have Americanized Spanish-speaking students by immersing them into English, resulting in the loss of the Spanish language. Because many preservice bilingual teachers did not receive bilingual instruction, and the opportunities to develop literacy in their native language were scarce or non-existent during their elementary and secondary schooling, they enter their bilingual teacher preparation programs with varied, and in some cases, less than adequate levels of academic literacy in Spanish (Ek & Sánchez, 2008; Guerrero, 2003a; Sutterby, Ayala, & Murillo, 2005). Moreover, many preservice bilingual teachers have a low perception of their own Spanish proficiency (Guerrero, 2003b; Rodríguez, 2007), or are "told that their Spanish is unacceptable" (Smith, Sánchez, Ek, & Machado-Casas, 2011, p. 180) given the variety or dialect of Spanish that they speak.

A number of factors influence the varieties of Spanish spoken in the United States. Among those factors are the countries of origin of the speakers of the language (Colombi, 1996), their social class, level of education, or region of the country (Smith et al., 2011). The variety of Spanish regarded as correct is considered the standard (Achugar, 2008). However, Achugar explains that what constitutes standard language is an arbitrary decision made by those in power. This is particularly relevant in bilingual contexts where two languages coexist and are consistently used in the communicative practices of bilingual individuals.

The work of García (2011) defines the specific practices of bilingual individuals as translanguaging, challenging the traditional definition of code-switching as the simultaneous use of two separate monolingual codes. She also challenges the notion of strict separation of languages for instruction in bilingual classrooms (Celic & Seltzer, 2011). The traditional monoglossic ideology and consequent language separation comes from an additive conceptualization of bilingualism where English was perceived as the language to add to students' repertoire. García and Kleifgen (2010) propose a non-linear, more dynamic understanding of bilingualism, where both (or more) languages are not seen as autonomous but intrinsically interwoven in bilingual people's practices. From this perspective, teacher preparation needs to move from the idea of simply accepting students' languages to nurturing those languages by using them as resources for teaching and learning (Creese & Blackledge, 2010; García, 2011). Cummins (2007) explains that translation is appropriate in bilingual classrooms as it facilitates the development of biliteracy and the acquisition of English. Creese and Blackledge (2010) argue for a flexible bilingual pedagogy that adopts a translanguaging approach. García (2011) asserts that in bilingual classrooms teachers can translanguage to make content instruction accessible and comprehensible for emergent bilingual students as they acquire academic language.

Teaching Language through Content

The literature exploring how to support emergent bilinguals' language development in English through content instruction is prolific and can contribute to understanding what is needed in bilingual teacher preparation (Janzen, 2008). This research considers how different content knowledge is constructed using language registers that differ from those used to interact in daily life (Schleppegrell & de Oliveira, 2006).

Freeman and Freeman (2008) identify four reasons to teach language through content instruction: students learn language and content simultaneously, students learn about language in a natural context, they have authentic reasons to use the social and academic language they acquire, and students learn the registers of the different content areas. In addition, Janzen's (2008) extensive literature review pinpoints research findings in regards to the critical role language plays in enabling students to reach higher levels of achievement. She concludes that research conclusively shows that

> The academic uses of language as well as the meaning of individual words need to be explicitly taught for students to fulfill the genre or discourse requirements privileged in academic settings and to understand the material they encounter in, for example, history textbooks or mathematical word problems. (p. 1030)

Situating language learning in the content classroom requires that teachers develop understanding of language, how language is used to construct meaning, and what strategies foster language development in the different content areas (Janzen, 2008; Rea & Mercuri, 2006; Schleppegrell and de Oliveira, 2006). Preservice teachers need to understand how the academic language encountered in content readings and needed to produce written texts differs in characteristics from one discipline to another, and from the language used in social interaction. For instance, several researchers have explored the complexities of content-based instruction (CBI) in different disciplines. Schleppegrell and de Oliveira (2006), drawing on functional linguistic theory, described how teachers can engage students in history meaning making through text analysis, even when the students' language proficiency and reading skills have not reached grade level proficiency. Hart and Lee (2003) argue that science instruction provides a meaningful context for teachers to foster English language and literacy development if opportunities for hands-on, inquiry-based science instruction, and authentic language use are provided. When these are used, students develop scientific understanding and engage in inquiry practices more actively than traditional textbook-based instruction.

The literature has also emphasized the strategies that support academic language development and providing comprehensible input for emergent bilingual learners' content understanding. Walqui (2006) discusses different ways to scaffold instruction in subject matter classes taught in English. She identifies six main types of instructional scaffolding: modeling, bridging, contextualization, building schema, re-presenting text, and developing metacognition. Rea and Mercuri (2006) provide detailed examples of lesson plans that integrate different scaffolds, such as modeling and contextualization.

Gottlieb and Ernst-Slavit (2013) recommend a curricular framework for integrating content and academic language development that builds on the Common Core State Standards and highlights the role of linguistic and cultural resources for learning. The framework shows "how academic language is part of content learning and how content provides the context for language learning" (p. 17) identifying strategies that scaffold language at the discourse level, sentence level, and word/phrase level. These levels correspond to the levels of academic language as identified by Freeman and Freeman (2009), who state that teachers of emergent bilinguals can address academic language at the text, paragraph, sentence, or word levels in their content lessons by planning language objectives in addition to content objectives. Adopting a CBI approach including both content and language objectives "provides a means for students to continue their academic development while also improving their language proficiency" (Stoller, 2004, p. 262 as cited by Schleppegrell & de Oliveira, 2006). Egbert and Ernst-Slavit (2010) explain that language objectives are needed to help emergent bilinguals attain the content objectives. That is, teachers of emergent bilinguals need to identify the language demands that the content lessons present to determine the lesson's language objectives. In addition, Egbert and Ernst-Slavit (2010) emphasize that developing academic language proficiency requires developing competency in the four language domains: listening, speaking, reading, and writing. Therefore, teachers of emergent bilinguals must also understand the complexities of each of the language domains to support their students in language development in all language domains as they learn content.

Academic language, then, is critical for preservice teachers to understand. However, research exploring specific aspects of content learning in Spanish-speaking classrooms is scarce and conducted mostly at the elementary level in dual language programs (see Musanti & Celedón-Pattichis, 2012; Lopez-Robertson, 2012, for examples of such studies).

Method

This is a qualitative study that explored preservice teachers' understandings of effective practices in the bilingual classroom and their use of Spanish academic language to express their ideas and to design lessons for teaching content in bilingual classrooms. We opted for a qualitative research design because as Merriam (1998) explains, researchers who choose qualitative studies "... simply seek to discover and understand a phenomenon, a process, or the perspectives and world views of the people involved" (p. 11).

Both the purpose and questions of this study derived from our experience teaching in an elementary bilingual teacher preparation program as well as from our beliefs about bilingual teacher preparation. The goal of this study was to gain insights into preservice bilingual teachers' understandings of teaching language through content by analyzing their lesson planning. In doing so, we also explored the role of academic language in a content methods course. This allowed us to identify their challenges as well as to produce recommendations to better support preservice bilingual teachers' learning while strengthening their academic language.

The Researchers

Alma Rodríguez is an experienced teacher educator who grew up in the border area and has in-depth knowledge of the local culture and traditions. Her first language is Spanish, and she received her elementary and secondary education in Mexico. She has taught different classes in the Bilingual and ESL elementary programs for over 9 years, and she has also been involved in the undergraduate curriculum committee, which gives her insider knowledge of the history of the program.

Sandra Musanti is originally from Argentina, her first language is Spanish and, even though she shares the Latino ethnicity with the community, she is new to the region. Her long experience in teacher education at the undergraduate level was mostly in Argentina. In the US context, she engaged in collaborative work with bilingual teachers teaching Mexican-origin students in a working class neighborhood doing post-doctoral research. She has taught the course selected for this research six consecutive semesters since her arrival at this university in 2011. As a newcomer to the region and the university, Dr. Musanti has prioritized gathering knowledge about her students, their linguistic traditions, and their ways of knowing.

Setting

We conducted this qualitative study at a' university located on the Texas—Mexico border serving a majority Latino population of Mexican descent. Most of the students define themselves as bilingual or second language learners of English. The Texas—Mexico border is a dynamic, fast-growing region with a population that has grown by 65% since 1980 compared to only a 24% growth rate nationally (Phillips & Cañas, 2004). The "region forms a uniquely intertwined, bi-national, bi-literate, and bi-cultural community" (Texas Center, 2010, p. 2).

Although Spanish is widely used in this region, schooling is predominately in English. Some schools offer early exit bilingual education that includes some use of Spanish in the early grades as a medium to transition students to English.

The university plays an important role in promoting bilingual education in a context that favors education in English by supporting and expanding the bilingual education undergraduate and graduate programs. Spanish is the language of instruction in a series of mandatory courses for the elementary bilingual education program including Emergent Literacy in the Bilingual Classroom, Teaching Reading in the Bilingual Classroom, and Content Area Methods in the Bilingual Classroom. These courses contribute to bilingual education in the region by stressing the importance of students' first language development.

The course under examination, Content Area Methods in the Bilingual Classroom, provides preservice bilingual teachers with an overview of current methods and theories of planning and teaching across content areas in bilingual classrooms from an interdisciplinary perspective with an emphasis on the development of academic Spanish. Dr. Musanti was the instructor for the course during the four semesters when data was collected. To organize the course she drew from the perspective of developing language through content using two texts, *Access to Academics: Planning Instruction for K-12 Classrooms with ELLs* (Egbert & Ernst-Slavit, 2010), and *Research-based Strategies for English Language Learners* (Rea & Mercuri, 2006). These texts provided principles and guidelines to develop lessons that integrate language development and content instruction and different scaffolds for teaching such as modeling, contextualizing, and reframing information.

A real challenge to designing and delivering this class was the lack of reading materials in Spanish. Central readings were all in English. This made it necessary for the instructor to develop materials for the class in Spanish including presentations, handouts, and graphics to support meaning making in both languages (Beeman & Urow, 2012). Therefore, instructor and students were constantly translanguaging to navigate the content between two languages (García & Kleifgen, 2010). For instance, students would read a passage from the textbook in English and then they would discuss the ideas presented in the passage in Spanish.

One of the goals of this course was to further bilingual teachers' academic language development, while they learned about content area instruction. Students had multiple opportunities to interact and work collaboratively in Spanish during and after class completing tasks or preparing materials to be shared with peers and the instructor. Dr. Musanti presented the content in an interactive manner using visuals such as videos, images, or graphics to support students' Spanish academic language development. Frequently, vocabulary was frontloaded and connected to the English academic vocabulary known by students, cognates were highlighted throughout the course, and specific content area vocabulary was emphasized including, for example, the term *equal* in mathematics, or the terms *scientific explanation* or *probe* in science. Especially during the first part of the semester, students were required to write responses in Spanish to the class readings. These writing tasks had the double purpose of identifying key concepts in the readings as well as having students use their Spanish language resources to interpret the English textbook content. Later in the semester, students' Spanish writing focused on lesson planning.

Participants

The participants in this study were 65 preservice bilingual teachers taking the core course Content Area Methods in the Bilingual Classroom in Spring 2012, Fall 2012, Spring 2013, and Fall 2013. Participation in the study was voluntary and students were recruited after the instructor informed them about the purposes of the study and the information that would be collected.

The participants were 63 female and 2 male students. Most of them came from working class families and had either full- or part-time jobs. All participants were bilingual with different levels of oral fluency, reading, and writing skills in both Spanish and English. Preservice bilingual teachers who attend the institution where this study was conducted fall under two broad categories: (a) students who received most or all of their elementary and secondary education in the United States and (b) students who received most or all of their elementary and secondary education in Mexico. It is important to note that the preservice bilingual teachers from south Texas did not benefit from sustained and quality bilingual education programs in US public schools, and many had difficulty with the Spanish language as compared to students who received some or part of their elementary and/or secondary education in Mexico.

Data Collection

The data analyzed for this study consisted of participants' lesson plans developed in the Spring 2012, Fall 2012, Spring 2013, and Fall 2013. Participants developed two lessons in the Spring 2012 semester ($N = 36$)

and five lessons in the Fall 2012, Spring 2013, and Fall 2013 semesters ($N = 235$). Each lesson addressed a different content area: mathematics, science, or social studies. All lessons had to connect the state standards, Texas Essential Knowledge and Skills (TEKS), and incorporate the English Language Proficiency Standards (ELPS) of the state of Texas to ensure that the needs of emergent bilinguals were addressed. Preservice bilingual teachers were required to provide a brief rationale for how their lessons helped emergent bilinguals develop language through content. For each lesson participants were required to identify content and language objectives, and describe strategies to support language development while teaching content. These included modeling strategies; contextualizing strategies such as using images, building background information, and using graphics. Students were expected to include a detailed description of the sequence of activities. In addition, students were asked to incorporate informal and formal assessment strategies in their lessons as well as extension activities to work with families and/or communities.

Data Analysis

Using a grounded approach, we read all the data separately using a method of constant comparison (Strauss & Corbin, 1998). We independently analyzed the data and open coded each element of participants' lesson plans looking at evidence that portrayed their understandings of how to develop language through content in the lesson objectives, the strategies that were included, and their use of academic language. We also analyzed the rationale participants' provided for their instructional decisions. This part of the analysis provided further insight into participants' understandings.

Initially, we coded the instances when students adequately or not identified content and language objectives. Based on our experience as faculty in the teacher preparation program, we know that a number of courses require students to design lessons in which they include content objectives. However, they are less familiar with language objectives. For many of them, this is the first course in which they have the opportunity to learn about and write language objectives. As a result, our analysis of objectives focused on language objectives rather than on content objectives. Therefore, in a second reading, we coded the types of language objectives included in each lesson, whether students integrated the levels of academic language (word, sentence, and text), and whether they considered different dimensions of language development (listening, speaking, reading, and writing). A third reading focused on analyzing the lesson activities, especially looking at the types of strategies students included. We coded for the different strategies to support language development: grouping students, vocabulary development, use of students' L1, translanguaging, modeling, contextualizing, building background knowledge, and sentence frames.

Even though analyzed data is limited to four semesters, our prolonged involvement and insider knowledge of the context and program contributes to the findings' trustworthiness (Lincoln & Guba, 1985). Both researchers have taught the selected course, and the researchers have been involved in the undergraduate program for more than 12 combined years and developed in-depth knowledge of the program and students' needs and characteristics.

Limitations

The generalizability of our findings is limited given the scope of the study. The study explores a course that is part of a bilingual teacher preparation program with characteristics that might differ from other programs. Another limitation derives from the context of the study. As it was mentioned earlier, our study was conducted in a very unique area of south Texas, where bilingualism is common in the community. In fact, the location of the institution makes our program accessible to students from both sides of the US—Mexico border. In addition, the sample of participants in this study consisted of only Latinas/os preservice bilingual teachers. In as much as the uniqueness of our program and our bilingual teacher candidates constitute limitations for the generalizability of our findings to contexts that would significantly differ from ours, we consider our uniqueness a valuable opportunity to explore effective practices in the preparation of Latina/o bilingual teacher candidates. In addition, in the future it would be important to explore the research questions in similar courses taught in English to expand the scope of the study.

Findings

Teaching Language through Content

In this section we discuss the first research question, which investigated how preservice bilingual teachers' apply their understanding of teaching language through content into their instructional planning. Participants learned that effective teachers of emergent bilinguals integrate language into their content lessons. Effective teachers begin the process by writing content and language objectives to guide their instructional planning (Egbert & Ernst-Slavit, 2010). Preservice bilingual teachers also learned that effective teachers of emergent bilinguals facilitate language development during content instruction when integrating multiple strategies that facilitate comprehension and support emergent bilinguals in their learning (Rea & Mercuri, 2006). Therefore, we analyzed participants' lessons to identify such understandings by focusing on the lessons' objectives and the lessons' activities. Throughout this analysis student quotes are written verbatim. Unconventional Spanish was not changed, and English translations attempt to reflect participants' original writing.

Language objectives. Participants included both language and content objectives in their lessons following Egbert and Ernst-Slavit's (2010) definition of objectives as "statements of attainable, quantifiable lesson outcomes that guide the activities and assessment of the lesson" (p. 56). Participants' content objectives focused on the content knowledge students were expected to acquire by the end of the lesson. For example, "*Los estudiantes serán capaces de identificar y nombrar los huesos del cuerpo humano.*" (Students will be able to identify and name the bones in the human body.) Although the quality of lesson objectives varied by cohort and by individual preservice teacher, participants generally had a clear understanding of content objectives.

There was greater variation in the quality of language objectives than in the quality of content objectives written by participants. This was due to two factors: First, participants had more opportunities learning to write content objectives than language objectives in previous courses. Second, the course requirements were different for the Spring 2012 and Fall 2012 cohorts than for the Spring 2013 and Fall of 2013 cohorts. Participants from the Spring 2012 and Fall 2012 cohorts were required to write three language objectives for each lesson: one at the text level, one at the sentence level, and one at the word level. Preservice bilingual teachers in these cohorts were able to produce language objectives that successfully addressed the text, sentence, and word levels as can be seen in the following examples:

- *Nivel de texto – Los estudiantes van a crear un plan detallado describiendo como van alcanzar su meta de corto plazo o de largo plazo.*
  [Text level – Students will create a detailed plan describing how they will reach their short-term and long-term goal.]

- *Nivel de oración — Los estudiantes tendrán que escribir en oraciones completas usando el vocabulario específico. La maestra les proporcionara marco de oraciones durante la evaluación.*
  [Sentence level — Students will have to write in complete sentences using specific vocabulary. The teacher will provide sentence frames during the evaluation.]
- *Nivel de palabra — Los estudiantes utilizaran vocabulario específico, señalización, y términos generales durante la lección al escribir y presentar. [Vocabulario] Específico: ganar, ahorrar, dinero, gastar, donar. [Palabras de] Señalización: primero (first), segundo (second), tercero (third), [Vocabulario] General: meta de corto plazo (short-term goal), meta de largo plazo (long-term goal), t-chart.* (Note: Student translated into English some of the words in the lesson plan.)
  [Word level — Students will use specific vocabulary, signal words, and general terms during the lesson when writing and presenting. Specific vocabulary: *earn, save, money, spend, donate.* Signal words: *first, second, third.* General vocabulary: *short-term goal, long-term goal, t-chart.*]

However, Sandra Musanti, who was the instructor for the course, noticed that *text* was understood by many preservice bilingual teachers as written text. Most participants (70%) focused on having students write when they were required to include language objectives at the text, sentence, and word levels as can be noted in the examples above. Some participants (36%) also included some level of oral production in their language objectives as is illustrated above in the third example. Musanti's informal assessment led her to make an instructional decision to emphasize the four dimensions of language in subsequent semesters to help students broaden their understanding of *text*. Participants from the Spring 2013 and Fall 2013 cohorts were required to include language objectives for each lesson that focused on giving students the opportunity to use the four language domains: listening, speaking, reading, and writing. As a result, 41% of preservice bilingual teachers in those semesters included other language domains such as reading or listening in addition to speaking and writing in their language objectives:

- *Los estudiantes escucharan a la maestra leer un texto y contestaran preguntas oralmente sobre la lectura.*
- [Students will listen to the teacher read a text and will answer questions orally about the reading.]

Although participants improved in developing language objectives integrating the four language dimensions, they struggled embedding the different levels of academic language. For example, 41% of preservice bilingual teachers struggled writing language objectives at the text and sentence level, but not at the word level. The following example is of a preservice teacher who attempted to write a language objective at the sentence level, but wrote an objective at the word level instead:

- *Nivel de oración: Los estudiantes nombraran los dibujos del bingo practicando el vocabulario.*
- [Sentence level: Students will name the bingo pictures practicing the vocabulary words.]

It was easier for preservice bilingual teachers to write objectives at the word level, which were consistent across cohorts. An example is provided below:

- *Nivel de vocabulario: Los estudiantes usan las palabras de vocabulario específico como, nieve, lluvia, granizo y aguanieve.*
  [Word level: Students use specific vocabulary words such as *snow, rain, hail,* and *sleet.*]

Finally, a small percentage of participants (9%) had difficulty writing language objectives altogether. That is, they were not able to focus on language and described activities related to content knowledge in what they intended to be language objectives as shown in the following example:

- *Los estudiantes dibujaran cada paso de crecimiento de la planta.*
  [Students will draw each step of the growth of a plant.]

Focusing on vocabulary. Vocabulary constituted a central component in participants' lessons. In fact, several participants expressed that language acquisition consists of acquiring vocabulary as was explained by one participant: "*Los estudiantes incrementaran su lenguaje en L2 mediante el aprendizaje de vocabulario nuevo.*" [Students will increase their second language by learning new vocabulary.] Other participants equated academic vocabulary with academic language, as did the participant who wrote, "*Esta lección es muy apropiada para una clase bilingüe por que se incorpora el uso de vocabulario y así incrementar el lenguaje académico.*" [This lesson is very appropriate for a bilingual class because it incorporates the use of vocabulary and, in that way, academic language increases.] Whether their intention was to help students acquire a second language or develop academic language in

Spanish, the majority of participants (81%) designed specific activities through which they would help students develop vocabulary. Interestingly, preservice bilingual teachers' beliefs on the centrality of vocabulary for learning seemed to trump the course's emphasis on redefining academic language from a broader perspective.

Most participants selected as part of their vocabulary-building activities word walls and the use of cognates. The following excerpt from a preservice bilingual teacher's lesson displays how she would use a word wall integrating the use of visuals with the written words:

> *Después la clase repasara los nombres de todos los lugares (Norte América, Estados Unidos de América, Texas, y Brownsville) que estarán escritos, tanto en inglés y español junto a su foto apropiada, en una pared de palabras ya preparada por la maestra.*

> [Then the class will review the names of all the places (North America, United States of America, Texas, and Brownsville) that are written both in English and in Spanish next to the corresponding picture, in a word wall previously prepared by the teacher.]

Many participants decided to use cognates to build vocabulary as did the preservice bilingual teacher who wrote the following as a vocabulary activity in her lesson: "*La docente también tendrá palabras de cognados en el pizarrón para que sus ELL estudiantes se apoyen mientras completen la investigación de grupo, (Pluto/Plutón, Jupiter/Júpiter etc., horas/hours, ... minutes/minutos, distance/distancia).*" [The teacher will also have cognates on the board to support her ELL students while they complete the group investigation, (*Pluto/Plutón, Jupiter/Júpiter*, etc. *hours/horas ... minutes/minutos, distance/distancia*).]

Integrating strategies. In addition to focusing on vocabulary, preservice bilingual teachers included a variety of strategies in their lessons. Fig. 1 displays the strategies that were selected by preservice bilingual teachers. The percent of preservice bilingual teachers who integrated each strategy in their instructional planning is also indicated.

Many participants believed these strategies would help them teach language through content, as was explained by the following preservice bilingual teacher: "*La lección desarrolla el lenguaje a través de contenido ya que se utiliza las estrategias de vista-previa/vista/revisión, modelado, trabajo cooperativo, y contextualización.*" [The lesson develops language through content because strategies such as preview/view/review, modeling, cooperative work, and contextualization are used.]

Participants had learned about the importance of contextualizing their lessons, or providing clues to meaning by reading and discussing this

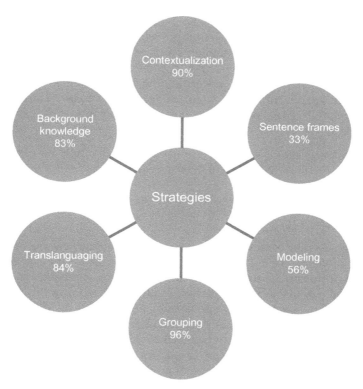

Fig. 1.   Scaffolding Strategies Selected by Preservice Bilingual Teachers to Teach
Language through Content in their Lesson Planning.

strategy as presented by Rea and Mercuri (2006). Contextualization allows
emergent bilinguals to anchor the new concepts and bridge language and
meaning. Participants selected a variety of contextualization strategies such
as visuals, songs, videos, and manipulatives. The following quote from a
participant explains how she planned to contextualize the lesson: "*[La lec-
ción] es contextualizada. Las actividades incluyen ideas, objetos y eventos
reales de los estudiantes para presentar o conectar información. También, los
estudiantes tienen materiales que pueden tocar, manejar y aplicar.*" [The
lesson is contextualized. The activities include ideas, objects, real events
from students' lives to present or connect information. Students also have
materials they can touch, manipulate, and apply.]

In addition to incorporating contextualization strategies in their lessons, participants included sentence frames, which give emergent bilinguals "a starting point for constructing syntactically well-formed sentences" (Egbert & Ernst-Slavit, 2010, p. 154). In addition the use of sentence frames helps students express their understanding of the content. Participants included activities in which they used sentence frames to provide scaffolding for emergent bilinguals' writing as is indicated in the following instructional sequence.

Los estudiantes completaran una hoja y escribirán la diferencia entre una piedra y un mineral … Con el siguiente marco de oración: "EL/La _____ se pude clasificar como (una roca) o(minerales) porque_____."

[Students will complete a handout and will write the difference between a rock and a mineral … with the following sentence frame: The _____ can be classified as (a rock) or (minerals) because _____.]

Another strategy selected by preservice bilingual teachers was modeling. Effective modeling for emergent bilinguals involves using language as procedures are demonstrated to maximize content learning and language development. Think-alouds, in which teachers model by verbalizing their thinking, are particularly beneficial for emergent bilinguals (Rea & Mercuri, 2006). Participants understood that it is important for teachers to show emergent bilinguals exactly what they are expected to do: "*La maestra modelará para que así los estudiantes vean lo que la maestra hace y lo que ellos deberán de hacer paso por paso.*" [The teacher will model so that students can see what the teacher does and what they are supposed to do step-by-step.]

The use of different grouping configurations was another strategy employed by preservice bilingual students in their lessons. They realized the numerous benefits that collaborative work has for emergent bilingual students as they are learning content. One of those benefits is language development.

Los estudiantes también fueron agrupados heterogéneamente, por niveles de lenguaje y habilidades, durante una actividad para que se apoyaran y aprendieran entre ellos mismos. Todos los integrantes del grupo tendrán diferentes niveles de lenguaje permitiendo al estudiante modelar el inglés a los demás integrantes para crear la lista de maneras de ahorrar.

[Students were grouped heterogeneously by language and ability levels during an activity to support each other and learn from each other. All group members would have different language levels allowing students to model English for other members to create the list on ways to save money.]

Participants also considered the use of students' first language in content lessons an important strategy to make content instruction comprehensible.

Many of them incorporated the first language through the Preview-View-Review strategy, which was well explained by one preservice bilingual teacher:

> *La lengua materna y la segunda lengua son utilizadas durante esta lección ya que la maestra empieza la lección usando la primera lengua ya que sirve como introducción o foco para motivar a los estudiantes. Luego, la maestra enseña el contenido de la lección en la segunda lengua y los estudiantes pueden entender ya que tuvieron una vista previa del contenido en su primera lengua. Finalmente, la maestra va a repasar lo que han aprendido durante la lección en su lengua maternal.*

> [The mother tongue and the second language are used during this lesson since the teacher begins the lesson using the first language because it serves as an introduction or focus to motivate the students. Then, the teacher teaches the content of the lesson in the second language and the students can understand because they had a preview of the content in their first language. Finally, the teacher reviews what they have learned during the lesson in their mother tongue.]

As can be noted, the Preview-View-Review strategy makes use of translanguaging in the bilingual classroom by integrating both languages into the lesson. Other translanguaging practices were also planned by preservice bilingual teachers: "*El L1 se utiliza ya que la maestra les da la opción de que hagan sus reportes en ingles o en español y también les pone como referencias libros en ambos idiomas.*" [The first language is used because the teacher gives them the option of making their reports in English or Spanish and also uses reference books in both languages.]

Making connections between new and previously learned material was another strategy that preservice bilingual teachers incorporated into their lessons. Egbert and Ernst-Slavit (2010) explain that "it is important to make academic and personal connections to the lesson objectives ..." (p. 72). Activating prior knowledge helps emergent bilinguals anchor the understanding of new concepts. In addition, students can use the language available to them to express what they know. Many participants opted for including a KWL chart in which the teacher begins the lesson by recording what students already know about the topic in the K column. The teacher then records what students want to learn in the W column, and after the lesson she records what students learned in the L column. Another example of how preservice bilingual teachers activated students' background knowledge follows: "*La maestra usara experiencias previas de los estudiantes con animales y sus crias, como visitas al zoológico.*" [The teacher will use students' previous experiences with animals and their young such as visits to the zoo.] As can be seen in the examples provided, participants combined the use of a variety of strategies in their lessons' activities as emergent bilinguals benefit from different forms of scaffolding within one lesson.

In summary, preservice bilingual teachers were able to design instruction to teach language through content. It was evident that participants emphasized vocabulary development and the incorporation of scaffolding strategies into their lessons to support emergent bilingual students in their content and language development. Nevertheless, participants struggled writing language objectives that integrated the four language domains – listening, speaking, reading, and writing – and the levels of academic language – text, sentence, and word. Despite their struggles with language objectives, the majority of participants were able to integrate different strategies that support language development into their lessons.

Academic Spanish in a Bilingual Content Methods Course

The second question explored the role of academic language in a content methods course taught in Spanish for preservice bilingual teachers. The analysis of preservice bilingual teachers' writing in Spanish showed that they made good attempts at writing academically, but it was also evident from their writing that many of them struggled with standard Spanish. As it was mentioned in the review of the literature section, academic language is "the special language used in school and the professions" (Krashen & Brown, 2007, p. 1). Preservice bilingual teachers used the language of school in their lessons as they wrote how they would deliver and explain content knowledge to emergent bilinguals in Spanish. However, standard language refers to the "norm against which usage is measured" (Díaz-Rico, 2008, p. 344). Although standard language norms are arbitrary, "grammar and usage books usually prescribe correct or standard language" (Díaz-Rico, 2008, p. 344). Participants' lessons revealed that their written Spanish did not always conform to the norm. After analyzing participants' lessons written in Spanish, three themes were identified: preservice bilingual teachers' efforts in using academic language in Spanish, preservice bilingual teachers' struggles with standard Spanish writing, and translanguaging.

Preservice bilingual teachers' efforts in using academic Spanish. Lesson planning required participants to use academic Spanish as they wrote about the content they would teach and the instructional strategies they would use. It is important to note that our study did not set out to measure participants' level of proficiency in academic writing in Spanish but to understand how preservice bilingual students used academic writing in Spanish to plan lessons focused on teaching language through content. In doing so, we identified that preservice bilingual teachers made great efforts to write academically in Spanish to plan academic content instruction. The following example demonstrates how one preservice teacher used academic Spanish as she explained science concepts.

> *La maestra les explicará que la presión atmosférica es el resultado del peso de pequeñas partículas de aire que empujan hacia abajo en un área. Aunque son invisibles a simple vista, (o sea, son microscópicas), ocupan un espacio y tienen peso.*

> [The teacher will explain that atmospheric pressure is the result of the weight of small particles of air that push downward in an area. Although they are invisible to the eye, (that is, they are microscopic), they occupy space and have weight.]

The previous example shows how this preservice bilingual teacher used specific academic terms such as *atmospheric pressure*, *particles*, and *microscopic*, which are scientific terms that are not often used in conversations outside of the science context. In addition, the last sentence in the example is a complex sentence with a dependent clause, and an independent clause. Moreover, academic language is more closely aligned with written text as opposed to spoken text as explained by Biber (as cited in Freeman & Freeman, 2009). An analysis of the example above using Biber's ideas, shows that the short excerpt includes little personal involvement and is written in a reported style, which are characteristics that align text to academic, and not conversational language.

The following example shows how a preservice bilingual teacher used academic language to explain the instructional sequence of her lesson:

> *La maestra pide a los alumnos que tomen su circulo y ella toma su circulo para señalar las características; la circunferencia es el conjunto de todos los puntos de un plano que están a una distancia fija de un centro, el diámetro empieza en un punto de la circunferencia, pasa por el centro y termina del otro lado de la circunferencia, el radio es la distancia del centro al borde. Se pide que los alumnos identifiquen cada parte del circulo y escriban su definición.*

> [The teacher asks the students to take their circle and she takes her circle to point out the characteristics. The circumference is the set of all points in a plane that are at a set distance from a center. The diameter starts at a point on the circumference, goes through the center, and ends at the other side of the circumference. The radius is the distance from the center to the edge. Students are asked to identify each part of the circle and to write their definition.]

This example also uses very specific mathematical vocabulary such as *radius* and *circumference*. In addition, the last sentence uses the passive voice which is more impersonal and uses a reported style, characteristics of academic language.

Preservice bilingual teachers' struggles with standard Spanish. As can be seen throughout the examples provided in this chapter, preservice bilingual teachers struggled with standard writing in Spanish. As was expected, they often used a variety of Spanish that is common in the community, which does not always conform to the norm. Some participants struggled with contractions. For example, it was common for participants to write *de el* [of the] instead of the standard form *del* [of the] or *a el* [to the] instead of the standard form *al* [to the]. This may have been done in an attempt to write formally, but resulted in a non-standard use of Spanish. For instance, in English, it is expected to minimize the use of contractions in formal writing. That is, students are expected to write *cannot* as opposed to *can't*. However, the contractions *del* and *al* are the standard in Spanish and should be used in formal writing as well as in conversation.

Preservice bilingual teachers also struggled with gender agreement between articles and nouns. For example, participants would write *la aula* [the classroom − feminine] instead of *el aula* [the classroom − masculine], *las mapas* [the maps − feminine] instead of *los mapas* [the maps − masculine], *la tema* [the theme − feminine] instead of *el tema* [the theme − masculine], and *la orden* [the order − feminine] instead of *el orden* [the order − masculine]. The last example is particularly complex because changing the gender of the noun changes its meaning. *La orden* [the order − feminine] can refer to an order as in a request or command. *El orden* [the order − masculine] refers to the order as in the arrangement or sequence of items. The other three examples (*aula, mapa,* and *tema*) are commonly mistaken for feminine nouns in the variety of Spanish that is spoken in the community where this study took place because they end with the letter *a,* and most nouns that end with *a* are feminine, but these are exceptions.

Another salient struggle with standard Spanish displayed by preservice bilingual teachers was the irregular use of conjunctions. In standard Spanish, the conjunction *y* [and] changes to *e* [and] when the following word begins with the letter *i.* Many participants did not apply this rule as they wrote *construir y interpretar* [build and interpret] instead of the standard *construir e interpretar* [build and interpret], or *español y inglés* [Spanish and English] instead of the standard *español e inglés* [Spanish and English].

All three of these common non-standard uses are often found in the Spanish the preservice teachers spoke in their communities. Nevertheless, we contend the fact that some aspects of preservice bilingual teachers' writing did not conform to the norm, was not an impediment for them to move toward more academic forms of writing by including content terminology, complex sentences, and a reported and impersonal style.

Translanguaging. As is common in bilingual communities, the preservice bilingual teachers who participated in this study engaged in dynamic bilingual discourse practices. They maximized their linguistic resources and regularly engaged in translanguaging. Participants often used English words and phrases that are common in the discourse of education in the United States such as *foldables, whole group, t-chart, checklist,* or *handout* when writing their lesson plans. They did so because they had discussed in class that this was an acceptable practice that facilitated meaning making, especially when they encountered terms that do not have an easy, one-word Spanish translation. For example, the concept of what a *foldable* is would have to be explained in Spanish using several sentences. It is important to point out that in most cases, participants enclosed the English words in quotation marks, which shows that they were well aware of how they were translanguaging. However, on a few occasions, participants did not use quotation marks for the English words or phrases. One example is, *"Ponga todos los objetos en una bolsa. Shake it up! Describa cómo ..."* [Put all objects in a bag. Shake it up! Describe how ...]. This may indicate that this preservice bilingual teacher did not realize she was using both English and Spanish, but just displayed her usual translanguaging in her writing. Another participant translanguaged writing the list of materials for one of her lessons as follows: "Materiales: colores, marcadores, construction paper, tijeras, pegamento, papel de 'bulletin board', 'posterboards'." [Materials: colors, markers, construction paper, scissors, glue, paper for the bulletin board, posterboards.] The analysis of bilingual preservice teachers' lessons displayed their ability to maximize their linguistic repertoires to convey meaning more clearly in the context of planning bilingual instruction to emergent bilingual students.

Conclusions and Practical Implications

When teacher educators are concerned with improving their practice and providing preservice teachers with quality experiences that will help them become effective educators, it is important to analyze the artifacts produced by their students and reflect on the implications of the findings. In the case of preservice bilingual teachers, the concern is two-fold because they not only need to acquire knowledge of content and pedagogy, but they need to develop the ability to impart such knowledge in two languages. For that reason, in this chapter we focused on analyzing bilingual preservice teachers' planning of instruction in terms of their understanding of effective practices to teach content to emergent bilingual students and their use of Spanish to convey such understandings.

Based on our experience as teacher educators who have worked with preservice bilingual teachers in this program for several years, we understand that participants' lesson planning was not only a direct result of the instruction they received in this course, but it was influenced by a number of factors. We must acknowledge that the broader context of participants' schooling experiences, the counter examples they see in schools, and the inherent difficulties of constructing knowledge in Spanish about content in English while developing the academic language, all played a role in the outcomes. Based on our interpretation of the findings and drawing from García and Kleifgen's (2010) concept of dynamic bilingualism, as well as on research on bilingual teacher preparation (Clark & Flores, 2001; De Jong & Harper, 2005; Menken & Antunez, 2001), we propose a dynamic bilingual curriculum for bilingual teacher preparation programs that

- Incorporates sustained opportunities across coursework for preservice bilingual teachers to strengthen their understanding of content teaching and academic language development for emergent bilinguals.
- Values preservice bilingual teachers' language varieties, develops metalinguistic awareness as they become aware of different language varieties, and fosters the ability to navigate between language registers for teaching and learning.
- Values translanguaging as a pedagogical strategy that provides access to content and language development.

Content Teaching and Academic Language Development for Emergent Bilinguals

The findings discussed show that preservice bilingual teachers were more successful writing content objectives than language objectives for their lessons. Participants struggled with complex concepts, such as writing language objectives at the text and sentence level while demonstrating greater ease writing language objectives at the word level. After receiving sustained scaffolding such as analysis of examples, small group discussion, and feedback on drafts of their lessons, preservice bilingual teachers were able to integrate the four dimensions of language (listening, speaking, reading, and writing) into their language objectives. Nevertheless, our findings show that achieving mastery in developing language objectives requires more than a semester long course.

De Jong and Harper (2005) emphasize the importance of preservice teachers becoming competent in the identification of language objectives. Based on the performance of our preservice bilingual teachers, we argue that teacher educators should provide multiple opportunities for students to access the complexities of creating language objectives that address both the language dimensions and the levels of academic language. Preservice bilingual teachers would benefit from sustained opportunities to grapple with such complex concepts during a course and across courses throughout their bilingual teacher preparation program.

Our findings also showed that preservice bilingual teachers focused on vocabulary as a key aspect of academic language development for emergent bilingual students when designing lesson activities even though a wide range of strategies involving work at the sentence and text level were discussed in class, modeled by the instructor, demonstrated in small group work, and available in the readings. Bilingual teacher preparation programs must work on a conceptualization of academic language that goes beyond teaching vocabulary. This is an important tension in teacher preparation given the prevalence of this narrower view of academic language, especially in schools. Menken and Antunez (2001) emphasize that bilingual preservice teachers need to develop a better understanding of language development and linguistics. Moreover, they must understand the complexities of academic language, which include not only vocabulary, but also grammar, syntax structures, and discourse elements (Egbert & Ernst-Slavit, 2010; Scarcella, 2003; Zwiers, 2008). Therefore, additional time must be devoted and instructional strategies integrated in bilingual teacher preparation programs to the exploration of academic language in its three levels providing multiple opportunities for preservice bilingual teachers to engage in discussions and analysis of academic texts. Ideally, bilingual teacher preparation programs should devote a particular course for bilingual teachers where academic Spanish across the content areas is covered in depth coupled with additional opportunities for extending their understanding of academic language development for emergent bilinguals across other required coursework.

Valuing Language Varieties and Fostering Metalinguistic Awareness

In terms of the role of academic language in a bilingual content methods course, our findings show that preservice bilingual teachers used their linguistic resources to express their ideas for instruction. Participants used academic Spanish both to explain academic concepts and to describe instructional procedures. In doing so participants integrated ways of using Spanish common in their community, which in some instances are considered non-standard forms of Spanish. Our interpretation of the findings afforded two important lessons as teacher educators who also engage in teaching language through content: (a) the importance of providing opportunities for preservice bilingual teachers to reflect on the role of academic language and (b) the importance of providing students with opportunities to reflect on their own uses of language as they learn the course's content.

Similar to Clark and Flores' (2001) recommendation that preservice bilingual teachers engage in critical reflections in which they explore their own cultural past, teacher educators can incorporate self-monitoring and self-reflection of preservice bilingual teachers' trajectory in regards to language development. Moreover, preservice bilingual teachers need opportunities to reflect on the role of academic Spanish in teaching and learning while still valuing the varieties of Spanish spoken in the community. Opportunities for preservice bilingual teachers to navigate across language varieties as required in social and academic contexts and reflect on such language uses would strengthen their metalinguistic awareness. That is, they would develop an "... understanding of how language works and how it changes and adapts in different circumstances" (Beeman & Urow, 2012, p. 4). We contend that metalinguistic awareness of language varieties would contribute to preservice bilingual teachers taking ownership of their language development and professional growth as bilingual educators.

Translanguaging as a Pedagogical Strategy for Content and Language Development

Preservice bilingual teachers were successful in maximizing their bilingual skills as they translanguaged and navigated the discourse of education in both English and Spanish. As García (2011) explains, "bilinguals adapt their language practices to the particular communicative situation in which they find themselves in order to optimize communication ..." (p. 2). For example, participants resorted to English in their lesson plans when referring to concepts or terms with which they were not familiar in Spanish. As teacher educators, we need to value all the linguistic resources that students bring to the classroom. Coursework and the curriculum need to reflect the translanguaging practices that occur naturally in the students' contexts and will be present in their future bilingual classrooms. Preservice bilingual teachers' use of both languages in their lessons is not a limitation, but a result of bilingualism (García, 2011). Teacher educators should encourage preservice bilingual teachers to engage in ongoing self-reflections of their own translanguaging to determine how it helps them as a resource for knowledge construction.

Moreover, bilingual teacher preparation programs should select materials and employ instructional strategies in English and Spanish that would bridge both languages (Beeman & Urow, 2012) and help foster the development of academic language as preservice bilingual teachers acquire knowledge of content and pedagogy. "Translanguaging as a pedagogical strategy offers more direct ways to teach rigorous content, at the same time that academic uses of language are developed" (García, 2011, p. 2). Ultimately, we propose a dynamic bilingualism approach to bilingual teacher preparation programs enacting the principles of translanguaging both in instruction and curriculum design.

Our findings revealed that preservice bilingual teachers possess valuable linguistic resources that should be emphasized and used to deepen their understanding of how to effectively teach language through content to emergent bilinguals. Our interpretation of the findings suggests that the use of multiple language varieties and translanguaging are important pedagogical strategies that have the potential to build bilingual teacher capacity. In addition, the results of our study made evident that sufficient time is needed for preservice bilingual teachers to reach deeper understanding of complex teaching concepts including the development of language objectives and the use of translanguaging. Therefore, bilingual teacher education programs should provide sustained support for bilingual teacher candidates to develop the necessary knowledge and skills to become effective teachers of emergent bilinguals.

References

Achugar, M. (2008). Counter-hegemonic language practices and ideologies: Creating a new space and value for Spanish in southwest Texas. *Spanish in Context, 5*(1), 1–19.
Barnwell, D. (2008). The status of Spanish in the United States. *Language, Culture and Curriculum, 21*(3), 235–243.

Batalova, J., & McHugh, M. (2010). *Top languages spoken by English language learners nationally and by state* [Migration Policy Institute]. Retrieved from http://www. migrationpolicy.org/research/top-languages-spoken-english-language-learners-nationally-and-state

Beeman, K., & Urow, C. (2012). *Teaching for biliteracy. Strengthening bridges between languages.* Philadelphia, PA: Caslon, Inc.

Capella-Santana, N. (2003). Voices of teacher candidates: Positive changes in multicultural attitudes and knowledge. *The Journal of Educational Research, 96*(3), 182–190.

Celic, C., & Seltzer, K. (2011). *Translanguaging: A CUNY-NYSIEB guide for educators.* New York, NY: CUNY-NYSIEB. Retrieved from www.cuny-nysieb.org

Clark, E. R., & Flores, B. B. (2001). Who am I? The social construction of ethnic identity and self-perceptions in Latino preservice teachers. *The Urban Review, 33*(2), 69–86.

Colombi, M. C. (1996). Spanish language: Variations across Latino groups. In R. Chabrán & R. Chabrán (Eds.), *The Latino encyclopedia* (pp. 1548–1556). New York, NY: Marshall Cavendish Corporation.

Creese, A., & Blackledge, A. (2010). Translanguaging in the bilingual classroom: A pedagogy for learning and teaching? *The Modern Language Journal, 94*, 103–115.

Cummins, J. (2007). Rethinking monolingual instructional strategies in multilingual classrooms. *Revue Canadienne de Linguistique Appliquee.* [Canadian Journal of Applied Linguistics.], *10*(2), 221–240.

Cummins, J. (2008). BICS and CALP: Empirical and theoretical status of the distinction. In B. Street & N. H. Hornberger (Eds.), *Encyclopedia of language and education* (2nd ed., Vol. 2, pp. 71–83). Literacy. New York, NY: Springer Science, Business Media LLC.

Darling-Hammond, L. (2006). *Powerful teacher education: Lessons from exemplary programs.* San Francisco, CA: Jossey-Bass.

Davis, V. (n.d.). *How good is good enough: Assessing the Spanish communications abilities of bilingual teachers.* Retrieved from http://images.pearsonassessments.com/images/NES_Publications/1995_09Davis_355_1.pdf

De Jong, E. J., & Harper, C. A. (2005). Preparing mainstream teachers for English-language learners: Is being a good teacher good enough? *Teacher Education Quarterly, 32*(2), 101–124.

Díaz-Rico, L. T. (2008). *Strategies for teaching English learners.* Boston, MA: Pearson.

Egbert, J., & Ernst-Slavit, G. (2010). *Access to academics: Planning instruction for K-12 classrooms with ELLs.* Boston, MA: Pearson.

Ek, L. D., & Sánchez, P. (2008). *Latina/o preservice bilingual teachers in Texas: Narratives of bilingualism and biliteracy.* In *Raising voices: U.S. Latin@s for linguistic, educational and political rights.* Symposium conducted at the 8º Congreso de Lingüística General. Madrid, Spain.

Freeman, D. E., & Freeman, Y. S. (2007). *English language learners: The essential guide.* New York, NY: Scholastic.

Freeman, D. E., & Freeman, Y. S. (2008). Enseñanza de lenguas a través de contenido académico. *Revista Educación y Pedagogía, 20*(51), 97–110.

Freeman, Y. S., & Freeman, D. E. (2009). *Academic language for English language learners and struggling readers: How to help students succeed across content areas.* Portsmouth, NH: Heinemann.

García, O. (2011). Theorizing translanguaging for educators. In C. Celic & K. Seltzer (Eds.), *Translanguaging: A CUNY-NYSIEB guide for educators* (pp. 1–6). New York, NY: CUNY-NYSIEB.

García, O., & Kleifgen, J. A. (2010). *Emergent bilinguals. Policies, programs, and practices for English language learners.* New York, NY: Teachers College Press.

Gee, J. P. (1992). Reading. *Journal of Urban and Cultural Studies, 2*(2), 65−77.

Gottlieb, M., & Ernst-Slavit, G. (Eds.). (2013). *Academic language in diverse classrooms: Promoting content and language learning: Mathematics, grades K-2.* Thousand Oaks, CA: Corwin Press.

Guerrero, M. D. (2003a). Acquiring and participating in the use of academic Spanish: Four novice Latina bilingual education teachers' stories. *Journal of Latinos and Education, 2*(3), 159−181.

Guerrero, M. D. (2003b). We have correct English teachers. Why can't we have correct Spanish teachers? It's not acceptable. *Qualitative Studies in Education, 16*(5), 647−668.

Hart, J. E., & Lee, O. (2003). Teacher professional development to improve the science and literacy achievement of English language learners. *Bilingual Research Journal, 27*(3), 475−501.

Janzen, J. (2008). Teaching English language learners in the content areas. *Review of Educational Research, 78*(4), 1010−1038. doi:10.3102/0034654308325580

Krashen, S., & Brown, C. L. (2007). What is academic language proficiency? *Singapore Tertiary English Teachers Society.* Retrieved from http://www.sdkrashen.com/content/articles/krashen_brown_alp.pdf

Lincoln, Y. S., & Guba, E. G. (1985). *Naturalistic inquiry.* Newbury Park, CA: Sage Publications.

Lopez-Robertson, J. (2012). Esta página me recordó: Young Latinas using personal life stories as tools for meaning-making. *Bilingual Research Journal, 35*(2), 217−233.

Menken, K., & Antunez, B. (2001). *An overview of the preparation and certification of teachers working with limited English proficient (LEP) students.* Washington, DC: US Department of Education. Office of Bilingual Education and Minority Languages Affair. Retrieved from ERIC database. ED455231.

Merriam, S. B. (1998). *Qualitative research and case study applications in education.* San Francisco, CA: Jossey-Bass Publishers.

Musanti, S. I., & Celedón-Pattichis, S. (2012). They need to know they can do math reaching for equity through the native language in mathematics instruction with Spanish speaking students. *Journal of Bilingual Education Research & Instruction, 14*(1), 80−94.

Perkins, I., & Flores, A. (2002). Mathematical notations and procedures of recent immigrant students. *Mathematics Teaching in the Middle School, 7*(6), 346−351.

Phillips, K. R., & Cañas, J. (2004). *Business cycle coordination along the Texas−Mexico border.* Research Department Working Paper No. 0502. Federal Reserve Bank of Dallas.

Rea, D., & Mercuri, S. (2006). Research-based strategies for English language learners. *How to reach goals and meet standards.* Portsmouth, NH: Heinemann.

Rodríguez, A. D. (2007). Prospective bilingual teachers' perceptions of the importance of their heritage language. *Heritage Language Journal, 5*(1), 172−187.

Scarcella, R. (2003). *Accelerating academic English: A focus on English language learners.* Oakland, CA: Regents of the University of California.

Schleppegrell, M., & de Oliveira, L. (2006). An integrated language and content approach for history teachers. *Journal of English for Academic Purposes, 5*, 254−268.

Schneider, B., Martinez, S., & Owens, A. (2006). Barriers to educational opportunities for Hispanics in the United States. In M. Tienda & F. Mitchell (Eds.), *Hispanics and the future of America* (pp. 179−227). Committee on Population, Division of Behavioral and Social Sciences and Education. Washington, DC: The National Academies Press.

Sheets, R. H., Flores, B. B., & Clark, E. R. (2011). Educar para transformar. A bilingual education teacher preparation model. In B. B. Flores, E. R. Clark, & R. Hernández-Sheets (Eds.), *Teacher preparation for bilingual student populations: Educar para transformar* (pp. 9–24). New York, NY: Routledge.

Smith, H., Sánchez, P., Ek, L. D., & Machado-Casas, M. (2011). From linguistic imperialism to linguistic conscientización: Learning from heritage language speakers. In D. Schwarzer, M. Petrón, & C. Luke (Eds.), *Research informing practice – practice informing research: Innovative teaching methodologies for world language teachers* (pp. 177–198). Charlotte, NC: Information Age Publishing, Inc.

Stoller, F. (2004). Content-based instruction: Perspectives on curriculum planning. *Annual Review of Applied Linguistics, 24*, 261–283.

Strauss, A., & Corbin, J. (1998). *Basics of qualitative research: Techniques and procedures for developing grounded theory* (2nd ed.). Thousand Oaks, CA: Sage Publications.

Sutterby, J. A., Ayala, J., & Murillo, S. (2005). El sendero torcido al español [The twisted path to Spanish]: The development of bilingual teachers' Spanish-Language proficiency. *Bilingual Research Journal, 29*(2), 435–501.

Texas Education Agency. (2012–2013). *ELL student reports by language and grade: PEIMS data 2012–2013*. Retrieved from http://ritter.tea.state.tx.us/cgi/sas/broker

The Texas Center for Border and Transnational Studies. (2010). *Report*. Brownsville, TX: University of Texas at Brownsville.

Walqui, A. (2006). Scaffolding instruction for English language learners: A conceptual framework. *The International Journal of Bilingual Education and Bilingualism, 9*(2), 159–180.

Zwiers, J. (2008). *Building academic language: Essential practices for content classrooms*. San Francisco, CA: Jossey-Bass.

CHAPTER 9

A SELF-STUDY OF TEACHER EDUCATOR PRACTICE: STRATEGIES AND ACTIVITIES TO USE WITH AUTHENTIC TEXTS

Mary Soto

Abstract

This chapter discusses the findings of a self-study of teacher education practices (S-STEP) conducted to investigate the ways the author supported teacher candidates, and first year teachers who were teaching emergent bilinguals in planning reading and writing activities around authentic texts. The purpose of the study was to determine in what ways the researcher supported the candidates' planning, in what ways the teacher candidates implemented the activities, and how the self-study informed the researcher as a teacher educator. The study looked at how the teacher candidates and first year teachers implemented the activities with their own students. Teacher candidates were supported by the researcher through a methodology class, class observations, informal meetings, and emails and text messaging. The teacher candidates and first year teachers reported that all of the activities and strategies that they learned from the researcher and then implemented with their own

Research on Preparing Preservice Teachers to Work Effectively with Emergent Bilinguals
Advances in Research on Teaching, Volume 21, 233–255
ISSN: 1479-3687/doi:10.1108/S1479-368720140000021008

students were effective. Both the teacher candidates and the first year teachers modified many of the strategies in order to meet the needs of their emergent bilingual students. Through this self-study investigation of how students used and modified the strategies and activities, the researcher gained valuable information that will inform work with future students. She will introduce fewer strategies and activities and explain how each one can be used to teach different content. In further study, the researcher will provide student teachers with a rubric to evaluate the effectiveness of each strategy or activity with different types of students.

Keywords: Secondary emergent bilinguals; authentic literature; thematic units; ELL strategies; preservice teachers

Introduction

At a large urban high school, 16 students sit quietly in their ELD (English Language Development) class. On each student's desk is a worksheet of vocabulary words that they have been asked to define and use to write sentences. Some students work quietly on their worksheet while others stare at the walls. One student nods off to sleep. The teacher sits at her desk correcting worksheets from the previous day.

When I first began working with teacher candidates and observing the classrooms where they were placed, I was surprised to see that the above scenario was typical. It was a great contrast from my own experience of teaching ELD (English Language Development) for over 16 years. In the classes I taught, students read and discussed authentic texts, created projects, wrote fiction and non-fiction, and worked collaboratively. The atmosphere of the class was lively and student centered. Students were motivated and engaged learners.

As I observed the ELD class placements my student teachers were in, I began to reflect on my own practice and draw both on what I knew about second language acquisition and what had worked for me as an ELD teacher. I decided to investigate whether the strategies and support I provided future teachers working with secondary emergent bilinguals were effective. Specifically, I examined the ways I was able to best support them as they engaged students in activities based on authentic texts. In addition, I was also interested in learning whether they continued using authentic texts and the strategies I taught them once they left the teacher education program and began teaching in their own classrooms. This chapter reports the results of my self-study of teacher education practice (S-STEP) (Pinnegar & Hamilton, 2011; Pinnegar, Hamilton, & Fitzgerald, 2010).

Purpose

As I reflected on the classrooms where my student teachers had been placed and on the theory and research on second language acquisition that I was sharing with student teachers in their education classes, I saw the disconnect between what was known to be good research-based practice and what the student teachers were observing. This led me to this self-study based on the five students I taught. I wished to answer the following questions:

1. In what ways did I support teacher candidates in planning reading and writing activities around authentic texts?
2. In what ways did teacher candidates and first year teachers implement these activities with their students?
3. How did this self-study inform me as a teacher educator?

Significance

In order to be successful in high school, adolescent emergent bilinguals need literacy skills (Daniels & Zemelman, 2004). Short and Fitzsimmons (2007) found that adolescent emergent bilinguals in grades 6–12 have not developed the skills necessary for academic success. The researchers believe that if these learners are provided with consistent, effective programs and materials, they can experience school success. Unfortunately, emergent bilinguals are usually provided with both programs and materials that are not effective (Short & Fitzsimmons, 2007).

Research on education and achievement has shown that schools and communities can change the course of academic achievement for emergent bilinguals (Gándara & Contreras, 2009). One of the greatest needs involves recruiting and preparing extraordinary teachers. However, many teachers are not adequately prepared to work with language minority students. They do not have the support, or strategies necessary to meet the needs of these students (García, Kleifgen, & Flachi, 2008; Olsen, 2010). Curriculum planning that focuses on the needs of emergent bilinguals is important for their academic success.

This S-STEP study was important to me as a teacher educator because I wanted to be certain that what I believed was critical in my teaching of future teachers was, in fact, evident in what my students were able to implement in both their student teaching practices and in their later teaching assignments.

Literature Review

Olsen (2010), Gándara and Contreras (2009), García et al. (2008) and others have found that many teachers are not prepared to work with adolescent emergent bilinguals. In most cases, they do not have the support or strategies necessary to meet their needs. However, when emergent bilinguals are provided with consistent effective learning opportunities, they can succeed academically (Daniels & Zemelman, 2004; Short & Fitzsimmons, 2007). A review of the approaches and strategies suggested by researchers for emergent bilinguals, the importance of engagement, and the type of reading instruction and materials that are appropriate create a picture of what adolescent emergent bilinguals need for academic success.

Approaches and Strategies for English Learners

Thomas and Collier (2002) and Freeman and Freeman (2002) describe current approaches appropriate for the academic success of English learners including cooperative learning, thematic units, using authentic texts, and drawing on students' interest and backgrounds. They go on to explain that teachers should scaffold the instruction by using a variety of strategies such as visuals, gestures, primary language support, and the use of visuals with the students.

Short and Fitzsimmons (2007) found that in order for emergent bilinguals to catch up to their English-speaking peers, teachers need to use research-based instructional strategies in their lessons. Horwitz et al. (2009) found that in successful schools for emergent bilinguals, there was comprehensive planning and adoption of language-development strategies for emergent bilinguals with a particular emphasis on improving reading and literacy for all students.

Adolescents who engage in reading and writing on a regular basis are able to develop a robust vocabulary.

Engagement. Guthrie and Davis (2003) and Meltzer and Hamann (2005) found that struggling readers are especially unmotivated. They are more likely to have low confidence in their reading. They often tend to feel socially marginalized, and be lower in intrinsic motivation and self-efficacy for reading. Guthrie and Davis (2003) found that even high achieving students who, when confronted with content they were not interested in, displayed weak cognitive strategies and low motivation. Therefore, the key to engagement is motivation. Moje, Overby, Tysvaer, and Morris (2008) state that "it is essential that educators determine how to build on what motivates adolescents' literary practices in order to promote the building of their social selves and improve their academic outcomes" (p. 107).

Reading materials and instruction. Ivey and Broaddus (2007) found that having reading material that was at the students' level was just as important as having reading material that was of high interest. Daniels and Zemelman (2004) support these conclusions as they argue that in schools, textbooks are overused. The authors explain that there are several reasons why textbooks are ineffective for all students. After an analysis of several textbooks from different subject matters and different grade levels, Daniels and Zemelman concluded that textbooks are superficial, exceedingly hard to read, badly designed, authoritarian, often inaccurate, too expensive, and finally, not written keeping students in mind. In other words, the texts are too difficult and do not draw on students' background and interests. Instead of relying exclusively on these ineffective materials, educators need to use culturally relevant texts (Ebe, 2012) and emphasize literacy for school success.

Krashen (2004) makes a case for the importance of reading for all students. He argues that reading helps students' cognitive development and critical thinking skills. Krashen presents research showing that reading is the key to helping students gain access to advanced levels of literacy. If educators understand the level of literacy that students ultimately need for school success and expose them to a variety of texts with increasing levels of difficulty, then more students' will experience academic success.

Meltzer and Hamann (2005) suggest instructional practices that facilitate student engagement in literacy. Three key practices include making connections with student's lives, creating responsive classrooms in which students are acknowledged, have voice, and are given choices, and having students interact with each other about text and with text.

García and Godina (2004) discuss some basic characteristics of literacy approaches that can aid in the academic success of adolescent emergent bilinguals. They argue for process literacy approaches. Some of the basic characteristics of process literacy approaches include:

> the use of trade books, writing from multiple drafts, integrating reading and writing, peer interactions, a student centered curriculum, giving students choice for reading and writing, inquiry based projects, and open-ended activities in which students are encouraged to explore the various meanings of texts (p. 310).

Process literary approaches, combined with strategy instruction and explicit instruction on topics students are not familiar with, are a key to engaging emergent bilinguals in literacy and giving them access to academic success (García & Godina, 2004).

Teaching the Strategies

In this study, I looked at how the support and strategies I gave my teacher candidates played a role in their teaching of emergent bilinguals. I was specifically interested in exploring how the support and strategies I gave them helped them develop effective reading and writing activities around authentic texts as suggested by the research. I also wanted to know whether students who graduated and became first year teachers continued implementing these reading and writing strategies in their own classrooms.

Table 1 lists the descriptions of the strategies that participants in the study learned about in my teacher education classes, and that were used by student teachers and/or first year teachers with their own students:

Methodology

Since I was investigating how my instruction and support affected the teaching practices of my students, I conducted what Pinnegar and Hamilton (2009) and Pinnegar et al. (2010) refer to as a S-STEP. In S-STEP investigations, the researcher collects and analyzes observational data. S-STEP findings might be referred to as "understandings, assertions for action" (p. 2). In some cases, the research leaves the researcher with more questions or wonderings. In S-STEP research, researchers not only

Table 1. Activities and Strategies.

Activity/Strategy	Description
Positive/negative graph	Students place events from something they have read onto a timeline graph and rank events according to how positive or negative they think they are.
I am poem	Students use a poetry template to fill in information about a character from a story.
Story board	Students create a storyboard of a series of events from a text.
Three scenario chart	Students write and draw about different scenarios that all relate to a theme.
Frontloading vocabulary	The teacher introduces students to potentially challenging vocabulary from a text before they read through a project. For example, they could have the students write the words, translate them into their native language, and draw a picture to represent them.
Charter analysis letter	Students write a letter to a character for the novel or write a letter from one character to another.
It says/I say	Students pick sections of a text that they like or find interesting. They share their section and then give their opinion about what it says.
Character graphic organizer	Students use a graphic organizer to keep track of different traits of the characters in the text.
Mandala	Students fill in different parts of a circle graphic organizer to show different aspects of a text, such as setting, character, and conflict.
Flipbook	Students create small booklets that they use to organize key concepts from a reading.
Authentic Venn diagram	Students compare and contrast themes and or story elements from different texts. Instead of the traditional circles, students draw a shape of something that represents the story.
Inside–outside circle	Students get into circles that face each other. They speak about a topic to the person in front of them. Every few minutes the inside circle rotates and students have a new partner.
Concept map	Students complete a graphic organizer that represents different concepts from a story.
How to	Students write about the process of doing something using a variety of signal words. Students add illustrations.
Story order sorting	Students are given strips of paper with events from a story they are reading. They put the story events in order.
Movie poster	Students create a movie poster based on a book they are reading. They include story elements, themes, and quotes from the book on their poster.
Concrete poem	Students pick out important words from a reading and then write the words in the shape of something that relates to the story.
Figurative language drawings	Students draw the literal meaning of figurative language and then write about what it means figuratively.
Textual evidence	Students use textual evidence to support their answers and opinions about a story they are reading.
Facebook project	Students create a Facebook page for a character they are reading about.

collect data based on their current experiences working with teacher candidates, but also develop recollections of their own experiences as teachers.

Pinnegar and Hamilton (2009) present an inquiry cycle that researchers engaged in S-STEP research tend to follow. S-STEP researchers ask questions such as: What am I interested in exploring? How could I explore these concerns and issues? Who are the most appropriate participants? What work in teacher education research (or other research fields) will guide my inquiry?

According to Pinnegar and Hamilton (2009) in S-STEP research the researchers decide on elements of a situation that they want to focus on in order to better understand their own practice. Data collected and participants involved vary from study to study. When considering the context of a study, Pinnegar and Hamilton argue that researchers should focus on characteristics that would "support interpretation, shape the contour of the experience, impact the data itself, or help the reader understand what the author asserts or understands" (p. 3).

In S-STEP research, the purpose of the study needs to be clearly stated since that will provide guidance in what research literature is needed. The review of the literature includes studies that are relevant to and show the importance of the investigation at hand (Pinnegar & Hamilton, 2009).

S-STEP researchers are considered to be participants in their own study (Pinnegar & Hamilton, 2009). Collaboration supports S-STEP researchers since it can help attend to places where others could claim misinterpretation or bias. They explain that authors need to be clear about what data they chose to collect, how the data were analyzed as well as how they reached conclusions based on their findings. When this is done, their findings are more likely to be valued and found trustworthy

Finally, Pinnegar and Hamilton (2009) discuss the importance of S-STEP researchers' reflecting on what they learn from the research process. The researcher must ask

> What have I learned that is significant and valuable not just for me and those engaged in my practice but that can deepen and extend the research conversation in teacher education specifically or educational research more generally (p. 5).

In my S-STEP research, I identified the questions I was interested in exploring, connected those questions to my own experiences and understanding of second language acquisition, determined appropriate participants, collected qualitative data, and reviewed the data to determine if I had answered my own questions.

Setting and Participants

This study was carried out at a university of approximately 15,000 students in Northern California. According to the 2010 census, the city that the university is located in is 81% White and 15% Hispanic. Surrounding areas are much more diverse. For example, in a nearby city where some of the student teachers in this study were placed, the population is 57% White, 28% Hispanic, and 17% Asian. The bilingual teacher education program at the university has between 15 and 30 students each year. Teacher candidates are about 80% Hispanic and 20% White.

The five teacher candidates involved in this investigation are all secondary single subject majors working with ethnically diverse student populations. Three of the teachers are Spanish majors, one is a social science major, and one an English major. All five teach ELD in addition to other classes related to their majors. Three teachers graduated from the bilingual teacher education program and are now teaching in Northern California secondary schools. The other two are currently student teaching in secondary schools close to the university. All names used are pseudonyms.

Violet. Violet is currently a student teacher at the university. After living in Costa Rica for a year and taking a linguistics class, she was inspired to become a bilingual teacher. She is in her second and final semester of student teaching. In addition to teaching one ELD class, Violet also teaches Spanish 2. Her student teaching placement is at a high school where the major ethnic groups are White (70%), Hispanic (14%), and Asian (7%).

In Violet's ELD class, students are in different grades from 9 to 12. The ethnic makeup of the class includes Hmong, Chinese, and Hispanic students. Students in the class have varying levels of English proficiency. Some are newcomers with very limited English, while others have been in the United States for many years. Some students were even born in the United States.

Perla. As an Hispanic undergraduate, Perla had the opportunity to tutor at several schools. Throughout these experiences, she was told many times how valuable she was since she was often the only bilingual person at the site. This is what inspired her to become a bilingual teacher. Perla, a student in the bilingual teacher education program, has just finished her second semester student teaching at a high school of approximately 1,166 students. The ethnic makeup of the school is 50% Hispanic, 26% White, and 17% Asian.

Perla taught classes for emergent bilinguals in her student teaching experience. She taught two ELD classes. One was an intermediate class and the other designed for students who have been classified at the school as long-term English learners. According to Olsen (2010) emergent bilinguals who have been in the United States for 7 years or longer become what are known as long-term English Language Learners (ELLs).

The ELD 3 class included students from grades 9 to 12. Eleven students in the class were Hispanic and one was Filipino. All students were at a very low level of English language proficiency. Perla's long-term ELL class had students in grades 11 and 12. Twelve of the students in the class were Hispanic and four were Hmong. All the students in the class had conversational English but struggled with the academic language needed in school. Cummins (1984) found that many emergent bilinguals have conversational fluency but do not develop academic language proficiency.

Damian. As a first generation Mexican American, Damian grew up hearing stories from his family members about the unfair treatment they received within the educational system. Especially after learning more about Mexican American history within the United States, Damian decided he wanted to become a part of the educational system and make changes. When Damian was in the bilingual student teaching program, he was placed at a middle school in a nearby town. The school had a fairly diverse population, and he worked with two ELD classes. Now, in his first year of teaching, he also teaches at a middle school with a very diverse population of 790 students. The student population is 61% Hispanic, 14% Filipino, 10% Asian, and 8% White.

Damian teaches Social Studies, Spanish, and ELD. The students in his ELD class are in 6th, 7th, and 8th grade. At the time this study was conducted, the class had a diverse population that included 4 Spanish speakers, 3 Filipino speakers, 2 Arabic speakers, 2 Vietnamese speakers, 1 Nepalese speakers, and 1 Chinese speaker. The students' English proficiency levels vary from newcomers with very limited English to early intermediate.

Paz. Throughout her own schooling experiences, Paz knew that she and her Hispanic classmates were not receiving the education they deserved. Subsequently, when she entered the university, she was not prepared and struggled. She wanted to become a teacher in order to create better educational opportunities for students like herself. Paz' student teaching experience was in a nearby town with a diverse population. She taught two ELD classes and a Spanish class that consisted of mostly Hispanic and

Hmong students, many of them long-term emergent bilinguals. In her ELD student teaching experience, she fell in love with her ELD students and got excited about creating authentic learning experiences for them. Paz graduated last year from the bilingual student teaching program and is in her first year teaching at a middle school with approximately 798 students. The student population is 78% Hispanic and 11% White. All students at the school are emergent bilinguals since it is a two way dual immersion school. All students learn in both English and Spanish.

One class that Paz teaches is for students recently excited from ELD. This 6th grade class includes 16 Hispanics, 2 Pacific Islanders, and one student from Pakistan. All students in the class are long-term English learners who have strong conversational English skills but struggle with reading and writing.

Miclo. Miclo, went into bilingual education because he wanted to help Hispanic students like himself who are misrepresented and misunderstood. Miclo's student teaching experience was at the same high school as Paz. He and Paz worked with many of the same students since students at the school had ELD 2 periods each day. Miclo is in his first year teaching at the same middle school as Paz. Like Paz, he also teaches students recently exited from ELD. This 7th grade English support class has 19 Hispanic students and 1 Pacific Islander. Students in the class are at intermediate and advanced levels of English proficiency.

I worked with these teachers and student teachers in different classes and as their student teacher supervisor. During the methodology class that met over five Saturdays, I introduced the student teachers to a variety of strategies and activities that they could use with their students. Since all of the student teachers taught ELD plus another subject, we discussed how each strategy could be used across subject areas as well as with emergent bilinguals. I had the students do many of the activities themselves in my class to give them a better understanding of how to do them with their own students. In addition, I showed many examples of my own high school students' work to give the student teachers an idea of what finished projects might look like. These activities are described along with the purpose of each activity in the data analysis section of this chapter.

During the first class session, student teachers learned about activities they could do with the students at the beginning of the year to get to know them and to help the students get to know each other. We discussed how these beginning of the year activities could be done throughout the school year to teach class content.

In the second class session, students learned about how to introduce figurative language, tone, and story elements to their students. We also discussed the use of graphic organizers, and I introduced the idea of using authentic texts with their students.

The next two sessions focused on creating thematic units based on authentic texts. We discussed and practiced a variety of reading strategies they could use as well as writing, projects, oral presentations, and other activities they could engage their students in as they read the authentic texts.

In the final session, the student teachers participated in several writing strategies they could use with their own students. We talked about how texts can inspire students to write and practiced writing activities inspired by texts.

After each session, I challenged students to try one or more of the activities/strategies they had studied in my class with their own students. At the beginning of each session, student teachers shared strategies and activities they had tried with their students. Overall, the student teachers had great success with using the strategies and activities with their students.

In addition to teaching the student teachers in the methodology class, I was also able to support them with activity and strategy ideas when I observed them teaching in their placements. After observing a lesson, I often gave them some specific strategy or activity they could do in the future to improve the lesson. During these post-observation meetings, student teachers would also often ask about upcoming lessons they planned to teach, and we would brainstorm strategies and activities together.

With all participants in this study, I communicated primarily through email and texting. Student teachers and the now first year teachers often email or text me that they have an idea for a lesson but need some strategies or activity ideas. These texts and emails have been archived for reference for this study.

The qualitative data for this study consisted of classroom observations, student teacher and first year teacher informal interviews, and surveys. These will be further discussed in the next section.

Data Collection

Class Observations

Merriam (1998) explains that through observation, we are able to learn about and make sense of our world as well as guide our future actions. I observed all of the participants as student teachers in their placements. I observed Violet and Perla six times each during one semester. I observed Damian, Adriana, and Miclo when they were student teaching observing each 12 times throughout the year. For each observation, I completed a detailed evaluation form that included comments and suggestions based on the lessons. During many of the visits to the participants, I was able to observe them teaching lessons and activities based on authentic texts. They often put into practice strategies they had learned in my methodology class or that I had introduced them to in individual meetings, by email, or text.

Informal Interviews

Menken, Kleyn, and Chae (2012) found that interviews were a key element in their data collection. Based on the results of interviews they carried out during their studies, they were able to make recommendations for improving the educational experiences of students. As I worked on this project, I conducted informal interviews. I communicated with all of the participants on a regular basis. I often needed more information about their students, how they implemented the strategies, and their feedback on the usefulness of the strategies. The majority of the communication was through texting since it was the most effective way to get a response quickly.

Additionally, I conducted informal interviews with the students in person during the methods class that I taught and after each of their observations. I took notes relating to questions and comments students raised that related to this study.

Survey

Olsen (2010) conducted a statewide survey in order to gather data for her research with long-term emergent bilinguals. Olsen found that the survey gave her valuable information that helped her to determine what schools can do to better serve the needs of these students. I also conducted a survey that provided important information (see appendix). Each participant completed a survey in which they reported on the implementation of the strategies that I had taught.

On the survey I created, students were asked to describe their current teaching situation in detail. They also reported on the authentic texts they used in their classrooms and strategies they used with these texts that they had learned in the teacher education methods classes they took from me.

On the survey I asked students to evaluate the usefulness of these strategies in teaching the content they wanted students to learn. Follow-up information was collected through text messaging. Through this survey and follow-ups, I was able to identify a variety of strategies that the teachers used and to see both how the strategies were implemented and how the teachers had modified them.

Data Analysis

Below, I show the results of the survey for each student individually. I first discuss student teachers and then first year teachers I had worked with as student teachers previously. I recorded the activity/strategies that each participant used, listed content skills they wanted to teach, and reported whether the teacher candidate or first year teacher judged the activity/strategy to be successful, partially successful, or not successful. I then present additional data based on the informal interviews. This data includes student comments on the strategies and ways they modified some strategies. The students felt that all the activities were effective. At the same time, they found ways to modify several of the strategies and to adapt them to the specific lessons they were teaching. Table 2 shows the strategies Violet used, the skills she taught, and her evaluation of the effectiveness of the strategy.

Violet described three strategies and activities I taught her that she used with her students as they read authentic texts. She felt that all of the strategies and activities were effective. For example, when discussing the character graphic organizer she wrote, "Students learned key words to describe a character. Rather than simply copying vocabulary from the book, the students were able to come up with their own words as well."

Table 2.   Violet's Strategies.

Activity/Strategy	What Skills Did You Want Students to Develop through This Strategy/Activity?	Is the Strategy Effective
Positive/negative graph	Recall information from a text	Yes
It says/I say	Students learned to form an opinion based on textual evidence to deepen understanding of a character	Yes
Character graphic organizer	Character analysis	Yes

She also wrote about the *It says/I say* strategy, "Students learned to make inferences based on the text, find textual evidence, and then form their own opinions."

Although Violet did not make any changes or modifications to the strategies, she has ideas about how she might do them differently in the future. With the character graphic organizer, she felt that there were too many characters on one graphic organizer. In the future she might have the students have several different graphic organizers or only write about the main characters from the story.

Table 3 lists the strategies Perla used.

Perla indicated that the eight strategies she engaged her students in were all effective. She wrote about the inside—outside circle, "The Students love to interact with each other and through this activity. They definitely grasped better knowledge and understanding of internal and external conflict." When describing why she thought the concept map was so effective she explained, "Building diagrams helps students have a way to visually organize their knowledge and understanding of important concepts."

Perla made modifications to all of the activities and strategies. For example, students first worked on the concept map as a whole class instead of as an individual assignment. By doing this, Perla explained that students gained a better understanding of how to create a concept map. Later, students were very successful when they created their own.

Table 3. Perla's Strategies.

Activity/Strategy	What Skills Did You Want Students to Develop through This Strategy/Activity?	Is the Strategy Effective
Inside—outside circle	Developing oral language Internal and external conflict	Yes
Concept map	Relationships between different concepts	Yes
Mandala	Literary elements	Yes
I am poem	Character analysis	Yes
Concrete poem	Reading comprehension Textual evidence	Yes
Graphic organizers	Story elements Character analysis Theme	Yes
Movie poster	Story elements Character analysis Theme	Yes
Figurative language drawings	Figurative language	Yes

Table 4 shows Damian's strategies.

Damian identified six strategies used for teaching authentic texts that he learned from me and has used in his own classroom. Through these strategies and activities, his students were able to develop reading comprehension, build vocabulary, learn about order and significance of story events, and analyze literary characters. According to Damian, all of the strategies and activities were effective.

In addition to identifying the strategies as effective, Damian commented on what specifically was effective about each one. About the storyboard activity he wrote, "It helped students recall events and analyze the narrative." About the three scenario chart he wrote, "Students were able to demonstrate their understanding of the theme of the narrative by writing and drawing about similar situations." In reference to the simulation letter he wrote, "It was a great assessment tool that engaged students in higher order thinking."

Not only has Damian had success with the strategies and activities I have taught him, but he has also found ways to make additions and modifications that fit his own teaching style and situation. For example, with the positive/negative graph, Damian added a writing component to justify the rankings for each event. For the frontloading of vocabulary activity, Damian had students do a pre-assessment where they showed their understanding of words through color coding.

Table 5 summarizes Paz's strategies

Paz felt that the 11 strategies/activities she used with her students were effective. What she especially liked about all of the strategies was that "They could be modified in many different ways for different purposes."

Table 4.   Damian's Strategies.

Activity/Strategy	What Skills Did You Want Students to Develop through This Strategy/Activity?	Is the Strategy Effective
Positive/negative graph	Character analysis	Yes
I am poem	Character analysis and description	Yes
Story board	Comprehension of a narrative	Yes
Three scenario chart	Synthesize alternative solutions to a theme from literature	Yes
Frontloading vocabulary	Vocabulary development	Yes
Simulation letter	Comprehension of the text and character analysis	Yes

Table 5. Paz's Strategies.

Activity/Strategy	What Skills Did You Want Students to Develop through This Strategy/Activity?	Is the Strategy Effective
Mandala	Story elements	Yes
Story board	Order of events	Yes
Flipbook	Story elements	Yes
Venn diagram	Theme	Yes
	Story elements	
Positive/negative graph	Order and importance of events	Yes
Story order sort	Order of events	Yes
What if? Poem	Inference	Yes
I am poem	Character analysis	Yes
Facebook project	Character and plot analysis	Yes
Graphic organizers	Story elements	Yes
Movie poster	Story elements	Yes

For example, after reading urban legends with her students, she had them create a storyboard of an urban legend they had heard from their own families.

Paz also commented that she liked the fact that many of the strategies and activities I taught her include a combination of writing and drawing. When students are limited in their English proficiency, she is able to assess their understanding of the readings through their drawings.

Table 6 lists the strategies Miclo used.

Miclo rated nine activities he described as effective and one as partially effective because students needed more support. One thing that he liked about all of these activities was that it gave students the opportunity to engage in higher order thinking. He also found that these activities drew on students' creativity which motivated them to participate, "When students participated in these activities, they were engaged." He explained that these particular strategies and ideas gave him the opportunity to assess what the students understood in the readings they were doing.

Miclo modified all nine strategies to fit in with the texts they were reading at the time. For example, with the *How to* project, students had to write a *How To* that would be useful to a character in the book they were reading. He found that the *What If? Poem* was a challenge for his students since they had not had many opportunities to use inference in the past. He explained that next time he does this activity, he would give students more support.

Table 6.   Miclo's Strategies.

Activity/Strategy	What Skills Did You Want Students to Develop through This Strategy/Activity?	Is the Strategy Effective
Positive/negative graph	Comprehension of story events	Yes
Mandala	Story elements	Yes
How to ...	Signal/transition words	Yes
I am poem	Character analysis	Yes
Story order sorting	Order of events	Yes
Textual evidence	Using textual evidence to support opinions	Yes
What if? Poem	Inference	Partially students needed more guidance
Facebook	Character and plot analysis	Yes
Graphic organizers	Story elements Theme	Yes
Movie poster	Story elements	Yes

Conclusions

For this study, I wanted to answer the following questions:

1. In what ways did I support teacher candidates in planning reading and writing activities around authentic texts?
2. In what ways did the teacher candidates and first year teachers implement these activities with their students?
3. How did this self-study inform me as a teacher educator?

In the following sections, I will write my conclusions based on my findings for each question.

In What Ways Did I Support Teacher Candidates in Planning Reading and Writing Activities around Authentic Texts?

I supported the teacher candidates in planning reading and writing activities around authentic texts in a variety of ways. One way that I supported them was through a methodology class. In that class, I taught students strategies and activities by describing the strategy, having the teacher candidates actually do the strategy in the methods class, and by showing examples of my own high school students work student work for each strategy.

I was also able to support the teacher candidates by observing their lessons and then meeting with them after those observations to conduct informal interviews. During this time I was able to give feedback and brainstorm more ideas. Finally, both the teacher candidates and first year teachers communicated with me on a regular basis by texting or email as they modified the strategies and created new strategies and activities.

In What Ways Did the Teacher Candidates and First Year Teachers Implement These Activities with Their Students?

The teacher candidates and first year teachers indicated that all of the strategies they learned from me and then implemented with their own students were effective. In most cases, both the current teacher candidates as well as the first year teachers modified many of the strategies and activities in order to best meet the needs of their students. In some cases, they added to the original strategy or activity. For example, Damian added a writing component to the positive negative graph. Another type of modification that was made was that participants found ways to use the activities and strategies in a number of different contexts. Paz explained that she used the Mandala activity at the beginning of the year to help students get to know each other and then again later in order to show comprehension of the story elements of a book they were reading.

I also found that the teacher candidates and first year teachers often implemented the same strategies in different ways. For example, Damian used the positive/negative graph to help students develop an understanding of character analysis. Perla used the same activity to help students learn about story events.

How Did This Self-Study Inform Me As a Teacher Educator?

One of my most important findings throughout this study is that I learned as much from my teacher candidates and first year teachers as they learned from me. After teaching the participants the activities and strategies, they not only used them in their own classrooms but they found creative ways to modify them so that they would be even more effective.

In the future, I would like to have more specific information about the ways that the strategies were effective or not effective. For example, were the strategies more effective for certain students? In what situations (such as individually, in pairs, or in groups) were the strategies the most effective? I could create a rubric where students could record strategies as they are doing them and comment on the above areas. This information would be very useful to me for teaching and supporting both teacher candidates, and also first year teachers as they use the strategies in their own classrooms.

As the teacher candidates and first year teachers shared with me their student's work based on these strategies and activities, I was constantly impressed with the way they took the original ideas and made them their own. I began collecting samples of that work to share with current and future teacher candidates. The student work that my first year teachers sent me was shared with my current student teachers in our methodology class. As the current student teachers tried the strategies in their placements, they brought student work to class and presented to each other. I realized that each year, teacher candidates and beginning teachers that I teach will continue to implement the strategies and activities I teach them and modify them to meet the needs of their own students. I expect this spiral effect to continue throughout the years that I work as a teacher educator.

I found that there were many benefits to conducting this self-study. Having the opportunity to first look closely at what I teach teacher candidates and then how effective what I teach them is in their own practice, has been a very educational process. When I reflected on what teacher candidates and first year teachers actually used in their own classrooms, I realized it was a small percentage of all of the strategies and activities I introduced them too. I have realized that giving them fewer strategies and activities in more in-depth, might be more effective.

Conclusion

In this study, I investigated the ways that I supported my teacher candidates by teaching them reading and writing activities that they could use as they taught authentic texts to their emergent bilingual students. I was interested in finding out whether the teacher candidates and first year teachers who just graduated from the bilingual teacher education program used the strategies with their own students and whether they found them to be effective.

Throughout the course of the study, I found that the teacher candidates and first year teachers implemented many of the strategies that I taught them. They also found the strategies to be effective. Not only did the teacher candidates and first year teachers use the strategies, they found ways to modify them to best meet the needs of their emergent bilinguals.

By reflecting on my own practice, I found that I learned as much from my students as they learned from me. I also realized that in the future,

I would like to create a rubric with more specific questions for the teacher candidates to use on a regular basis to record the strategies that they use. Having more specific information about how the strategies were implemented, who they were most effective for, and what settings worked the best, would be useful information that I could use to inform my own practice.

References

Cummins, J. (1984). Language proficiency and academic achievement revisited: A response. In C. Rivera (Ed.), *Language proficiency and academic achievement* (pp. 71–76). Clevedon: Multilingual Matters Ltd.

Daniels, H., & Zemelman, S. (2004). *Subjects matter: Every teacher's guide to content-area reading*. Portsmouth, NH: Heinemann.

Ebe, A. (2012). Supporting the reading development of middle school English language learners through culturally relevant texts. *Reading & Writing Quarterly, 28*(2), 179–198.

Freeman, Y., & Freeman, D. (2002). *Closing the achievement gap: How to reach limited formal schooling and long-term English learners*. Portsmouth, NH: Heinemann.

Gándara, P., & Contreras, F. (2009). *The Latino education crisis: The consequences of failed school policies*. Cambridge: Harvard University Press.

García, G., & Godina, H. (2004). Addressing the literacy needs of adolescent English language learners. In T. Jetton & J. Dole (Eds.), *Adolescent literacy research and practice* (pp. 304–320). New York, NY: The Guilford Press.

García, O., Kleifgen, J. A., & Flachi, L. (2008). *From English language learners to emergent bilinguals*. New York, NY: Teachers College.

Guthrie, J., & Davis, M. (2003). Motivating struggling readers in middle school through an engagement model of classroom practice. *Reading & Writing Quarterly, 19*, 59–85.

Horwitz, A. R., Uro, G., Price-Baugh, R., Simon, C., Uzzell, R., Lewis, S., & Casserly, M. (2009). *Succeeding with English language learners: Lessons learned from the Great City Schools*. Washington, DC: The Council of the Great City Schools.

Ivey, G., & Broaddus, K. (2007). A formative experiment investigating literacy engagement among adolescent Latina/o students just beginning to read, write, and speak English. *Reading Research Quarterly, 42*(4), 512–545.

Krashen, S. (2004). *The power of reading*. Portsmouth, NH: Heinemann.

Meltzer, J., & Hamann, E. (2005). *Meeting the literacy development needs of adolescent English language learners through content-area teaching: Part two: Focus on classroom learning and teaching*. Providence, RI: The Education Alliance at Brown University.

Menken, K., Kleyn, T., & Chae, N. (2012). Spotlight on long term English language learners: Characteristics and prior schooling experiences of an invisible population. *International Multilingual Research Journal, 6*, 121–142.

Merriam, S. B. (1998). *Qualitative research and case study applications in education*. San Francisco, CA: Jossey-Bass Publishers.

Moje, E. B., Overby, M., Tysvaer, N., & Morris, K. (2008). The complex world of adolescent literacy: Myths, motivations, and mysteries. *Harvard Education Review, 78*(1), 107–154.

Olsen, L. (2010). Changing course for long term English learners. *Leadership, 40*(2), 30–33.

Pinnegar, S., & Hamilton, M. L. (2009). Creating representations: Using collage to explore our work. In *Research methods for self-study of practice*. Dordrecht: Springer.

Pinnegar, S., & Hamilton, M. L. (2011). Self-study inquiry practices. In S. Schonmann (Ed.), *Key concepts in theatre/drama education* (pp. 345–350). New York, NY: Springer.

Pinnegar, S., Hamilton, M. L., & Fitzgerald, L. (2010). Guidance in being and becoming self-study of practice researchers. Paper presented at the Proceedings of the Eighth International Conference on Self-studies of Teacher Education Practices: Navigating the Public and the Private: Negotiating the Diverse Landscapes of Teacher Education, Herstmonceaux Castle, UK.

Short, D., & Fitzsimmons, S. (2007). *Double the work: Challenges and solutions to acquiring language and academic literacy for adolescent English language learners — A report to Carnegie corporation of New York*. Washington, DC: Alliance for Excellent Education.

Thomas, W. P., & Collier, V. P. (2002). A national study of school effectiveness for language minority students' long-term academic achievement. Retrieved from http://www.crede.usc.edu/research/llaa/1.1_es.html. Accessed on April 9, 2002.

Appendix

Name:

Current or most recent teaching placement (location):

Number of students at the school:

Ethnic make-up of the student population of the school (percent of Hispanic, etc.):

Please fill out the following chart according to your current or most recent teaching experience. *Only fill it out for the classes you teach for emergent bilinguals.*

Name of Class	Grade(s) of Students in the Class	Ethnic Makeup of the Class	English Language Level(s)-Anywhere from Newcomers to Long-term ELs	Other Information You Would Like to Share (Optional)

Please fill out the chart based on any strategies/activities that you used while reading authentic texts that you learned from me or in our class.

Activity/ Strategy	What Content/ Skills Were You Hoping Students Would Develop through This Activity/Strategy?	Do You Think the Students Gained a Better Understanding of Concepts/Skills through the Activity/Strategy?	Were There Any Modifications You Made to the Activity/ Strategy? Or Have You Thought of Modifications You Might Try to Incorporate in the Future?

CHAPTER 10

ANNOTATED LESSON PLANS: THE IMPACT ON TEACHER CANDIDATE PREPARATION FOR EMERGENT BILINGUAL STUDENTS

Craig A. Hughes

Abstract

This chapter explores the concept of annotated lesson plans. Teacher candidates annotated why modifications were made to their lesson plans to support emergent bilinguals. They included the research and theory to support such modifications. This research demonstrates the impact of annotated lesson plans on candidates in connecting their understanding of learning and language acquisition theories to actual classroom practices. Two questions guided the research: (1) Would annotated lesson plans assist teacher candidates in connecting language and learning theories to the modifications made in their lesson plans? (2) What was the impact of creating the annotated lesson plan on the teacher candidates, as expressed through their self-reflection of the process? Founded on the base of naturalistic inquiry (Lincoln & Guba, 1985), the data

Research on Preparing Preservice Teachers to Work Effectively with Emergent Bilinguals
Advances in Research on Teaching, Volume 21, 257–286
ISSN: 1479-3687/doi:10.1108/S1479-368720140000021009

collected was contextualized within the frame of a teacher candidate course. Annotated lesson plans and accompanying reflection papers were gathered as data. These items were analyzed based on the guidelines established by Lincoln and Guba (1985) and Spradley (1980). Teacher candidates connected theories to their planned lessons. They demonstrated and expressed better understanding of related theories and methods. While a minority of the candidates expressed concerns with their overall preparation to educate emergent bilingual students, the majority of the candidates felt the lesson plans provided them with greater confidence in meeting the needs of such students. The implications of the study are that annotated lesson plans can better prepare preservice teachers for teaching emergent bilinguals.

Keywords: Teacher preparation; lesson plans; annotations

Introduction

The first day of school had arrived at the middle school. A new English as a Second Language (ESL) teacher was walking around his room, prepping for the classes yet to come. It was first period. The ESL teacher had arranged for a 1st period prep so that any assessment for placement of new students could be conducted before they were placed in classes. He had checked to make sure no assessments were needed that day, and he was assured that all new students had been assessed by the district office.

He was checking things, once again, to make sure all of the books and activities were ready to go when, all of a sudden, his door flew open and a student rushed in. "Quick," he yelled, "Mr. Jones needs you in his room." The ESL teacher wondered what kind of emergency had caused this urgent appeal.

The ESL teacher entered the classroom. He looked around. Sitting on the floor at the front of the room was a young Latina crying. What had happened? The ESL teacher looked at Mr. Jones, whose face showed much concern and confusion. Mr. Jones explained, "I had finished calling roll and I saw her there. I asked her what her name was and she just looked at me. I asked again, and she started crying. I checked and nobody in here speaks Spanish! I didn't know what to do, so I sent the student for you."

Research Guiding Questions

This scenario reflects one of the major issues in schools today. Teachers have completed their training. Most have received basic information on how to differentiate their teaching to meet the needs of the diverse students found in their classrooms. However, generally this training has not provided them with the theoretical knowledge or the skills and/or the ability to connect that knowledge with effective classroom practices (Professional Educator Standards Board, 2008).

As a teacher educator I have worked to help my teacher candidates understand how effective methodologies and techniques emerge from strong language acquisition and cognitive learning theories. Opportunities to put theory into practice seldom occur since theories are commonly presented in a college classroom setting while the actual development of methodology occurs in a school classroom setting (Hammerness et al., 2005).

Annotated lesson plans can be advanced as one means to facilitate this connection of theory to practice. Morris and Hiebert (2011) include annotated lesson plans as a fundamental tool for increasing shared instruction products. For their purposes, the annotations of such plans would include updates and information needed to facilitate the use of lesson plans in different contextual settings. Knowledge of two kinds was contained in the plans. The first was the "what to do," or the methods and techniques teachers can use. The second was "why" and "how to do it." The "why" provided a grounded theory for its implementation and the "how to do it" included the information needed for other teachers to effectively implement it.

For this project, the annotated lesson plans had a similar purpose. Annotations were used in such a way that teacher candidates would (a) include explanations of modifications provided for emergent bilingual students and (b) provide theory and research support for their modifications.

Consequently, there were two questions that I addressed. The first question was, "Would annotated lesson plans assist teacher candidates in connecting language and learning theories to the modification made in their lesson plans?" The second question was, "What was the impact of creating the annotated lesson plan on the teacher candidates, as expressed through their self-reflection of the process?" I wanted to know if the candidates would recognize how adding annotations to their plans influenced what would occur in their classrooms.

Significance of the Study

There are several areas of significance for this study. First, teacher preparation is being critically examined from multiple perspectives (Darling-Hammond, 2009). Efforts have been made to remove most, if not all, of the pedagogical preparation of teacher candidates and focus instead on content knowledge. (Darling-Hammond, 2009). While content knowledge is essential for all teachers, understanding the conditions and approaches needed to increase the learning probability of students is required as well (Hammerness et al., 2005).

Second, emergent bilingual students are a growing population in our school systems. Nationwide, the population of English Language Learners (ELL), grew by more than 500,000 students, or 1.1% (National Center for Educational Statistics [NCES], 2012). The achievement gap between ELL students and non-ELL students has not significantly narrowed between 2002 and 2011 (NCES, 2013). Teacher preparation programs need to prepare their candidates to better meet the educational contexts that exist today.

Setting and Participants

The participants in this study were teacher candidates taking a course entitled, *Principles and Practices for Educating Linguistically Diverse Students,* a course required for all teacher certification candidates at a regional university in the northwest. This course is normally taken at the midpoint of the certification program and is the only direct exposure such candidates receive in preparing them for emergent bilingual students. Constructivism is the theoretical foundation for this particular teacher preparation program. Consequently, this course includes opportunities for teacher candidates to connect what they are learning and developing with what they have learned in previous courses.

In this particular cohort, there were 24 teacher candidates majoring in elementary education and minoring in literacy in the course. Twenty-one of the participants were female and three were male. There was one male of African descent, one female of Asian descent. All other participants were of White European descent. Three of the female students were non-traditional in regards to age.

Annotated Lesson Plans

The annotated lesson plan I developed came from my concern that students implement practices that were theoretically sound. (A sample plan completed by one of the participants can be found in Appendix A.) To begin with, I required no single format for such lesson plans. In my courses, teacher candidates are encouraged to use lesson plans they had already developed for previous courses. The rationale for this was that it would allow the candidates the opportunity to recognize the modifications needed to successfully educate emergent bilingual students. Each of the previous courses had developed particular lesson plan formats emphasizing key components of the planning process. Although different formats had been developed, they could still be modified. There were certain elements to be included in each lesson plan:

- Language proficiency levels of emergent bilingual students in the class for which the plan was developed. This required the candidates to recognize that not all students are at the same level of English proficiency.
- Content and language objectives. Following the work of several researchers (Freeman & Freeman, 2011; Gottlieb, 2006; Short, 1999) teacher candidates need to be able to identify the language objectives that correlate with the content objectives to be taught.
- The standards upon which the learning objectives are based.
- The materials to be used in the lesson.
- The sequence of activities involved in the lesson.
- The assessment procedures to be used connected to the objective taught.

As they are developing or modifying their lesson plans, the candidates also need to include the annotation component of the plans. There are two types of annotations: annotations to explain the modifications being used to meet the needs of emergent bilinguals at different levels of English proficiency and annotations to explain the research support for the modifications being implemented. Students italicized the items to be annotated in their lesson plans and then added the annotations at the end of the lesson plan (see Appendix A). The italicized sections were hyperlinked to the associated annotation to facilitate movement to and from the annotations.

The following two sample boxes demonstrate the association of the lesson plan component and the annotation. In Table 1, the lesson plan item is a rough demographic breakdown of the projected class. The two italicized items indicated that an annotation was linked (in this case, two

Table 1. Lesson Plan Component and Associated Annotation.

Lesson plan Component	Student population
	The classroom is extremely diverse. Native English-speaking students and English language learners (ELL) create the classroom population. English language development is focused toward students who are at the *advanced beginning*, and *intermediate* levels of English proficiency.
Annotation	Ability level expectations: advanced beginning
	A student at the advanced beginning level of English proficiency is capable of participating in academic discussions on familiar topics, begins to use academic vocabulary, expresses self, using words and/or phrases to identify main idea and details, and begins to write based on model or frame (OSPI, 2010).
	Ability level expectation: intermediate
	Students at the intermediate level of English proficiency is capable of participating in academic social discussions, uses appropriate social and academic vocabulary for different audiences, responds to and asks why- and yes/no questions, increases vocabulary through reading across content areas, infers and makes generalizations from text, and writes simple sentences (OSPI, 2010).

annotations). The annotations provide an overview of the expected language capabilities for students at the two designated levels.

In Table 2, the candidate is providing an overview of the activities being used in the lesson. Once again, the italicized segment indicates a link to an

Table 2. Lesson Plan Component and Associated Annotation.

Lesson plan component	Explore
	Students will work together as a group to read and discuss each data set. Students will use the strategy think-ink-pair-share. Students will use a graphic organizer provided to record all ideas, and points found within each data set that it presented. The teacher will present each data set, and read through the information using *comprehensible input* one time.
Annotation	Comprehensible input
	"Slowing down the rate of speech slightly and pausing between thoughts gives learners time to process what they've learned and catch up" (Rothenberg & Fisher, 2007). According to Krashen's theories, in order to help ELL students understand the information being presented, it is important that when the teacher is presenting the information, the teacher speaks slow, articulates important ideas, repeats key words and/or phrase, pauses frequently, and uses gestures when appropriate. This will allow ELL students the necessary time to process the information being said and make sense of it.

annotation. The annotation provides support for the chosen modification (there are additional annotations in the complete lesson plan found in Appendix A).

The inclusion of the annotations provide the opportunity for the instructor to analyze the connection the teacher candidates can make between the theories they have learned and the plans they are developing.

Literature Review

The literature review relevant to this study included literature related to the importance of linking learning theories and second language acquisition theories to classroom methodologies and the role of lesson plans in teacher preparation. California led the movement toward a more professional base for teachers by recognizing a diploma from a normal school, a teacher preparation college, as meeting the requirements for licensure. This movement continued until by 1930, most states had a minimum education requirement for their teachers and that teacher training had to be included. By 1930, educational psychology (or educational theories) connected to classroom practices was a requirement for teacher licensure (Elsbree, 1939; James, 1892, 1939).

Recently, Elliot (1993, 2012) compared the relationship of theories to practice by exploring the rationalist view and the hermeneutic view of teacher education. In a pure rationalist view, theory comes before practice. Teacher candidates should have a strong grasp on the theories and their applications before entering the teaching phase. The hermeneutic view places teacher preparation as the result of situational understanding, or learning from what occurs in the actual classroom. Theory can be useful, but it should be the theory that is created by the candidates and examined through collaborative interaction. Academic research is viewed as of limited in value in a hermeneutic view.

More contemporary approaches to teacher preparation hold that theory and practice should be developed together (Hammerness et al., 2005; Timperly, 2008). The National Academy of Sciences developed three principles to improve teacher preparation. The second one, as cited in Hammerness et al. (2005), states teachers must have a deep theoretical foundation, understand how the theories come together in a conceptual framework, and then be able to organize this information in such a way that they can retrieve it and implement it in their classrooms. This indicates that for teachers to be effective, they need to combine their content knowledge with their knowledge of learning and language theories in the production of productive classroom activities (Hammerness et al., 2005).

Timperley (2008) conducted a meta-analysis of studies dealing with teacher professional learning and development. Ten key principles were identified. Of interest to this study was Principle 3: Integration of Knowledge and Skills (p. 11). The synthesis of existing studies found that teachers must integrate their knowledge of the content with their knowledge of teaching the content area, including appropriate assessment procedures, "This integration allows teachers to use their theoretical understandings as the basis for making ongoing, principled decisions about practice" (p. 11).

Timperley summarized the finding of the meta-analysis in regards to the two approaches Elliot (1993, 2012) presented by recognizing that a skills-only approach can provide a false sense of theory-based practice while teaching theory without connecting it to actual classroom practices is ineffective as well.

In addition to learning theories, teachers of emergent bilingual students should have a foundational base in language and second language acquisition theories. Fillmore and Snow (2002) postulated that public school teachers need to have a certain level of language knowledge in order to serve any student, especially emergent bilinguals. They recommended a series of courses that would provide the needed level of understanding. Included in this listing were Language and Cultural Diversity, Sociolinguistics for Educators in a Linguistically Diverse Society, and Second Language Learning and Teaching. The overall purpose of these three courses would be to provide any classroom teacher with the basic linguistic foundations needed to address the language needs of such students in a complex socially, culturally, and politically embedded school community.

Understanding how someone acquires a second language is not easy to grasp. Brown (2007) demonstrated the complexity of this issue by presenting a series of questions beginning with who, what, how, when, where, and why the second language was to be acquired. Freeman and Freeman (2011) demonstrated the complexity of understanding second language acquisition (SLA) by presenting how it is studied from the perspectives of psycholinguists, neurolinguists, and sociolinguists. Psycholinguists study the structure of language developed by an individual as they develop the second language. Neurolinguists explore where and how the new language is placed in the brain. Sociolinguists examine the impact of sociocultural factors on the development of a new language. These and other noted factors need to be considered in the development and application of second language theories (Ellis, 1985; Freeman & Freeman, 2011).

As can be seen in the existing research, the importance of teacher candidates developing an understanding of learning and language theories is needed. Without such an understanding, they are limited in how to make modifications in their teaching methods when the need arises.

Lesson plan development is a second area of focus for this study. Lesson planning began to appear in teacher preparation programs in the 1950s, but obtained the presence found today through efforts to reform America's education crisis during the 1960s and 1970s. While the formatting of lesson plans tends to reflect a behaviorist foundation (John, 2006), they offer structure to future teachers to help them handle the complexity in the classroom.

Lederman and Niess (2000) reflected on the struggles teacher candidates have in developing their lesson plans. One of these issues is that candidates see lesson plans as more of an evaluation of their progress in their coursework than as something they can use. Due to lack of opportunities for candidates to actually practice their teaching, lesson planning becomes an evaluation tool for teacher preparation coursework. An important observation that Lederman and Niess (2000) make is that more capable teacher candidates are able to plan without the written detail required for most lesson plans while less able candidates function through writing the plans without necessarily thinking about them. Lesson plans need to be viewed as a tool, not a burden.

In summary, the review of existing literature demonstrates the need teacher candidates have in learning and applying learning and SLA theories. This preparation provides them with the foundation needed to make informed instructional decisions. Lesson plans play several key roles in teacher preparation. The one most important for this study is their use by candidates to connect theories with actual classroom practices.

Research Methodology

Lincoln and Guba (1985) presented an overview of the distinctions between the established research paradigm (positivism) and their proposed entry into the post positivism era, naturalistic inquiry. Naturalistic inquiry recognizes that multiple realities are constructed by those involved. Such realities cannot be broken into fragmented parts, rather they should be viewed as multiple components intertwined into a complex whole. Rather than believing that all change occurs as the result of some preceding cause, all entities interact in such a way that they are in a state of constant change. And, of particular importance to this study, the research being conducted does not exist in a time and/or context free environment. Rather, to fully understand the research being conducted a researcher must fully understand the context in which it takes place.

This study followed the guidelines established by Lincoln and Guba (1985) in that it was time- and context-embedded. Data were collected as part of the normal teacher preparation program with the researcher serving as instructor. The data collected were the annotated lesson plans and reflection statements on the impact of the lesson plan development and modification. Two of Lincoln and Guba's characteristics of operational naturalistic inquiry are particularly relevant: Grounded Theory and Emergent Design. Grounded Theory, defined by Lincoln and Guba (1985) as "theory that follows from data rather than preceding them" (p. 204) guided the development of this project. Emergent Design occurs when the research design is allowed "to emerge (flow, cascade, unfold) rather than to construct it preordinately" (Lincoln & Guba, 1985, p. 41).

Data Analysis

The data were analyzed using a system similar to the process proposed by Spradley (1980). NVivo, a qualitative data processing software, was used to facilitate the analysis. The first step was coding data into domains and taxonomies using some that were predetermined and others that appeared through the coding processes. Domains, as Spradley presented them, "are categories of meaning" (p. 88). Domains are broad in meaning with any item that can be viewed as having a semantic relationship being included. Taxonomy is the next step where focus domains are examined looking at the semantic relationships (Spradley, 1980). Fig. 1 presents a sample taxonomy chart where the domain of "theories" was categorized into two taxonomies, "second language acquisition theories" and "cognitive theories." Each of these was then broken into specifically related subcategories. Such charting allows for the relationships to be evident.

At this stage the data were reanalyzed and coded based upon the taxonomies that had emerged. Next, the coded data were organized into meaningful themes. These themes bring together the elements that demonstrate

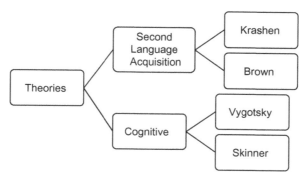

Fig. 1. Sample Taxonomy Chart.

the relationships that exist in the subject(s) being studied. This implies that research coding demonstrated the appearance of certain traits within and between the different subgroups.

Fig. 2 demonstrates the flow of a theme. This sample uses the theme of "Candidates' Use of Theory." Two participants are shown in the figure. The theme flows to the participants, then to the distinction between knowledge of a theory and its correct implementation in the lesson plan. The

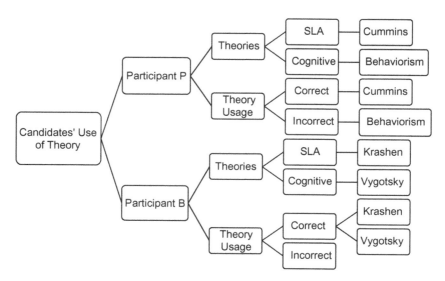

Fig. 2. Sample Theme Development Chart.

theories are then divided into second language acquisition theories and cognitive theories. Finally, the actual theory or researcher is referenced.

Each of the emerging themes flowed through this process. The major themes that emerged through the data analysis were:

- candidates' use of theories,
- ease of developing or modifying the lesson plan, including the annotations, in relation to potential impact in the classroom,
- new knowledge learned as a result of the process, and
- self-reflection of their potential as a teacher.

Findings

This research project was designed to answer two questions. The first was to see if the use of annotations would lead to candidates connecting language acquisition theories and learning theories to the lesson plans they developed for the course. The analysis of the first theme, candidate's use of theories, was used to answer this question. The data analysis of the remaining three themes were used to answer the second question, "What was the impact of creating the annotated lesson plan on the teacher candidates, as expressed through their self-reflection of the process."

Candidates' Use of Theories

The data in Table 3 document that the participants overwhelmingly connected learning and second language acquisition theories to their planned lessons.

The findings, as seen in Table 3 are positive in nature. None of the candidates failed to include a connection to at least one theory. When the

Table 3.   Reference to Learning and/or Second Language Acquisition Theory.

	Only Learning Theories	Only Second Language Acquisition Theories	Both	Neither
Number of participants that included theories	8%	38%	54%	0%

individual theory and both types of theories are combined, 62% of the candidates included at least one learning theory, while 92% included at least one second language acquisition theory. It is interesting to note the inclusion of second language acquisition theories at a higher rate than learning theories. One could correlate this to the emphasis placed on the language acquisition theories in the coursework for the class. However, the candidates had been exposed to learning theories in other coursework with a particular focus on constructivism. As mentioned previously, constructivism is the underlying framework upon which the teacher education program at this university is founded. However, only 11 of the 24 candidates included an annotation connected to constructivism or one of its chief theorists, Bruner and Vygotsky.

While most of the participants were able to support their lesson plans with appropriate theories, considering they are teacher candidates with limited classroom experiences, there was a variation in the depth of understanding of theories presented in the annotations. For example, Participant B demonstrated how the principle proposed by Brown (2007), that learning should be meaningful, would be incorporated into the lesson by engaging students in small groups to create their own versions of "The Hungry Caterpillar" (Carle, 1969, 1987):

> Brown's principles of language teaching and learning include 5 ways of teaching content to ELL students. Brown's 2nd principle meaningful learning, states that memorizing facts or rote learning will not promote long term retention. Learning will take place with meaningful connections to the student's reality and interests. This lesson will go beyond rote learning and have students engaged and turn abstract learning into concrete knowledge. (Participant B)

Other candidates chose to include a direct quotation from a text with a detailed explanation of how this appears in the lesson plan:

> "If students don't understand what they are hearing or reading, we cannot expect them to then produce comprehensible language" (Rothenberg & Fisher, 2007, p. 41). This lesson provides a high level of comprehensible input through the use of manipulatives, mixed use of written and oral expression, and exploration of physical examples that relate to the concept. Specifically, during the explanatory portion of the lesson, students are able to directly observe and relate the objects that are being passed around with the provided explanation. Given comprehensible input, language acquisition happens naturally and unavoidably. (Participant G)

Other candidates provided basic, unreferenced explanations, "In reference to the constructivism theory students can use the pictures and text in the passage to make predictions related to the text and this will aid to

build their schemas to connect to their interests and prior knowledge."
(Participant F)

In addition to this range of detail provided, not all annotations met the expectations for the course. This can be divided into two categories: (a) the idea is correct but not properly referenced and (b) theory is applied incorrectly. The first of these two can be seen in statement made by Participant A, "According to Krashen, allowing students to respond in the way most appropriate to their level of English competency allows for comprehensible output, which is the practice with English speaking peers and is just as important as comprehensible input." The participant has internalized the connection of the work conducted by Krashen (1981) with the term "comprehensible." Consequently, Krashen, in place of Swain (1985), was referenced as a source of support for comprehensible output.

Participant I can be seen as an example of the cited theory not being properly applied. In this case, the candidate is implying that written instructions on the board will provide the support needed for comprehension to take place. While such an action has been documented as helping emergent bilingual students, this particular annotation did not indicate that any action would be taken to facilitate the comprehension of the written language used in the described instructions.

"This accommodation is inspired by the comprehensible input theory of Krashen. Providing Liza and Manny with written instructions on the board will help them put in to perspective not only the order of the tasks, but will help them relate what they remember the tasks to be, to words on the board." (Participant I)

Table 4 documents the percentage of candidates who correctly or incorrectly applied the theories. The learning theories are correctly applied at a lower rate than the SLA theories, largely due to the lack of inclusion of the learning theories in the annotations. SLA theories are applied correctly by the candidates at a higher rate.

Along with the correct usage of the theories, Table 4 demonstrates that theories were incorrectly applied on a regular basis. SLA theories and learning theories were applied incorrectly by 21% of the candidates. This

Table 4.   Correct and Incorrect Application of Theories by Candidates.

	Learning Theories	SLA Theories
Correctly applied	58%	92%
Incorrectly applied	21%	21%

documents that the candidates did correctly apply the theories at a much higher rate than incorrect application. However, these trends do document that these candidates need further preparation in understanding and applying theories to their practice.

In response to the first research question, this particular population of teacher candidates was able to connect the theories with classroom practices. Although the strength of their understanding of such theories was not clearly visible at all times, all of the candidates demonstrated their ability to connect their classroom expectation and procedures to the theories they had learned.

Once again I used the three themes that emerged from the data to answer the second research question, "What was the impact of creating the annotated lesson plan on the teacher candidates, as expressed through their self-reflection of the process?" The three themes were (a) ease of developing or modifying the lesson plan; (b) development of new knowledge; and (c) professional self-reflection.

Ease of Developing or Modifying the Lesson Plan

The first theme that emerged was the ease of developing and/or modifying the lesson plans as well as the perceived benefits of this process. All of the teacher candidates had developed lesson plans in previous classes using multiple formats. The recommendation I made to the candidates was that they take a lesson plan previously developed and modify it, which would allow them to see the results of their efforts. One candidate, after assuming it would be relatively simple to modify a lesson plan that had previously been developed, discovered it took more effort than she originally believed:

> Altering a lesson I had previously authored to accommodate the diverse needs of ELL students with varying levels of proficiency in the English language was more challenging than I'd imagined. Having to examine content, language requirements, directions, and tasks with ELL students in mind required me to assess my delivery and the comprehensibility of the lesson input. However, in doing so, I was able to apply my knowledge of learning and second language acquisition theories, and modify strategic portions of the lesson to accommodate ELL students. (Participant Y)

A second candidate also expressed the difficulty in meeting the needs of diverse learners in planning lesson. As shown by this reflection, the concern does extend beyond the lesson plan alone, but the effort to try and include additional accommodations for students with limited English ability has become a concern for her.

> There are so many ways to teach a class when you know for the most part that everyone understands what you are saying. Trying to figure out how to plan when someone doesn't understand is something that even after making the accommodations, I still don't know if I would actually be effective at teaching them what I want them to learn. (Participant K)

Other teacher candidates found that including emergent bilingual students to be a relatively simple process, "By developing an annotated lesson plan designed to accommodate linguistically diverse students, I have learned that simple adjustments within a lesson can be exceptionally beneficial for English learning students" (Participant C).

Notwithstanding the perceived ease or difficulty in completing the assignment, all of the teacher candidates found the effort to be worthwhile. Participant Y, quoted above, recognized the positive impact of the activity as well as the difficulties involved. As was stated, the connection of theories to practice required her to analyze and assess how emergent bilingual students would have comprehensible access to the planned instruction.

Another participant presented her reflection of the assignment which indicated that, at least for one, the annotated lesson plans met its objective and had a positive impact.

> Using a lesson I had already created was beneficial because it helped me see what I had learned from taking this ELL course. There were many things that I overlooked or didn't account for in my original lesson. Through this assignment, I made additions and adaptations to the lesson plan that would better benefit a diverse group of students. (Participant M)

Not all of the candidates found the modification of the plans and the addition of the annotations to be easy. However, they did note the benefits they found through the process of explicitly connecting theories to practices.

Development of New Knowledge

The analysis of the third theme, new knowledge learned as a result of the process, showed that many of the teacher candidates recognized growth in their development of new knowledge. The first area of knowledge growth demonstrated by the student reflections was that of coming to know language and learning theories. Participant G stated, "I am now familiar with several second language acquisition theories and am able to combine the information I learned with learning theories to apply in meaningful ways in my classroom." Participant L expanded this view by stating, "I have the resources and knowledge to complete further investigations to increase my knowledge in English language development instruction."

The second area of increased knowledge was instructional methods and practices. This cohort of teacher candidates was completing the final quarter in the first year of a two-year program. During their first year, they had received instruction in methods and strategies, but without an explicit focus on emergent bilingual students. The focus on second language acquisition theories and teaching methods in this course provided them with new knowledge.

Participant U, in reflecting on the impact of modifying a previously developed lesson plan stated:

> By completing this accommodation lesson plan I was able to strengthen my own understanding and knowledge of different effective methods of instruction and theories for ELL students. This lesson not only gave me a clear picture of how accommodations for ELL students play out in a lesson plan, but it also challenged me to re-evaluate a lesson that I had previously written to make it more conducive to ELL learning styles. (Participant U)

One aspect of lesson planning that emphasized in the course was the relationship of language and learning objectives to assessment. Participant H spoke of this:

> I have also learned to carefully examine my assessment rubrics to make sure that I am not grading for something that is not part of the learning objective. For instance, in my original lesson plan my rubric for the commemorative stamp was grading for art elements, even though art was nowhere in my learning objectives. (Participant H)

The teacher candidates had developed an appreciation for methods and practices that would be effective for emergent bilingual students. One final item of interest in regards to the development of new knowledge in methods was that the methods and practices appropriate for English learners would be beneficial to all students, not just the emergent bilinguals. Participant L summarized this concept, "Through the creation of this lesson plan, I have been introduced to multiple instructional strategies that aid in the teaching of English language learners. These strategies relate not only to English language development, but are beneficial to all students across ability levels."

Several of the teacher candidates acknowledged the relationship between learning the new theories and the development of new methods and practices. Participant W acknowledged the research needed to make the development of her plan effective:

> In completing the ELL annotated lesson plan, I learned how to better take into account the extra focus needed for ELL students. I learned how to gear my lesson towards a small group instruction, keeping in mind how I would best fit the needs of my ELL students. Furthermore, a great deal of research took place to make this lesson compatible to my ELL students. (Participant W)

Participant L states the overall goal of this assignment that the teacher candidates see themselves capable of exploring the research related to bettering the educational experiences of their students, "The strategies that I have gleaned from this activity will be very useful in my future classroom. Additionally, I have the resources and knowledge to complete further investigations to increase my knowledge in English language development instruction."

Professional Self-Reflection

The final area of analysis in the refection part of the study has to do with the self-reflection of the teacher candidates. The data comes from analysis of the third theme, self-reflection of their potential as a teacher. While the annotated lesson plans caused three of the candidates to question their abilities to properly educate emergent bilingual students, most of the students felt the lessons helped them to feel better prepared to work with English learners.

The expression of concern of the candidates questioning their abilities was that, even after learning the theories and methods presented in the class, preparing the lesson plans helped them realize how unprepared they felt:

> After writing this lesson plan I began to doubt my ability to modify and make the necessary accommodations for ELL students. There is so much research supporting the modifications that it was hard to keep it all straight as to who said and thought what. (Participant B)

Most of the teacher candidates saw how the annotated lesson plans provided them with an understanding of the modifications needed for emergent bilingual students, an understanding of the importance of critically analyzing their methods and materials, and feelings of confidence when looking at their future careers. Participant C commented on how this opportunity impacted her. "Preparing a lesson plan that integrates specific accommodations for students who are not English-proficient has opened my eyes to what my future lesson plans need to include." This concept was echoed and expanded by Participant A, who stated, "In using the accommodations I was able to notice how important and beneficial accommodations and modifications are in each and every part of the day."

The teacher candidates also noted how they had to be aware of lesson plans and activities previously planned and commercially produced activities, "While doing this lesson I have learned that I cannot just take a lesson that comes out of a book, from another teacher, or offline and just use them. I need to make sure I meet the needs of the students who need help" (Participant X).

The development of this new understanding strengthens their ability to critically examine what they will do with the emergent bilingual students, "The creation of this lesson plan provided the opportunity to reflect on what I was doing, why I was doing it, and how I could make it better" (Participant L). Several of the candidates appreciated how modifying lesson plans they had developed for previous classes made such changes even more visible:

> The feature of this assignment that gave me the most benefit was reviewing a lesson that I had previously written and evaluating how well I accommodated the different learning styles of ELL students. As I was evaluating this lesson on observation that I wrote during my first quarter in the ... teaching program, I realized that I knew very little about accommodating ELL students. My accommodations listed in the original lesson were very broad and did not give helpful information as for how to adapt the lesson elements for different language needs. (Participant U)

The ability to critically review these areas was recognized by the candidates. Participant M stated, "I found this assignment to be well worth my time. It challenged me to think critically about new concepts and helped me make connections to things I have already learned and experienced." This assignment allowed for the candidates to take ownership and responsibility for their future students. "I could definitely implement this lesson in a classroom and feel comfortable and confident that I was meeting the needs of my ELL students" (Participant O). This self-reflective attitude was best expressed by Participant Y, "Perhaps the greatest thing I learned in this exercise was to self-assess and self-monitor how I present materials, directions, and content to ELL students."

In addition to the ability to critically assess their future plans and activities, the candidates recognized how this new understanding and capabilities will have an impact on their future classrooms. Participant L previously noted that the project required him to reflect on his plans, continued with this statement, "As a teacher, I will complete similar evaluations of my lesson plans to ensure that they encompass the needs of all learners."

The future importance of these abilities necessary to complete the annotated lesson plans was emphasized by one of the candidates:

> When this class first began I had given little thought to how my instruction would have to be tailored to meet the needs of the English language learning students. I always had assumed that there would be special instruction classes for them and they would not be included in general education classrooms. After looking closer at the composition of classrooms I visited and the stories I hear from classmates I realize that I will have to be prepared to meet the needs of these students in every class I teach. (Participant P)

Overall, in exploring the results of the second research questions, the teacher candidates found themselves to be better prepared to educate emergent bilingual students. The lesson planning, while not always considered easy, did cause them to explore the knowledge they had developed and link it to the needs of the students. It provided them with the opportunity to reflect on what they had developed in previous classes, as well as realize they must focus on the needs of all students in their classrooms.

Practical Implications and Recommendations

Annotated lesson plans have the potential to assist teacher candidates in their preparation. Giving candidates the opportunity to see the connection of the theories they have learned with the actual application of them in the classroom should assist them in becoming education professionals. In other words, they will have the power and confidence needed to make decisions on how to best educate all students in their classroom(s).

From the perspective of the course instructor, the implementation of the annotated lesson plans has provided a new window into the pedagogical understanding of the teacher candidates. For example, when a candidate includes an annotation that links comprehensible input (Krashen, 1981) with an assessment focused on grammatical accuracy, further instruction is needed.

The implementation of annotated lesson plans could occur in any course where lesson plans are required. The instructor could make modifications as to what is an acceptable annotation, as well as consider content-specific requirements. While my students have been required to submit their plans electronically in a format that allows for interactive footnotes or endnotes, traditional paper versions could be created as well.

Grading the annotated lesson plans would follow the same pattern as any lesson plan. The development of the plans must align with the course outcomes. A grading rubric can be developed that would include all outcome-based expectations. The rubric used in this course is included in Appendix B.

Limitations of the Study

This study has several limitations. First, this is a study based on Naturalistic Inquiry (Lincoln & Guba, 1985). Consequently, the generalizability of this study is limited. Replication is possible as other teacher educators take the initiative in their own local context. As with other such studies, replication of the use of annotated lesson plans would provide a greater understanding of the effectiveness of annotated lesson plans in other contexts (Johnson, 1997).

Second, in this study, all of the teacher candidates were preparing to become elementary level teachers. To strengthen our understanding of the impact of such lesson plans, additional studies would need to be conducted with secondary teacher candidates preparing for content-specific areas including math, science, and language arts, as well as for candidates preparing to work in specialization areas such as special needs and literacy.

Finally, the world of lesson planning in teacher preparation programs is becoming more and more regulated by state and national agencies. Twenty-three states and the District of Columbia have joined together in using a student teaching assessment tool called edTPA. One aspect of the edTPA is the development of lesson plans. While no single format of the plan has been established, the requirements needed to successfully pass the assessment are complicated enough that schools are establishing planning systems that would be less open for the inclusion of "non-edTPA" items in the plans. However, even with such frameworks, the concept of annotating the plans would provide important information for evaluators about the preparation of teacher candidates to meet the needs of diverse students.

Conclusion

Educating emergent bilingual students is a complex, highly contextualized effort that occurs at all levels and in all states. Preparing preservice teacher candidates to effectively mentor and instruct such students requires both preparation in the content areas as well as proven pedagogies. Too often teacher candidates develop the pedagogical techniques and methods without truly understanding the theoretical bases upon which they are built.

In this particular setting, annotated lesson plans helped students connect theory and practice. Through the use of annotated lesson plans, the professor could better assess the candidates' ability to use research-based methods and techniques. It allowed the candidates to understand why the activities they included should be used. The candidates were also able to better recognize their weaknesses and prepare to address such weaknesses. Finally, as viewed through the candidates' reflection statements, the annotated lesson plans increased the self-confidence of the candidates in working with emergent bilingual students.

References

Brown, H. D. (2007). *Principles of language learning and teaching*. White Plains, NY: Pearson Longman.

Carle, E. (1969, 1987). *The very hungry caterpillar*. New York, NY: Scholastic.

Darling-Hammond, L. (2009). Teacher education and the American future. *Journal of Teacher Education, 61*(1−2), 35−47.

Elliot, J. (1993, 2012). Three perspectives on coherence and continuity in teacher education. In J. Elliot (Ed.), *Reconstructing teacher education*. New York, NY: Routledge.

Ellis, R. (1985). *Understanding second language acquisition*. Oxford: Oxford University Press.

Elsbree, W. S. (1939). *The American teacher*. New York, NY: American Book Company.

Fillmore, L. W., & Snow, C. E. (2002). What teachers need to know about language. In C. T. Adger, C. E. Snow, & D. Christian (Eds.), *What teachers need to know about language* (pp. 7−53). Washington, DC: Center for Applied Linguistics.

Freeman, D. E., & Freeman, Y. S. (2011). *Between worlds: Access to second language acquisition*. Portsmouth, NH: Heinemann.

Gottlieb, M. (2006). *Assessing English language learners: Bridges from language proficiency to academic achievement*. Thousand Oaks, CA: Corwin Press.

Hammerness, K., Darling-Hammond, L., Bransford, J., Berliner, D., Cochran-Smith, M., McDonald, M., & Zeichner, K. (2005). How teachers learn and develop. In L. Darling-Hammond & J. Bransford (Eds.), *Preparing teachers for a changing world: What teachers should learn and be able to do* (pp. 358−389). San Francisco, CA: John Wiley & Sons.

James, W. (1892, 1939). *Talks to teachers on psychology*. New York, NY: Henry Holt Company.

John, P. D. (2006). Lesson planning and the student teacher: Re-thinking the dominant model. *Journal of Curriculum Studies, 38*(4), 483−498.

Johnson, R. B. (1997). Examining the validity structure of qualitative research. *Education, 118*(2), 282.

Krashen, S. D. (1981). Bilingual education and second language acquisition theory. In California State Department of Education (Ed.), *Schooling and language minority students: A theoretical framework* (pp. 51–78). Los Angeles, CA: Evaluation, Dissemination and Assessment Center, California State University.

Lederman, N. G., & Niess, M. L. (2000). If you fail to plan, are you planning to Fail? *School Science and Mathematics, 100*(2), 57–60.

Lincoln, Y. S., & Guba, E. G. (1985). *Naturalistic inquiry.* Beverly Hills, CA: Sage Publications.

Morris, A. K., & Hiebert, J. (2011). Creating shared instructional products: An alternative approach to improving teaching. *Educational Researcher, 40*(1), 5–14.

National Center for Educational Statistics. (2012). Graph illustration from Digest of Educational Statistics. *Table 47: Number and percentage of public school students participating in programs for English language learners, by state: Selected years, 2002–03 through 2010–11.* Retrieved from http://nces.ed.gov/programs/digest/d12/tables/dt12_047.asp

National Center for Educational Statistics. (2013). *The condition of education.* Retrieved from http://nces.ed.gov/programs/coe/indicator_cgf.asp

Professional Educator Standards Board. (2008). *Supporting English Language Learners: Recommendations for teacher preparation and professional development in Washington State.* Retrieved from http://www.pesb.wa.gov/publications/reports

Short, D. (1999). Integrating language and content for effective sheltered instruction programs. In C. Faltis & P. Wolfe (Eds.), *So much to say: Adolescents, bilingualism, and ESL in the secondary school* (pp. 105–137). New York, NY: Teacher College Press.

Spradley, J. P. (1980). *Participant observation.* New York, NY: Holt, Rinehart & Winston.

Swain, M. (1985). Communicative competence: Some roles of comprehensible input and comprehensible output in its development. In S. M. Gass & C. G. Madden (Eds.), *Input in second language acquisition.* Rowley, MA: Newbury House.

Timperley, H. (2008). *Teacher professional learning and development.* Educational Practices Series – 18. Brussels: International Academy of Education.

Appendix A: Teacher candidate sample lesson plan and annotation

Unit1: Washington State History

Lesson Topic: What were the main events that caused the Pig War?

Length of Lesson: 120 minutes (2 days)

Prerequisite Knowledge
Students should understand that major events in history are often times a result of other smaller problems leading up to the larger issue. Students should be able to extract the main ideas out of a document. Students should be able to work in a group and discuss ideas in order to help answer the inquiry question.

Student Population
The classroom is extremely diverse. Native English-speaking students and English language learners create the classroom population. English language development is focused toward students who are at the *advanced beginning2*, and *intermediate levels3* of English proficiency.

Outcomes
Content Objectives: Students will be able to write a thesis that includes all key points in the class document describing the main events that led to the Pig War.

Language Objectives:
Students will be able to discuss in a group setting each document presented. Students will be able to define content-specific vocabulary.

Standards

- Social Studies: 5.4.1
- Reading: 3.1.1.4.1
- Communication: 2.3.1

Materials
Engage Materials
Explanation Materials
Evaluative Materials

Preparation Activities
Engage
Student will come to this lesson with a wide range of comprehension abilities. Being able to comprehend and select main points from each data set it a main component of this lesson. The lesson deals with understanding that many smaller events in history often lead to a larger more major event. *Linking lessons4* will help students to better understand the new material. Once the lessons have been linked, students will use *personal student friendly dictionaries5* to define unknown words in table groups. The words will be important to helping understand the main points of each data set that students will be working with.

Instructional Activities
Explore
Students will work together as a *group7* to read and discuss each data set. Students will use the strategy *think-ink-pair-share6*. Students will use a graphic organizer provided to record all ideas, and points found within each data set that it presented. The teacher will present each data set, and read through the information using *comprehensible input9* one time. Students will express what the group talked about in front of the class. Students are working toward answering the inquiry questions, "What were the main events that caused the Pig War?" The teacher will capture the ideas that the students found most important from each data set in a class document for all students to see, and have access to. After all the ideas have been captured, students will work to write a hypothesis. Individuals will have the opportunity to share their hypothesis with the class. Students will repeat this process for each data set presented. Students will read through the data set, capture the main ideas using a *graphic organizer10*, share findings with the class, create a hypothesis to answer the inquiry question, and share the hypotheses with the class.

Explain
Students will vote as a class on the main points that students feel best answers the inquiry question. Each student will write all of the main points down on a graphic organizer. Students' will then work to create a final thesis that answers the inquiry question, including all of the points discussed as a class. On the last page of the inquiry worksheet/graphic organizer students will find a place to write their final thesis. Students will then write a one paragraph explanation that discusses why the main points best answer the inquiry question using evidence gathered from the data sets.

Review8

Once all of the data sets have been presented, together as a class the inquiry question will be revisited. The lesson will end with an oral and written review of what was learned. The teacher will ask the students, "What is the question we are trying to answer today? Please write the question at the bottom of your graphic organizer or highlight the question on your graphic organizer." Students will then be asked to answer exit questions orally and written. Students will answer the questions in partners, and then complete the exit ticket.

Assessment

- Formative: I will know students are working toward the learning goals based on the students' initial hypothesis, and the revision of the initial hypothesis. I will know that this is happening by roaming from table group to table group eyeing the students' work, listening to table conversation, and asking questions to the student to ensure understanding. Questions are as follow:
  - I like what you have written as your hypothesis so far. Will you please explain to me what information you used to create your hypothesis?
  - (For my students who may be stuck, or unsure) What information did we just talk about in the last data set? What new idea did you learn? Is this important to helping answer the inquiry question? Why is the information important?
  - Students will be able to orally produce answers as well as in writing.
- Summative: I will be assessing the students' thesis. The student will be assessed on the strength of his or her thesis, and whether or not the main points highlighted in the classroom document are included in the thesis statement. This assessment will allow me to see if my students can connect the idea of using data sets to acquire new information in order to produce a well-rounded thesis.

    I will know that my students will have reached the listed objectives based on the written thesis. Students will demonstrate an understanding of creating a conclusion based on obtaining information from various different data sets through the creation of a thesis.

Notes

1. **Authenticity**
    "Language acquisition is enhanced when students are engaged in meaningful activities and their anxiety levels are low. Students must feel

comfortable enough to risk producing imperfect language. Students who are in the process of learning English must be able to speak within the comfort and safety of friends, and yet participate in activities that require them to use more explicit formal language" (Rothenberg & Fisher, 2007). This lesson is structured in a way that supports English language development by providing a classroom environment that is conducive to practicing proficiency but utilizing partners and group learning. Students collaborate, and share ideas in order to come to a better understanding. Utilizing groups, students can work more freely and not have high anxiety as with whole group discussions. This lesson relies on small group communication.

2. **Ability Level Expectations: Advanced Beginning**
A student at the advanced beginning level of English proficiency is capable of participating in academic discussions on familiar topics, begins to use academic vocabulary, expresses self using words and/or phrases to identify main idea and details, and begins to write based on model or frame (OSPI, 2010).

3. **Ability Level Expectation: Intermediate**
Students at the intermediate level of English proficiency is capable of participating in academic social discussions, uses appropriate social and academic vocabulary for different audiences, responds to and asks why- and yes/no questions, increases vocabulary through reading across content areas, infers and makes generalizations from text, and writes simple sentences (OSPI, 2010).

4. **Linking Lessons**
"Lessons benefit from reviving students' past learning, linking it to concepts to be presented. The more frequently you revisit conceptually important pieces of information, the more opportunity students have for learning" (Reiss, 2012). The lesson will be linked to the previous days learning. Students will be asked to turn and talk with their table partners about what was discussed the day prior. "What did we talk about yesterday when we were discussing Washington State becoming an actual state?" Students will discuss in partners, and then share their understanding with the class. ELL students will benefit from this strategy because they can share their understanding of the previous days material with a partner, and learn how both lessons are connected in order to help the student construct meaning of the newly presented information.

5. **Student Friendly Personal Dictionaries**
"Personal dictionaries benefit all students. No matter the form, they help students remember new words and phrases that are academically

useful and/or personally meaningful or interesting" (Reiss, 2012). This lesson introduces students to new, important academic and process vocabulary words. Students will work together in pairs to define the new words in their personal dictionaries to help the students remember the new language. ELL students will benefit greatly because they will be working with partners to understand and define unknown words that are important to know during the lesson.

6. **Think-Ink-Pair-Share**

"Think-Ink-Pair-Share is a strategy that encourages participation at the same time that it activates students' prior knowledge. It is a way of getting students actively and immediately involved in learning new concepts and topics" (Reiss, 2012). This strategy is used throughout the entire lesson in order to help students, especially students who are working toward becoming proficient in the English language. This lesson requires students to think critically about each data set, and by given the students the opportunity to discuss thoroughly what was read, all students will come to a better understanding of the material.

7. **Purposeful Grouping**

"Classrooms that provide maximum opportunities for students to talk are those that are organized around a variety of grouping configurations. Students frequently work collaboratively with others, in pairs or small groups, to develop skills, complete a task and construct meaning" (Rothenberg & Fisher, 2007). Students work in pairs or groups throughout the entire lesson. The lesson is structured in such a way that student voice drives the lesson. By allowing students to discuss and make meaning, students are in more control of their learning. Grouping students and asking students to discuss and talk about various documents during the lesson allows students to be actively engaged in the learning process, which allows the students to ELL students to construct meaning with the help and support of peer discourse.

8. **Reviewing**

"If background knowledge forms the building blocks of learning, then review is the cement that holds those blocks together. Mini-reviews during a lesson and a final review at the end will benefit all students. Frequent review during and at the end of every class period reinforces learning; it far exceeds the value the minutes devoted to it" (Reiss, 2012). At the end of the lesson, students are to answer exit questions to reinforces the objectives of the lesson, and to bring understanding to the purpose of the entire lesson. Students are offered two ways of doing so, orally or in writing. The students are given a choice to help support ELL students. A student at the advanced beginning stage may not be able to fully write out what was learned, but he or she can communicate what was learned via spoken language.

9. **Comprehensible Input**

   "Slowing down the rate of speech slightly and pausing between thoughts gives learners time to process what they've learned and catch up" (Rothenberg & Fisher, 2007). According to Krashen's theories, in order to help ELL students understand the information being presented, it is important when the teacher is presenting the information, the teacher speaks slow, articulates important ideas, repeats key words and/or phrase, pauses frequently, and uses gestures when appropriate. This will allow ELL students the necessary time to process the information being said and make sense of it.

10. **Graphic Organizers**

    "Graphic organizers help students understand complex text and ideas. They are especially useful as a during-reading or after-reading activity" (Rothenberg & Fisher, 2007). Providing the students with a structured graphic organizer will help to identify key points of each data set, and help to keep all of the information organized. ELL students will benefit from using a graphic organizer because it will help to make the text more comprehensible.

Works Cited

Reiss, J. (2012). *120 content strategies for English language learners, teaching for academic success in secondary school* (2nd ed.). Boston, MA: Allyn & Bacon.

Rothenberg, C., & Fisher, D. (2007). *Teaching English language learners, a differentiated approach*. Columbus: Prentice Hall.

Washington State OSPI. (2010, May). Retrieved from http://www.k12.wa.us/MigrantBilingual/pubdocs/MasterELD_0510.pdf

Appendix B: Annotated lesson plan grading rubric

	Exceeds	Meets	Falls Below
Theory and application	More than two different theories are documented with basic information included in the explanations, and/or two different theories are documented with comprehensive information included in the explanations.	Two different theories are documented with basic information included in the explanations.	Less than two different theories are documented with basic information included in the explanations.
Language proficiency modifications	Modifications for and differentiation for ELL students at three or more different language proficiency levels are included.	Modifications for and differentiation for ELL students at two different language proficiency levels are included.	Below expectations: modifications for and differentiation for ELL students at less than two language proficiency levels are included.
Teaching techniques	All of the following criteria are effectively included in the lesson planning: (1) student population language expectations; (2) objectives and/or outcomes (a) subject area (required), (b) language (required), (c) skill/strategy development (optional); (3) standards; (4) materials; (5) preparation activities; (6) instructional activities; (7) review; and (8) assessment.	All but two of the following criteria are effectively included in the lesson planning: (1) student population language expectations; (2) objectives and/or outcomes (a) subject area (required), (b) language (required), (c) skill/ strategy development (optional); (3) standards; (4) materials; (5) preparation activities; (6) instructional activities; (7) review; and (8) assessment.	More than two of the following criteria are not effectively included in the lesson planning: (1) student population language expectations; (2) objectives and/or outcomes (a) subject area (required), (b) language (required), (c) skill/ strategy development (optional); (3) standards; (4) materials; (5) preparation activities; (6) instructional activities; (7) review; and (8) assessment.

CHAPTER 11

"PERFORMING GOOFINESS" IN TEACHER EDUCATION FOR EMERGENT BILINGUAL STUDENTS

Mary Carol Combs

Abstract

This chapter explores an approach to instruction in pre-service classes called "goofiness pedagogy." Embedded in teaching and learning theories, goofiness pedagogy is designed to model creative teaching to help emergent bilingual learners academically, linguistically, and socially. Currently in Arizona, highly restrictive language policies limit curricular and pedagogical choices for students acquiring English. As a result, pre-service teachers are often reluctant to work with them, and worried that their own creativity will be constrained. This chapter thus discusses a multi-year study of goofiness pedagogy — theatrical drama, play, and performance — that helps pre-service teachers develop an alternative vision of exceptional teaching for and with emergent bilingual learners. Data sources include student and author reflections on the practice of performed goofiness in Structured English Immersion classes at the University of Arizona, video-taped performances of students engaged

Research on Preparing Preservice Teachers to Work Effectively with Emergent Bilinguals
Advances in Research on Teaching, Volume 21, 287–312
Copyright © 2014 by Emerald Group Publishing Limited
ISSN: 1479-3687/doi:10.1108/S1479-368720140000021010

in drama and improvisation, and analysis of student written artifacts. Findings indicate that while some pre-teachers hesitate to participate in "performed goofiness," the majority believe that theatrical activities encourage them to try out innovative teaching strategies, take risks, make mistakes, and analyze those mistakes in a supportive community of practice. Equally important, pre-service teachers begin to understand that learning in general, and language learning in particular, are social pursuits and that teachers should create social spaces in their own class-rooms to support the academic and language development of emergent bilingual students. Goofiness pedagogy also has transformed the author's own teaching practices, and consequently represents a "pedagogy of hope" within a rigid state context.

Keywords: Performed goofiness; pre-service teachers; restrictive language policies; teacher risk-taking; drama in teaching

I'm a senior in college now, and I have been through more teachers than I can remember. The ones who made an everlasting impression on me are the teachers who made me feel comfortable in my own skin by making complete fools of themselves. They showed me that you are never too old to embrace humility and learn from it. I want the children I teach to recognize what these teachers showed me. Humility is strength and when embraced instead of feared, it puts the world at your fingertips. (Jessica Juarez ("Jay Jay"))

When Jay Jay sent me this comment about the Structured English Immersion (SEI) methods class she took with me recently, my first reaction was: Is that how I came across – as a complete (and old) fool? On the other hand, she seems to recognize her own inner silliness as a potential tool for good teaching.

My teaching in this course *was* unusual, some would even say eccentric. But the word I use most often to describe my style is "goofy," so my teach-ing incorporated a kind of elaborate and intentional "goofiness" that I tried to perform at least once in every class. I say *perform* because the kind of dramatic techniques I use take practice, experimentation, risk and, as Jay Jay rightly noted, a large degree of humility. I have been actively perform-ing goofiness activities in my pre-service classes for four years. Even after considerable trial and error, I'm still practicing and learning how far I can push my pre-service students out of their comfort zones; essentially, how to help them "get over themselves" in order to teach content creatively, even "outrageously" (Progrow, 2009).

In this chapter, I define goofiness pedagogy and what it means to perform goofiness, how this instructional tool is embedded in theories of learning and teaching, and how it can potentially help emergent bilingual students socially, academically, and linguistically. In this chapter, I use the labels "English language learner" and "emergent bilingual" interchangeably. I am mindful of the privileging of *English* in "English language learner," as well as the more positive endorsement of the potential for the development of bilingualism in "emergent bilingual." However, I live in a state whose legislators seem determined to prevent even superficial bilingualism among this population of students. The use of the term "emergent bilingual" is hopeful, but "English language learner" is probably more realistic, at least in Arizona.

I have implemented the goofiness activities described here in my teacher preparation courses since 2010, and while the reactions to them from pre-service teachers are mostly enthusiastic, my ideas about this kind of teaching are still evolving. Between 2010 and the present, I have undertaken a multi-year self-study of my own teaching practice with pre-service teachers. I developed and implemented explicitly "goofy" content and language focused lessons in my SEI classes in part to explore how far I could push myself and my students into performance. Primarily however, I wanted to see whether drama and performed goofiness helped pre-service teachers develop a vision of exceptional teaching for and with emergent bilingual learners. This chapter thus proposes instructional settings that teachers can create and makes the case for multiple linguistic and social benefits for students who are acquiring English as a second language. I end the chapter with suggestions for how pre-service teachers can think about and begin to design lessons that incorporate goofiness.

Context Is Everything (But It Doesn't Have To Dominate)

My explorations into the goofiness paradigm originated from an ideological dilemma that I and other English as a second language and bilingual teacher educators in Arizona experience. The dilemma is whether to significantly alter our pre-service education programs in order to integrate ELL curriculum and pedagogy derived from seriously flawed state language and education policies, or whether to defy state law and promote the continued use of effective teaching practices for emergent bilingual students. Contrary to research in second language acquisition that supports the use of students' first language in their acquisition of academic content and English, Arizona has adopted a rigid English only, skills-based approach. All English language learners in the state, with few exceptions, are segregated for four hours each day into a euphemistically named "English language development" (ELD) block. This block consists almost exclusively of grammar, vocabulary, and reading instruction. The teaching of content areas like math, science, social studies, and language arts — which all students need in order to pass state achievement tests and which are routinely provided to non-ELL students — is openly discouraged by state education officials (see Fig. 1). To be sure, some ELD teachers manage to incorporate content subjects into their language instruction in innovative ways. Their efforts to provide an equitable education to English learners, in spite of top-down, a theoretical policy mandates, should be supported and affirmed.

The rationale for this dubious program rests largely in a fallacy: the best and quickest way for students to learn English is to immerse them in it for extended period of time. This time on task principle of language acquisition advances three general assumptions: first, that immersion in English is more effective than other alternatives, second, that immersion classrooms will enable English language learners to acquire the language in one year, and third, that young children are ideally suited for immersion because they are better at learning languages than older children or adults (Combs,

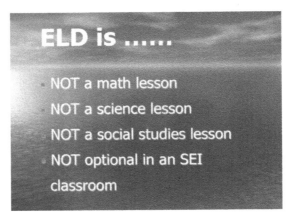

Fig. 1. What English Language Development Is NOT. *Source*: Arizona Department of Education (2009).

2012). While ostensibly logical, these assumptions have been consistently disproved by research studies in second language acquisition (see, e.g., Collier, 1987, 1988, 1995; Cummins, 1992, 1996; Hakuta, Butler, & Witt, 2000; Hawkins, 2005; Kasper & Roever, 2005; Krashen, 1996; Krashen, Rolstad, & MacSwan, 2007; Martinez-Wenzl, Pérez, & Gándara, 2012; Wong Fillmore & Snow, 2002).

Since 2009, when Arizona officials forced all school districts in the state to implement the ELD block, the growing number of research studies and evaluations about the program has been uniformly negative. English language learners are not acquiring English in one year, as required by state law, and because they have not received instruction in other subject areas, by the time they are reclassified and transferred to mainstream classrooms, they are academically behind their English-speaking peers. Finally, lengthy segregation of students into special language blocks has affected their self-esteem (Blum & Johnson, 2012; Combs & Nicholas, 2012; DaSilva, Combs, & Moll, 2012; Florez, 2012; Gándara & Hopkins, 2010; Gándara & Orfield, 2012; Heineke & Cameron, 2013; Johnson, 2012; Leckie, Kaplan, & Rubinstein-Avila, 2013; Mackinney & Rios-Aguilar, 2012; Rios-Aguilar, González, & Moll, 2012; Rios-Aguilar, González, & Sabetghadam, 2012).

Researchers have not disputed the need to teach grammar and vocabulary development to emergent bilingual students. Rather, they emphasize the importance of embedding linguistic features of English in meaningful context (Goldenberg & Coleman, 2010; Saunders & Goldenberg, 2010). The question is whether teaching grammar and vocabulary alone is sufficient preparation to prepare students for regular classrooms. Most serious ELL practitioners, fortified with learning theory and social justice principles, would answer that question with a resounding no.

Purpose of the Project

Given the top-down and contested nature of Arizona language policies, teachers of emergent bilingual students are often uncertain about what they can and cannot do in an ELD classroom, for example, whether teachers are permitted to use students' first language, whether or how to teach content within the rigid parameters of the program, or indeed whether they can stray from the strict time designations for teaching oral English, grammar, reading, vocabulary, and writing. My pre-service teachers also wonder how they can possibly make the direct teaching of these subjects engaging for students, and whether their own creativity, albeit developing, will be constrained.

Because Arizona's policy mandates for the education of emergent bilingual students are clearly intended to restrict the curricular and pedagogical choices of ELD or SEI teachers, I have sought ways in my teacher preparation classes to counter the trepidation some students express about working with English learners. I incorporate theatrical and improvised dramatic performances as a way to model the kinds of creative possibilities teachers can use with students acquiring English as a second language.

Although initially my goofiness activities were designed to model ways to engage K-12 emergent bilingual learners even under oppressive circumstances, the activities consistently yielded a happy residual effect as well — considerable levity and fun in my SEI classes. Over time, these kinds of activities have become a principal focus in my pre-service SEI classes. Indeed, the students' final project in the class is to teach a sheltered lesson in a content area in which students incorporate numerous features of goofiness pedagogy. This endeavor is related to my continuing research interest in locating and promoting "pedagogies of hope" (Freire, 2007) within the rigid constraints of Arizona language policies.

Participants: Pre-Service Teachers In SEI Classes

I incorporate goofiness projects in both undergraduate and graduate pre-service SEI methods classes required by the state for certification and graduation. At the University of Arizona, undergraduate pre-service teachers typically major in elementary education, while graduate pre-service teachers study different content areas for secondary teaching. Undergraduate students enroll in SEI classes at different stages in their program; for some it is the first teacher education class they take. Others take the class immediately before they begin student teaching and or during their student teaching placements. Students typically enroll in these classes on campus or at school sites. The demographics of the teacher education program in the College of Education mirror that of other institutions: our students are mostly white, middle class, and female. In the 2014 spring semester a total of 790 students were enrolled in the College of Education's teacher preparation program. Of this number, 706 students were female, and 84 were male; 524 students described themselves as white, 103 as mixed race,

53 as Hispanic/Latino, 67 as Mexican American/Chicano, 15 as African American, 10 as Asian (the remaining students either did not indicate ethnicity or checked the "other" category).

These pre-service teachers overwhelmingly student-teach in the Tucson, Arizona, metropolitan area in K-12 schools in which students of color predominate. According to Milem, Bryan, Sesate, and Montaño (2013), in Pima County, where the University of Arizona is located, white students comprise only 39 percent of the K-12 population compared to nearly 48 percent of Latino students. The remaining percentages include Native American, African American, and Asian American students. With few exceptions, growing numbers of emergent bilingual students are present in nearly every Tucson school and student teachers will encounter and work with them. If pre-service teachers are placed in ELD classrooms, 100 percent of their students will be emergent bilinguals. Even if pre-service teachers leave the area for other school districts in Arizona, they will encounter English language learners: statewide, Arizona schools serve approximately 166,000 of these students, or about 15 percent of all K-12 students in the state (Batalova & McHugh, 2010). This figure is contested. The Arizona Department of Education reports that the number of English language learners declined significantly, from 162,136 in 2004 to 75,970 in 2012. The department reported a 51 percent decrease among Latino ELLs and an 89 percent decrease in Indigenous ELLs (Milem et al., 2013). The validity of the state's ELL proficiency test – the Arizona English Language Learner Assessment (AZELLA) – was challenged by the U.S. Office for Civil Rights and the Department of Justice because the test's cut scores for student reclassification as fluent had been manipulated to reclassify English learners as proficient when they had reached only an intermediate level of proficiency as determined by the state's own ELL performance standards (Florez, 2012). In addition, a change in the Home Language Survey, used by schools to identify students for English proficiency testing, resulted in a serious undercount of ELLs in Arizona (Goldenberg & Rutherford-Quach, 2012). Milem et al. (2013) argue that these developments "created an environment that made it more difficult for ELL students to be eligible to receive services and easier to be reclassified and transitioned out of the ELL program" (p. 19).

Whether or not our pre-service teachers decide to pursue teaching positions at schools serving emergent bilingual students, the sociocultural, historical, and linguistic information provided in the SEI courses gives pre-service teachers a deeper understanding of the social context of education for emergent bilingual students and their communities. The theoretical basis for goofiness pedagogy and its practical application in K-12 class-rooms can thus benefit *all* students.

Methodology

In the fall of 2010, I began a systematic self-study of my teaching practices with pre-service teachers in SEI classes. As a teacher educator seeking ways to improve my own practice, I wanted to "walk the talk" by bringing together my own understanding of good pedagogy with emergent bilingual students and the actions I undertook in pre-service classes to model this pedagogy (Hamilton & Pinnegar, 2000, p. 239). If I believed that implementing drama and goofiness was a useful tool to develop students' language and content knowledge, I had to make it an important focus in my teacher education courses.

Known in the literature as S-STEP — self-study of teacher education practices — this methodology is grounded in a study of "personal practice in the space between self and others in the practice" (Pinnegar, Hamilton, & Fitzgerald, 2010, p. 1). I wanted to examine my own practice and to collaborate with my students in this practice. Thus, my approach was consciously introspective and interactive (Dinkelman, 2003; Pinnegar & Hamilton, 2009). The data for this study comprised personal critical reflection on the practice of performed goofiness across undergraduate and graduate pre-service teacher education programs and in the SEI courses I taught, student reflections and reactions to goofiness pedagogy, video-taped performances of me and my students engaged in drama, and analysis of written artifacts. My first set of self-study research questions considered my own goofiness practice, that is, how did I operationalize goofiness pedagogy? How "edgy" or "goofy" was I prepared to be in making connections between performance and content instruction? Did goofiness pedagogy improve my instruction with future teachers of emergent bilingual students? Subsequent questions in the study focused on how I would determine whether students were responding positively to performance activities, and how I would handle pre-service teachers who were reluctant to participate. I also provided students with several questions at the end of the semester, to which they could answer anonymously:

1. Was it easy or difficult for you to participate in the drama games we did in class? If it was difficult, please explain why. If it was not, explain why not.

2. How comfortable do you feel implementing drama and goofiness in your own classrooms?
3. Are there benefits for teaching this way for yourself and for your students?
4. Have you ever taught a dramatic or "goofy" lesson? Would you like to? About what subject?

Students' answers to these questions, which contained both praise and critique, have helped me refine my ideas and implementation of performed goofiness activities. I have also kept a reflective journal of notes about student reactions to the variety of goofiness activities I conduct. Various colleagues have video-taped me introducing students to performed goofiness as an academic construct and leading them in drama and goofiness activities. The videos present a unique opportunity for analysis and self-critique. Recently, I have collected written artifacts from students, including collaborative ideas about goofiness activities, scripts and informal dialogue for roleplaying, simulations and games related to content subjects, as well as photographs of students performing individually or in groups. Throughout the duration of my self-study, I have conducted a literature review of the use of drama and improvisations in K-16 classrooms, in second language classrooms, and with emergent bilingual students.

What Is Performed Goofiness?

What I call performed goofiness could just as easily be described with labels used by other educators: "captivating instruction" (Bontjes, 2013), "outrageous teaching" (Progrow, 2009), "performance pedagogy" (Cahnmann-Taylor & Souto-Manning, 2010), "dialogic drama" (Edmiston, 2014), or "theater game workshops" (Spolin, 1986). The term *goofiness* signals the playfulness inherent in this approach. Goofiness teaching is performative because it does not come naturally to most teachers. Performing goofiness requires us to overtly assume an alternate persona for a brief period of time. For some pre-service teachers, this persona initially feels peculiar because it requires physical exertion, for example, exaggerating or distorting body positions and hand gestures, or raising their voices in dramatic ways. For others, the alternate persona may be an extension of their own personalities and thus manifest more easily (Bontjes, 2013). Because goofiness teaching is expressive and dramatic, it involves risk and emotion, and must be practiced, revised, and ultimately performed.

Etymology of the word *goofy***.** The word *goofy* implies a degree of silliness, to be sure, but in a cheerful way. An internet search of the word turns up mostly positive associations: wacky, nutty, zany, mildly ludicrous, harmlessly eccentric, and silly in a funny or pleasant way (Dictionary.com; Merriam-Webster.com). The etymology of *goofy* is more obscure. The Oxford English Dictionary reports that the word was probably borrowed from the Middle French *goffe*, meaning awkward or stupid. *Goffe*, and later *goff*, meant a fool, dolt, or foolish clown. One of the earliest appearances of *goofy* in the North American popular press occurred in the national weekly *Collier's* in February 1921, in which a man was reported to have a "goofy grin." Dashiell Hammett was among the first to use the noun *goofiness* in his detective novel *Dain Curse*, published in 1930. Hammett wrote, "Evidence of goofiness is easily found: the more you dig into yourself, the more you turn up" (Oxford English Dictionary Online, 2013). The Disney character Goofy first appeared in 1932 as a clumsy, not too smart, but good-natured talking dog. The Walt Disney Archives describes Goofy this way: "Goofy is good-natured. Though he can be a bit clumsy and trips himself up from time to time, he never loses his willingness to try his best at anything" (mickey.disney.com, n.d.).

Why do we like goofy people? When most of us recall our own schooling experiences, we typically think of the teachers we had in binary categories – the ones who frustrated or disciplined us, and the ones who challenged or made us laugh. When I ask my students to describe a favorite teacher, they invariably put the teacher's ability to engage or entertain them at the top of the list. Their favorite teachers are "funny, humorous, wild, eccentric, original, creative" and, in fact, "goofy." My own favorite teacher was my high school world history teacher, who taught history as an extended narrative on the often bizarre, heroic, and tragic exploits of individuals and nations. Her voice would rise and fall depending on the courage or folly of these exploits, culminating with a kind of shuffle, slap on the knee, and loudly pitched rhetorical question, "Can you BELIEVE that?"

Performed "Goofiness": Embedded in Multiple Disciplines

Drama and improvisation in K-16 classrooms. There is an extensive literature on drama and improvisation in K-16 education classrooms. Spolin's (1986) classic *Theater Games for the Classroom* is designed for classroom teachers as a supplement to the general curriculum. Spolin's approach to drama teaching begins with the premise that theater games are rooted in play. As such they are highly social and collaborative: students and teachers meet in theater workshop spaces as fellow players in creative and intellectual games. Because children's worlds are controlled by adults, Spolin writes, classroom theater games are among the few places outside of play "where children can contribute to the world in which they find themselves" (1986, p. 3).

Cahnmann-Taylor and Souto-Manning (2010) argue that bringing theater into classrooms has the potential to break down barriers to social change. Using a professional development approach that brings together theories of critical pedagogy from Paulo Freire (1970) and teaching strategies from Augusto Boal's *Theater of the Oppressed* (1979), Cahnmann-Taylor and Souto-Manning feature theatrical exercises that help teachers use their political agency to bring about social change. The process of change is not one-sided, however. If teachers are to create positive change in their students' lives, they have to begin with themselves; hence, theater exercises provide teachers with "opportunities to rehearse alternative, edgier personas and to feel they've got a supporting cast behind them" (2010, p. 5).

Bontjes (2013) carries the character and cast analogy even further by suggesting that teachers need to think like entertainers: "Entertaining is the *key* to education. You cannot educate a student whose attention you do not hold. You cannot educate a student whom you do not *entertain!*" (p. 5, emphasis in original). Bonjes recommends that teachers adopt a character who is everything they are not ... a character that has all of "your strengths but more so and one that has none of your weaknesses ... the character is you but better" (p. 13).

Progrow (2009) draws from cognitive theory, neuroscience, and imagination and learning theory to advance the case for "outrageous teaching," or content area pedagogy that incorporates humor and dramatic technique and inventive storylines as a way of connecting to students and helping them retain content material. He describes outrageous lessons taught in math, English, and social studies by several of his pre-service teachers, analyzing strong and weak features from each lesson. In addition to captivating students' attention, these pre-service teachers themselves were transformed by the realization that they were capable of exuberant teaching.

Similarly, Wright (2001) argues that teacher preparation programs must move beyond merely teaching *about* drama and improvisation to teaching *how* to incorporate it into their practice teaching. Teachers must learn how to combine teaching strategies with drama and thus "think drama on their feet" (p. 206). She concludes that teacher education programs should

include demonstrations of drama in methods classes, opportunities to participate with other pre-service teachers in dramatic enactments and theater
games, and finally, activities that help teachers develop, practice, and teach
drama lessons (p. 209).

Drama, improvisation, and games in the second language classroom.
Role-playing and language games also have been important components
of second language classrooms. These activities provide extended opportunities for second language learners to develop oral communication as well
as listening, reading, and writing in second languages. Because drama and
improvisation activities invariably require students to adapt an alternative
persona, students are more willing to take risks, and indeed, are often less
inhibited and less aware of making grammatical mistakes (Ernst-Slavit &
Wenger, 1998). Language games can be a principal focus of a lesson, or an
extension activity to supplement more conventional teaching about the
grammatical features or vocabulary of the second language (Marsland,
1998; Pollard & Hess, 1997; Wright, Betteridge, & Buckby, 2006). English
as a second language and foreign language teachers organize dramatic or
humorous scenarios as spaces where students collaboratively use language
for real as well as imagined purposes (Chappell & Faltis, 2013). These scenarios engage student's emotions, build their vocabulary and reinforce
content knowledge while allowing them to explore complex issues they
encounter in multiple texts (Medina, 2004). For older emergent bilingual
youth, language play gives them permission to act silly and may help them
overcome reluctance to perform in front of their peers.

Drama and improvisation as an extension of sheltered instruction. In
the early 1980s linguist and second language researcher Steven Krashen
(1982) theorized that adults have two distinct ways of acquiring a second
language. The first way is to actually *acquire* the language in ways that children acquire their first language – as a natural and subconscious process.
The second way to develop competence in a second language is to *learn* it,
which implies a more conscious knowledge of the linguistic rules (the grammar) of the language, knowing when to apply these rules and how to talk
about them. Krashen's acquisition-learning distinction is part of a larger
conceptualization of second language acquisition theory he calls the
Input Hypothesis. Krashen argues that language *acquisition* does not
require conscious study of grammatical rules or tedious drills. However, for
language acquisition to happen naturally, teachers must use instructional
methods that supply "comprehensible input in low anxiety situations, con-
taining messages that students really want to hear" (p. 7). Comprehensible

input — messages that are understandable to second language learners — allow learners to move from proficiency stage i to proficiency stage $i+1$. This means that teachers should teach the second language using structures just beyond the students' level of understanding (Krashen, 1982).

The pedagogical question for second language teachers, then, is how to make the $i+1$ approach comprehensible so that learners do in fact make progress. Curtain (1986, 1991) conceptualized a teaching approach based in large part on Krashen's Input Hypothesis. This approach, called "sheltered instruction" focused on meaning rather than form, avoided overt error correction, used simplified speech and controlled vocabulary, and context clues to convey meaning, conversational interaction important to students, and not forcing students to speak before they felt ready.

Conventional sheltered strategies include increased wait time, slow but natural levels of speech, clear enunciation, short, simple sentences, repetition and paraphrasing, controlled vocabulary and idioms, visual reinforcement, demonstrations, hands-on experiences, and frequent comprehension checks (Echevarría & Graves, 2011; Echevarría, Vogt, & Short, 2013; Levine & McCloskey, 2013). Less conventional sheltered strategies are those which teach language and content through exaggerated gestures and body language, improvisation and drama, costumes, wigs, hats, and masks related to academic content lessons (Combs, Betts, & Fisher, 2013; Reyes, 2013).

I view collaborative classroom drama and improvisation as an extension of good sheltered instruction. When pre-service teachers participate in theater games, they begin to understand how the language development of emergent bilingual students is linked to social interaction. Although still novices, pre-service teachers learn to create fun, stress-free activities that allow their own students to express themselves verbally or to interpret and perform passages from texts. Pre-service teachers thus see the potential that these performances have to help emergent bilingual students internalize English linguistic patterns and develop sociolinguistic competence. Even the more reluctant participants come to see the benefits of risk-tasking by emergent bilingual students when they take risks themselves. Drama activities connected to particular content areas can also help develop academic language and concepts related to these areas.

Sociocultural Theory and Goofiness Pedagogy

One of the principal tenets of sociocultural theory is that learning is a socially situated activity. This idea is embodied in Lev Vygotsky's well known theory of the zone of proximal development (ZPD), a kind of metaphorical space or activity in which a child develops linguistically or cognitively through problem solving with adult guidance or collaboration with peers. Vygotsky (1978) conceptualized the ZPD as the difference between what individuals can accomplish when acting alone and what they might accomplish when acting in collaboration with others. Vygotsky was a keen observer of children engaged in play activities; he argued that play created a zone of proximal development in which a child "always behaves beyond his average age, above his daily behavior ... and as though he were a head taller than himself" (1978, p. 102). Cazden (1981) applied Vygotsky's ZPD to classroom contexts in which teachers assist children in development of classroom discourse. She observed that child discourse under guidance from a teacher was often more advanced than what the child could produce independently. Cazden called this phenomenon "performance without competence," concluding that assisted performance contributed to subsequent development (1981, p. 7).

I would argue a similar analogy can be made that emergent bilingual learners develop language during drama play. Under adult guidance in drama activities children are capable of more advanced discourse than what they may be able to produce on their own. Assisted performance has the potential to facilitate the development of language and new ways to engage the world. Performance gives students permission to experiment and take risks with language, and to make mistakes without embarrassment or repercussion. In organized and spontaneous play, including semi-structured dramatic play, emergent bilingual learners create imaginary situations, switch between roles, and engage in social interaction with others. This dramatic play, similar to Vygotsky's ZPD, represents a space where learners can perform above their average age and be a head taller than themselves. Goofiness pedagogy also has the potential to create what Lantolf (2000) calls the "collaborative construction of opportunities" in which people who work collaboratively on tasks and projects co-construct contexts in which expertise emerges as a feature of the group (p. 17).

What Does Performed Goofiness Look Like in Pre-Service Teacher Education Classes?

Getting students ready to perform goofiness. Simply asking pre-service teachers to perform goofiness in a theater game does not mean they all approach the task easily. If students are shy or embarrassed by displays of emotion, their participation, whether scripted or improvised, will be half-hearted. That is why I model the kind of goofiness that I want students to practice. I never ask my pre-service teachers to participate in drama activities that I would not willingly undertake myself. If I expect students to take risks, which for many of them mean emoting in unaccustomed ways, I have to model emotion, even if I look pretty silly.

We often begin by practicing exaggerated facial expressions and body language. First in small groups and then as a whole class I provide random prompts like "angry" or "sad" or "euphoric." Or students will pantomime a routine action that others have to identify, for example, drinking a hot cup of tea, reading a scary book, cracking and frying an egg, or lighting a candle. Students perform these emotions and actions as a way to practice visual scaffolding for the emergent bilingual students in their classrooms. We then move to theater games that require verbal and movement improvisation.

"Making you laugh" and the "industrial machine". Two activities I use in this introductory phase are often used in conventional drama classes. The first leverages the emotions students have already practiced in small group as a way to make others laugh. Three students sit on chairs at the front of the classroom, and a classmate performs different facial expressions and gestures as a way of getting the seated participants to laugh. The first two students who laugh have to get up and leave; the one who has not laughed is the winner. The second activity is the "industrial machine," where one student becomes the central part of a machine, moving her arms and legs in a machine-like pattern and making a sound related to the part. Another student attaches himself to the machine as an additional part, moving in tandem with the first student and performing a different sound. Eventually, up to six or seven students constitute an entire moving and whirring machine. Both activities are designed to introduce students into comic performance.

Performed goofiness as a warm-Up activity. I have occasionally deviated from gentle guidance into theater games, though when this happens students are typically used to my eccentricities. A dramatic introduction to a particular content lesson can be unexpected, startling, but nearly always memorable. For example, in a sheltered science lesson on plate tectonics and the human cost of earthquakes, I acted the part of a distraught earthquake victim; I wore ragged clothes, a dusty wig, and ran into the classroom screaming. In a sheltered social studies lesson on evolution and intelligent design, my teaching assistant and I performed a dialogue between Charles Darwin and a Catholic priest to model that science and faith did not have to be in conflict. In a lesson on music and cultural icons, I dressed up as Jimi Hendrix; my teaching assistant was a flower child (we wore bell bottoms, tied-dyed shirts, love beads, and granny glasses). We entered the classroom with a boom box blasting Hendrix's anthem of the 1960s — *Purple Haze*. In a sheltered lesson on the planets, we wore huge alien glasses and Styrofoam antennae to simulate extra-terrestrial life.

Students enjoy these simple performances in three ways. First, the performances create a dramatic tension or playful mood in the class and focus students' attention on the lessons. Subsequent de-briefing of the humor, cultural references, or "shock effect" allows students the opportunity to react (both positively and negatively) to what they have witnessed. Second, the dramatic activities can be riveting and connect the performance to the content subjects being taught. Finally, as noted above, when students see me taking and modeling both playfulness and dramatic creativity, they feel more comfortable engaging in performance themselves.

Performed goofiness as "expressive microbursts". According to Progrow (2009), a common method of classroom management is to use dramatic techniques to capture students' initial attention or to refocus them after a noisy activity. Often these refocusing techniques are performed as "expressive microbursts," or "exaggerated tonal or facial expressions or gestures used by teachers to covey the importance of something that is happening or that has just happened" (Progrow, 2009, p. 42). Expressive microbursts can be dramatic gestures of facial expressions that praise or dissuade students, but they can also give emphasis to a word or a key idea related to a content subject. They can also be sounds; in order to grab students' attention, I often use a vuvuzela, which is a long, brightly colored plastic horn used by South African soccer fans during the 2010 World Cup soccer matches. Expressive microbursts tend to be brief, occurring within a single moment, but they can also be extended. When modeling a vocabulary and geographical literacy lesson on the Sonoran Desert and desert animals in Spanish, for instance, I sometimes lead my pre-service teachers around the classroom in a conga line. We chant the new vocabulary in unison while kicking out our legs and moving our hips.

Performed goofiness as authentic assessment. Drama and performed goofiness can be used as a way to assess learning. Teachers can organize imaginative and kinesthetic activities to review and evaluate how much students recall about a subject. In my SEI methods courses students have an opportunity to show what they have learned about different topics in several ways. One assessment is the "speed dating" approach to processing new or reviewed content. Students line up facing one another. I give them a prompt, for example, to review demographic shifts, "Where in the U.S. has the ELL population grown the most in recent years?" or "Which three U.S. states have the highest numbers of English language learners?" They have one minute to respond and discuss the prompt with their counterpart. After signaling that time's up with my vuvuzela or a cued YouTube music video, students rotate so they are facing a different person. I provide another prompt; students discuss it and so it goes. At the end of the review, the parallel line becomes a dance line that students move through in pairs, dancing to the music video.

Another assessment activity that students enjoy involves PowerPoint images of individuals or places related to a content area. For example, in a middle school social studies lesson on U.S. presidents, images of several presidents are flashed on the screen. Three or four students stand with their backs to the screen facing the rest of the class. Students in the audience — who can see the images — give their peers clues about the identity of the presidents. The standing students then must guess the identity of the individual based on clues. This activity is designed to model different ways to assess whether emergent bilingual students have learned the content taught.

In a graduate SEI methods class, we reviewed principles of second language acquisition and sociocultural theory by staging a "dating game" based on the 1970s television show with that name. Students dressed up in a variety of costumes, wigs, and hats. Then at the front of the room three contestants sat in a row. The date then asked each of them prepared questions about the different theories we had studied. The date then made his or her choice based on the accuracy or eloquence of the answers to review questions about second language acquisition or sociocultural theory.

Performed goofiness as an entire lesson. While I enjoy incorporating drama games in every class I teach, I am not opposed to conventional instruction, like the common lecture and discussion format. Indeed, teachers of emergent bilingual students need to expose students to all kinds of instruction because they will encounter different approaches as they move through the grade levels. There have been occasions when my entire SEI class (between 2 and 2½ hours) has focused on drama and creative performance, but has incorporated conventional lecture as well. I offer two examples, both modeled for a secondary English class.

Planet personal advertisements. The first lesson is an integrated astronomy and English lesson on the planets in our solar system, the Greek and Roman names given to them, and a number of commercial products whose names also have been taken from Greek and Roman mythology. In order to introduce the lesson, I ask students to close their eyes and imagine lifting off from earth and shooting into space. As they move into the earth's upper atmosphere and eventually into orbit, I ask them to describe what they see "outside of their spaceship's viewing window." As the ship moves past the planets and the sun, students – still with their eyes closed – describe the moons and gas rings they see. Their descriptions may include an alien or two, or even another spaceship. When they finally open their eyes, I am wearing an alien mask and antennae! We then divide up into nine groups and I assign a planet to each group (including Pluto, which has been downgraded to a "planetoid") and distribute pictures and astronomical information about each planet to the appropriate group.

After reviewing the information as well as the Greek and Roman origins of the names, I tell students that their planet is lonely and needs visitors. We then look at examples of personal advertisements from local newspapers and national magazines (I sometimes have to edit them for language and appropriate content). Modeling how the pre-service teachers might work with emergent bilingual students, we deconstruct some of the abbreviations found in the ads, for example: ISO (in search of), LTR (long-term relationship), S (single), SOH (sense of humor), NS (non-smoker), WAA (will answer all), etc. Subsequently, I give each table a list of astronomical "personal" abbreviations, which group members can use in their personal planet ads: CAS (crust and surface), DFTS (distance from the sun), EAP (enormous atmospheric pressure), EO (elliptical planet), GG (gas giant), HF (huge fireball), IR (infrared radiation), SD (sonic disturbances), and others. Students then get to work and when they finish the personal advertisement, perform it for the whole class.

Teaching about bravado and boasting in shakespeare's Romeo and Juliet through Reggaetón. Nearly all of the secondary English pre-service teachers in my SEI classes have to teach Shakespeare's tragedy *Romeo and Juliet.* First, the study of Shakespeare is required by the Arizona state language arts standards for the secondary grades and, second, the themes in *Romeo and Juliet* are universal even in contemporary times. Nonetheless, novice teachers worry about how to connect the literary and academic concepts in the play to the lived experiences of 9th and 10th graders. Elizabethan English is challenging for native speakers of English and nearly impenetrable for students acquiring English. In addition, teachers need to clarify or explain Shakespeare's metaphorical language and his historical references. I developed a lesson that focused on the Shakespearean themes of rivalry and bravado in *Romeo and Juliet* by comparing the conflict between the Montagues and Capulets to the famous rivalry between Puerto Rican reggaetón artists Daddy Yankee and Don Omar. Secondary goals were to model the teaching of academic vocabulary in context and to provide an example of how teachers might use Spanish translations of the vocabulary to provide additional scaffolding to emergent bilingual youth (I wanted to show pre-service teachers that using a few lesson-related Spanish phrases would neither violate state language policies nor jeopardize their teaching certificates). After I asked students to imagine that they were students at one of Tucson's urban high schools, we began by previewing academic concepts in English and Spanish. We then viewed several photographs of Daddy Yankee and Don Omar from various internet sites, discussing the genesis of their rivalry (envy, historical distrust, and perceived insult), and that the resulting feud had produced a number of collaborative, brilliant, and humorous call and response "dis" tracks. We returned to *Romeo and Juliet*, Act II, Scene IV which features the spirited exchange between Benvolio and Mercutio (Romeo's friends) about Tybalt (Juliet's cousin), in which Mercutio masterfully insults Tybalt: "More than Prince of Cats, I can tell you. O' he's the courageous captain of compliments ... The pox of such antic, lisping, affecting fantasticoes – these new tuners of accent!" (Shakespeare, 1969). We find examples of bravado and boasting in Shakespeare's passage and then compare them to excerpts from Daddy Yankee's song *El Jefe* and *Tira'era pa Daddy Yankee* by Don Omar. We listen to both reggaetón tracks on YouTube, identifying examples of bravado and boasting on a handout of the lyrics; because most of my pre-service teachers do not speak or understand Spanish, I provide translations. Once again we return to *Romeo and Juliet*, this time to Act III and the duel between Mercutio and Tybalt. Finally, the students create a kind of T Chart comparing an excerpt from Romeo and Juliet to the *Tiradera* between Daddy Yankee and Don Omar. We conclude the lesson with aerobic dance and Zumba moves to Daddy Yankee's track *El Jefe* (http://www. youtube.com/watch?v=VXRo1VOdZ1Y&feature=related). After the lesson we examine the lesson through theoretical and practical lenses. What were the sheltered strategies used? Was goofiness pedagogy evident in the lesson?

Does a comparison between Shakespeare and popular cultural icons make sense? Are references to drugs and the use of profanity too risky to use in a high school English class? What other comparisons could teachers use? And so on.

Analysis

Engaging in goofiness activities has had some observable benefits in my SEI classrooms. One of the most tangible is the way it has transformed my own teaching. Incorporating drama and performance has allowed me to leverage my own goofiness —however natural or performed — and has inspired opportunities for me to be creative. Goofiness pedagogy has reanimated teaching for me. Teaching pre-service teachers is a joyful experience when we engage in academic silliness together, and I look forward to every class. Because I often write about the difficult and depressing political climate in which emergent bilingual learners are educated in Arizona, goofiness pedagogy has become a pedagogy of hope in my own practice. While I lament the ideological restrictions against bilingual education in our state and consider the forced segregation of English language learners in multi-hour grammar blocks a form of educational malpractice, I can at least show ELL pre-teachers another vision for teaching for this population.

Goofiness pedagogy has also benefited many of the pre-service teachers in my SEI classrooms. Goofiness activities create a less stressful classroom environment and lower students' affective filters (Krashen, 1982). The activities help students get to know one another, laugh together, try out innovative teaching strategies, take risks, make mistakes, and analyze those mistakes in a supportive community of practice (Lave & Wenger, 1991; Wenger, 1998). Pre-service teachers are engaged in a situated experience which is social, dynamic, and at times spontaneous. As such, they begin to understand that learning in general and language learning in particular are social pursuits. Pre-service teachers learn to create social spaces for language and content development in ways that can ultimately support emergent bilingual students.

Some students have found participation in drama and goofiness activities to be challenging. Each semester a few pre-service teachers express embarrassment about assuming alternative personas. They would not ask their own students to engage in drama or performance because they did not want the students to be uncomfortable. As shy or inhibited individuals themselves, they understood the goal of goofiness pedagogy but questioned the wisdom of this approach with other shy or inhibited young people. Others questioned their ability to incorporate drama into more advanced content classes.

Getting There (but Not Quite There yet)

Over the years I have practiced goofiness pedagogy, pre-service teachers for the most part seem excited about the prospect of experimenting with drama and performance, but are uncertain about how to use it with their own students. Some of them stated a willingness to participate in performed goofiness activities only because they knew and trusted other members of their teaching cohort. This perspective is exemplified in the following comment by a secondary education teacher: "[Performing goofiness] was easy for me, but I feel that much of it was because I have known everyone in the program for months now. I don't warm up to people quickly and I believe that I would have had trouble with this earlier."

Another common sentiment among graduate pre-service teachers in particular was genuine interest in goofiness pedagogy, but uncertainty about how much to implement in their classroom: "I'm not entirely sure I'll ever be able to do full justice to a performed goofiness activity in my own class, again because I'm not entirely comfortable with it myself. Maybe that's something I'll be able to work up to as I teach more and feel more at ease in my classroom. In the meantime, I would like to do it here and there, and over time perhaps progress to activities like those from class." Table 1 provides a sample of student comments about goofiness pedagogy, taken from different mid and end-of-semester reflections.

Practical Implications And Recommendations

If teachers and teacher-educators themselves are uncomfortable with drama, they will be far less likely to use it with students. Reluctance to stray from the familiar into the unfamiliar can be a strong impediment, as is the fear that most novice teachers have about looking silly to students, or worse, incompetent. These fears are understandable. I had them too when I was a new teacher just starting out. My recommendation for any

Table 1.   Comments about "Performed Goofiness."

What You Liked about PG	What You Did Not Like about PG (or Suggestions for Improvement)
I thought the goofiness activities were very creative and informative.	I wanted more instruction on how to create the activities you showed us in class.
I liked the engaging, interactive activities we did.	It was hard to relate some of the more simple lessons to a higher level class that is more conceptual.
I really enjoyed the roleplays.	Don't spend quite so much time on roleplays of activities.
I loved the goofiness factor. I love learning to be silly.	I didn't clearly see the connections between learning how to teach [in a] Structured English Immersion classroom and some of the learning activities we did.
I do see some definite benefits with activities like [performed goofiness] if only because it lowers everyone's affective filters enough that we're all contributing. This would be especially beneficial in a class where students are reluctant to participate such as ELLs.	I am not a fan of performed goofiness. As an educator I understand the purpose behind it, but … I feel that it alienates those in the class that maybe shy; I understand that part of the purpose is to get students out of their comfort zones, but for me this went too far.
[Drama and goofiness] turns class into something that many will enjoy and it holds their attention.	I am nervous to use too much. I have a very deadpan personality and I feel that if I used this with students out of the blue that it would not work well. In terms of having my students use this, I'm very careful about how adventurous I get in student teaching.
I could see myself using this with younger students (and actually did a lot of goofy activities when I worked with young kids). I also think that it could be useful in language classes when simulating real life roleplays.	I'm naturally a shy person, and so activities like we did in class are always a bit more difficult for me to get involved in, only because I'm not a big fan of having the attention focused on me. However, I think there's something to be said about all of the activities being done with multiple people, as it feels like there is a sense of safety in numbers.

Source: From Pre-service Teachers in Foundations and Methods of SEI.

teachers or teacher-educators wishing to experiment with goofiness pedagogy is to start small. Brief and exaggerated facial expressions or an "expressive microburst" here and there can disrupt more conventional routines, surprising students and redirecting their attention from off-task behaviors. If the activities are different, creative, and fun, students will respond positively. Another recommendation for the reluctant but interested teacher is to invite a more animated colleague or guest speaker into the class to engage in performance pedagogy related to different content subjects. If the students are excited teachers can try out short, then longer dramatic or goofy activities.

If teachers need ideas about different activities to implement in their classrooms, there is no shortage of articles or books about teaching and performance. I recommend that teachers explore these texts, trying out ideas that appeal, and revising or reworking activities that need work. Finally, emergent bilingual students acquiring English need opportunities to play with the language in a way that allows them to take risks, make mistakes and perform "a head taller than themselves" (Vygotsky, 1978, p. 102). I believe that goofiness pedagogy provides one way for students to do this.

To conclude, goofiness pedagogy has invigorated my own work with pre-teachers and has helped me implement more meaningful SEI classes. The goofiness and performance activities provide pre-teachers them with a vision of good instruction with and for emergent bilingual students. Once pre-service teachers experience the pleasure of performing with peers in teacher education classes, they will be less reluctant to try it out themselves. That is my hope.

References

Arizona Department of Education. (2009). *Administrator's model implementation training.* PowerPoint presentation. Retrieved from https://www.ade.az.gov/oelas

Batalova, J., & McHugh, M. (2010). *Number and growth of students in U.S. schools in need of English instruction.* Washington, DC: Migration Policy Institute.

Blum, A., & Johnson, E. J. (2012). Reading repression: Textualizing the linguistic marginalization of nonnative English-speaking teachers in Arizona. *Journal of Language, Identity, and Education, 11*(3), 167–184.

Boal, A. (1979). *Theatre of the oppressed.* New York, NY: Theatre Communications Group.

Bontjes, C. (2013). *Create captivating classrooms.* Lanham, MD: Rowman & Littlefield Publishers.

Cahnmann-Taylor, M., & Souto-Manning, M. (2010). *Teachers act up! Creating multicultural learning communities through theater.* New York, NY: Teachers College Press.

Cazden, C. B. (1981). Performance before competence: Assistance to child discourse in the zone of proximal development. *The Quarterly Newsletter of the Laboratory of Comparative Human Cognition, 3*(1), 5–8.

Chappell, S. V., & Faltis, C. J. (2013). *Arts and emergent bilingual youth: Building culturally responsive, critical and creative education in school and community contexts.* New York, NY: Routledge.

Collier, V. (1987). Age and rate of acquisition of second language for academic purposes. *TESOL Quarterly, 21*, 617–641.

Collier, V. (1988). *The effect of age on acquisition of a second language for school.* Washington, DC: National Clearinghouse for Bilingual Education. ERIC Number: ED296580. Retrieved from http://eric.ed.gov/?q=The+effect+of+age+on+acquisition+of+a+second+language+for+school&id=ED296580. Accessed on January 2, 2014.

Collier, V. (1995). *Promoting academic success for ESL students: Understanding second language acquisition for school.* Elizabeth, NJ: New Jersey Teachers of English to Speakers of Other Languages-Bilingual Educators.

Combs, M. C. (2012). Everything on its head: How Arizona's structured English immersion policy re-invents theory and practice. In M. B. Arias & C. Faltis (Eds.), *Implementing educational language policy in Arizona: Legal, historical and current practices in SEI* (pp. 59–85). Bristol: Multilingual Matters.

Combs, M. C., Betts, J. D., & Fisher, P. (2013). Acted and enacted lives: Language play, theater, and language development at the border. In S. V. Chappell & C. J. Faltis (Eds.), *The arts and emergent bilingual youth* (pp. 63–67). New York, NY: Routledge.

Combs, M. C., & Nicholas, S. E. (2012). The effect of Arizona language policies on Arizona indigenous students. *Language Policy, 11*(1), 101–118.

Cummins, J. (1992). Bilingual education and English immersion: The Ramírez report in theoretical perspective. *Bilingual Research Journal, 16*(1–2), 91–104.

Cummins, J. (1996). *Negotiating identities: Education for empowerment in a diverse society.* Ontario, CA: California Association for Bilingual Education.

Curtain, H. A. (1986). Integrating language and content instruction. *ERIC/CLL News Bulletin, 9*(2), 1, 10–11.

Curtain, H. A. (1991). Methods in elementary school foreign language teaching. *Foreign Language Annals, 24*(4), 323–329.

DaSilva, I. A. C., Combs, M. C., & Moll, L. C. (2012). In the arid zone: Drying out educational resources for English language learners through policy and practice. *Urban Education, 47*(2), 495–514.

Dictionary.com. *goof.* Retrieved from http://dictionary.reference.com/browse/goof. Accessed on January, 20, 2014.

Dinkelman, T. (2003). Self-study in teacher education: A means and ends tool for promoting reflective teaching. *Journal of Teacher Education, 54*, 6–18.

Disney Mickey. (n.d.). *Goofy.* Retrieved from http://mickey.disney.com/goofy. Accessed on March 30, 2014.

Echevarría, J., & Graves, A. (2011). *Sheltered content instruction* (4th ed.). Boston, MA: Pearson.

Echevarría, J., Vogt, M. E., & Short, D. (2013). *Making content comprehensible for English languages* (4th ed.). Boston, MA: Pearson.

Edmiston, B. (2014). *Transforming teaching and learning with active and dramatic approaches.* New York, NY: Routledge.

Ernst-Slavit, G., & Wenger, K. J. (1998). Using creative drama in the elementary ESL classroom. *TESOL Journal, 7*(4), 30–33.

Florez, I. R. (2012). Examining the validity of the Arizona English language learners assessment cut scores. *Language Policy, 11*(1), 33–45.

Freire, P. (1970). *Pedagogy of the oppressed.* New York, NY: Seabury Press.

Gándara, P., & Hopkins, M. (2010). *Forbidden language.* New York, NY: Teachers College Press.

Gándara, P., & Orfield, G. (2012). Why Arizona matters: The historical, legal, and political contexts of Arizona's instructional policies and U.S. linguistic hegemony. *Language Policy, 11*(1), 7–19.

Goldenberg, C., & Coleman, R. (2010). *Promoting academic achievement among English learners: A guide to the research.* Thousand Oaks, CA: Corwin Press.

Goldenberg, C., & Rutherford-Quach, S. (2012). The Arizona home language survey: The under-identification of students for English language services. *Language Policy, 11*(1), 21–30.

Hakuta, K., Butler, Y. G., & Witt, D. (2000). *How long does it take for English learners to attain proficiency?* Santa Barbara, CA: University of California, Linguistic Minority Research Institute. Retrieved from http://www.stanford.edu/~hakuta/Publications/%282000%29%20-%20HOW%20LONG%20DOES%20IT%20TAKE%20ENGLISH%20LEARNERS%20TO%20ATTAIN%20PR.pdf. Accessed on January 2, 2014.

Hamilton, M. L., & Pinnegar, S. (2000). On the threshold of a new century: Trustworthiness, integrity, and self-study in teacher education. *Journal of Teacher Education, 51*(3), 234–240.

Hawkins, M. (2005). ESL in elementary education. In E. Hinkel (Ed.), *Handbook of research in second language teaching and learning* (pp. 25–43). Mahwah, NJ: Lawrence Erlbaum.

Heineke, A. J., & Cameron, Q. (2013). Closing the classroom door and the achievement gap: Teach for America alumni teachers' appropriation of Arizona language policy. *Education and Urban Society, 45*(4), 483–505.

Johnson, E. J. (2012). Arbitrating repression: Language policy and education in Arizona. *Language and Education, 26*(1), 53–76.

Kasper, G., & Roever (2005). Pragmatics in second language learning. In E. Hinkel (Ed.), *Handbook of research in second language teaching and learning* (pp. 317–334). Mahwah, NJ: Lawrence Erlbaum.

Krashen, S. (1982). *Principles and practice in second language acquisition.* Oxford: Pergamon.

Krashen, S. (1996). *Under attack: The case against bilingual education.* Culver City, CA: Language Education Associates.

Krashen, S., Rolstad, K., & MacSwan, J. (2007). *Review of "Research summary and bibliography for Structured English Immersion programs" of the Arizona English Language Learners Task Force.* Retrieved from http://www.elladvocates.org/documents/AZ/Krashen_Rolstad_MacSwan_review.pdf

Lantolf, J. P. (Ed.). (2000). *Sociocultural theory and second language learning.* Oxford: Oxford University Press.

Lave, J., & Wenger, E. (1991). *Situated learning: Legitimate peripheral participation.* Cambridge: Cambridge University Press.

Leckie, A. G., Kaplan, S. E., & Rubinstein-Avila, E. (2013). The need for speed: A critical discourse analysis of the reclassification of English language learners in Arizona. *Language Policy, 12*(2), 159–176.

Levine, L. N., & McCloskey, M. L. (2013). *Teaching English and language and content in mainstream classes* (2nd ed.). Boston, MA: Pearson.

Mackinney, E., & Rios-Aguilar, C. (2012). Negotiating between restrictive language policies and complex teaching conditions: A case study of Arizona's teachers of English learners. *Bilingual Research Journal, 35*(3), 350–367.

Marsland, B. (1998). *Lessons from nothing: Activities for language teaching with limited time and resources.* Cambridge: Cambridge University Press.

Martinez-Wenzl, M., Pérez, K. C., & Gándara, P. (2012). Is Arizona's approach to educating its ELS superior to other forms of instruction. *Teachers College Record, 114,* 1–32.

Medina, C. L. (2004). Drama wor(l)ds: Explorations of Latina/o realistic fiction. *Language Arts, 81*(4), 272–282.

Merriam-Webster.com. *goofy.* Retrieved from http://www.merriam-webster.com/dictionary/goofy. Accessed on January 20, 2014.

Milem, J. F., Bryan, W. P., Sesate, D. B., & Montaño, S. (2013). *Arizona minority student progress report, 2013.* Tucson, AZ: Arizona Minority Education Policy Analysis Center.

Oxford English Dictionary Online. (2013). *goff,* n.2. Oxford University Press. Retrieved from http://www.oed.com/view/Entry/79712. Accessed on January 20, 2014.

Pinnegar, S. E., & Hamilton, M. L. (2009). *Self-study of practice as a genre of qualitative research: Theory, methodology, and practice.* Dordrecht: Springer.

Pinnegar, S. E., Hamilton, M. L., & Fitzgerald, L. (2010). Guidance in being and becoming: Self-study of practice researchers. In L. Erickson, J. Young, & S. Pinnegar (Eds.), *Proceedings of the eighth international conference on self-studies of teacher education practices: Navigating the public and the private: Negotiating the diverse landscapes of teacher education* (pp. 203–206). Herstmonceaux Castle, UK: Self-Study of Teacher Education Practices SIG.

Pollard, L., & Hess, N. (1997). *Zero prep: Ready-to-go activities for the language classroom.* Burlingame, CA: Alta Book Center Publishers.

Progrow, S. (2009). *Teaching content outrageously.* San Francisco, CA: Jossey-Bass.

Reyes, S. A. (2013). *Engage the creative arts.* Portland, OR: DiversityLearningK-12.

Rios-Aguilar, C., Gonzalez, C. M. S., & Moll, L. C. (2012). A study of Arizona's teachers of English language learners. *Teachers College Record, 114,* 9.

Rios-Aguilar, C., Gonzalez, C. M. S., & Sabetghadam, S. (2012). Evaluating the impact of restrictive language policies: The Arizona 4-hour English language development block. *Language Policy, 11*(1), 47–80.

Saunders, W., & Goldenberg, C. (2010). *Improving education for English learners: Research-based approaches.* Sacramento, CA: California Department of Education.

Shakespeare, W. (1969). Romeo and Juliet *[1597].* New York, NY: Scholastic, Inc.

Spolin, V. (1986). *Theater games for the classroom.* Evanston, IL: Northwestern University Press.

Vygotsky, L. S. (1978). *Mind in society.* Cambridge, MA: Harvard University Press.

Wenger, E. (1998). *Communities of practice.* Cambridge: Cambridge University Press.

Wong Fillmore, L., & Snow, C. E. (2002). What teachers need to know about language. In C. T. Adger, C. E. Snow, & D. Christian (Eds.), *What teachers need to know about language* (pp. 7–53). McHenry, IL: Delta Systems.

Wright, A., Betteridge, D., & Buckby, M. (2006). *Games for language learners* (3rd ed.). Cambridge: Cambridge University Press.

Wright, L. (2001). Preparing teachers to put drama in the classroom. *Theory into Practice, 24*(3), 205–210.

ABOUT THE CONTRIBUTORS

Lori Czop Assaf is Professor at Texas State University. She teaches undergraduate and graduate courses in literacy methods, teacher research, and cultural and linguistic diversity. As the Director of the Central Texas Writing Project, she leads professional development for teachers in Central Texas and facilitates the Invitational Summer Institute. She is a co-editor for English in Texas and graduate advisor in the Reading Program at Texas State. Her research focuses on language and literacy learning in the diverse classroom and teacher identity. Additionally, she conducts research with students and teachers in countries such as Pakistan and South Africa.

María Estela Brisk is Professor of Education at Boston College. Her research and teaching interests include writing instruction, bilingual education, bilingual language and literacy acquisition, and preparation of mainstream teachers to work with bilingual learners. She is the author of numerous articles and six books: *Bilingual Education: From Compensatory to Quality Schooling*; *Literacy and Bilingualism: A Handbook for ALL Teachers*; *Situational Context of Education: A Window into the World of Bilingual Learners*; *Language Development and Education: Children with Varying Language Experiences* (with P. Menyuk); *Language, culture, and community in teacher education*; and *Engaging Students in Academic Literacies: Genre-based Pedagogy for K-5 Classrooms*.

Mary Carol Combs is Associate Professor in the Department of Teaching, Learning, and Sociocultural Studies, University of Arizona. She teaches graduate and undergraduate courses in bilingual education, English as a second language methods, Indigenous language revitalization, and language policy and planning. Her research interests include education policy and law, sociocultural theory, immigration and education, second language acquisition, sheltered instruction and ELL teacher preparation.

Peter Farruggio is Associate Professor of Bilingual Education at the University of Texas Pan American. During a 25-year K-12 teaching career, he worked as a bilingual teacher, a teacher trainer, a community outreach coordinator, and a Reading Specialist in New York City and Northern

California. Prior to his teaching career, he worked for 15 years in the West Coast longshoremen's union (ILWU), specializing in education and organizing projects in the Latino immigrant communities in the San Francisco Bay Area. He earned a Ph.D. in Language, Literacy, and Culture from the Graduate School of Education at the University of California at Berkeley in 2004.

Mary Fuchs is a Special Education and Secondary English teacher who has taught in the Netherlands, the United Kingdom, and the United States. She holds a graduate degree in teaching from Montclair State University and a graduate degree in theology from Harvard Divinity School. She combines inclusive and translingual pedagogies with assistive technology to drive student success.

Anne Homza is Assistant Professor of the Practice in the Teacher Education, Special Education, Curriculum and Instruction Department at the Lynch School of Education at Boston College. A former bilingual teacher and biliteracy specialist, she has worked in school districts and higher education in Massachusetts since 1986. She works in both teacher professional development and pre-service teacher preparation and presents work related to effective instruction for bilingual learners regionally and nationally. With a social justice foundation, her current efforts are collaborative and endeavor to promote asset views of bilingualism/biliteracy and the infusion of linguistically responsive pedagogy.

Craig A. Hughes is Professor of Bilingual Education/Teaching ESL at Central Washington University. During his tenure at CWU, he has served as Title VII Grant Director, Program Coordinator, and Department Chair. He has taught Spanish and ESL at a high school in California, as well as ESL at a middle school in Colorado. He presents regularly at national and state bilingual conferences and has published articles and book chapters on bilingual and ESL education.

Tatyana Kleyn is Associate Professor in the Bilingual Education and TESOL programs at the City College of New York and associate investigator for the CUNY New York State Initiative on Emergent Bilinguals. She received an Ed.D. in international educational development at Teachers College, Columbia University. She is author of *Immigration: The Ultimate Teen Guide* (Scarecrow Press, 2011) and co-author with S.A. Reyes of *Teaching in Two Languages: A Guide for K-12 Bilingual Educators* (Corwin Press, 2010). She is the director of the documentary "Living

Undocumented: High School, College and Beyond." She was an elementary school teacher in San Pedro Sula, Honduras and Atlanta, Georgia.

Althier Lazar is Professor of Education at Saint Joseph's University in Philadelphia, PA. Her research focuses on the ways teachers and teacher candidates evolve in their understandings of culture, literacy, and language, and how these understandings translate to social equity teaching. Her books include: *Bridging Literacy and Equity: The Guide to Social Equity Teaching* (2012), with co-authors Patricia Edwards and Gwendolyn Thompson McMillon; *Practicing What We Teach: How Culturally Responsive Literacy Classrooms Make a Difference* (2011), with coeditor Patricia Ruggiano Schmidt; and *Learning to Be Literacy Teachers in Urban Schools: Stories of Growth and Change* (2004).

Minda Morren López is Assistant Professor of Literacy in the College of Education at Texas State University. She teaches undergraduate and graduate courses in reading, writing, and language acquisition. She also serves as the Elementary Education Teacher Preparation Program coordinator. In 2008, Minda completed her Ph.D. in Culture, Literacy, and Language from the University of Texas, San Antonio. Her mixed-methods research concerns equity, ideologies, literacies, and language acquisition. For her, these areas intersect most significantly in the fields of bilingual and literacy education.

Sandra I. Musanti is Assistant Professor in the Department of Language, Literacy and Intercultural Studies at The University of Texas at Brownsville. She prepares elementary preservice teachers in the bilingual program and also teaches graduate courses in bilingual education, sociocultural foundations of education, and qualitative research. She is a former postdoctoral fellow of the NSF-funded Center for the Mathematics Education of Latinos/as (CEMELA). Her research interests include exploring pedagogical practices that support the mathematics learning of emergent bilinguals, as well as issues of language, culture, and identity in bilingual teacher preparation and development.

Alcione N. Ostorga is Associate Professor of Curriculum and Instruction and the Director of the Office of Field Experiences at the University of Texas Pan American. She has more than 35 years of experience as an educator at various levels. Currently, her research focus has been on the preparation of teachers, especially bilingual teachers of Latina/o cultural backgrounds. Her research focuses on teacher professional development, teacher action research, critical reflection, and the application of adult learning theories to the preparation of teachers.

Alma D. Rodríguez is Associate Professor and Chair of the Language, Literacy, and Intercultural Studies Department at the University of Texas at Brownsville. She has over 15 years of experience working with Hispanic emergent bilinguals in the United States at all levels, elementary, secondary, and higher education. She has held teaching as well as administrative positions at the elementary and secondary levels in schools with high numbers of emergent bilinguals. Currently, as a teacher educator, Dr. Rodríguez specializes in the preparation of bilingual and ESL teachers at the undergraduate and graduate levels. She has published articles and book chapters on bilingual teacher education in English and Spanish.

David Schwarzer is Associate Professor in the Department of Secondary and Special Education at Montclair State University in New Jersey. He teaches undergraduate and graduate level courses on innovative ways to engage students in learning and teaching. His research interest focuses on the role of the monolingual teacher in the multilingual classroom. He has published several books and articles on multiliteracy and world language education. More recently, he has become interested in redefining the boundaries between literacy, biliteracy, and multiliteracy. He is exploring the idea of "translingual" and "transliteracy" education as a possible solution.

Suniti Sharma is Assistant Professor in the department of teacher education at Saint Joseph's University, Philadelphia. She teaches ESL pedagogy, English language arts methods and assessment and evaluation. Her research interests include identity, culture, and curriculum; multicultural global education; and qualitative research. Her research has been published in *Issues in Teacher Education*, *Teachers College Record*, and *Race, ethnicity and education*. Her work on at-risk youth has been published in a book, *Girls Behind Bars: Reclaiming Education in Transformative Spaces* and an edited collection on preparing multicultural teachers is entitled *Internationalizing Teacher Education for Social Justice: Theory, Research and Practice*.

Janet Smith consults with higher education institutions and non-profit organizations to evaluate teacher education initiatives and programs for high-risk youth. She has been involved in education for over 30 years, including as a secondary Spanish teacher, instructional designer for computer-based learning, adult ESL teacher and Peace Corps volunteer. Her work has taken her from Boston to Costa Rica, Australia, Montana, Nicaragua, Zambia, and Haiti. She earned a Ph.D. in education at Boston

College where her dissertation examined parent engagement from the perspective of immigrant Latino parents and identified school practices that marginalized families based on home language.

Mary Soto is the multiple and single subject coordinator for the Center for Bilingual and Multicultural Studies at California State University, Chico. She teaches courses for the teacher preparation as well as the master's program. In addition, she supervises student candidates. She taught English to high school English learners in California, Guadalajara, Mexico, and Texas for 17 years. She has published her research on long-term English learners in *Language Magazine* and *The NABE Journal of Research and Practice.* Her research interests center on effective practices for English learners.

Jan Valle is Associate Professor and director of the Childhood Education program at the City College of New York. She is the author of numerous articles and book chapters that address issues in both general and special education. As a DSE scholar, Jan has a particular interest in schooling and the cultural politics of difference. She is the author of *What Mothers Say about Special Education: From the 1960s to the Present* (Palgrave, 2009) and co-author with David Connor of *Rethinking Disability: A Disability Studies Approach to Inclusive Practices* (McGraw-Hill, 2011).